Fourth Canadian Edition

Small Business
Management
Fundamentals

Andrew J. Szonyi, Ph.D., P. Eng., M.B.A.
Formerly Professor of Management
University of Toronto

Dan Steinhoff, D.S.Sc.
Late Professor of Business Management
University of Miami

McGraw-Hill Ryerson Limited
Toronto Montreal New York Auckland Bogotá Caracas Lisbon
London Madrid Mexico Milan New Delhi Paris San Juan
Singapore Sydney Tokyo

To Michael and Eric

SMALL BUSINESS MANAGEMENT FUNDAMENTALS
Fourth Canadian Edition

ISBN: 0-07-551135-5

2 3 4 5 6 7 8 9 10   D   0 9 8 7 6 5 4 3

Printed and bound in Canada

Care has been taken to trace ownership of copyright material contained in this text. The publishers will gladly take any information that will enable them to rectify any reference or credit in subsequent editions.

Sponsoring Editor: Jennifer Mix

Supervising Editor and Copy Editor: Margaret Henderson

Cover and Text Design: Hania Fil

Technical Artist: Hania Fil

Typesetting and Page Make-Up: Southam Business Communications, Inc.

Printing & Binding: John Deyell Company

Text set in: Times

Canadian Cataloguing in Publication Data

Szonyi, Andrew J., Date
   Small business management fundamentals

4th Canadian ed.
Includes index.
ISBN 0-07-551135-5

1. Small business – Management.   2. Small business – Canada – Management.
I. Steinhoff, Dan.   II. Burgess, John F.   III. Title.

HD62.7.S96 1991   658.02′2   C91-093409-6

C O N T E N T S

Chapter 4 Buying an Existing Firm Versus Starting a New One 58

Chapter 5 Franchising 71

Chapter 9 Surveying the Market to Be Served: Finding Its Limits, Its Nature, and Its Sales Potential   134

Chapter 10 Understanding the Basic Financial Statements from a Management Viewpoint   156

Chapter 11 Sources of Financing for New Small Firms   174

Chapter
15 Layout 234

Chapter
16 Pricing Policies 245

Chapter
17 Advertising and Promotion 254

Chapter **Day-to-Day Management of the Ongoing**
29 **Business Firm** **423**

P A R T
7 **CASE STUDIES** **433**

Preface

This fourth Canadian edition of *Small Business Management Fundamentals* reflects many of the suggestions from instructors in the more than one hundred educational institutions from coast to coast who have used the previous edition. Particularly, I would like to acknowledge the contributions of Linda Boisvert, Northern Alberta Institute of Technology; Gerry McCready, St. Lawrence College, Kingston; Hilda Main, Vancouver Community College; Anita Metcalfe, Seneca College; and Ron Wolch, Northern Alberta Institute of Technology. Their valuable advice, based on experience in the field and in the classroom, led to the changes and improvements to the text.

The objective of this textbook is to present a straightforward, fundamental approach to managing a small firm in Canada. The reader will benefit from the clear, logical presentation of the necessary steps in planning, operating, and evaluating a small business in Canada. The text is suitable for community colleges and universities, as well as for practising business planners and managers.

In this edition we have placed stronger emphasis on the series of entrepreneurial activities involved in the early startup period. Students will see a new Chapter 3 on venture search and selection and two chapters discussing the various kinds of businesss: new businesses, established businesses, and franchises.

In Part 2, on the planning process, there is a new discussion of the strategic goals of the business plan (Chapter 6). In the section on accounting, we have increased coverage of the control aspects of small business, especially finance and accounting, including ratio analysis and cash flow analysis. Extensive discussion and treatment of both the Canada–United States Free Trade Agreement and the Goods and Services Tax are included in this new edition. In Part 7, we have now added four substantial and comprehensive cases to fourteen of the small case studies in the previous edition. And, to further assist students, a business plan outline and an illustrative sample business plan have been included in Appendixes 2 and 3.

Every effort has been made to maintain the text's readability by using a straightforward, fundamental approach to planning and operating a small firm. The language will be easily understood by college students at all levels. The much applauded logical sequence of the steps in planning a new small business is maintained. Following the example of the fifth American edition by John F. Burgess, chapter objectives have been added to assist in the learning process.

The authors are satisfied that the approach and format have been effective in student accomplishment. Large classes each semester have demonstrated student appreciation of the approach and the grasp of the total management area. Planning chapters can be studied in sequence or in isolation, but it is believed that the total sequence is most valuable to students. The emphasis on basic accounting principles and statements reflects our conviction that managers of small firms need this knowledge for more effective decision making.

Dan Steinhoff's death in December 1984 sadly ended the collaboration that was for me an especially enjoyable, instructive, and rewarding experience. It was my privilege and honour to have had Dan Steinhoff as a co-author and a friend. I will always strive to live up to his high standards in future work on this book.

The cooperation, patience, and assistance of an outstanding team at McGraw-Hill Ryerson was invaluable. Thank you Jennifer Mix, Margaret Henderson, Betty Tustin, Norma Christenson, and Laurie Graham. Without your dedication to the task, this new edition would not have happened.

Andrew J. Szonyi

1

INTRODUCTION

1

The Small Business Scene

LEARNING OBJECTIVES

After reading this chapter, you will be able to:

1. **U**nderstand that in many ways small businesses dominate the business scene
2. **K**now how important small businesses are to larger firms and how that importance is nurtured by larger businesses
3. **U**nderstand that there is a trend for more and more small businesses even though fewer people are self-employed than there were in the past
4. **K**now the general definitions of just what it takes to be considered a small business
5. **U**nderstand the importance of adapting sound management principles to small business
6. **K**now the activities and objectives of the many types of small businesses
7. **U**nderstand the characteristics of an entrepreneur, who they are and what makes them tick
8. **U**nderstand how the federal government supports small business

It is currently estimated that there are over one million business firms of all sizes in Canada, excluding small, independent farmers. All studies of these statistics show that at least 95 per cent of these firms are "small," regardless of which measure of "smallness" is applied. We will investigate these measures of size in this chapter. Meanwhile, we can recognize that the small business scene in this country comprises about 900 000 individual firms.

These small firms have been established to manufacture, distribute, and retail innumerable goods and services for our population at home and to export products as well. The vast majority of these firms concentrate on selling material products, but many firms provide a service. Although most service firms operate for local markets, services, too, are exported. Recent years have seen a great increase in the export of management consulting, medical, and technological services.

The truth of these statements often comes as a surprise to those who have the impression that the world of business consists chiefly, or only, of business giants. It is true that we do have many giant corporations in our country and that they are essential in making economies possible through mass production and mass distribution. Without these mass facilities, the present standard of living in Canada could not have been reached. Many small firms are dependent on larger firms for raw materials or finished products, which would be much more costly without the economies of mass production or not even available without the larger business firms that produce and distribute them.

But large firms are likewise dependent upon small firms. Mass-production industries recognize that they could not distribute their goods and services without the hundreds of small firms which do that job. It has been estimated that an average of 500 small suppliers and 3000 retailers support every major manufacturing firm in the country.

Big businesses are taking a page from the small business book and many are moving to smaller operations with fewer layers of costly management, better employee–employer relationships, quicker decision/response time, and, generally, more flexible operations.

To understand the small business scene, we must recognize that of the more than one million business firms in Canada, fewer than 0.5 per cent employ as many as 2500 people. Among manufacturing firms, more than 90 per cent employ fewer than one hundred people and 66 per cent employ fewer than twenty people. When we look at distributors, retailers, and service firms, these percentages are even more surprising in demonstrating the numerical preponderance of small firms.

The great majority of Canadian business firms are small and independently owned and operated by small business proprietors. Numerical evidence is abundantly available to support this fact, both in Canada and in most other countries of the Western world. Study of this evidence makes it clear that small business firms actually constitute the backbone of the free enterprise economies.

In 1987 there were some thirty-six small business firms for every 1000 persons in our total population. Small firms employ about 4.2 million people and produce over 30 per cent of the total gross national product. They employ about 50 per cent of the total work force in the private sector and produce goods and services with a value of about $160 billion each year. Despite the importance of our large corporations—which play an essential role in our total economy—in terms of the number of business units, the volume of business, and the percentage of paid employment, the small firm remains a significant factor in Canada and most of the Western world.

WHAT IS A SMALL BUSINESS?

A small business is one that possesses at least two of the following four characteristics:

1   Management of the firms is independent. Usually the managers are also the owners.
2   Capital is supplied and the ownership is held by an individual or a small group.
3   The area of operations is mainly local, with the workers and owners living in one home community. However, the markets need not be local.
4   The relative size of the firm within its industry must be small when compared with the biggest units in its field. This measure can be in terms of sales volume, number of employees, or other significant comparisons.

This definition of a small business was developed years ago by the Committee for Economic Development (CED) based upon a cross section of characteristics. It is this CED definition of the small business we will have in mind throughout the text. Of the four characteristics just cited, however, the authors believe that the fourth (relative size) is probably the most important. Any firm can be considered small when its sales volume, total employees, capital investment, and so forth are much smaller than the corresponding figures for the largest firms in its field. Under this relative size concept, American Motors has been considered small in government circles because it is only a fraction of the size of General Motors or Ford Motor Company. Similarly, a chain of food markets might still be considered small if compared to the Loblaws Company chain of grocery stores.

It will be obvious that our definition of small business encompasses a wide gamut of firms, from Mom and Pop stores to substantial manufacturing plants, distributors, retailers, and service firms. Our emphasis will be on the small firms that desire to grow. Management principles are common to all types and sizes of businesses, as we shall see.

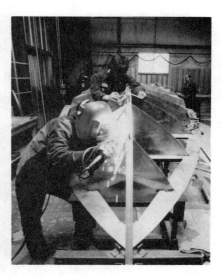

Small businesses are prominent in manufacturing, mining, wholesaling, retailing, and service-oriented firms. *Courtesy Government of Canada, Regional Industrial Expansion.*

Courtesy Industry, Science and Technology

Courtesy Government of Canada, Regional Industrial Expansion

Courtesy Government of Canada, Regional Industrial Expansion

Courtesy Industry, Science and Technology

Courtesy Ontario Bus Industries Inc.

*Courtesy Government of Canada,
Regional Industrial Expansion*

The subject of what a small business is can receive an unwarranted amount of space, time, and discussion, which is not appropriate to the objectives of this text. Nevertheless, some facts bear mentioning here because the definitions are often important in connection with legislation that has been passed to provide assistance to small firms.

Definitions of a small firm, for these purposes, demand some measurement of its size compared with that of large firms. Various measures, including the number of employees, the volume of sales, the nature of firm ownership, and the area of operations, have been used. Within these measures of size, differences are often noted when comparing manufacturing, wholesaling, and retailing firms.

The somewhat time-honoured dollar measures of a small firm, which originated with the U.S. Small Business Administration, were as follows in 1989:

- In retailing, a firm is considered small if its annual sales do not exceed $3.5 million. However, in some industries this total may reach $13.5 million.

- Among service firms, a firm is considered small if its annual receipts do not exceed $3.5 million. Certain firms may go up to $14.5 million.

- In wholesaling, a firm is considered small if it has less than 500 employees.

- In manufacturing, a firm is considered small if it does not have more than 1500 employees. Again, some industry variations exist.

- In transportation and warehousing, a firm is considered small until its annual receipts exceed $3.5 million; in some industries: $12.5 million.

- In construction, a firm is considered small unless its income exceeds $7 million in Specialty Trade Contracting or $17 million in General Contracting.

- In agriculture, a firm is considered small if its annual receipts do not exceed $100,000. Depending on the nature of the operation, this figure may be as high as $3.5 million.

- Special circumstances may justify variations from these limits.

It should be hurriedly added, however, that these measures are subject to frequent changes. They do not, for example, fully reflect the inflationary trends of the decade of the seventies that continued into the eighties. Each year the size limits for eligibility for SBA service may change several times.

An excellent definition of a small business is contained in the Small Business Act passed by the United States Congress in 1953. That definition says a small business is "one which is independently owned and operated and not dominant in its field of operations." The feature of "dominance in its field" has come to be of greatest importance in most attempts to specifically define a small business.

It should be noted, however, that due to the much smaller scale of the Canadian economy, as well as the relatively greater importance of world competition, it is possible that many firms could be dominant in their field in Canada, and yet should still be considered small because the volume of their sales, assets employed, and the number of employees in these firms are small relative to world competition.

The Canadian government uses the following definition for small business: a firm whose gross annual revenue is less than $2.0 million or where the firm employs less than fifty employees, if in the service sector, *or* less than 100 in the manufacturing sector. In addition to this definition, the *Small Business Loan Act* (SBLA), originally passed in 1960, sets $2 million annual gross revenue as the upper limit for consideration. In the area of management counselling, firms are eligible to use the Counselling Assistance to Small Enterprises (CASE) program if they have no more than seventy-five full-time employees.

In recent publications by the Minister of State (Small Businesses and Tourism), small business is referred to as manufacturing firms employing fewer than one hundred workers or having annual sales of $2 million or less, and firms in other sectors employing fewer than fifty people or having annual sales of less than $2 million.

A very important definition of eligibility exists in the Canadian *Income Tax Act* passed by parliament in 1971, with periodic changes and updates in regulations. Currently, according to section 125, all Canadian-controlled private corporations (of any size) qualify for a "small business deduction" and pay a lower tax rate of 25 per cent on the first $200,000 of active business income per year.

Meanwhile, provincial governments have their own ideas of what constitutes a small enterprise. Manitoba draws the line at fifty employees or less than $100,000 in sales, while Saskatchewan, when deciding eligibility, leans in the direction of the firm that is owned and managed/operated by the same individual. Moreover, Saskatchewan looks to the federal government for guidance in that it will consider the definition given by Revenue Canada *or* the SBLA definition when it sees it as appropriate to do so.

Every small business owner and every student of small business management has a very clear conception of what is considered to be a small business. The interest in volumes such as this is to get into the "nitty-gritty" of planning and operating a small firm, of developing devices to solve specific problems, and of learning ways to bring all phases of management into a cohesive whole.

ADAPTING VERSUS ADOPTING MANAGEMENT PRINCIPLES

An important observation can be made with regard to this matter of size. The same principles of business management apply to the largest firms in the country as well as to the smallest. This does not mean that a principle should be *adopted* uniformly in all cases, but that principles should be *adapted* to the particular needs of the firm. The fundamental truths of business management must be recognized regardless of size. Division of labour and the delegation of responsibility are cases in point.

TYPES OF ACTIVITY OF SMALL BUSINESS

The areas of activity for most small firms can be classified as follows:
   Manufacturing
   Mining
   Wholesaling
   Retailing
   Service

Manufacturing   Manufacturing firms engage in gathering of raw materials necessary for the creation of consumer and industrial products and in giving them useful form through their manufacturing processes. Most small manufacturing firms then pass their finished products on to wholesalers or other distributors (jobbers, sales agents, brokers, commission merchants, or manufacturers' agents) who handle their further distribution to the eventual users of these products. The use of manufacturers' agents to represent small factories in this process increased in the 1980s and continued into the 1990s. This is particularly true in the machinery and heavy industrial goods industries. Very few small manufacturers of home-consumer products engage in the distribution process beyond normal wholesale channels.

Primary manufacturing is the processing of basic raw materials such as nickel ore, uranium, petroleum, beef, and milk; a smelter would be a good typical example. Secondary manufacturing is the production of fabricated parts, materials, finished goods utilized by industry (for example, a milling machine or a conveyor belt), or by the final consumers (a toaster or a dress). Canadian primary manufacturing industries have been long established with substantial exports to the United States and to overseas markets; secondary manufacturing industry relies heavily on the domestic market for the sale of its output.

Service industries that directly support the manufacturing sector, such as computer services, engineering services, and scientific services, are sometimes classified as tertiary manufacturing industry. Canada has always been considered at a disadvantage in the area of secondary manufacturing; the economies of scale (size of production runs), limited domestic market, and long delivery lines all have adverse effects and influences. On the other hand, the tertiary industries are far less vulnerable to these factors. With their high content of sophistication, they are decidedly skills and management intensive.

Mining   Mining firms engage in gathering raw material from the earth, sea, or air. They either process the raw materials into consumer goods as part of their normal operation or sell them to other firms which convert them into usable form. An example of the former is the small salt mine where the salt is gathered and packaged in its own operation. The latter is exemplified by the small oil-well operator who drills for a product but sells it to a refinery.

Wholesaling   Wholesaling for the distribution of both consumer and industrial goods is a large part of the small business scene. For most consumer goods, marketing experience in business has demonstrated the economic benefits of using established wholesale channels of distribution. Let us consider a pork-and-beans cannery attempting to distribute its product to all the individual stores that would like to have it on their shelves. By using wholesalers, the costs of distribution are greatly reduced. In addition, one wholesaler handles many other products in a particular area of activity—in this case, groceries—providing further benefits to the individual stores, which can obtain other products at the same time from the same source.

Retailing   Retail stores represent a large percentage of all small firms. Small retailers are to be found in every area of products and services we can imagine. Perhaps this is because more people feel competent to attempt independent firm ownership as a retailer. All retail firms buy their products from wholesalers, jobbers, or other distributors in final form for use by the consumer. The function of retailers is to give these products *place utility*, that is, to add to their value by making them available to consumers at a convenient location. Creation of this place utility and provision of other services to the consumer are the economic justification of the retailers' profits.

Service   Service firms are numerous and varied. They are engaged in rendering an essential service to their customers. Pure services are not tangible products that may be inventoried, but they are in great demand by many people in many areas. Doctors and dentists provide services. Consultants and accountants provide services. Many common types of services are supplied by firms which do not work on products that are owned by their customers, for example, repairing TV sets or washing machines, or dry-cleaning clothing for customers. Other service firms perform such services as barbering or obtaining tickets to the current hit play in town. The essential characteristic of all service firms is that they do not provide a consumable product for their customers, but a special, nonmaterial service.

ENTREPRENEURSHIP: A KEY TO SMALL BUSINESS SUCCESS

The term *entrepreneur* is a derivative of the French word *entreprendre*, which means "to undertake." The entrepreneur is the one who undertakes a venture, organizes it, raises capital to finance it, and assumes all or a major portion of the risk. Entrepreneurs also appear to be the prime change agents in a society.

The entrepreneur is the source of innovation and creativity, the schemer, the heart and soul of economic growth.

Typically, the entrepreneur is seen as an individual who owns and operates a small business. But simply to own and operate a small business – or even a big business – does not make someone an entrepreneur. If an individual is merely a caretaker involved in ordering, scheduling, and administration, then he or she should be considered a manager. If this person is a true entrepreneur, then new products are being created, new ways of providing services are implemented.

There are many misconceptions about entrepreneurs and their function in business development. In the strictest sense of the word, an entrepreneur is an organizer, the coherent force between capital and labour that "puts it all together and makes it happen." An entrepreneur is usually innovative by nature, frequently creating new forms of financing, marketing, or corporate structures to exploit their own or someone else's innovative concept.

Who are the entrepreneurs? What makes them tick? Researchers have identified characteristics that are common to all entrepreneurs to a greater or lesser degree. Here are a few the personality traits of individuals who have a propensity to behave entrepreneurially:

- *Good physical health*
  As anyone who has done it will attest, starting and establishing a business requires long hours of hard work, so physical stamina is important.

- *Superior conceptual abilities (Problem Solving)*
  To identify quickly relationships in complex situations allows the entrepreneur to learn rapidly and resolve complex situations. This results in faster identification of solutions and facilitates crisis management.

- *The broad thinking of a generalist*
  Successful entrepreneurs are able to maintain a constant overview of the entire situation, thus allowing them to integrate detail, and to support and reinforce the main thrust of their project at all times. They are wearing many hats, often at the same time.

- *High self-confidence*
  This quality helps offset adversity and permits the entrepreneur to turn anxieties into effective action.

- *Strong drive*
  Persistence coupled with a strong sense of urgency means the entrepreneur will get things done. When tenacity is added to this drive, it is almost impossible to distract the entrepreneur from the chosen path.

- *A basic need to control and direct*
  Most entrepreneurs are very good at bringing together all the components of a venture to make it achieve its goals. They are normally thought of as take-charge people. The successful

entrepreneur must be in control, rejecting authority over him or her. Entrepreneurs dislike structures, wanting to create their own, and will personally bear maximum responsibility and accountability.

- *Moderate risking*
  The entrepreneur is neither risk averse nor a high risk taker and, certainly, not a "gambler"; but he calculates the risks by analyzing actions and consequences prior to making decisions. If the elements are right, the entrepreneur will assume the risks necessary to do the job.

- *Very realistic*
  The entrepreneur generally accepts things the way they are and deals with them in a practical manner, but she wants to know the status at all times. Cautious and suspicious at times, her word is dependable and expects others to be the same.

- *Moderate interpersonal skills*
  "People" (interpersonal) skills are mandatory for the professional manager, but they are not required to the same degree in entrepreneurs. As they run their own show and set company goals, they rarely delegate decisions or go for in-depth team participation. If they possess highly developed interpersonal skills *in addition* to the other necessary characteristics, this will be a plus, especially useful as the business grows larger.

- *Orientation to excellence*
  Entrepreneurs often desire to achieve something that is outstanding, that they can be proud of — something first class.

- *Sufficient emotional stability*
  Successfully establishing and running a new enterprise creates incredible pressures at times, so the ability to remain cool and maintain self-control under trying conditions is almost essential.

In addition to the characteristics identified, all of which may or may not be fully present in any individual entrepreneur, specialized training and experience will significantly enhance their probability of success.

Of course, nothing is ironclad about the above noted traits and characteristics. If one or more are missing in the entrepreneur, they can be offset by carefully selected partners and associates who possess the missing elements. In a study of the twenty-one inductees into the Babson Academy of Distinguished Entrepreneurs, including such notables as An Wang (Wang computers), Wally Amos (Famous Amos' Chocolate Chip Cookies), and Soichiro Honda (Honda Motors), only three attributes and behaviours were mentioned by all twenty-one as the principal reasons for their success, and they were all learnable:

- responding positively to all challenges and learning from mistakes
- taking personal initiative
- having great perseverence

Indeed, if you have these in you, your chances of success are great!

Entrepreneurship is not the prerogative of the few but an opportunity for all. It is the entrepreneurs who play the principal note in determining their success or failure. The entrepreneur is the centre of the system, but he or she depends on good satellite support.

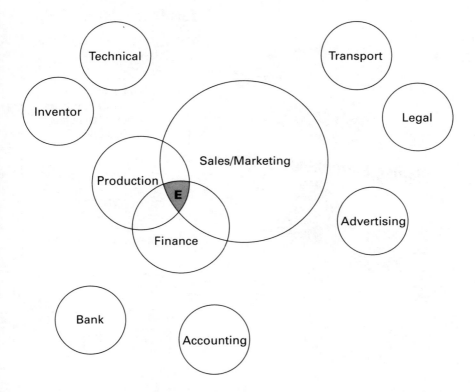

The success of entrepreneurs depends above all on their own efforts and ingenuity. But governments can have a significant influence on the business environment through their policies. The next section will explain this.

THE FEDERAL GOVERNMENT AND SMALL BUSINESS

The federal government has a major and long-standing commitment to small business; its present level of financial support of this segment of our economy is estimated at well in excess of $500 million per year. The provinces, as well, are providing financial assistance to the small business community through a variety of support programs administered by provincial development corporations.

Government supports small business. *Courtesy of Federal Business Development Bank and Ministry of Industry, Trade and Technology.*

Since its inception in 1944, the Industrial Development Bank (IDB) provided debt capital (term loans) to small firms and served as an important source of financing for new and expanding small business. In 1975, it was replaced by a new Crown corporation, the Federal Business Development Bank (FBDB), with a greatly expanded mandate, converting it from a somewhat conservative term lender to a supplier of everything from education to equity capital for the independent business community: more branch offices, faster turnaround time in loan applications, and an improved attitude to risk taking. During the 1990 fiscal year, the FBDB authorized some 5600 loans for a total amount of over $900 million and made thirteen equity

A sample of publications that provide information about small business. *Courtesy of Bank of Montreal and Canadian Federation of Independent Business.*

investments totalling $11.6 million, mostly in high technology undertakings. For a nominal fee, management assistance is also made available.

The *Small Business Loans Act* (SBLA) is another federal program to help small firms: it actually utilizes private sector (banks, trust companies) funds by guaranteeing loans made by these institutions for small business start-ups and expansions. In 1988, $684 million was made available to 18 640 small business firms under the SBLA.

The federal government has made a concerted effort to make itself more accessible to small business and to simplify procedures. It is no secret that small business often finds dealing with government to be difficult and time-consuming. In response to such perceptions, the government has restructured the departments and agencies responsible for delivering programs at the local level. At that time, the activities of various departments are being harmonized and coordinated.

One of the principal advocates working for small business in the federal government is Industry, Science and Technology Canada (ISTC). The department has been given a broad mandate to promote the international competitiveness, technological capabilities, productivity, and efficiency of Canadian industry. As part of this broad mandate affecting all Canadian businesses, whatever their size, ISTC has been given a specific mission to "develop and implement national policies to foster entrepreneurship and the start-up, growth and expansion of small businesses."

ISTC also has a role in promoting and supporting the marketing of Canadian goods, services, and technology at home and abroad. And it promotes investment in Canadian industry, science, and technology. Most of ISTC's functions relate to small business in one way or another.

The creation of ISTC has been accompanied by a conscious effort to get closer to the small- and medium-sized firms that do not always have the resources to find their way to the many services offered by government. Within the government, the Minister of State (Small Business and Tourism) and ISTC's Entrepreneurship and Small Business Office (ESBO) have a responsibility to ensure that the interests of Canada's small businesses are represented and reflected in the actions and policies of ISTC and other federal government departments and agencies.

Small business plays a critical role in regional development. Statistics show that small business activity is distributed across Canada in direct proportion to the distribution of the population at large. Also, studies have shown that the resilience of small business has played a critical role in sustaining regional economies, especially during economic downturns.

The federal government has recognized the regional importance of small business in the mandate it has given to several new organizations that focus on regional development. A local orientation allows government services to be focused on specific regional concerns, it permits greater flexibility, and it fosters increased responsiveness. The most important federal regional programs are delivered through three organizations: Western Economic Diversification Canada, Atlantic Canada Opportunities Agency, and ISTC itself.

Western Economic Diversification Canada (WD) covers the four western provinces and seeks to encourage activity outside of traditional resource-based industries. In carrying out its mandate to encourage the development of new products, technologies, and markets in the western provinces, WD provides financial assistance to projects that contribute to the diversification of the western economy; helps businesses to find the most appropriate source of government assistance for their projects; and acts as an advocate for the West in national economic decision-making. Although not exclusively geared to small businesses, WD programs benefit many smaller companies.

The Atlantic Canada Opportunities Agency (ACOA) fosters development in the four Atlantic provinces. Small business has traditionally been and remains an important part of the region's economy. ACOA is based on the principles of partnership, shared risk, investment, and working with all levels of government to promote the interest of the Atlantic region. ACOA cooperates with the private sector, provincial and municipal governments, universities, and industrial commissions on programs to develop the region. It acts as a coordinator for the efforts of all federal government departments with an impact on the Atlantic region. It also promotes Atlantic interests in the formulation of federal policy.

From the viewpoint of small business, ACOA's most important function is its Action Program, through which small- and medium-sized businesses can obtain direct financial assistance, loan guarantees, and interest buy-downs to modernize, expand, design a new product, develop technology, or carry out feasibility and marketing studies.

ISTC retains responsibility for regional development in Ontario and Quebec. Its objective is to promote economic development in areas of Quebec and Ontario where low incomes and slow economic growth prevail or where opportunities for productive employment remain inadequate, to emphasize long-term economic growth, and to foster the development of small- and medium-sized businesses. In northern Ontario, FedNor is a government agency designed to spur economic growth through a range of assistance programs mostly aimed at small business. In Quebec, the main vehicle of government assistance is the Canada-Quebec Subsidiary Agreement on the Economic Development of the Regions of Quebec, signed in June 1988. The Agreement provides for federal and provincial assistance to both the central and the resource regions of the province.

SELLING TO THE FEDERAL GOVERNMENT

The federal government is the single largest purchaser of goods and services in Canada. Through its purchasing policies, it has an important impact on the small business sector. As a source of business, the federal government is a customer that no small business can afford to ignore.

Supply and Services Canada (SSC) is responsible for approximately half of all federal government purchases. Up to 70 per cent of its purchases involve high technology products. Public Works Canada is the contracting authority for the majority of construction contracts relating to federal public works and installations. Responsibility for the remainder of government purchases, many of which consist of services, is delegated by the Treasury Board of Canada to individual departments.

The annual value of SSC contracts awarded to small firms rose from $780 million to $1.85 billion between 1980–81 and 1986–87. In the latter year, some 32 000 small companies sold goods and services directly to SSC. These firms accounted for one-third of the value of all SSC contracts.

In 1986, SSC introduced a Small Business Action Plan in order to improve small business access to government contracting. This included a one-stop sourcing registration system and adoption of a short-form contract for purchases below $25,000. These were adopted to make it easier for small firms to bid for and win federal business.

In 1988, SCC and ISTC announced the Access Small Business Program. This program includes a number of initiatives aimed at helping small business gain improved access to government contracts.

Doing business with SSC is different from dealing with a private company. In the majority of cases, SSC solicits bids from source lists of companies or individuals who have registered as potential suppliers.

However, for requirements falling under GATT (General Agreement on Tariffs and Trade) or the Canada–U.S. Free Trade Agreement, opportunities to bid are posted in a new weekly publication called Government Business Opportunities. Small firms wishing to sell to federal departments and agencies should begin by registering with their regional SSC office. These offices will make information available on what the government is buying in their region. SSC reflects regional development considerations in its procurement policies and processes. For example, the Area Buy Policy requires that SSC's regional offices solicit bids within their area to ensure adequate competition, the required level of service to customers, and fair value for the taxpayer's dollar. Small businesses are major beneficiaries under the Area Buy Policy.

Small business now has a political voice in the federal Cabinet through the post of Minister of State (Small Business and Tourism). This is an important development in the relationship between the small business community and the federal government, which, hopefully, will lead to a strong permanent department-level civil service to protect and to further the interests of small businesses.

The value of good, healthy competition is recognized in our society. Competition is deemed essential for keeping a strong free enterprise system. If we recognize that more than 90 per cent of the more than one million firms in Canada employ fewer than fifty people, we can appreciate the statement that thousands of small firms act both as suppliers of materials and products to our large firms and as distributors of products for these firms.

From this review of the small business scene, the reader can probably appreciate that the big firm is the exception and not the rule in our business community.

SUMMARY

Small business firms are an integral part of the total business scene in Canada and in most countries of the Western world. In all major areas of business activity—manufacturing, mining, wholesaling, retailing, and service business-es—small firms account for a large part of the total dollar sales.

Entrepreneurship is the key to small business success. Entrepreneurs take risks when they operate small businesses. They have invested time and money into the venture in the hope of making a profit.

Special people become successful entrepreneurs. They must have a vision for their business, be willing to take risks, and have the ability to plan, organize, and follow through. In addition, entrepreneurs must work hard and put in long hours, and they must maintain good relations with customers, employees, and with the other businesses they deal with, such as banks, insurance companies, service firms, and suppliers.

The preservation and development of a healthy small business community is an avowed policy of our governments. Industry, Science and Technology Canada and the Minister of State (Small Business and Tourism) are charged with specific activities to aid small firms. Their support ranges from management and financial assistance to help in securing government contracts.

Big business recognizes its dependence on small firms and gives more than lip service to help preserve their strength and profitability. Many suppliers of parts and materials to large corporations are very small firms. Mass-production factories could not distribute their output without the services of thousands of small retailers. Purchasing policies of many of our largest industries specify special consideration for buying from small firms.

QUESTIONS FOR CLASS DISCUSSION

1   Can you name a large manufacturing firm whose products are sold in more than 3000 retail stores?

2   How many small firm suppliers of parts and materials would you suspect sell their products to the Ford Motor Company of Canada Limited?

3   How many small businesses are there in Canada per 1000 population? Is this more or less than we have had in the past?

4   How does the Committee for Economic Development measure a small business?

5   Do large business firms that employ more than 2500 people represent 30 per cent, 20 per cent, 10 per cent, or less than 0.5 per cent of the total firms in the country?

6   Does the Government of Canada support small business firms? How?

7   Is it worthwhile to sell to the Government?

8   Can you name an example of a manufacturing firm? A mining firm? A wholesaling firm? A retailing firm? A service firm? A firm in the field of finance?

9   What is meant when we say that principles of management are adaptable even though not always adoptable?

10   Can you name three service firms whose services you have used?

11   Are more small firms engaged in retailing than in manufacturing? Why do you think this is so?

12   Why would giant companies be interested in the welfare of healthy small companies?

13   Which are the three most important characteristics of a successful entrepreneur, in your opinion?

Projects for Home Assignment and/or Class Discussion

1   There are approximately thirty-six small business firms in Canada per 1000 population.
   a. Does this mean that a small town of 1000 people would support thirty-six different small firms? Explain.
   b. Prepare a list of thirty-six firms that would serve a cross-section of 1000 people in a large city.

2   Prepare a written evaluation of the definitions of small business given in the U.S.A. Small Business Act, by the Committee for Economic Development, and by the various Canadian government programs and legislations. Which definition do you prefer? Why?

3   Write a brief essay demonstrating the difference between adaptability and adoptability of a particular principle of management.

4   Identify a successful entrepreneur in your community. Interview that person, prepare a brief report, and try to have that person visit your class.

REFERENCES FOR FURTHER READING

Archer, M., *An Introduction to Canadian Business*, 5th ed., McGraw-Hill Ryerson Ltd., Toronto, 1986, Chapters 1 and 17.

Beckman, M.D., W.S. Good, and R.G. Wyckham, *Small Business Management*, John Wiley & Sons Canada Ltd., Toronto, 1982, Chapter 1.

James, J.D., *Starting a Successful Business in Canada*, 7th ed., International Self-Counsel Press Ltd., North Vancouver, B.C., 1982.

Kao, R.W.Y., *Small Business Management: A Strategic Emphasis*, Holt Rinehart and Winston of Canada Ltd., Toronto, 2nd ed., 1984, Chapter 1.

Knight, R.M., *Small Business Management in Canada*, McGraw-Hill Ryerson Ltd., Toronto, 1981, Chapter 1.

Peterson, Rein, *Small Business—Building a Balanced Economy*, Press Porcépic Limited, Erin, Ontario, 1977.

Tate Jr., C.E., L.C. Megginson, C.R. Scott Jr., and L.R. Trueblood, *Successful Small Business Management*, 3rd ed., Business Publications, Inc., Plano, Texas, 1985, Chapter 1.

Canadian Small Business Guide, CCH Canadian Limited, Don Mills, Ontario.

. . . .

2

The Individual Small Firm:

Its Advantages, Rewards, and

Requirements for Success

LEARNING OBJECTIVES

After reading this chapter, you will be able to:
1. **R**ecognize the advantages of running a small business
2. **A**ssess the chances for success
3. **K**now the rewards of a small enterprise
4. **F**ocus on the requirements for successful small firm management

ADVANTAGES OF SMALL FIRMS

The fact that small firms are such an important part of our economy is not an historical accident. It is not only the result of government programs to aid small firms or a benevolent policy of large firms. Competition in our society is recognized as desirable in order to serve the population better. Small firms actually have advantages over large firms in many cases. All large firms were once small. They grew because they were well managed with dynamic leadership. Many of today's small firms will become giants in tomorrow's business world.

Some of the situations in which small firms have distinct advantages are the following:

1   *When new products or ideas are being tried out.* The freedom to attempt new types of business ventures is one of our cherished rights, and when one is engaging in such a business, it is much better to start with a small firm. Growth can always come with success. The acceptability of the new product or idea may need market testing. It is often better to check market reaction before investing a great deal of money in a new product or idea. Management requirements may be uncertain and financial needs unknown in the starting period of the new firm.

2   *When the personal attention of the owner is essential to daily operations.* A fine restaurant is an example. If the owner's presence as host or as executive is important to the growth of the business, it will be more successful if it is small enough for one person to supervise.

3   *Where personal services, either professional or skilled, are dominant.* Firms that offer the professional or nonprofessional services of their employees in offering their product or service to the public usually have a distinct advantage if they are small. Examples include beauty parlours, real estate offices, interior decorating firms, TV repair shops, and major heavy-equipment repair firms. Any possible advantages of large size in these areas are usually offset by greatly enlarged overhead, less efficiency on the job, and loss of the personal touch of the smaller firm. Medical and dental services are usually rendered by small firms.

4   *When the market for the product or service is mainly local.* In some types of firms, it just is not economical to attempt a scale of operation that exceeds the local market demand. The making of bricks or concrete blocks for the construction industry is an example. Transportation costs are prohibitive for moving such products. The independent real estate firm specializing in residential sales usually falls in the category of firms that do better on a smaller, local scale.

5 *When the firm deals in perishable materials or products.* Small florists may join together to have their "flowers by wire" services, but still the greatest volume of business is done through local orders. Dairy products are now sold in wider markets, but the local firms have distinct advantages in dealing with these perishable products. Local canneries still do much of the canning of fruits and vegetables in closely supervised small firms.

6 *When only a limited market is available or sought.* One example is custom tailoring. And neighbourhood groceries with alert managers have successfully competed with the trend toward large supermarkets.

7 *When the industry is characterized by wide variations in demand or in styles.* Examples include ladies' dress lines, ornamental candlemakers, and custom-made chandeliers and lamp shades. These circumstances just do not invite large firm development in most cases. Large production plants need stable markets and the ability to plan production quantities of products in economical lot sizes. The small, flexible firm usually can adjust to the necessary variations much more easily.

8 *When close rapport with personnel is essential.* Small firm owners usually have the valuable advantage of being close to employees. They do not have to receive grievances through a committee or hold formal hearings on them. They know problems from daily conversations and can adjust employment to abilities better because of this close association. As a result, they are usually able to maintain better morale and efficiency in the firm, which is important in any business.

9 *Where product is highly specialized or customized.* An immediate example that comes to mind is the furniture shop that builds customized furniture. The customer can only be at ease in the small business environment where he or she deals only with the owner/manager/craftsman/artist. There is a clear line of communication in such a situation, one which is indispensable and unachievable in the large business environment. In the situation where art/furniture is being personalized, the importance of closeness and communication cannot be over-emphasized.

10 *Autonomy* or *absolute control.* To many entrepreneurs, this is the most critical element of being self-employed. In the small business, the one-man or one-woman show, that inherent personality trait, is satisfied in the only way it can be. Not being told what to do, when to do it, and how to do it is the ultimate expression of achievement to many entrepreneurs. This can only be achieved in the small business environment. As a business grows, one person can only do so much. At some point the entrepreneur will have to

delegate authority and responsibility. If the entrepreneur is to relish the condition described, he or she will then surely keep the business a small, controllable one.

11   *Ease of movement.* In a small business, unlike a large one, the entrepreneur has a great deal of freedom. He or she can open and close the shop and alter the line of business as he or she so chooses. The commitment isn't so large that exercising the above liberties is restricted by impractical movement.

The individual firm has benefited from having these and other advantages. In addition to the types of firms cited, small firms in such fields as construction, wholesaling, retailing, and the service industries have faced up well to their larger firm competition. Insurance and smaller finance firms have also been very successful. The profitable firms have not relied on the inherent advantages of small firms as such, but have combined these advantages with alert and competent management to achieve their success.

REAL AND ALLEGED DISADVANTAGES OF SMALL FIRMS

It is very easy for persons who have failed in a small business to blame it on the disadvantages of being small. In many cases, however, their failures were likely due to lack of management ability, lack of proper planning, or simply the fact that the type of firm established did not have a chance in the first place.

Small firms are often said to labour under such disadvantages as inability to secure competent employees, tax burdens, inability to finance expansion that has been proved to be practicable, limited vendor goodwill, inability to cope with monopolistic practices, lack of support by "vested interests," discriminatory practices by large shopping-centre developers, lack of time for the small proprietor to handle multiple assignments, lack of research facilities, and the problems of making a new firm or product known in its market.

While it cannot be denied that there is substance to some of these alleged disadvantages (such as shopping-centre developers desiring chain stores instead of small local firms for tenants), it can also be contended that many of these problems are a direct result of improper planning and operation, which will be outlined in succeeding chapters. Large firms share many of the problems that small firms have. The adage that "an ounce of prevention is worth a pound of cure" was never more aptly demonstrated than in the planning stage of a new firm. So many of the business failures that occur every year could have been avoided if the firm had been properly planned. Many would likely not have been established. (See Figure 2-1.)

We have cherished the right of all citizens to go into business for themselves. We have probably given more attention to preserving this right than to the matter of helping those starting new firms prepare to be successful.

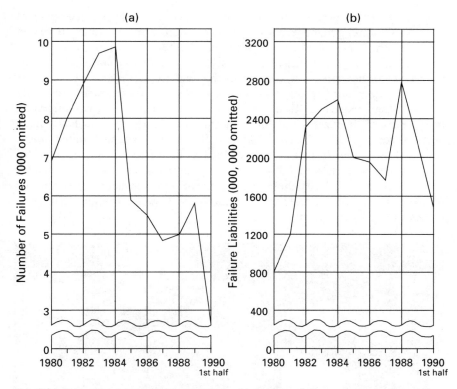

F I G U R E   2 - 1 • (a) The number of business failures have been on the rise since the late 1970s. (b) For firms that do fail, the average liabilities increased substantially during the 1980s and into the 1990s.

Adapted from Dun & Bradstreet Canada Limited/Limitée and Superintendent of Bankruptcy, Monthly Insolvency Report.

Fortunately, not all Canadians believe that they would be successful managers of their own firms. Respect for the responsibilities of ownership and management of a business is a first requirement for success. When this respect exists, the person contemplating setting up a new firm will recognize the need for education in management as the first step in planning.

PREPARATION FOR SMALL FIRM OWNERSHIP

There is no better way to prepare for a successful business operation than by learning the ingredients of good planning, having some experience in the particular line, and knowing the essentials of good management. This truth is aptly demonstrated by the fact that the most common causes of small firm failures are incompetence, improper experience, and lack of management training. Obtaining managerial competence and experience requires time and effort. There is no substitute for training whether at a school, community college, university, or management institute; nor is there a substitute for the experience to be gained by working in the field for an organization.

What is important to many small businesses is survival during the early years of their existence. Every effort must be directed towards this goal, because those businesses that make it through the early years have much better success records. In a 1985 Dun & Bradstreet Canada Limited study, results showed that firms in existence for less than four years accounted for 30 per cent of total failures, those in existence for five to six years accounted for 18 per cent of the failures, those in existence for seven to ten years accounted for 23 per cent of the failures, and those in existence for over ten years represented 29 per cent of the failures.[1]

The satisfaction of being one's own boss is an important reward to many. *Courtesy Industry, Science and Technology.*

---

[1]These facts represent findings from detailed studies made by the Business Economics department of Dun & Bradstreet Canada Limited, Toronto. This fine research firm serves business, government, and educational institutions with many reports on operational phases of the business community. (Quoted by permission.)

THE REWARDS OF SUCCESSFUL SMALL FIRM OWNERSHIP

The rewards of success in operating one's own business are seen differently by different people. The retired couple who wish only to maintain a small income while they enjoy other activities in their senior years will measure rewards quite differently from the young college graduate who opens his or her new firm with big ideas for expansion and growth. The entire approach of this text will be toward enabling the new small firm not only to survive but to grow.

All proprietors seek the reward of *good profits*. Many small firms realize excellent profits. Most small firm owners also find a great reward in the *satisfying nature of their work*. The *ability to be one's own boss* is an important reward to many. Additionally, the *status in the community* that comes with being a successful firm owner ranks high on the list of rewards for most proprietors.

While these rewards are the ones that most owners seek, other owners may gain satisfactions of quite a different nature. *Family pride, money to educate children well, preservation of family tradition*, and an *outlet for creativity* are some additional benefits.

Regardless of motivation, it is clear that successful ownership of one's own business can be a most satisfying and profitable experience. Furthermore, the right to start your own firm is guaranteed in our country. If this freedom is coupled with competence in planning and operation, then the individual's desire for reward can be achieved. The creation of such success stories is the objective of this book.

REQUIREMENTS FOR SUCCESSFUL SMALL FIRM MANAGEMENT

The requirements for successful small firm management do not include only the personal characteristics of the individuals involved. They also include good customer relations and an awareness of the consumerism movement; good community relations as part of a total public relations policy; good business ethics and a demonstrated social responsibility; the ability to deal with vast government regulations; and, in many cases, a willingness to operate the small firm as a wholly regulated business. These requirements for success can be summarized as follows:

1 Personal characteristics
2 Good customer relations and knowledge of consumerism
3 Business ethics and social responsibility
4 Compliance with vast government regulations
5 Willingness to operate as a completely regulated firm

As we proceed with our study of management details, the existence of these success requirements will be presumed and not reiterated with each subject of our investigation. Therefore, brief comment on each is made here.

1 Personal Characteristics

In Chapter 1 we described and discussed briefly the major personality traits of an entrepreneur. We are now extending that description to include the personal characteristics of successful small firm managers. Many of the manager's traits overlap with the entrepreneur's; however, there are some additional and distinct skills for successful small firm managers: strong "people" skills and communication and administrative abilities, which are very important to an ongoing operation.

Many studies have been made in search of the definitive list of personal characteristics that an individual should have in order to succeed in small firm ownership. No generally agreed-upon composite of characteristics has resulted, which is to be expected when one is dealing with human beings. Different characteristics appear in greater or lesser degrees in different people. Offsetting features may be more dominant in one person than in another. Still, we can attempt to make a list of those characteristics that have been found generally desirable in studies of successful small firm owners.

Especially prominent characteristics of successful managers of small firms include:

Energy

Initiative

Willingness to take some (calculated) risks

Ability to organize

Personality

Technical competence

Administrative ability

Good judgement

Restraint

To communicate well

Leadership qualities

Patience

Preownership experience

Experienced small firm owners will agree with any list of success characteristics such as the above. They will hurriedly point out, however, that they believe the chief characteristic for success is *willingness to work hard*. Being one's own boss means that you do not punch a clock, your hours are not 9 to 5, but instead you must do what is necessary in the total management of the firm. That usually means hard work and long hours, and, at least in its early years, hours beyond those when the firm is open for business. Experienced business owners will also point out that different types of firms will require a different combination of some of the characteristics listed above. Taking risks is a part of all firm ownership.

We can note in passing that the American philosopher William James summed up the requirements for success in any endeavour as consisting of three essential components:

The idea

The act

The will to act

As we shall learn in detail through our study here, *the act* of starting a new small business involves much planning and a detailed knowledge of every phase of total management.

2 Good Customer Relations and Knowledge of Consumerism

Good customer relations (as distinguished from public relations) have always been a key to successful ownership of any firm; but today's business world has seen wide-ranging developments in the consumerism movement. Consumer groups have vociferously expressed concerns about the conduct of the business world. Consumerism goes beyond concern with services offered. These groups speak of value, adequacy and safety of products, and price policies. In the 1990s, consumers concerned with the protection of the environment encouraged the creation of "green" products; nonpolluting packaging, container recycling, and the like will provide many opportunities to innovative small firms.

Much legislation was passed in the 1970s to protect consumer rights in such matters as credit arrangements, customer complaints about merchandise, financial responsibility, and related matters. In the 1980s, many amendments were made to update those laws passed in the 1970s. More recently, a move has been made to review all legislation that governs consumers' rights. The government is, however, in the midst of administering protection funds, such as the Auto Protection Fund, the General Insurance Fund, and the Travellers Insurance Fund. These funds are, in a sense, self-regulating. Participants are the business people who contribute premiums to protect consumers. Therefore, by minimizing the so-called "rip-offs," the business owners minimize their premiums. Both the movement to review all legislation and the movement to create more of these funds began in 1985. It seems apparent that, in the coming years, the rights of the consumer and a concern for the environment will be in the forefront of government consideration. A knowledge of the applicable legislation and current demands of consumers is essential to success.

3 Business Ethics and Social Responsibility

The problem of earning a profit in business goes far beyond the details of management techniques. Not the least point to consider is community expectations concerning business ethics and the social responsibility of the business world. The typical small business owner assumes that good ethics are reflected in his or her daily dealings. But the question of responsibility of the business world for all of the economic ills of the society has divided both academicians and business leaders. Entire college courses are now offered under the title "The Social Responsibility of Business." Some critics hold the business community responsible for unemployment, crime in the streets, and the plight of the ill-clothed, ill-housed, and ill-fed. Others believe that it is the responsibility of the business world to create jobs, produce products, and pay taxes to the government so that it can employ experts to cope with social problems.

It behooves even small firm owners to be aware of social issues involved, to practise honest business ethics, and to become good citizens of the community.

4 Compliance with Extensive Government Regulations

New small firm owners are often not familiar with the extent to which government rules and regulations reach into almost every phase of their operations. The extensive tax structure is only one part of this problem. Frustration, expense, and time are involved in complying with the avalanche of government regulations in effect today. Chapter 22, "Small Business and the Law," will expand this subject for us later.

5 Willingness to Operate as a Completely Regulated Firm

Government regulations extend even further into the operations of many types of small firms. These can be small utility companies, such as local water companies, or firms like taxi companies, ambulance services, or towing companies. The very basics of daily operations are indicated by government agencies in such cases. Rate charges, quantity of service available, and areas to be served can all be dictated. Such regulations go well beyond the licences or qualification certificates needed for beauty parlour operators, barbers, or truck drivers. Rugged individualists who desire to make all their own decisions will find it necessary to compromise many of their convictions when engaging in these types of business activities. The ability to operate under strict regulation remains a requirement for success in such fields.

SUMMARY

There are many circumstances in business in which the small firm has distinct advantages over the larger firm. These include cases where new products or ideas are being tried, when personal attention of the owner is necessary for success, where personal services are dominant, when markets are mainly local, where perishable materials or products are handled, where only limited markets are sought or available, and when close rapport with employees is essential.

Many of the alleged disadvantages of small firms could be overcome with better planning. An ill-conceived business, whether large or small, has little chance of success if its operations has not been properly planned. Good research in the planning stage can reveal opportunities for success. It can also indicate when a business that is contemplated should not be undertaken.

The rewards for successful small firm ownership can be significant. The personal satisfactions will vary with the individual owner. Good profits, satisfying employment, being one's own boss, community status, family pride and tradition, and having an outlet for one's creativity are some of them.

But the rewards are never automatic or guaranteed. Success makes many demands upon the operator of the firm. Personal characteristics and other requirements for successful ownership of small business firms have been enumerated, but sound business knowledge and willingness to work hard stand at the head of any list. Knowing the causes of failures can protect the owner against them.

QUESTIONS FOR CLASS DISCUSSION

1 Do you agree that "competition is desirable in order to serve the population better"? Explain.

2 Do you know of a business firm where the personal attention of the owner is important to the firm's success?

3 Why do brickyards usually have a market that is essentially local?

4 Do you think that small firms can keep competent employees? How?

5 Why is it that not all Canadians believe they would be successful owners and managers of their own business?

6 How would you explain that small firm failures declined in the last decade but that the average debts of those failing increased?

7 Which two rewards of success would you place first if you had your own small business?

8 Would you include preownership experience in your list of requirements for successful management?

9 What do you like about a particular small business that you patronize?

10 Do large firms share the same problems that small firms have? Explain.

Projects for Home Assignment and/or Class Discussion

1 Write a description of a small firm, with which you are familiar, where the personal appearance of the owner is considered important by its customers. Explain why this is considered important.

2   Prepare a short paper explaining your impressions of the chief disadvantages of small firms. Explain how you believe these disadvantages can be overcome.

REFERENCES FOR FURTHER READING

Beckman, M.D., W.S. Good, and R.G. Wyckham, *Small Business Management*, John Wiley & Sons Canada Ltd., Toronto, 1982, Chapter 2.

Knight, R.M., *Small Business Management in Canada*, McGraw-Hill Ryerson Ltd., Toronto, 1981, Chapter 2.

Tate Jr., C.E., L.C. Megginson, C.R. Scott Jr., and L.R. Trueblood, *Successful Small Business Management*, 3rd ed., Business Publications, Inc., Plano, Texas, 1985, Chapters 2 and 3.

3

Venture Search and Selection

LEARNING OBJECTIVES

After reading this chapter, you will be able to:

1. **R**ecognize the need to conduct a systematic search for ventures
2. **E**stablish business selection criteria
3. **S**creen potential ventures
4. **D**istinguish different types of firms
5. **U**nderstand where to find ideas

The search for a potentially profitable product or service is a first step towards a successful venture. In fact, there are many examples to indicate that the product idea is the single most important factor in business success. The "golden key" to success is: get in the right business at the right time. The advice is simple; the accomplishment of it is not. The business will also have to be "right" for you, so a systematic and disciplined preliminary screening should eliminate the prospects that simply do not suit or meet your needs. Those business prospects remaining must be subjected to an objective assessment of their potential followed by a careful feasibility analysis. In order to increase the likelihood of finding a successful product idea, as many candidates as possible should be considered.

In this chapter, we discuss systematic approaches to idea generation, screening, and evaluation. Figure 3-1 shows a model for the process.

F I G U R E   3 - 1

MODEL FOR VENTURE SELECTION

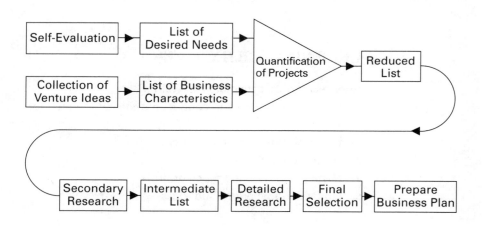

BUSINESS SELECTION CRITERIA

In order to put you on the right track, start with your "capability assessment" as shown in Table 3-1. This will enable you to focus and build on your strengths.

Now we can move on to the next step: developing your own business selection criteria.

Business selection criteria are made up of several elements that deal with financial and personal goals, business work requirements, and the impact of a small business on the owner's lifestyle.

TABLE 3-1

CAPABILITY ASSESSMENT

HEALTH AND PHYSICAL CAPABILITIES

-
-
-

CAPABILITIES DEVELOPED IN FORMAL EDUCATION

•	•	•
•	•	•
•	•	•
•	•	•

CAPABILITIES DEVELOPED AS AN EMPLOYEE

•	•
•	•
•	•
•	•

CAPABILITIES DEVELOPED IN HOBBIES AND OTHER ACTIVITIES

•	•
•	•
•	•
•	•

INVESTMENT CAPABILITY

- Net Worth $_____
- Family Contingency Fund $_____
- Total Cash Actually Available for Investment $_____

OTHER PEOPLE'S OPINIONS OF YOU, HOW THEY SEE YOU

-
-
-

The student of small business management will find it very helpful to list on paper his personal business selection preferences. The business selection criteria, what the potential small firm owner wants from the business, will be used later on to screen a large group of different types of businesses. In this way, the student will be able to select the type of business that comes closest to meeting his criteria. The criteria should be divided into three major selections:

Goals

The work

Lifestyle impact

Goals

Annual Income   How much do you want to earn each year after your business is running smoothly? It is important to decide on an income goal because different types of businesses have different income potentials. A fast-food restaurant has one income potential and a small manufacturing business may have quite another. The potential small business owner should make sure that goals are set realistically. The easiest way for a person to set a personal income goal is to answer the question: How much do I want to be making per year five years from now?

Personal Achievement   Now that an income goal has been established, let's move on to a type of goal that is quite different: personal achievement, which is really nothing more or nothing less than what the potential small firm owner, as an individual, wants to be. The most obvious personal achievement goal is to build a successful business, which is quite an achievement in itself. But after thinking about it, additional personal goals may become obvious. Here are some examples of goals that others have expressed.

- To provide work opportunities for minorities
- To build a business that will provide for family
- To contribute something worthwhile and lasting to society
- To maximize the percentage of enjoyable time each day
- To travel and see the world
- To express personal artistic creativity

This list is obviously not complete; it is only intended to start you thinking.

Importance of Status   Everyone knows what status is, and most profess not to be interested in it. Yet, we are all concerned with what other people think of us. They influence our choice of clothing, the car we drive, the neighbourhood we live in, and even where, when, and how often we go on vacation. All of us are status seekers to at least a modest degree. Some seem to thrive on it. Businesses have their status, too. There are high status businesses and low status businesses. Junk collecting is an obvious low status business and being a Mercedes-Benz dealer is an obvious higher status business. But there are more subtle differences. There is a different status in owning a Burger King franchise than owning a Red Lobster or Swiss Chalet franchise, even though all are restaurants. And it is true in manufacturing also. A manufacturer of surgical instruments has a higher status than a manufacturer of nuts and bolts. Some people are very interested in the status of their business and others are not interested at all. Neither group is "right," but it may be an important consideration in selecting the type of business for you. The key is to choose a business that has a status with which *you* will feel comfortable.

The Work

Content   The key to defining the business selection criteria as they relate to work content is to isolate the types of work enjoyed most. Making things with your hands? Paper work? Personal persuasion and selling? A strong preference for working indoors or outdoors?

People Contact   What about working with other people? Is it enjoyable or would working alone be more satisfactory?

How Much Time Are You Willing to Spend?   Starting a small business takes a lot of hard work; in fact it may consume most of the small business owner's waking hours in the first few years.

Samples of publications covering new venture ideas. *Courtesy of Ernst & Young, Scotiabank, and Federal Business Development Bank.*

TABLE 3 - 2

SCREENING-TABLE FORMAT

BUSINESS SELECTION CRITERIA

POSSIBLE TYPES OF BUSINESSES	GOALS				THE WORK			LIFESTYLE		TOTAL YES
	INCOME	PERSONAL ACHIEVEMENT	STATUS	CONTENT	PEOPLE CONTACT	HOW MUCH	BUSINESS HOURS	OTHER IMPACTS		
1.	( )	( )	( )	( )	( )	( )	( )	( )		( )
2.		( )	( )	( )	( )		( )	( )		( )
3.										
4.										
5.										
6.										
7.										
8.										
9.										
10.										

TABLE 3-3

SAMPLE SCREENING TABLE

BUSINESS SELECTION CRITERIA

POSSIBLE TYPES OF BUSINESSES	GOALS		STATUS	THE WORK		HOW MUCH	LIFESTYLE		TOTAL YES
	INCOME ($50K)	PERSONAL ACHIEVEMENT (Minority group hiring)(Travel)( )	(Moderate)	CONTENT (Hand)(People)(Things)	PEOPLE CONTACT (All except personal selling)( )	(Eventual)(Part-time)	BUSINESS HOURS (M-F)(9-5)	OTHER IMPACTS (25 km)(No emergency)( )	
1. Real Estate	Yes	No	Yes	No	No	Yes	No	Yes	4
2. Camera Shop	No	No	No	Yes	Yes	No	No	Yes	3
3. Bicycle Shop	No	No	No	Yes	Yes	No	No	Yes	3
4. Lock Manufacturing	Yes	Yes	Yes	Yes	No	Yes	Yes	Yes	7
5. Antique Shop	Yes	No	Yes	Yes	Yes	No	Yes	No	5
6. Dog Kennel	No	No	No	No	Yes	No	No	No	1
7. Auto Repair Franchise	Yes	No	No	Yes	Yes	No	No	No	3
8. Machine Shop	Yes	Yes	Yes	Yes	No	Yes	Yes	Yes	7
9. Mail Order	Yes	No	Yes	Yes	Yes	Yes	Yes	Yes	7
10. Travel Agency	Yes	Yes	No	No	No	No	No	No	2

Lifestyle Impact

Business Hours   A 9-to-5, Monday-to-Friday employee might not have given much thought to the hours that many small businesses are open. If you enjoy a normal work week and do not want to give it up when you start your business, you will have to be careful when you choose your business.

Other Business Impact   You have seen how business hours can have a major impact on lifestyle, but there are many more subtle ways a business can affect lifestyle. For example, being a manufacturer's representative may require heavy, out-of-town travel, which means nights and evenings away from family. Personal selling businesses may also require entertaining customers on evenings or weekends. Another area of major impact is the location of a specific business. Many businesses, to be successful, must be near a large concentration of potential customers. There is the effect of emergency calls or customer complaints on the owner's lifestyle.

Now that the business selection criteria have been developed, small business goals have been defined, types of work you enjoy have been chosen, and a certain lifestyle has been chosen, proceed with a very simple method of isolating one or maybe more types of businesses that come closest to meeting the goals, work requirements, and lifestyle desires specified.

SCREENING POTENTIAL VENTURES

The first step in the comparison process is to set up a screening table. Table 3-2 will show you the screening table format guide.

Once the screening table format has been set up, begin to fill in the parentheses under each column. For example, in the parentheses below the heading Income, fill in the dollar income goal arrived at when developing the business selection criteria. After completing the Business Selection Criteria columns, fill in the horizontal lines: the possible types of businesses. As indicated earlier, the screening process involves comparing the business selection criteria made with each of the types of businesses on the list. Basically, the process involves comparing one type of business at a time. Take the first business type and work across the page. Put a *Yes* under each column where the criterion is satisfied by that particular type of business. If the business does not meet the criterion, put a *No*. A typical screening table that has been filled in is shown in Table 3-3.

After completing the screening table, count up each *Yes* for the different businesses chosen. Totalling them up, you will probably begin to see some interesting results; some business types will have mostly *Yes* and some will have only a few.

The next step will analyze the results and implications of the screening process. The results of the screening table may make a selection very obvious. If only one business type has a high total score, then this is probably the business type for you—and it may be your own first choice for business type.

However, it is quite likely that three or four business types will have high scores. Don't be concerned about this situation. The purpose of the screening process is to take a large number of business types and, by using the business selection criteria, reduce them to a manageable number, say down to four. The next step is to assign an importance factor to the various criteria – in technical jargon this is called "weighting" – and then go through the entire exercise again. Eventually, through the elimination process, a final selection will be reached. Of course, depending on the weight assigned to the various factors, the last four can be easily manipulated; that is where real intuition, or what is called a "gut-feel," takes over. Table 3-4 and Table 3-5 show you how to tabulate the results.

T A B L E   3 - 4

TABULATION OF INPUTS

SCREENING TABLE INFORMATION

BUSINESS SELECTION CRITERIA ELEMENTS	IMPORTANCE FACTOR	LOCK MANUFAC- TURING	MACHINE SHOP	MAIL ORDER
Income Goal	5	Yes	Yes	Yes
Personal Achievement	2	Yes	Yes	No
Status	3	Yes	Yes	Yes
Work Content	3	Yes	Yes	Yes
People Contact	5	No	No	Yes
How Much Work	2	Yes	Yes	Yes
Business Hours	3	Yes	Yes	Yes
Other Lifestyle Impacts	1	Yes	Yes	Yes

T A B L E   3 - 5

TOTALING IMPORTANCE FACTORS

BUSINESS SELECTION CRITERIA ELEMENTS	LOCK MANUFACTURING	MACHINE SHOP	MAIL ORDER
Income Goal	Yes – 5	Yes – 5	Yes – 5
Personal Achievement	Yes – 2	Yes – 2	No
Status	Yes – 3	Yes – 3	Yes – 3
Work Content	Yes – 3	Yes – 3	Yes – 3
People Contact	No	No	Yes – 5
How Much Work	Yes – 2	Yes – 2	Yes – 2
Business Hours	Yes – 3	Yes – 3	Yes – 3
Other Lifestyle Impacts	Yes – 1	Yes – 1	Yes – 1
Totals	19	19	22

There are some additional factors that play an important part and they should be included in the selection process. These factors can be grouped in the following three categories:

1 *Head-start factors.* The head-start factors would include advantages such as technical know-how, personal contacts, physical resources, venture concept, or even customer orders encountered by coincidence in the course of pursuits other than the venture itself.

2 *The price of the venture.* The notion of downside risk often plays an important role in the venture choice, with the entrepreneur exploring the question, "What can I lose?"

3 *Pay-offs.* Particularly an important concept in assessing most ventures is the notion of upside potential. Here the question for the entrepreneur to explore is, "How much can I win?"

Earlier, we discussed the degree of personal appeal in the work. Closely related is the issue of personal talents, and resources versus requirements of the venture. That is to say, what are the potential small business owner's financial and personal resources? Do they meet and match the requirements of the venture? It is very important that the entrepreneur either have or be able to obtain sufficient resources, particularly money, to carry the enterprise through; and this, therefore, needs to be weighted early in the screening process.

Finally, the preliminary analysis must contain some sort of potential profitability estimate. The starting point here is usually the question of margin. If the margin cannot be seen to compare favourably with what is typical for companies in similar lines of work, then the venture idea must either be modified to improve margins or must be dropped. For consumer products manufacturing, for instance, a rule of thumb is that the product must sell at retail for at least four to five times the cost of labour and materials or it will lose money. The reasoning here is that wholesalers typically receive around 50 to 60 per cent off retail price as a discount, which cuts the manufacturer's share of that price to less than half. Cost of administration, overhead, and selling typically at least equal those of labour and material, so what is left for labour and materials and profit is less than half the manufacturer's selling price, or less than one-quarter of the retail price; hence the required ratio between four and five to one. For service firms, the typical rule is three times labour cost. Another way of looking at this is to note that a manufacturer has to receive about double the labour and material costs in order to cover administration, overhead, and selling and still make a profit. This is true for commercial as well as retail products, but it is only a very rough first approximation for manufacturers.

In practice, a considerably wider range can be found, as illustrated in Table 3-6, which shows actual operating figures for five small manufacturing companies in different lines of businesses. The gross margins range from 23 to 45 per cent and sales as a multiple of labour and materials to selling price ranges from 1.4 to 2.5. Margin figures for still other lines of work, including

T A B L E   3 - 6

EXPENSES OF FIVE SMALL MANUFACTURING COMPANIES (AS % OF SALES)

	COMMERCIAL ELECTRONIC INSTRUMENTS	CONSUMER HI-FI AMPLIFIERS	WOODEN FURNITURE	RESTAURANT EQUIPMENT	SAWMILL MACHINERY
Labour Materials	10%	13%	41%	19%	28%
	30	33	18	36	42
Manufacturing Overhead	15	10	9	14	7
(Cost of Sales)	(55)	(56)	(68)	(69)	(77)
Gross margins*	45	44	32	31	23
Selling	10	20	15	8	3
Administrative	15	7	15	13	3
Engineering	4	5	0	0	2
Pretax Profit	16	12	2	10	15
Sales as a Multiple of Labour and Materials	2.5	2.17	1.69	1.82	1.43

* Sales Revenue Minus Cost of Sales

Financial Ratios. (Philadelphia: Robert Morris Associates, 1988).

TABLE 3-7

A SAMPLING OF INCOME STATEMENTS

TYPE OF COMPANY	COST OF SALES AS A PERCENTAGE OF SALES		PRETAX PROFITS AS A PERCENTAGE OF TANGIBLE NET WORTH	
	COMPANIES WITH SALES UP TO $250,000	ALL COMPANIES	COMPANIES WITH SALES UP TO $250,000	ALL COMPANIES
Manufacturing				
Cutlery and Hand Tools	74.5%	70.7%	17.8%	22.1%
Auto Parts	72.7	76.9	20.7	28.4
Sporting Goods	69.0	71.2	23.1	29.9
Jewelry	68.2	70.5	15.9	23.3
Men's and Boys' Pants	—	77.6	—	17.0
Millwork	79.2	81.6	15.5	17.9
Surgical, Medical Instruments	53.5	59.5	—	27.9
Drugs	63.5	58.2	5.4	28.0
Nonferrous Foundries	71.5	80.5	29.8	27.2
Wholesaling				
Hardware and Paints	69.2	75.3	21.6	20.4
Auto Equipment	68.0	72.3	27.7	22.2
Sporting Goods	76.8	76.3	12.3	17.5
Jewellery	76.9	77.1	23.5	22.2
Men's Clothing	81.3	75.0	14.2	16.9
Lumber and Millwork	87.8	85.7	23.1	21.2
Drugs	73.5	80.5	31.1	18.1
Retailing				
Hardware	65.7	69.1	19.7	19.2
Tires, Batteries, Accessories	64.8	68.9	29.6	25.9
Sporting Goods	67.2	68.1	29.6	21.6
Jewellery	56.8	56.2	24.5	19.3
Men's and Boys' Clothing	60.0	62.9	14.4	13.8

nonmanufacturing, can be found in the library from public sources such as those of Robert Morris Associates, Dunn and Bradstreet, and Statistics Canada. Table 3-7 shows you a sampling of income statements from various businesses.

A more complete list of check-out questions, beginning with those raised earlier, appear in Table 3-8. Ultimately, however, the questions must be determined by the nature of the particular entrepreneur situation and venture, and no general list can fit all cases without being overly voluminous and boring. Rather than picking into every fine detail about starter feasibility, it may be better to return to the most generally important success factor, nature of the business, and to the question of whether it fits the entrepreneur's objectives.

TABLE 3-8

SOME VENTURE IDEA CHECKOUT QUESTIONS

BASIC FEASIBILITY

1. Can the product or service actually work?
2. Will it be legal?

COMPETITIVE ADVANTAGES

1. What will be the specific competitive advantages of the product or service?
2. What are those of the companies already in business?
3. What will the competitors' countermoves likely be?
4. How will the initial competitive advantage be maintained?

BUYER DECISIONS

1. Who will decide to buy from the company and why?
2. How much will each such person buy and how many such people are there?
3. Where are these people located and how will they be sold?

MARKETING

1. How much will be spent on advertising, packaging, selling?
2. What share of the market will the company get and by when?
3. Who will personally perform the selling functions?
4. How will prices be set and how will they compare to competitors' prices?
5. How important is location and how will it be determined?
6. What channels will be used—wholesale, retail, agents, mail, direct?
7. What specific sales targets should be met?
8. Can any orders be obtained before starting the business? How soon?

PRODUCTION

1. Will the company make or buy what it sells?
2. Are sources of supply at suitable prices available?
3. How long will needed delivery take?
4. Have adequate lease arrangements for premises been lined up?

5. Can needed equipment be available on time?
6. Are there special problems with plant setup, clearances, insurance?
7. Who will have the appropriate operating skills?
8. How will quality be controlled?
9. How will returns and servicing be handled?
10. How will pilferage, waste, spoilage, and scrap be controlled?

PEOPLE

1. How will competence in each area of the business be ensured?
2. Who will have to be hired when? How will they be found and recruited?
3. How will a banker, lawyer, accountant, and other advisors be chosen?
4. How will replacements be obtained if key people leave?
5. Will special benefit plans have to be arranged?

CONTROL

1. What records will be needed at what stages?
2. Will any special controls be needed? Who will take care of it?

FINANCE

1. How much will be needed for development of product or service?
2. How much will be needed for setting up operations?
3. How much will be needed for working capital?
4. Where will money come from? What if more is needed?
5. To which assumptions are profits more sensitive?
6. Which assumptions in financial forecasts are most uncertain?
7. What will be the return on equity, on sales, and compared to the industry?
8. When and how will investors get their money back out?
9. What will be needed from the bank and how does the bank feel about that?

LONGER TERM PROSPECTS OF THE VENTURE

Most new companies begin small, but among small firms there is an enormous amount of variety, some elements being more attractive than others. Although most are bound to remain small, a few companies will grow larger. Generally, those with higher growth potential offer greater economic payoffs; but those are not the only kinds of payoffs that are important. Some stable small ventures provide very pleasant and lucrative employment. For convenience here, three types of ventures will be considered as follows:

1   *Lower pay, stable, small ventures.* Sometimes called "lifestyle ventures." These include most "one man shows" and "mom and pop" ventures, taverns, gas stations, restaurants, dry-cleaning shops, independent small retail stores. Typically their owners make modest investments in fixed assets and inventory, put in long hours, and earn considerably less income and fringe benefits than the average unskilled auto worker or union craftsman. Upside potential in resale also tends to be low.

2   *High pay, stable, small ventures.* Many small manufacturing firms, larger restaurants and retail firms, small chains of gas stations, and other multi-establishment enterprises are in this category. Usually they involve substantial capital investments from roughly $200,000 on up. Some owners put in long hours while others do not. Most enjoy a variety of fringe benefits, such as company paid cars and travel. Upside potential in resale can be high to a buyer who sees both an attractive job and a profitable investment.

3   *High growth ventures.* More rare than either of the previous two, although these days they are much more publicized, these are small firms that have the capability to become large ones. They include many high-technology companies; they are formed around new products with substantial potential markets. Often ventures of this type are bought up and absorbed by larger companies. Very high upside potential and resale often results.

Table 3-9 illustrates the difference between higher payoff and lower payoff types of businesses.

Table 3-10 shows investments and payoffs of typically stable small firms.

STRATEGIES OF SIZE

Not all stable small firms are low payoff. Those that offer greater rewards are ones that manage to exploit some sort of competitive advantage. A concept often associated with the small firm that identifies and obtains for itself a particular competitive advantage is the notion of "industrial niche." This refers to a specialized activity in service or manufacturing in which the company concentrates and becomes very good relative to its competitors. Some advantageous specialties small companies have over larger ones include:

1   When demand is limited either by a small national market, as for some medical instruments manufacturers, or where the market tends to be regionally dominated, as in heat-treating and plating or concrete block manufacturing, where local convenience is a major factor. Big companies usually avoid small markets because coping with them demands too many bureaucratic inefficiencies.

2   When flexibility and innovation are at a premium. Big firms have a penchant for tidiness, order, and, hence, regimentation that works against change—especially rapid change. Small companies, especially new ones, have much less to lose and may have everything to gain by introducing innovations. Consequently they can excel in the areas of fast change.

TABLE 3-9

HIGH VERSUS LOW PAYOFF FIRMS

HIGHER PAYOFF TYPES	*LOWER PAYOFF TYPES*
Harder to find or enter	Easy to think of and enter
Small minority of small firms	Most small firms
Higher capital investment	Lower capital investment
Higher skill and specialization	Lower skill, more generally available
Tight patents, trademarks, or secrets	Nothing very proprietary, easily copied
Established and respected reputation	Not particularly well-known
Strong customer ties or contracts	Easily formed customer relationships
Leadership position	Not a leader
More innovative but not radical	Ordinary or highly eccentric
Examples:	Examples:
high technology firms, successful franchise chains, very high-skill manufacturers	most single outlet retail and food establishments, single operator services, small contractors

TABLE 3-10

INVESTMENTS AND PAYOFFS OF TYPICAL STABLE SMALL FIRMS

TYPE	*INVESTMENT REQUIRED*	*ANNUAL SALES ($000 omitted)*	*OWNER INCOME*
1. Construction Contracting	20	40	20
	100	600	50
2. Beauty Shop	10	15	9
	50	150	17
3. Janitorial Service	10	30	15
	25	100	40
4. Machine Shop	5	60	20
	50	250	40
5. Mobile Catering Truck(s)	15	100	20
	30	325	35
6. Photo Portrait Studio	6	35	10
	20	75	25
7. Contract Dressmaking Plant	20	125	15
	40	375	35
8. Industrial Laundry	30	70	20
	100	300	40
9. Dry Cleaning	40	60	20
	65	120	30
10. Children's Clothing Store	50	120	20
	100	300	32
11. Convenience Store	70	150	15
	150	100	27
12. Bowling Alley	150	6	25
	500	250	45

3 When close supervision and very careful work without excessive costs are vital. Chain restaurants are fine for producing dependable mediocrity; but for exceptionally outstanding cuisine, a gourmet must turn to independent enterprises. High-quality, artistic outputs similarly call for small producing units.

4 When custom or personalized service is important. Architects, portrait photographers, private schools, and custom tailors are examples.

5 When government policies are designed to aid small firms because there are so many small businesses. In total, they represent an appreciable political "clout." Responding to this, the federal and provincial governments, and even big firms, have adopted policies within certain areas deliberately intended to foster and assist small firms. Certain federal contracts are set aside for small companies in particular. Certain types of financing are available to small firms that are not available to larger ones, such as the *Small Business Loans Act*. Certain tax benefits, such as preferential tax rates, and types of assistance are available only to small firms.

HIGH PAYING, STABLE SMALL FIRMS

Although the types of firms shown in Table 3-10 generally yield only low returns for their owners, there are almost always exceptions. Sometimes the key will in large measure be associated with greater investment, which makes possible expanded operations. Thus, while the owner of a single beauty shop may be able to earn only $20,000 per year, the same entrepreneur might, by expanding to two or three shops and hiring subordinate managers, be able to raise that income to $50,000 or more. Higher incomes are not always dependent upon having larger investments, however. Even among low-investment and low-skill businesses there are always some that manage to pay off highly. Often these businesses exploit one or more of the above small business competitive advantages and other special competitive advantages or tricks of doing business that other similar businesses are unable to exploit—an unusually good location, more effective advertising, lack of competitors in the immediate area, temporary surges in demand, and so forth.

HIGH GROWTH VENTURES

The highest economic payoffs of all tend to be associated with high-growth ventures. Virtually every large company started out as a small company; along its history of expansion, that company made many people wealthy. Those companies with potential for growth include many high technology companies formed around new products with large potential markets. Also, service-oriented companies in rapid growth industries, such as management, transportation, and communications.

Samples of government publications that assist new enterprises. *Courtesy of Ontario Ministry of Industry, Trade and Technology and Alberta Economic Development and Trade.*

IDEA SOURCES

Earlier, the strength and capabilities of the potential new firm owner were assessed and, with that information, the real search for the "right business" can proceed effectively. Table 3-11 summarizes the various sources that could stimulate your own thinking process. The table is far from exhaustive; it is designed to give direction only.

TABLE 3-11

IDEA SOURCES

MENTAL GYMNASTICS	*PERSONAL CONTACTS WITH:*	*VISITS TO:*
Ideas from a Previous Employment	Potential Customers	Trade Shows
Brainstorming (friends & acquaintances)	Potential Suppliers	Libraries
Observation of Daily Living Situations	Business Brokers	Museums
Seeking New Twists	Business Owners	Plants
	Successful Entrepreneurs	Invention Expositions
	Property Owners	Universities
	Professors	Research Institutes
	Graduate Students	Government Offices
	Patent Attorneys	
	Product Brokers	
	Former Employers	
	Prospective Partners	
	Bankers	
	Venture Capitalists	
	Chambers of Commerce	
	Corporate Licensing Departments	
	Editors	
	Management Consultants	
	Technology Transfer Agencies	
	Development Agencies (federal, provincial and municipal)	
	Government Departments Dealing with Industry and Trade	

READING OF:

Trade Publications
Trade Directories
Bankruptcy Announcements
Business Opportunities
Classified
Old Books and Magazines
Other Commerce Department Publications
Patents and Patent Gazette
New Product Publications
Doctoral Dissertations
Idea Books and Newsletters
Best Seller Lists
New Technology Publications
Licensing Information Services
Government Publications
   (*New Products Bulletin, The Market Place*)

OBSERVATION OF TRENDS

Materials Shortages
Energy Shortage
Waste Disposal
New Technology
Recreation
Nostalgia
Fads
Legal Changes
Pollution Problems
Health
Self-development
Personal Security
Foreign Trade
Social Movements

As a general guide here are the major areas of business opportunities:

- Replacing an existing product or service; e.g., vertical blinds
- Developing a new product or service; e.g., electric toothbrush with rotary bristles
- Developing a new way of making an existing product; e.g., using microbes for mineral extraction
- Developing a new use for an existing product or service; e.g., video recording service for insurance purposes
- Developing a new way of distributing a product or service; e.g., reduced calorie fast-food restaurant

Obviously, new and high technology is not a major factor in new business formation. Many successful business ventures are based on an adaptation or modification of established technologies. The range of business ideas is limitless; you will discover a number of other potential business opportunities through inquiry, systematic search, and careful observation. Table 3-12 is a starter list of possible types of business. There are many more.

TABLE 3-12

A STARTER LIST OF POSSIBLE TYPES OF BUSINESSES

RETAIL TRADE

1. Food
   a. General grocery
   b. Fast food
   c. Convenience
   d. Snack bar or restaurant
   e. Bar or lounge
   f. Specialty food store
2. General Merchandise
3. Apparel and Clothing
4. Furniture and Appliances

5. Hardware and Building Materials
6. Specialty Stores (flowers, computers, etc.)
7. Door-to-Door Sales
8. Party Plan or Home Parties
9. Mail Order
10. Rental Business
11. Craft Shows and Fairs
12. Swap Meets and Flea Markets

EXTRACTION INDUSTRIES

1. Agriculture
   a. Ranching
   b. Mixed farming
   c. Livestock farming
   d. Horticulture
2. Commercial Trapping and Fishing
3. Mining
   a. Minerals
   b. Sand and gravel
   c. Petroleum

4. Forestry
   a. Logging
   b. Tree farming
   c. Sawmilling

MANUFACTURING AND PROCESSING

1. Metalworking
   a. Sheet metal
   b. Machine shop
      i. general
      ii. special
   c. Foundry or mill
2. Plastic
   a. Formulation
   b. Extrusion
   c. Application

3. Food Processing
   a. Meat
   b. Vegetables
   c. Prepared and frozen foods
   d. Baked goods
   e. Specialty products

CONSTRUCTION

1. General Contracting
2. Subcontracting
   a. Carpentry
   b. Masonry
   c. Plumbing and heating
   d. Electrical
   e. Floor covering installation
   f. Painting and wallpaper
   g. Roofing and siding
   h. Cabinetry
   i. Drywall

3. Land Development
   a. residential
   b. commercial
   c. industrial
4. Repair and Renovation
5. Interior Decoration

TRANSPORTATION

1. Trucking
2. Rental or Charter Services
3. Bus, Taxi, and Limousine Services

4. Commercial Aviation
   a. Charter service
   b. Crop spraying
   c. Emergency transport

COMMUNICATIONS

1. Broadcast or Print Media
   a. Commercial printing
   b. Newletters
   c. Audio-visual production

2. Photography
3. Commercial or Industrial
   Communications

SERVICES

1. Professional Services
   a. Doctor
   b. Lawyer
   c. Dentist
   d. Architect
   e. Chiropractor
   f. Health care
   g. Psychologists
   h. Music and other teachers
2. Financial Services
   a. Mutual funds
   b. Financial planning
   c. Brokerage and real estate
   d. Public accounting
   e. Insurance agency

3. Business Services
   a. Advertising and promotion
   b. Janitorial
   c. Security
   d. Equipment rental
   e. Temporary help
   f. Training and education
   g. Employment services
   h. Travel services
   i. Equipment maintenance and
      repair
   j. Management consulting
   k. Research and development

4. Personal Services
   a. Barber and beauty shops
   b. Funeral homes
   c. Floor covering and upholstery
   d. Jewelry repair
   e. Shoe and watch repair
   f. Dry cleaning and laundry
   g. Appliance repair
   h. Automobile service and repair
   i. Temporary help
   j. Referral services
   k. Training and education programs
   l. Catering

5. Recreational and Leisure Services
   a. Accommodation
   b. Equipment rental
   c. Theatres and shows
   d. Bowling alleys
   e. Skating rinks
   f. Swimming pools and spas
   g. Ski resort
   h. Golf course
   i. Tennis club
   j. Private lakes and parks
   k. Marinas
   l. Camp grounds
   m. Horse ranches
   n. Gymnasiums
   o. Recreation clubs
   p. Health clubs
   q. Weight control clinics
   r. Dance classes

DISTRIBUTIVE TRADES

1. Manufacturer's agent
2. Jobber
3. Broker
4. Merchant wholesaler

Source: Walter S. Good, *Building a Dream: A Comprehensive Guide to Starting a Business of Your Own*, Scarborough: McGraw-Hill Ryerson, 1989.

SUMMARY

Most entrepreneurs and small business owners succeed by pursuing ideas that are not only sound business opportunities but also "fit" with their personal criteria, goals, desired lifestyle, and values. Identifying personal criteria speeds up the search process by narrowing the focus and providing guidance on what to disregard. It keeps you out of trouble.

In this chapter we also identified leading sources of business ideas and a simple method to help the search.

QUESTIONS FOR CLASS DISCUSSION

1   Rank in order of importance the most important criteria in selecting a business.
2   Select the questions you have to answer when checking out the viability of a business.
3   Which are the easiest and more readily available sources for ideas?

4   What are your career plans? What industry do you want to be working in five years from now?

5   Is there any advantage to growing big? Why?

Projects for Home Assignment and/or Class Discussion

1   Interview at least three people who are self-employed as small business owners, one of whom is in your own area of interest. Find out how and why they chose their business.

2   Generate as many new business ideas as possible; do not try to evaluate them, just list them.

3   Make a formal venture search based upon selection criteria set up according to your own values.

REFERENCES FOR FURTHER READING

Eckert, Lee A., J.D. Ryan, R.J. Roy, and R.J. Bracey, *Canadian Small Business: An Entrepreneur's Plan*, Harcourt Brace Jovanovich, Toronto, 1987.

Good, Walter S., *Building a Dream: A Comprehensive Guide to Starting a Business of Your Own*, McGraw-Hill Ryerson Ltd., Toronto, 1989.

Timmons, J.A., L.E. Smollen, and A.L.M. Dingee Jr., *New Venture Creation: A Guide to Small Business Development*, 3rd ed., Richard D. Irwin Inc., Homewood, Illinois, 1990.

· ·

4

Buying an Existing Firm Versus Starting a New One

LEARNING OBJECTIVES

After reading this chapter, you will be able to:

1. **C**ontrast the advantages and the disadvantages of buying an existing business
2. **O**utline the methods for evaluating or determining if an existing business has good potential
3. **E**xplain the methods used to determine the financial value of an existing business
4. **C**ompare the advantages to the disadvantages of starting up a new business
5. **D**etermine whether or not a startup company is a good idea and has a reasonable chance for success

For persons who want to own and operate a small firm, there are several ways to achieve their wish. They may follow all steps covered in the process of planning and establishing a new firm, or they may purchase an existing one in their desired line of business. Many students of management may even inherit a business from their parents or relatives. Our interest here is in choosing between the first two possibilities.

Whether to buy an existing firm or set up a new one is not a clear-cut decision. Each case must be decided on its merits. There are advantages and disadvantages to each. The realities of business suggest caution and competence when considering either route to ownership.

ADVANTAGES OF BUYING AN EXISTING BUSINESS

If an existing business can be purchased at the proper price (a matter that will be discussed later in this chapter), it usually has the following advantages:

1   A going concern with a good history increases the likelihood of successful operation for the new owner.
2   It has a proven location for successful operation.
3   The need to spend time, money, and energy to do a thorough planning job for a new firm is eliminated. Profits can be earned sooner.
4   It already has an established clientele.
5   Its inventory is already on the shelves and suppliers are established.
6   Its equipment is already available, and its resources and capabilities are known in advance.
7   Financing the purchase of the business is restricted to a single purchase transaction.

While these advantages appear at first reading to be very significant, they must be studied very carefully in each case of possible business ownership.

DISADVANTAGES OF BUYING AN EXISTING BUSINESS

Against the preceding list of advantages, even if they all stand the test of careful study, there are some important disadvantages.

1   The buyer inherits any ill will of the existing firm.
2   Lines of merchandise are already established and may not conform to the buyer's best judgement.

3   Certain employees may be inherited who are not assets to the firm.
4   The inherited clientele may not be the most desirable, and changing the firm's image is usually difficult.
5   Precedents set by the former owner are well established and may be difficult to change if the new owner doesn't like them.
6   The building itself and the layout inside the firm may not conform to modern standards and may entail substantial expense in modernization.
7   The landlord's attitude and practices may not be conducive to a pleasant and profitable relationship.
8   The purchase price may not be justified and may therefore create a burden on future profits.

Buying an existing firm does not always have disadvantages; but potential disadvantages must be investigated thoroughly when a purchase is being considered.

IDENTIFYING ACQUISITION CANDIDATES

Internal Eyes and Ears

Entrepreneurs should tap their knowledge or friends' knowledge concerning

- customers
- suppliers
- competitors
- companies using complementary technology

External Eyes and Ears

The entrepreneur should correspond directly on a regular basis with

- banks
- accountants
- lawyers
- business brokers
- the provincial government
- consultants
- investment bankers

Specific Industry Research

Candidates can be identified in specific industries by researching through the following sources:

- Canadian Trade Index
- Dun & Bradstreet Canadian Key Business Directory
- Scott's Industrial Directories
- Fraser's Canadian Trade Index
- *Financial Post* Surveys
- *Financial Post* Directories
- Yellow Pages
- Trade association membership listings and journals

Other Activities

Other search activities could include
- reviewing newspapers and journals for leads
- reading various acquisition publications, such as *Business Opportunities Quarterly* by the Bank of Nova Scotia
- attending trade shows
- "acquisitions wanted" advertising

HOW TO GET STARTED

There are six essential steps to follow to make an acquisition.
- define your acquisition objectives and criteria
- find, screen, and rank candidates
- contact and evaluate the most promising candidates
- set a price and negotiate a deal
- arrange financing
- accomplish transition of ownership

SETTING ACQUISITION CRITERIA

The acquisition criteria must be compatible with personal objectives.

Acquisition criteria should be set encompassing at least the following criteria:
- business activity (i.e., manufacturing, distribution, retail, extraction, processing, etc.)
- industry
- size
- profitability
- management capability and retention
- product depth, seasonality

- technology
- markets/customers served

Acquisition criteria must be consistent and realistic. Everybody is looking for a profitable, growing, market-leading, stable company that has proprietary products or services and technology, and sells only to blue chip companies – so the competition is keen for those companies. On the other hand, perhaps look into a company where your contributions may be the missing quality or ingredient to turn a "so-so" business into a successfully thriving one.

EVALUATING AN OPPORTUNITY TO BUY

The problem for the prospective buyer is, "How to confirm the advantages and the disadvantages in order to make a sound evaluation?" Any evaluation should begin with the potential buyer asking very specific questions and finding very specific answers. The following is a list of questions and suggestions for finding the answers.

1 *What has been the trend of profits for the firm?* At least five years should be reviewed to establish the trend. To find the answer we (*a*) ask for copies of financial statements; (*b*) review the firm's books; (*c*) study copies of bank deposits for the period; and (*d*) study copies of income tax returns for the past five years. If the seller (or business broker who has the firm listed for sale in his or her office) is not willing to provide these items, the buyer should be suspicious of the claimed profitability.

2 *Is the business growing, declining, or relatively stable?* The prime measure here is sales volume. Authenticity of sales claims should be verified. Audit reports are most valuable. Sales records, both cash and credit, are essential.

3 *Are profits consistent with sales volume?* We know now about comparative statistics that are available for almost every line of business. Any significant variation, up or down, from standard profits for this type of firm should be investigated.

4 *Why does the present owner wish to sell?* There may be entirely legitimate reasons for the decision, such as health, age, or a desire to move to Florida. The potential buyer must be sure that the current owner is not merely looking for a chance to sell at an inflated price or is selling because of serious problems in the firm's operation.

5 *Does the balance sheet for the firm reflect a sound current financial condition?* By applying the basic current ratio, quick ratio, and proprietorship ratio rules (to be discussed in Chapter 10), you have a first approximation of financial soundness. From this point, you must confirm the soundness of the assets. Are the accounts receivable current or a collection of long past due accounts? Is the

inventory composed of fresh, modern merchandise, or does it include much obsolete merchandise that will be hard to sell? Only investigation of the accounts receivable ledger and inspection of the inventory will turn up the answers.

6 *Are the fixed assets properly valued, considering their cost and depreciation charges?* Are they modern? Are they in good condition? The answers are to be found in purchase invoices, amounts of depreciation charges for past years, recognition of modern versus old equipment, and thorough checking of its condition by inspection and operation.

7 *Are expenses in line with average statistics for this type of firm?* The answer here is to refer again to comparative statistics while recognizing that there may be reasons for variations in the particular case.

8 *If the store is rented, what is the nature of the lease?* Can it be renewed? For what periods of time? Is it a percentage lease? What are those percentages? (To be discussed in Chapter 26.) What is the landlord's attitude toward the business? If one of the chief advantages in buying the firm is the location involved, the lease and an option to renew become of great importance. Options should be in writing.

9 *What is the competition in the area?* By buying instead of organizing a new firm, one competitor has been eliminated. The nature of remaining competition is still important. It should be known. Chances for successful competition with other firms should be reviewed as carefully as if a new firm were planned.

10 *What are the present owner's plans after the sale?* Too often new buyers find that the seller is in competition with them soon after the sale. The best assurance against this is a clause in the sales agreement stating that "the seller agrees to not engage in the same business within 15 km for five years." Such a clause is widely used today.

11 *Will I need any of the present employees?* Are they satisfactory? Honest sellers will usually give a prospective buyer an honest evaluation of their personnel. They may even assist in choosing only superior employees if they are going out of business for good. Interviews with employees and observations of their activities on the job can assist the potential buyer in making any necessary decisions.

12 *What are the prospects for increasing profits?* Even though the business has been profitable in the past, the competent buyer will analyze the floor space, the layout, the lines of goods carried, the market area, and the services now rendered in terms of whether or not a greater volume of sales and profits would be possible. Chain stores that purchase one-unit firms have a remarkable record of

increasing sales after purchase. Individual buyers of such firms can do the same thing.

13   *What is the customer and neighbourhood attitude toward the firm?* Interviews with customers within or outside the store and door-to-door neighbourhood surveys are the vital devices to find answers to this question. Some ill will may be discovered, but ways to overcome it may be devised. The important thing is to know what customers and neighbours think of the firm.

14   *What is the reputation of the firm among businesspeople in the area?* Visits to surrounding firms, the chamber of commerce, or service clubs will provide answers. The seller may be known as a "poor payer" in the trade, a dealer in shoddy merchandise, a "sharpie," or one who is lacking in community support or renders too few services. Again, if any of these opinions are discovered, they should not in themselves cancel the idea of purchasing the firm, but ways should be devised to change its reputation if possible. Information is important.

15   *Are there any nationality, religious, or political factors in the area that would discourage purchase?* Despite advances made in promoting goodwill among all peoples, it remains true that if a community is predominantly of one religious group, one nationality group, or even one political group, businesspeople who are not members of that group have a tougher time in developing successful business firms. Check the facts.

16   *Do suppliers regard the seller favourably?* Although any critical attitude discovered may be overcome, relations with suppliers are a measure of business competence. If the firm owns valuable distributorships, it is important that their maintenance is assured. The same is true for franchises.

17   *Is the community to be served growing?* Population growth means new potential customers. It also means new competitors in most cases. Being established gives existing firms the first chance to maintain pre-eminence.

18   *Are all liabilities correctly stated on the balance sheet?* Individual contracts and other obligations may be checked in detail. The best protection for the new buyer is a clause in the sales agreement providing that any other claims or liabilities are those of the seller. Purchase of the specific assets and stated claims by a separate legal entity may be appropriate.

19   *Would the investment make as high a return as could be made by starting a new firm?* The answer usually is found in the purchase price, to which we will now turn our attention. We know that profits can be realized sooner, but we must also consider the future situation.

HOW MUCH IS A BUSINESS WORTH?

When the desirability of buying an existing firm has been confirmed, the important question becomes, "What is the price?" Such terms as goodwill value, capital earnings basis, and replacement cost of assets must be discussed. *Note:* The majority of sales of small firms are made on the basis of asset value less liabilities, with some possible adjustment for profits in excess of a good salary for the owner, plus a satisfactory return on his or her investment.

Potential buyers will recognize from these remarks that goodwill value, capitalized earnings, and replacement values usually leave something to be desired in arriving at a precise price for a particular business. It will also be seen why the purchase prices of most small firms represent an agreed net asset value (assets minus liabilities assumed), with possibly some adjustment for profits in excess of the desired profit for the buyer, plus a satisfactory rate of return on the investment.

Current market prices of assets of all types have dominated firm values in the 1980s, which began with unheard-of inflation in the early years.

Goodwill as a Basis of Value

Goodwill may be described as the asset value of established patronage and an established name or image that is publicly recognized. It is usually assumed to give a firm profits above the average. The product names "Speedy Muffler" and "Levis" have great asset, or goodwill, value; "Smitty's Drugstore" has very little in comparison. Most small firms have little or no goodwill as an asset of sale. Their goodwill usually derives from the owner's personality, which is not part of the sale. However, some businesses may have special assets, such as a long-term lease in a prime location or a coveted distributorship, and can command high prices.

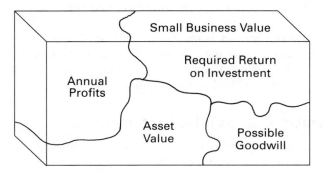

FIGURE 4-1 • Many factors need to be considered when valuing a business. These methods include, among others, using annual profits, or determining a required return on investment, or using the asset value. Accounting for goodwill is also an important factor in many cases.

Capitalized Earnings as a Basis of Value

Capitalized earnings as a basis of value are sometimes used alone for determining the value of a business. For example, if a firm regularly earns an annual net profit of $22,500 after the owner's salary and interest on the investment have been deducted, and the rate of capitalization (often called the *CAP rate*) is 15 per cent, the value of the business is said to be $150,000. By formula, we would solve the equation $0.15x$ equals $22,500 and solve for x to find it is $150,000.

$$
\text{Capitalized value} = \frac{\text{Net profit}}{\text{CAP rate}}
$$
$$
= \frac{\$22,500}{0.15}
$$
$$
= \$150,000
$$

The rate of capitalization varies with the riskiness of the particular type of business. If risks are believed to be normal, a rate of 20 per cent is popularly used. Firms considered to have less risk, such as a local water company, may use a lower capitalization rate with a consequent higher value. For example, a water company earning net profits of $20,000 capitalized at 10 per cent would be valued at $200,000. (The $20,000 is 10 per cent of $200,000, computed as just shown.)

When the risk is considered to be very high, the rate of capitalization is higher. Many neighborhood beauty shops, service stations, or dry-cleaning firms facing rough competition may be capitalized at a rate as high as 100 per cent. This would mean that the value is equal to one year's profits.

When only capitalized earnings are used as a basis of value, the net value of assets is ignored in finding value. It is recognized that adequate assets exist to produce the earnings. Liabilities, of course, are confirmed as the value of the assets and other items that have been reviewed in analyzing the firm to be purchased, but these do not enter into the determination of sale price when this method is used exclusively.

It should be emphasized again that only the profits in excess of what the buyer expects as salary for the time and effort expended in operating the firm and a desired rate of return on invested capital are the basis for using the capitalized earnings method of determining value.

Replacement Cost as a Basis of Value

Replacement cost of assets is a poor basis on which to determine their value for purposes of sale of the firm. Only in very rare circumstances, such as an extremely scarce supply situation, would assets ever have nearly the value of new assets to replace them. *Book value* (the original cost less reasonable depreciation) is often a sound basis for sale value. This is the value used for many small firm sales.

A Practical Way of Finding Value

Using a realistic example, let us see how the value of a small firm can be determined. A business has $60,000 net assets, with reasonably expected profits of $30,000 per year. The potential buyer values her time and energy at $20,000 and desires 10 per cent as a return on her investment. She would be willing to pay a premium for the profits in excess of the amount sufficient to cover her salary and interest. If a purchase price of $80,000 is offered, she would need $28,000 to cover salary ($20,000) and interest ($8,000, or 10 per cent of $80,000) if she invested the entire amount on the date of sale. This would be an attractive price because she can still contemplate $2,000 of extra profits. If the price is still being negotiated, she would be prepared to capitalize this extra $2,000 at 20 per cent, or $10,000, if risks are only normal. She would have a maximum price of $90,000 in mind during the negotiating sessions.[1]

STARTING A NEW BUSINESS

There are many factors to consider when an entrepreneur contemplates starting a new business. The primary question that needs to be asked is whether this is an idea that has never been tried or whether it is a proven concept. Real pioneering is needed for a completely new concept, and caution would be recommended. When the concept has been proven, the startup is much easier.

Advantages and Disadvantages of Starting a New Business

Several advantages are evident with a completely new business.
1   New businesses have no negative reputation.
2   The entrepreneur can make all the choices.
3   There is freedom of operations.

Some of the disadvantages include
1   Unproven operations; will the business run successfully?
2   The possibility of improper or inadequate planning;
3   No history to show suppliers, vendors, or banks;
4   No knowledge of how competitors will react.

---

[1]For another detailed example of arriving at a sales price, see Bank of America's *Small Business Reporter*, Vol. 8, No. 11, "How to Buy or Sell a Business."

Evaluating the Startup Business Opportunity

The primary consideration in evaluating a new business idea or opportunity is whether or not real profit potential exists. Without a chance for profit, the business is not worth the risk and effort it requires.

It follows, then, that the identification of a satisfactory market size with a substantial customer base is necessary to ensure adequate sales. In addition, the right time to start the business should be determined after studying economic trends. New businesses have a better chance of succeeding when the economy is growing than during periods of recession or economic downturn.

The reaction of competitors is important, too. Can those competitors afford to cut prices in order to retain customers? If they do, what will that do to the new firm's profits?

New businesses need operating sites, facilities, and equipment. These require the development of leases, agreements, and business relationships. All the planning steps discussed in Chapter 6 are important.

No new business can start without adequate capital and operating funds. Determining these amounts is a very important function for the entrepreneur. These dollar amounts, along with sales income projections and probable operating expenses, need to be included in a *proforma statement*, which is the document used in discussions with banks and suppliers. This proforma needs to be analyzed and verified as best as possible. Extra work in this important planning stage may save thousands of dollars or more of mistakes.

SUMMARY

There are many possible advantages to buying an existing business. It is possible to know the history of the firm and to check existing data about sales, expenses, customer base, the market in general, suppliers, and employees. These factors could be an advantage for purchasing one firm and a disadvantage for another, depending on what the investigation uncovers.

The advantages and disadvantages of a new organization are two sides of the same coin. Freedom to determine operations and the lack of any ill will from previous customers, suppliers, bankers, and employees can be advantages. However, operating without experience or previous relationships with the above groups could be disadvantages.

When considering a new startup firm it is important to learn as much about the product or service as possible and to estimate how customers, competitors, and financial people will react. Time spent developing an understanding of these issues may save the firm thousands of dollars in the long run.

Finally, all of the fifteen comprehensive planning steps discussed in Chapter 6 should be applied to plans for both purchasing an existing firm or developing a startup company.

QUESTIONS FOR CLASS DISCUSSION

1 What is meant by determining the value of a business on the basis of capitalized earnings?

2 If a business earns $25,000 per year consistently and has only normal risks, how much would it be worth on a basis of capitalized earnings?

3 If you are considering the purchase of an existing firm, why would you be interested in seeing its tax returns for the past five years?

4 What are some reasons for saying, "Buying an existing business increases the certainty of successful operation for the new owner?" Is this necessarily always true?

5 Can time be saved by purchasing an existing firm rather than by doing a thorough job of planning and establishing a new firm?

6 Can the ill will of an existing firm be overcome if you purchase the firm? How?

7 What are the advantages of an official audit report, in comparison with an owner-produced report, when evaluating a firm for purchase?

8 How can bank-deposit records be useful in firm evaluation?

9 What ratios would you look for on the books of a firm you planned to purchase?

10 Would you be interested in the cost and depreciation charged off on fixed assets by a firm you wished to buy? Why?

11 Would you want to know the details of the lease if you were buying an existing firm? Why?

12 Do you believe in protecting yourself when buying a firm by having the seller agree in writing not to be in competition within 15 km for five years? Is this a violation of the seller's civil rights?

Project for Home Assignment and/or Class Discussion

If you were contemplating the purchase of an existing small business, do you think it would be too drastic to ask to see bank deposit slips and income tax returns for the past five years? Explain how these items could assist in determining a fair purchase price. Would you be demanding in your requests for other information and records?

REFERENCES FOR FURTHER READING

Beckman, M.D., W.S. Good, and R.G. Wyckham, *Small Business Management*, John Wiley & Sons Canada Ltd., Toronto, 1982, Chapters 4 and 5.

Cunningham, G., *Buy Yourself A Job & Be Your Own Boss*, McGraw-Hill Ryerson Ltd., 1990, Chapter 4.

Kao, R.W.Y., *Small Business Management: A Strategic Emphasis*, 2nd ed., Holt, Rinehart and Winston of Canada, Ltd., Toronto, 1984, Chapter 14.

Kingston, J.P.R. and P.E. McQuillan, *Valuation of Business*, 3rd ed., CCH Canadian Ltd., Don Mills, Ontario, 1986.

Knight, R.M., *Small Business Management in Canada*, McGraw-Hill Ryerson Ltd., Toronto, 1981, Chapter 4.

Tate Jr., C.E., L.C. Megginson, C.R. Scott Jr., and L.R. Trueblood, *Successful Small Business Management*, 3rd ed., Business Publications, Inc., Plano, Texas, 1985, Chapter 5.

Minding Your Own Business, Federal Business Development Bank, Montreal, 1982, Vol. 1, Chapter 3.

5

Franchising

LEARNING OBJECTIVES

After reading this chapter, you will be able to:

1. **U**nderstand how a franchise works and know the responsibilities of the franchise operator
2. **E**xamine the advantages and disadvantages of owning a franchise
3. **I**dentify the steps necessary to evaluate a franchise opportunity
4. **D**etermine whether or not to purchase an existing franchise that is already operating at a specific location
5. **R**ecognize the different types of franchises available and how each functions

The recent growth of franchising as a major factor on the business scene merits giving the subject serious attention in our study. It is true that the vast majority of small firms started in our country every year are newly established, independent firms. A small percentage of new firm owners have purchased existing firms. Although the basic emphasis of this book is on the creation and management of a new firm, the concern of *this* chapter is franchising.

Good planning, financing, and management are essential to any type of small firm. This is true whether the firm is a franchise, a newly created firm, or the purchase of an existing firm. That franchises have a lower failure rate than other new small businesses is due in most cases to the managerial assistance provided by the franchisors. Failures can occur in any type of small firm when management does not apply continued good practice in the operation of the firm.

THREE BASIC METHODS OF ACQUIRING SMALL FIRM OWNERSHIP

The three basic methods of becoming a small firm owner are

1   To buy a franchise
2   To buy an established business
3   To create a new business firm

Persons desiring to go into business for themselves will often find all three methods available in the particular location they have decided upon. Availability varies with the type of business involved. Each method has advantages and disadvantages in a particular situation. When all three possibilities exist, the prospective owners should carefully evaluate the facts they have discovered before making their choice among the alternatives. We will take a look here at the details of franchising, along with its advantages and disadvantages.

FRANCHISING

Franchising became very popular in the decade of the seventies, and this growth continued in the eighties. Most people recognize such names as Kentucky Fried Chicken, Holiday Inn, or Harvey's as firms that have many units around the country that represent individually owned franchises of a parent firm. But franchising has now reached into many other types of business activity.

Franchising is basically a system for distributing products or services through associated resellers. The franchise gives rights to the franchisee to perform or use something that is the property of the franchisor. The parent company (Foodcorp Limited, for example) is the franchisor. The small business owner (Harry Jones) who buys a franchise is the franchisee. Foodcorp gives rights to Jones to operate a Swiss Chalet restaurant in accordance with the terms of the contract that is signed. This franchise agreement (contract) is a contractual relationship with the rights and privileges of both parties defined. Most franchises specify a time period of operation that may be renewed at the end of that period.

The objective of franchises is to achieve efficient and profitable distribution of a product or service within a specified area. Both parties contribute resources. The franchisor contributes a trademark, a reputation, known products, managerial know-how, procedures, and perhaps equipment. The franchisee invests capital in the purchase of the franchise and provides the management of the operation in accordance with rules set down by the franchisor. Marketing procedures may be specified and a common identity is established.

Historically, franchising has been successful when the franchisee receives a workable business plan and then works that plan. Success comes when all parties do their part. Unfortunately, not all plans presented by the franchisor contain tested and tried ideas, techniques, and operations methods. Also, not all franchisees follow through with good management and decision making.

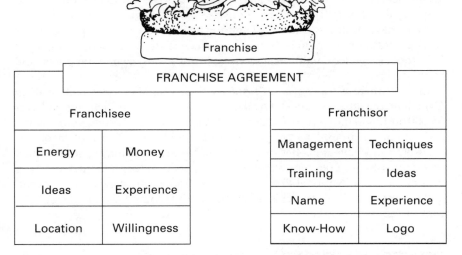

F I G U R E   5 - 1 • The franchise agreement holds the franchise and is a bridge between the franchisee and the franchisor. Both parties benefit from a well-run franchise.

However, franchises are successful for the most part. That's because they have as their objective the achievement of efficient and profitable distribution of products or services within a specified area or territory, and because both parties contribute resources that they want properly used.

The franchisor will contribute such things as a trademark, a reputation, known products, managerial know-how, training, and perhaps equipment and sometimes financing. The franchisee invests capital for the "rights" to the franchise and for equipment and facilities.

The franchisee then operates the business following the rules established by the franchisor. These rules are a part of the franchise agreement signed by both parties. The contract is a legal document that spells out the items discussed above and explains the duties of each in detail.

GROWTH OF FRANCHISING

The recent popularity of franchising might indicate that the idea is relatively new. That is not true. In the fields of fast food, restaurants, and motels this growth has been steady since World War II. But business had practised franchising in other fields for many years before this. Firms like the Ford Motor Company, General Motors, Singer Sewing Machine, Rexall Drugs, and Coca-Cola have had franchises outstanding for many years. Some have existed since the turn of the century.

There seems to be a distinction between the "older franchise groups" and the "new industry groups" that have gone heavily into franchising. The older group includes auto and truck dealers, service stations, soft-drink bottlers, and tire supply shops. The newer industry groups that have entered into franchising are almost endless. They include car wash, auto parts, repair services, restaurants, motels, hotels, convenience stores, drive-ins, employee help services, water conditioner services, hearing aids, swimming pools, and many others.

In 1989 there were some 700 franchisors in Canada, about half of them Canadian, the other half mostly American. The Canadian franchisors had over 55 000 outlets in the country with sales of franchise-related products exceeding $60 billion, or around 43 per cent of total retail sales. The growth of this industry is most dynamic. Between 1981 and 1989 franchising averaged annual sales increases of 15 per cent versus less than 8 per cent for retail sales and 7 per cent in the Gross National Product. In 1989, franchising grew by 12 per cent, and it is estimated that franchise operations will account for more than 65 per cent of the retail market within the next five to ten years.

DIFFERENT TYPES OF FRANCHISES

As franchising expanded into so many different fields of business activity, it was natural that different arrangements had to come forth for their contractual agreements. Most franchises can be classified into one of the three categories that follow:

1 *Straight-Product-Distribution Franchises*   Under this type of franchise, which is the most popular today, franchisors merely supply the franchises with their products in saleable form and the franchises sell them in the same form. Auto agencies, tire shops, and Color Your World paint and wallpaper stores are prominent examples. With this type of arrangement, the franchises operate under their own name, usually pay no franchise fee, and earn their profit from resale of the products. The franchisors earn their profit from the price at which they sell to the franchisee.

2 *Product-Licence Franchises*   These are typified by Burger King or Pizza Hut franchises. In these cases, the franchises use the franchisor's name but manufacture their products to comply with the franchisor's requirements. The franchisors provide brand identity and usually specify methods of manufacturing and/or distributing the product. Many franchisors in this category may also require that certain materials and supplies be purchased from the franchisor. A new franchise may be very expensive, and costs to the franchisee continue throughout the period of the franchise.

3 *Trade-Name Franchises*   Under this type of franchise, the franchisor licenses its trade name to the franchisee but seldom exercises any control over the product or service being marketed. Equipment distributors often use this method of franchise. Costs to the franchisee are usually limited to a monthly fee for use of the trademarked equipment. Equipment for a car wash is an example of this type of franchise.

Franchise firms have become popular in many lines of business. *Photo courtesy of Dan Kewley.*

Courtesy of Treats.

Courtesy of Tilden.

Courtesy of Molly Maid
International Inc.

ADVANTAGES OF FRANCHISING

Franchising offers its maximum advantages when undertaken with due consideration for the interests of the franchisee as well as the franchisor. The following table lists advantages to both parties.

TO THE FRANCHISOR	TO THE FRANCHISEE
1. Expanded distribution without increased capital investment.	1. Sound management procedures, training, and decision-making assistance made available by franchisor.
2. Community acceptance of product enhanced when local franchisee ownership is held.	2. Less risk with market-tested products and popular products.
3. Marketing and distribution costs shared by franchisees.	3. Pre-established promotion and advertising programs provided.
4. Some operating costs may be transferred to franchisee.	4. Being part of large system of retailers.
5. Flat fees often collected each month from franchisees.	5. Possible financial aid for part of purchase price at low interest.
6. Selling supplies or materials to franchisees can be profitable.	6. Credit available in buying inventory and supplies.
7. Retains quality control of product via franchise agreement.	7. Benefits of volume buying.
8. Keeps percentage of profits from sales.	8. Assistance with site identification.

DISADVANTAGES OF FRANCHISING

Although it would normally appear that most of the advantages accrue to the benefit of the franchisor, a close look at many of our nationally franchised operations will indicate that there are still some disadvantages applicable to both parties to the franchise contract. These include the following:

TO THE FRANCHISOR	TO THE FRANCHISEE
1. Long distance control over franchisees.	1. Usually gives up much freedom in management decisions.
2. Undue involvement in credit extensions to the franchisees for both investment and supply and inventory purchases.	2. Obligatory purchases from franchisor, even if better prices are available elsewhere.
3. Expenses of training and keeping on the road travelling supervisory personnel.	3. Profits always shared with franchisor, as either a percentage or a flat fee.
	4. Franchises have become very expensive.

There are many publications by banks, chartered accounting firms, and governments to provide more information about franchising.

FRANCHISES NEED PLANNING TOO

Despite the great growth and popularity of franchising in recent years, it should be noted that not all franchises have been successful. There are cases on record of huge prices being paid for a popular name franchise that folded because the market had been misjudged by both the franchisor and the franchisee. Great care should always precede any decisions to buy a franchise. Hundreds of buyers of franchises for a new proposed fried-chicken outlet lost their entire investment when the parent firm went into bankruptcy before the first unit was opened.

Prudence suggests that those planning to enter into a franchise agreement should carefully investigate the franchisor firm, the composition of the contract, and confirm the market to be served. Sincere and honest people may be the targets of fraudulent business practices, false promotion schemes, and claims of exaggerated profit potentials. The International Franchising Association is doing good work in organizing ethical franchisors and establishing standards and codes of ethical procedure. Franchising is relatively unregulated in Canada; only Alberta has legislation specifically governing this business method. Ontario is planning to introduce legislation to regulate franchising. The intention of the law is to ensure that prospective franchisees benefit from full disclosure of relevant information.

In other respects, franchising is subject only to the federal and provincial laws that govern all business activity, including the *Income Tax Act*, the *Competition Act*, the *Trademarks Act*, the various provincial Consumer Protection and Business Practices Acts and, in Quebec, provincial language regulations. Foreign franchisors planning to bring their systems into Canada are, of course, subject to Ottawa's *Foreign Investment Review Act*.

It is obvious that franchising has taken an important place in the small business field in our country. Many Canadian franchisors have extended their franchises to Europe, Asia, and around the world. This significant development, when handled with proper consideration for both parties, can provide real advantages to both franchisors and franchisees.

CHECKLIST FOR EVALUATING A FRANCHISE

Concerning the Franchisor

- How many years has the company been in the franchise business?
- What is the company's earnings history? Has it shown steady growth?
- What is the company's current financial condition?
- Who are the company's directors and officers?
- What is their business experience and reputation?
- What is the turnover of management, directors, and employees?

- Is the franchisor in the business of selling franchises or selling goods and services using franchisees?
- Does the company have a reputation of repossessing successful franchises or otherwise terminating the franchise contracts of successful franchisees?
- Have any outlets failed in the past seven years? If so, what were the reasons?
- Has the franchisor been involved in litigation in the past seven years? If so, what did it concern, and what are the details?
- Can the potential franchisee examine the franchisor's audited financial statements for the last three years or so?
- Can a potential franchisee examine the books and records of existing franchises?
- Can a potential franchisee examine the franchisor's profit and cash flow forecasts for your franchise?
- On what assumptions are the forecasts prepared? Are they reasonable?
- How do the forecasts compare with the actual results of existing franchises?
- Is the franchisor willing to help potential purchasers finance the purchase of the franchise?
- Are the interest rates competitive?
- What is the credit rating of the franchisor?
- Does the franchisor have a good marketing plan?
- Does the franchisor provide adequate national and local advertising?
- What portion of the advertising does the franchisee pay?
- Do new franchisees have any control over local advertising?
- Does the franchisor provide pre-opening advertising?
- Are initial and continuing training programs provided by the franchisor? Are they of high quality? Who pays for them? How long do they last?
- Does the franchisor exercise quality control by regular inspection of operations at each outlet?
- Is there an efficient system of inventory control in place?
- Are the franchisor's sales techniques and other facets of the operation up to date?
- Is a comprehensive, updated staff training and operating manual available?
- What is the franchisor's history of innovations in the business over the last ten years or so?
- Is there a standardized and simple bookkeeping and reporting system available for all outlets?

- Is the franchisor readily available with advice and help when problems arise?
- Will the franchisor help you recruit key personnel at the outset?
- How many outlets does the company now have?
- What is the breakdown between company-run and franchised outlets?

Concerning the Franchisee

Before investing in a franchise, operators of existing franchises should be approached to help in determining the reliability and reputation of the franchisor, the profitability of the franchise, the workload and lifestyle involved, and so on.

- How much equity capital (investment) was required?
- What was the final total cost of the franchise, and how does this compare with the initial projected cost?
- What items caused the total cost to exceed the projected cost?
- Is there a minimum sales quota? If so, is it reasonably attainable?
- How long did it take for the franchise to become profitable?
- Was there an adequate training program for the franchisee before the outlet opened? How long did it run?
- Was there a good training program for staff members? How long did it run? How often is it offered?
- Is there adequate continuing training for the franchisee and his staff?
- Who pays for the staff training?
- Were the franchisor's sales and profit forecasts accurate?
- What reports are required by the company, how often, and how long do they take to prepare?
- Does the franchisor respond quickly and fully to questions you may have or advice you seek?
- Does the franchisor provide adequate promotional and advertising assistance?
- What portion of the promotional and advertising costs is the franchisee required to pay, and what amount is involved?
- Have the lifestyle and working hours had any serious negative effects on the franchisee's home life?
- What changes would the franchisee make to the franchise agreement if one were starting out again?
- Is the franchisor fair and good to work for?

Concerning the Product or Service

- How long has the product/service been on the market?
- What is the annual sales growth rate over the past ten years?
- Are the sales seasonal? If so, what is the seasonal pattern?
- Is it a luxury/fad item, or an item of more stable demand through economic ups and downs?
- Taking into consideration both the price and the quality of the product/service plus the average income level, age, and ethnic mix of people in the desired location, is the product/service readily marketable?
- Are competitive products/services available in the area? If so, how do the prices compare?
- Is the product/service unique, or can it be readily duplicated by others?
- Is the product protected by a patent or trademark? If so, for how long? Can it be easily copied?
- Are there product/service guarantees or warranties? Who backs them?
- What is the warranty experience with the product/service?
- Who does repairs under warranty, and who bears the costs involved?
- Does the product/service have a high profile: is it well known or will a great deal of promotion and advertising be required, with unknown results?
- Is the franchisee allowed to buy inventory from suppliers other than the franchisor or those designated by her?
- Who controls the selling price?
- Are price wars common in the industry? If so, how does the franchisor protect his franchisees?

Concerning Location

- Who chooses the location? Is it the franchisor or franchisee?
- Is the location of the chosen franchise based on a market study?
- Does the franchisor have a long history of choosing good locations for franchises?
- How many franchises are closed each year because of poor results?
- Can franchisees lease the property initially with the right to buy, or must they buy now?

- Does the franchise agreement allow the franchisee to sublease, or even move the franchise if desirable?
- What are the company's expansion plans for the desired area?
- Is the area clearly defined?
- Is the area sufficiently large that competitors from the chosen franchisor will not be too close?
- What other competition is there in the area?
- How do the competition's product quality, acceptability, and price compare with those of your product?
- What is the current and projected potential user population in your area?
- Is the outlet in a growth area?
- Are new highways or shopping centres planned that will affect the business? If so, what is the expected effect?
- What is the average income level in the desired area?
- Does this income level suit the product or service?
- How are other businesses doing in the chosen area?
- Are many stores in the desired area "closing their doors" each year? If so, why?
- Have you talked to other store managers/owners in the area about the level of business?
- Is there adequate parking?
- Is there room for expansion should this prove desirable?

Concerning the Contract

The franchise agreement should spell out to each party's satisfaction answers to the following questions, among others:

- Is the franchise area precisely defined?
- Have exclusive rights to the area been granted, or has simply first refusal on future outlets in the area been granted?
- Can the franchise area be changed unilaterally by either the franchisor or the franchisee in the future?
- Is the franchisee limited as to the goods or services that may be offered for sale?
- Are there restrictions on customers to whom such goods or services may be sold?
- For what period does the franchisee have exclusive rights to the territory?
- Is the term of the franchise a specific period or is it indefinite?
- Is there a "right to renew" clause for both the contract and the building if it is leased? Do they expire concurrently?

- Is the term of the franchise and the renewal period sufficient to permit the amortization of the franchisee's investment?
- Is there a franchise renewal fee?
- Does the franchisee's family have the right to continue the operation in the event of death? If not, what provisions are there for this situation?
- What events will trigger a termination?
- How can the franchisee terminate the franchise?
- When and under what circumstances can the franchisor terminate the franchise?
- In the event of a termination, what are the provisions for the repurchase of inventory and equipment, and how would the price be determined and payment made?
- How will the franchisee be paid for any goodwill that has been developed, and how will the amount be arrived at?
- Is there a right to resell or reassign the franchise subject to the franchisor's approval and a provision that such approval will not be unreasonably withheld? If so, what are the restrictions and conditions?
- Does the franchisor have a right of first refusal?
- Does the franchisor have the right to repurchase or repossess the franchise? If so, under what conditions and how is the price determined?
- Is the training program (nature, duration, who pays, etc.) clearly outlined?
- Are all the services the franchisee requires specifically listed?
- Does the franchisor incur any specific penalty if he does not live up to the franchise agreement?
- Are the obligations of the franchisee clearly stated?
- Are penalties for nonperformance clearly listed?
- Must the franchisee purchase products or supplies from the franchisor? Must the prices be competitive? Are there minimum quantities that must be purchased each year?
- Are volume rebates and lower prices for large volume purchasing passed on to the franchisee?
- Can the franchisee accept the restrictive covenants listed?
- Is there a sales quota?
- Who pays for promotion and advertising?
- Does the franchisor control the selling prices?
- Does the franchisee control the hiring of employees at his outlet?
- Does the franchisor control the pay rates for employees of the franchisee?

- Is the method of determining the costs of services, inventory, equipment, and anything else to be provided by the franchisor clearly stated and acceptable?
- Is there an initial franchise fee?
- If there is a regular royalty payment, is it reasonable?
- What are the insurance costs?
- Is there a specified sales level below which no royalty is payable?
- Are all the franchisor's verbal promises included in the contract?
- Has the franchisee a right to all innovations the franchisor might make?
- Is the franchisee forced to accept any such innovations whether or not she wants them?
- If there are costs associated with mandatory innovations, who bears them?
- Who will manage the franchise in case of prolonged illness?
- In the event that you leave the franchise, are you prohibited from entering a similar business within a specified distance of the former franchise outlet for a specified time period?
- Are you allowed to engage in other business ventures while you are a franchisee?
- Is there a procedure for settling disputes that is acceptable to both parties?

EVALUATING AN OPPORTUNITY

It is vital that you, as a potential franchisee, fully understand what you are getting into and undertake a thorough investigation of the franchisor and all aspects of the franchise operations. The preceding checklists are rather extensive, but absolutely essential. They can assist the franchisee in identifying the areas that need consideration and decisions.

The franchise contract needs to be studied first. It is wise to consult a lawyer for review and advice. Contracts contain clauses and conditions that can be best interpreted by a professional. Thorough study will produce answers to questions about procedures and rights, obligations, and duties of the franchisee.

The franchisor's reputation in the business community is very important to check out. The following are good sources of information:

- *Banners*, which shows the company's financial condition
- Credit Rating Agencies, such as Dun & Bradstreet: the company's credit-worthiness
- Better Business Bureaus: any complaints by the public against the company

- Franchisor Organizations, such as the Association of Canadian Franchisors
- Government Agencies: federal and provincial consumer ministries maintain data on franchisors operating in their jurisdictions

The checklists on pages 80 to 86 suggest that the entrepreneur should study the market for the proposed product or service. This should include identifying the number of possible customers and their buying habits in the proposed territory. Consideration should be given to the future growth or decline of the population as well. The extent of competition should also be determined. Whether or not the new business can compete must be determined.

Finally, a potential purchaser should consider working in one of the franchise outlets. The viability of the franchise concept and the effectiveness of the franchise system should thus become clear, as should the potential suitability of this often rigorous and demanding life before a franchise contract is signed.

BUYING AN ESTABLISHED BUSINESS

We noted at the beginning of this chapter that another way to become a small business owner is to purchase an existing business. This method, too, may have distinct advantages and disadvantages in any particular case. There are many things to be noted in evaluating a small business firm that is considered for purchase. But it is one thing to note the general advantages of buying an existing firm—it is quite another thing to confirm the existence of those advantages. Even more important is the true evaluation of the business—to confirm the value of its assets, confirm its past profitability, and determine how to overcome any inherited disadvantages that may come with the firm. The final step in this process is to arrive at a fair purchase price. Too often, ambitious small firm buyers have become victims of the "small business opportunities" racket. This racket involves those who would profit from selling existing firms at inflated prices under a camouflage of exaggerated claims, exaggerated profits, and exaggerated values for assets of the firm.

SUMMARY

Franchising is an important way for an entrepreneur to go into business. More and more businesses are starting that way. Many very well-known organizations, such as McDonald's, Tilden, Coca-Cola, Chevrolet, and many others, have franchises in their distribution system.

The franchise is an arrangement between the parent company, called the franchisor, and the entrepreneur, called the franchisee. The arrangement has many advantages to both parties. The franchisor expands operations, receives additional capital, and has an additional profit source. The franchisee receives a program that has been tried and proven to be successful. Potential disadvantages include for the franchisor reduced control and for the franchisee a loss of freedom.

About one-quarter of all franchises are in the restaurant business. Sixty large franchisors control more than 50 per cent of all franchises. There are about 17 000 franchising companies in total.

The different types of franchises include straight-product-distribution, product-licence, and trade-name arrangements.

It is important to evaluate each franchise opportunity very carefully. The checklists on pages 80 to 86 identify areas to investigate. Franchisors are required by law to provide a disclosure statement listing detailed information about their operation. A thorough study of this data can also help determine the potential for success.

Buying an existing operating franchise is a second way to enter the world of franchising. An evaluation process similar to that used for starting a franchise should be used for this method, too.

QUESTIONS FOR CLASS DISCUSSION

1 How would you define a franchise?

2 What does the franchisor give to the franchisee under a franchise arrangement?

3 What does the franchisee give to the franchise arrangement?

4 Is the current popularity of franchises something really new on the business scene?

5 How would you start a franchise offering business?

6 How can we distinguish between straight-product-distribution franchises and product-licence franchises?

7 What is a trade-name franchise?

8 What do you think is the chief advantage of franchising to the franchisor?

9 What is the chief advantage of franchising to the franchisee that justifies the usually large investment in a franchise?

10 Do you agree that long distance control, credit involvement, expenses of training, and keeping auditors on the road are true problems and disadvantages to the franchisor?

11 If the franchisee gives up freedom in decision making, makes obligatory purchases from the franchisor, and always shares profits with the franchisor, are these items always disadvantages?

12 How can a potential franchisee check the company from which a franchise might be purchased?

Projects for Home Assignment and/or Class Discussion

1 Which method of becoming a small firm owner appeals most to you? Why?

2 If you owned a franchise for a fast-food chain organization, explain how your "giving up much freedom in management decisions" might be an advantage rather than a disadvantage. Explain how your answer would draw a distinction between well-trained owners with prior experience and the owner just entering into business for the first time.

3 If you or your instructor can obtain a copy of a franchise agreement, study it and report to your class on its provisions.

REFERENCES FOR FURTHER READING

Beckman, M.D., W.S. Good, and R.G. Wyckham, *Small Business Management*, John Wiley & Sons Canada Ltd., Toronto, 1982, Chapter 6.

Bond, R.E., *The Source Book of Franchise Opportunities*, Dow Jones-Irvine, Homewood, Illinois, 1985.

Coltman, M.M., *Franchising in Canada: Pros & Cons*, 2nd ed., International Self-Counsel Press, North Vancouver, B.C., 1987.

Cunningham, G., *Buy Yourself A Job & Be Your Own Boss*, McGraw-Hill Ryerson Ltd., 1990, Chapter 4.

Kao, R.W.Y., *Small Business Management: A Strategic Emphasis*, 2nd ed., Holt, Rinehart and Winston of Canada, Ltd., Toronto, 1984, Chapter 15.

Tate Jr., C.E., L.C. Megginson, C.R. Scott Jr., and L.R. Trueblood, *Successful Small Business Management*, 3rd ed., Business Publications, Inc., Plano, Texas, 1985, Chapter 24.

Zaid, F., *Canadian Franchise Guide*, Richard De Boo, Don Mills, Ontario, 1984.

Minding Your Own Business, Federal Business Development Bank, Montreal, 1982, Vol. 3, Chap. 1.

The 1986 Franchise Annual Handbook and Directory, Info Press, Inc., St. Catharines, Ontario.

2

THE PLANNING PROCESS OR ORGANIZATIONAL PLANNING

6

Steps in Planning a New Business: A Comprehensive Business Plan

LEARNING OBJECTIVES

After reading this chapter, you will be able to:

1. **U**nderstand the importance of the strategic planning process to the small business owner or manager
2. **I**dentify why markets, money, and motivation are essential to the total planning process for small business
3. **U**nderstand the ``determination-of-desired income'' technique for starting a new business
4. **K**now how the fifteen steps are used to develop a comprehensive business plan
5. **U**nderstand the need for anticipation of changes in customer wants and desires and how to deal with them

Chances of success for any new business are greatly increased when attention is first directed to a comprehensive business plan. A complete business plan provides a visualization of the firm before operations are started. When financial assistance from bankers, trade creditors, or investors is necessary, their first request is to see the total business plan. With it they can visualize the creditworthiness of the business. In this chapter we will investigate the key parts of such a total business plan.

Because there are so many areas in total management, so many decisions to be made in proper overall planning, we must recognize at the beginning that there is no one sequence of steps in planning that is agreed upon by all authorities in the field. The most important thing in planning a new small firm is that all phases of its operation be considered in the planning stage. As previously stated, there is no better application of the adage about an ounce of prevention versus a pound of cure. Mistakes in the planning stage of a new firm, or lack of proper attention to planning, can cause severe handicaps from which a new firm may never recover.

In this text we subscribe to what is known as the *desired income approach* to the entire planning process. In the most basic language, this approach suggests that the planner's first question should be, "How much profit do I expect to receive from this business in return for investing my time and money in it?" This approach is based on a conviction that this queston has been neglected much too often by new firm planners. No commitments, contracts, or obligations relative to a new business should be undertaken without a clear idea of what profits are possible over at least the first year of operation.

It is very important to recognize that strategic planning is an absolutely essential prerequisite to success.

DEFINING STRATEGIC PLANNING FOR SMALL BUSINESS

When intelligent people start on a long trip, they always make plans. They decide where they are going and how they plan to get there. Generally, the longer the trip, the more they plan.

Small business owners and operators should do the same thing. Since they normally will run the business for years and years, it follows logically that they should make plans on a long-term basis.

This is called *strategic planning*. It is a process by which the organization determines how it will try to achieve its long-term objectives. A complete strategic business plan provides a total picture of the firm before operations are started.

Most often, strategic planning should include the development of a comprehensive business plan. When the firm prepares to get its financial structure developed, bankers, trade creditors, and investors will all want to see the plan. Well-developed strategic business plans have made it possible for hundreds of small businesses to arrange for thousands of dollars of credit and investment funds before they ever started.

THE ESSENTIAL INGREDIENTS: MARKETS, MONEY, AND MOTIVATION

The total planning process is very complex, so much so that there is no one sure-fire way to succeed. However, three items are essential to success. They are markets, money, and motivation.

The strategic plan should definitely determine who will buy the product or service and how much must exist for the firm to be successful. Who will want the product? How many items will be bought? Is there competition to fight? How does the customer find out about the business?

The strategic plan must also consider money. It takes capital to purchase equipment and raw materials. Money is needed to pay employees' wages, rent or mortgage payments, and other necessary business expenses. Where should it come from? How much is needed? When will it be available? Will there be enough money? Will the business make enough profit so that the risks of running the business are worthwhile?

Finally, motivation is a major ingredient for business success. The entrepreneur must find ways to keep himself or herself going long hours when success may not be a sure thing. What keeps a person working hard in the face of discouragement? Of fatigue? When finances are bad? What will it take to motivate employees to treat customers so that they will come back?

These are just some of the questions small business planners need to consider during the planning process.

THE STRATEGIC GAME PLAN

The person preparing to manage a business, new or established, should develop a strategic game plan. That means he or she should have definite ideas about sales potential, the customer base, profit potential, financing, accounting methods, merchandise plans, location, hiring practices, training and supervision, customer relations, operation methods, advertising and promotion policies, expense control, credit sales, break-even point, legal requirements, depreciation policies, inventory and quality control, and possibly more.

The above paragraph presents a pretty imposing list. However, a well-conceived strategic business plan will address each point. By anticipating the need for answers in all these areas, the manager greatly improves the success probabilities.

The strategic business plan also provides the business with definite goals and methods of reaching them outlined on paper. Without goals and operational methods (tactics) spelled out in advance, most businesses "flounder on the rocks of hard times." The business may make it, but not without hardship.

Finally, a person should not make commitments, contracts, or business obligations without having a clear idea of how they will be met and paid. Profits must be a prime objective, too, or it is not worth the effort. A strategic business plan clarifies your objectives prior to making a firm commitment.

FIFTEEN BASIC STEPS IN A COMPREHENSIVE BUSINESS PLAN

Having understood the necessity of strategic planning, the following fifteen basic steps are designed to cover most of the decision areas of business planning. They begin by determining how much income the business owner feels is important and necessary. As mentioned earlier, this is called the *desired income approach*. Using this approach, the fifteen major steps in planning will be discussed here briefly; some additional items will follow that may be appropriate in some cases. Full chapters are devoted to each of these steps.

Zenon Environmental Inc., a company specializing in environmental quality services and products, started ten years ago with sales of less than $100,000. In 1990 this Canadian-controlled firm earned sales of well over $20 million. *Photo: Tom Bochsler Mainway Studio. Permission granted by Dr. Barry Loescher, President, Zenon Environmental Laboratories Inc.*

Step 1 *Determine what profit you want from this business, recognizing the time you will give and the investment you will have. Then complete a projected income statement based upon your decision.*

With the profit figure clearly in mind, it is possible, using business statistics now abundantly available, to calculate the sales volume that is necessary to produce that particular profit. The planner should complete a projected income statement for a typical first year of operation, and standard statistics will help in doing this. This statement, when it achieves its final form (a budgeted income statement) in the planning process, can serve as a budget during the coming year. How to prepare a projected income statement is discussed in Chapter 7.

Step 2 *Survey and test the market you plan to serve to ascertain if the necessary sales volume required to produce the profit called for in Step 1 is obtainable.*

The basic objective of Step 2 is to find out what can reasonably be expected in sales if the business is established within the intended market area. Market surveys are very important to business success. If the market survey shows that the necessary sales volume to produce the profit called for in Step 1 is not available, the planner can avoid working time and money by canceling plans at this point. Good maket surveys would probably have prevented many business failures for firms that never had a chance in their area of operations. The techniques for making market surveys have been vastly improved in recent years. Specific market data information is essential to determine dependable or attainable sales potential. The process of making a market survey is covered in Chapter 9. With its results known, the planner can also refine his or her projected income statement into a budgeted income statement covering the first year of operations.

It is always good news in the second step to find that the reasonably attainable sales volume exceeds the minimum required to produce the profit desired. In the majority of market surveys the authors have participated in over many years, the results have shown sales volume attainable to be in excess of that required in Step 1. It must be hurriedly added, however, that about one case in three has demonstrated that the business being considered should not be established. These facts demonstrate the importance of Step 2. When adequate sales and profits appear likely, proceed to Step 3.

Step 3 *Prepare a statement of assets to be used.*

A statement of assets to be used is a list of the assets that are essential to the operation of the business. Values in dollar amounts should be attached to each asset needed by the business. This step has the value of giving students and business people an appreciation of the workings of the business economy as they later determine how these assets are to be provided for the new firm.

For example, if the business needs machinery, equipment, tools, dies, delivery trucks, merchandise and raw material inventory, land and buildings, store equipment, office equipment, and cash, specific dollar amounts must be attached to each. This step requires careful thinking by the planner to be sure that all needs are thoroughly considered. This step can also involve policy decisions on such matters as whether or not you plan to carry your own accounts receivable or even sell on credit.

If credit sales are contemplated and you plan to finance your own accounts receivable, an added investment will be needed by the firm. This must be planned in a later step. The procedure for developing a statement of assets to be used will be further explained and illustrated in detail in Chapter 12.

Step 4   *Prepare an opening day balance sheet.*

Step 4 involves close study of the asset needs of the business as determined in Step 3 and decisions on how they are to be met. Here you decide whether to rent or buy the business building; whether to buy or lease the equipment; whether to buy delivery trucks, on what terms, or whether to hire a delivery service or even eliminate such service; and how you will finance the inventory from choices available. Every asset to be used, every liability to be incurred, and the resulting necessary investment by the proprietor must be clarified in this step. This will involve knowing the various types of financing available in providing each asset and how much you can safely use. Basic information relative to the nature of a balance sheet and of an income statement is necessary to do this task well. These statements will be discussed in Chapter 10. Sources of financial aid are covered in Chapter 11. Details of building the opening day balance sheet will be further discussed and illustrated in Chapter 12.

Step 5   *Determine the sources of funds to acquire the assets needed.*

There are many sources from which to raise capital for the firm. Regardless of the source, however, funds must be obtained either by borrowing or by selling some of the stock or partnership interest.

Borrowing usually comes from financial institutions, such as banks, or from trade credit from suppliers or equipment sellers. Other sources for borrowing money exist, and these will be discussed in Chapter 11. Selling a part of the stock or partnership interest has some advantages and disadvantages. They, too, will be discussed later.

Step 6   *Study the location and the particular site chosen in relation to specific characteristics.*

Too many small firms are located in space that "just happened" to be available, without any analysis of that space as a suitable location for the specific type of firm planned.

General location and specific site can be large factors in the success or failure of many businesses. This matter merits close study by the small firm planner. Details of measuring good versus poor locations and sites will be explained in detail in Chapter 13.

Step 7   *Prepare a layout for the entire space to be used for business activity.*

Have you ever wondered why the dessert section in a cafeteria is usually first in line? Have you observed where the prescription counter is located in a drugstore? Have you commented that some stores "seem like a jungle" without pattern or purpose in the way merchandise is presented to customers? The reasons for each location are to be found in a study of the good and bad things in layout. Reasons of a very positive nature explain the first two locations. Lack of recognition of good layout principles accounts for the third situation.

Every planner should create an actual floor-plan drawing of the operation that will reflect good layout principles. The rules of layout for different kinds of small firms will be reviewed in Chapter 15.

Step 8   *Choose your legal form of organization.*

The fact that most small firms are proprietorships, rather than partnerships or corporations, does not assure that proprietorship is the best legal form of organization. The authors believe that many small firms should be using the other legal forms. Planners should not only study the characteristics of the three major legal forms of organization, but should also seek out the true management advantages of each. The idea that the corporate form of organization is designed only for large firms can be seriously questioned. Different circumstances in different firms may call for advantages of one legal form rather than another. These considerations will be detailed in Chapter 8.

Step 9   *Review all aspects of your merchandising or marketing plan.*

Merchandising is a broad term generally used in business circles. It covers plans for presenting products to customers, the various channels of distribution that a firm may use to get its products to consumers, inventories in terms of dollar amount and lines of goods, sales promotion plans, advertising plans, pricing policy, public relations, markups, markdowns, seasonal variations in business, planned special sales, and many associated activities. It is in the study of these factors that many previous convictions or impressions of new business planners are seriously jarred or adjusted.

Step 10   *Analyze your estimated expenses in terms of their fixed or variable nature.*

When the budgeted income statement has been completed, it will show all operating expenses in detail. Of great value to the owner in making management decisions for the firm will be close scrutiny of these expenses in terms of their fixed or variable nature. The relation of risk to expenses should be known. This subject will be developed and illustrated in Chapter 26.

Step 11   *Determine the firm's break-even point.*

In simplest terms or in a more sophisticated formula, the old concept of a break-even chart is just as important to the small firm as to the large one. Most students know the concept in broad terms but cannot actually make a break-even chart from an income statement for a specific business. We will do that for a contemplated firm in Chapter 26.

Step 12   *If you are even considering sales on account, review the advantages and administrative decisions involved. Then establish a credit policy.*

The process of selling to customers on credit has many more implications than generally assumed. There are various types of credit plans available. Most are used by large firms. Small firms can do the same. Investment capital is necessary to carry your own receivables. Credit-card sales cost money. Open accounts risk uncollectibility. This subject, too, is a large one for small firm planners. Its many ramifications are discussed in detail in Chapter 27.

Step 13   *Review the risks to which you are subject and how you plan to cope with them.*

We all face risks in our daily activities. Small business firms are also subject to many risks every day. The more the planner knows about the risks, the better he or she can prepare the firm to protect itself against them. Such terms as "insurable interest" and "incidence of risk" should become a part of all small firm owners' vocabularies. We will look at details in this regard in Chapter 28.

Step 14   *Establish a human resources (personnel) policy at the outset.*

Small business has been accused of not being able to keep good employees. Everyone recognizes that good workers are the most valuable asset any business organization can have. Their importance may be even greater to small firms than to their large competitors. What will your policy be in this regard? How will you attract and keep good employees? Will you understand employee desires? How will you establish policies regarding them? This whole matter will be covered in Chapter 18.

Step 15   *Establish an adequate system of accounting records.*

Good accounting records are essential to decision making in any business. They are necessary for government reports, tax returns, and operations analysis. Every new firm should provide for an adequate system of accounting records in the planning stage. Details of the makeup and use of the basic financial statements are covered in Chapter 10. Establishing a basic system of records is illustrated with actual transactions in Chapters 23 and 24.

ANTICIPATING CHANGE IS VITAL

Customer wants and needs change daily, and for the small business to be successful, it must adapt itself to meet those changes. Not only must the small business be able to anticipate the shifts or trends of consumer preference, but it must have new or updated products ready when the changes occur.

Anticipation of customer desires often needs to be done months or even years in advance. Lead time is needed to develop new products or update old ones. Successful business operators give the topic of change much of their planning time.

OTHER ITEMS TO CONSIDER

The preceding fifteen steps in planning are deemed appropriate to almost every new small firm. Depending upon the size of the operation undertaken, other items may be considered in the planning stage. Larger firms may need to consider machine accounting, computer terminal services, use of quantitative techniques, or special financial reports, such as cash flow statements or source and application of funds statements. Cash flow statements are explained and illustrated in Chapter 24. The average small firm can have good management control if the fifteen steps just outlined are followed conscientiously. As the firm grows, investigation of these additional areas will become appropriate. For the average owner of the existing small firm and for student introduction to the subject of small firm management, we will confine our basic discussions to the fifteen steps listed here.

Whether the reader's objective is academic study of small firm management, preparation of a contemplated new firm, or analysis of an existing firm in line with established principles, competence in the field will be enhanced by the study of each of the steps outlined here.

SUMMARY

The strategic business plan for small business is used to assist in the goal-setting process and for demonstrating to financial institutions, equipment dealers and suppliers, and potential investors that the business knows where it is going.

The essential ingredients for success are: knowledge of the customer market; how much money will be used and where it will come from; and, finally, how motivation is needed to keep the human resources of the business going long hours and during periods of disappointment.

The chapter presents the fifteen steps that can be used to develop a comprehensive business plan. The first step is to use the desired income approach to determine the amount of profit the owners will need from the venture. These comprehensive steps are of great value to the planning process.

Finally, the small business entrepreneur should anticipate change. Customers will change their preferences, and the business must be ready with new or updated products or services when that happens.

QUESTIONS FOR CLASS DISCUSSION

1 What is the advantage of developing a comprehensive plan before starting a new business?
2 What is the danger of starting a new firm without adequate financing?
3 Do you think it is advisable for someone planning a new firm to think about what profit it will produce before beginning operations? Why?
4 What is the objective of a market survey?

5　Are people who operate their own small business entitled to both a salary and a profit on their investment?

6　What is a statement of assets to be used for?

7　What do we mean by "planning a new business"?

8　Do you agree with the steps needed for developing a comprehensive business plan as outlined in this chapter? How would you change them?

9　Could a neighbourhood grocery store justify the expense of a computer? Why?

10　What is a legal form of organization?

11　Do you believe that all small business firms should sell on credit? Why?

12　What do you like about the small firms you do business with?

Projects for Home Assignment and/or Class Discussion

1　Explain in a short paper what the term the *desired income approach* to planning a new firm means to you.

2　Do you think it is advantageous for new firm planners to have some idea of the amount of sales that can reasonably be expected in the first year? Explain.

3　Explain how you would determine how much profit you would expect as your salary and return on your investment if you were planning a new small business.

REFERENCES FOR FURTHER READING

Archer, M., *An Introduction to Canadian Business*, 5th ed., McGraw-Hill Ryerson Ltd., Toronto, 1986, Chapters 13 and 17.

Beckman, M.D., W.S. Good, and R.G. Wyckham, *Small Business Management*, John Wiley & Sons Canada Ltd., Toronto, 1982, Chapter 13.

Kao, R.W.Y., *Small Business Management: A Strategic Emphasis*, 2nd ed., Holt, Rinehart and Winston of Canada Ltd., Toronto, 1984, Chapter 6.

Knight, R.M., *Small Business Management in Canada*, McGraw-Hill Ryerson Ltd., Toronto, 1981, Chapter 3.

Tate Jr., C.E., L.C. Megginson, C.R. Scott Jr., and L.R. Trueblood, *Successful Small Business Management*, 3rd ed., Business Publications, Inc., Plano, Texas, 1985, Chapter 7.

Minding Your Own Business, Federal Business Development Bank, Montreal, 1982, Volume 2, Chapter 1 and Volume 3, Chapters 2, 5, and 6.

"Starting a Business," *Your Business Matters*, The Royal Bank of Canada, 1985.

. . . .

7

The Desired Income Approach to Business Planning: Making a Projected Income Statement

LEARNING OBJECTIVES

After reading this chapter, you will be able to:

1. **U**nderstand how the desired income approach is helpful in planning the new firm
2. **F**ind the kinds of industry data and governmental information that are available to help the small firm planner
3. **D**etermine the three statistical factors needed to calculate a projected income statement
4. **R**ecognize that the amount of income desired from the business is the starting point for calculating the projected income statement
5. **D**evelop a plan for a service firm and for a manufacturing firm

UNDERSTANDING THE DESIRED INCOME APPROACH FOR PLANNING

It should seem obvious to you by now that planning is extremely important to small business success. If an entrepreneur is going to invest money and energy into a venture, there should be some assurance the investment will pay off in the long run. Proper planning, then, is a must.

The desired income approach is a tool many small business planners have used successfully. It can be used to develop a projected income statement, which shows the entrepreneur what to expect in terms of sales income, total expenses, and profits.

LEARNING FROM THE EXPERIENCE OF OTHERS

"Intelligent people learn from others; only a fool learns from his or her own experience." Whether we agree fully with that statement is questionable; the point is, we can gain much from the experience of others.

Today's entrepreneurs have literally volumes of information available to use in planning their businesses. Our society has moved into the information age; we have all kinds of data to use that was not around just a few years ago.

The most important type of information is statistical. It is data collected from other businesses as they operate. Statistical information is generally current and can be found to match just about any size firm in any industry. Among other things, data is available showing a business's actual income, expenses, and profits.

PLANNING STATISTICS AND THEIR SOURCES

Once the new firm planners determine their desired income, continuing planning is made easier by the abundant statistics available that were not in existence when our grandparents were merchants. All potential new firm owners should become familiar with the statistics for the types of firms they plan to have. Previous employment in the type of firm planned is recommended for all prospective proprietors. This experience should enable them to gain valuable information about the statistics and operation of the type of business at first hand. But even without this experience, planners have many sources for gathering basic facts about their type of firm. Trade associations, chambers of commerce, government departments, Canadian Census, Annual Census of Manufacturers, Federal Business Development Bank, Statistics Canada, and business service organizations like Dun & Bradstreet Canada Limited are some sources readily available. Many publications of the government agencies are free of charge. Most are available in local libraries. Other agencies make only a minor charge for specific data reports.

Dun & Bradstreet regularly issues a publication that provides specific ratios and other financial data for 166 different lines of business. This publication covers firms in retailing, wholesaling, manufacturing, and construction. Comprehensive data ranging from the current ratio to the relationship of sales to fixed assets are presented. The figures are averages for hundreds of different firms in each line and include both profitable and unprofitable concerns. (See Figure 7-1.)

Among the other excellent sources of data of operating statistics for all types of business firms we should note at least the following.

For Canadian Firms:

Derived from actual financial statements filed with Revenue Canada by incorporated businesses of different classifications, informative aggregated balance sheet and income statement details are published annually by Statistics Canada (Catalogue No. 61-207). Another valuable quarterly by Statistics Canada (Catalogue No. 61-003) worthy of note focuses on corporations operating in Canada, and provides comparisons and trends by broad groupings of the financial transactions reflected on the balance sheet, statement of retained earnings, and statement of income, together with other selected items and a brief financial overview. The report covers the total industrial corporation sector of the Canadian economy.

For U.S.A. Firms:

Annual Statement Studies, published by Robert Morris Associates, Philadelphia National Bank Building, Philadelphia, PA 19107.

Barometer of Small Business, published by the Accounting Corporation of America, 1929 First Avenue, San Diego, CA 92112.

Annual Statement Studies covers manufacturing, wholesaling, retailing, service, and construction firms in each area. Both balance sheet and income statement data are included. *Barometer of Small Business* is a semi-annual publication that concentrates on retail firms of many types. Complete income statements are presented with percentages of sales for each item instead of dollar amounts. The data is classified for firms of different sales volume. Even trends, geographical variances, and seasonal data are provided. Complete balance sheets are presented in detail for each of the various types of firms reviewed.

A visit to the closest Federal Business Development Bank office and the provincial government department agency dealing with industry, trade, or commerce should be made by all who plan to open a new firm. Small business owners can also benefit from such visits by finding data by which to compare their specific situation with the principles set forth in the available reports. Many searchers will be surprised to find the information available for most lines of business. They may even find a pamphlet on their particular type of business. Often it will contain additional information that can be of value in planning or checking the status of an existing firm.

LINE OF BUSINESS (and number of concerns reporting) DOMAINE D'EXPLOITATION (et nombre d'entreprises étudiées)	Cost of Goods Sold Coût des marchandises vendues Per Cent	Gross Margin Marge bénéficiaire brute Per Cent	Current Assets to Current Debt Coefficient du fonds de roulement Times	Profits on Sales Coefficient du profit sur les ventes Per Cent	Profits on Equity Coefficient du profit sur l'avoir Per Cent	Sales to Equity Coefficient des ventes sur l'avoir Times	Collection Period Période de recouvrement Days	Sales to Inventory Coefficient des ventes sur les stocks Times	Fixed Assets Equity Coefficient des immobilisations sur l'avoir Per Cent	Current Debt Equity Coefficient des exigibilités sur l'avoir Per Cent	Total Debt Equity Coefficient de la dette totale sur l'avoir Per Cent
Non-Met. Min. Products, Other Produits miniers non métalliques, autres 311	75.6%	24.4%	1.8	4.6%	12.4%	2.7	50	6.4	69.5%	56.8%	95.1%
Orn. Iron Works Fer forgé 793	74.5%	25.5%	1.6	4.9%	18.1%	3.7	72	7.7	46.6%	86.6%	149.5%
Paint & Varnish Peintures et vernis 131	70.0%	30.0%	1.9	6.5%	19.1%	3.0	46	5.8	61.1%	58.5%	95.6%
Paper Boxes & Bags Boîtes et sacs de papier 319	78.7%	21.3%	1.5	2.9%	10.1%	3.5	53	8.6	73.7%	69.3%	130.5%
Paper Products, Other Produits de papier, autres 246	77.0%	23.0%	1.9	3.3%	9.5%	2.9	43	6.4	84.8%	53.5%	93.9%
Pet. & Coal Products, Other Produits du pétrole et du charbon, autres 51	85.7%	14.3%	1.2	3.1%	21.8%	7.0	24	20.6	96.9%	92.3%	153.4%
Pet. Refineries Raffineries de pétrole 80	85.4%	14.6%	1.5	4.7%	8.5%	1.8	46	6.4	54.9%	57.2%	98.5%
Pharmaceuticals Produits pharmaceutiques 141	49.7%	50.3%	2.5	10.5%	26.4%	2.5	69	5.3	36.2%	49.3%	68.6%
Publishing Only Edition 1,250	36.1%	63.9%	1.0	3.9%	18.2%	4.7	43	14.4	42.8%	167.6%	204.8%
Publishing & Printing Edition et imprimerie 730	12.1%	87.9%	1.2	7.0%	19.0%	2.7	49	26.1	57.4%	57.0%	142.7%
Pulp & Paper Mills Moulins de pulpe et papier 111	83.6%	16.4%	1.5	1.8%	3.5%	1.9	37	6.5	124.7%	47.1%	144.6%
Radio & TV Receivers Récepteurs radio/TV 49	76.7%	23.3%	1.4	1.0%	3.8%	4.0	42	5.6	42.0%	130.9%	178.0%
Refrigeration, Coml. Réfrigération, secteur commercial 37	79.6%	20.4%	1.7	2.7%	12.5%	4.7	68	4.4	34.2%	130.6%	156.9%
Rubber Products Produits de caoutchouc 156	78.3%	21.7%	1.8	3.4%	9.9%	3.0	46	5.6	76.1%	57.8%	120.2%
Sash, Door & Millwork Plants Produits usinés 1,463	76.9%	23.1%	1.5	3.2%	21.3%	6.7	44	6.8	93.3%	141.3%	237.4%
Sawmills & Planing Mills Scieries et moulins de dressage 1,236	84.9%	15.1%	1.5	3.9%	13.8%	3.6	36	5.5	128.0%	85.0%	216.0%
Scientific & Professional Equipment Equipement scientifique et professionnel 1,194	67.7%	32.3%	1.9	4.2%	11.9%	2.8	68	5.5	37.7%	69.1%	81.5%
Smltg & Refining Affinage et raffinage, laminage 206	90.0%	10.0%	1.5	-4.4%	-7.6%	1.7	30	4.8	156.3%	41.4%	153.1%
Soap & Cleaning Compds Savons et nettoyeurs 125	65.7%	34.3%	1.4	5.2%	12.3%	2.4	35	6.9	62.8%	45.4%	74.5%
Soft Drinks Boissons gazeuses 182	62.7%	37.3%	1.1	1.0%	5.1%	5.0	45	11.4	106.2%	114.8%	188.6%
Sporting Gds & Toys Articles de sport et jouets 374	73.8%	26.2%	1.7	2.3%	10.1%	4.4	65	4.4	39.0%	128.9%	167.7%
Structural Steel Acier de structure 309	77.9%	22.1%	1.4	3.0%	5.3%	1.8	53	6.0	28.4%	51.7%	91.4%
Textile Products, Other Produits textiles, autres 706	70.1%	29.9%	1.9	4.7%	20.2%	4.3	47	5.6	54.8%	92.4%	143.1%
Textiles, Synthetic Textiles, synthétiques 50	82.8%	17.2%	1.5	-0.6%	-2.0%	3.4	47	7.2	78.1%	68.3%	131.5%
Tobacco Products Tabac 12	61.6%	38.4%	2.5	13.1%	11.3%	0.9	36	1.8	15.5%	34.2%	51.1%
Toilet Preparations Produits pour la toilette 115	49.2%	50.8%	1.6	4.6%	16.0%	3.5	62	5.1	34.0%	97.7%	111.1%
Transportation, Misc. Transport, divers, 566	85.6%	14.4%	1.2	2.3%	7.4%	3.2	39	2.7	121.9%	171.9%	305.9%
Truck Bodies Carrosseries de camions 332	82.5%	17.5%	1.6	3.8%	15.8%	4.1	41	5.5	53.0%	94.0%	139.5%
Veneer & Plywood Bois de placage et contre-plaqué 60	90.0%	10.0%	1.4	-0.9%	-3.9%	4.1	38	5.7	106.8%	96.6%	200.7%
Wineries Vins 41	64.2%	35.8%	2.1	6.4%	11.1%	1.7	42	2.0	55.6%	56.4%	87.7%
Wire & Wire Products Fils métalliques et produits connexes 300	76.8%	23.2%	2.0	7.6%	14.8%	2.0	50	3.8	45.5%	46.2%	102.9%
Wood Products, Miscellaneous Produits du bois, divers 465	82.2%	24.3%	1.2	3.7%	22.9%	6.2	46	8.7	107.1%	131.9%	192.9%

FIGURE 7-1 • Sample of Dun & Bradstreet's financial statistics for manufacturing. Similar information is available for wholesaling, retailing, and construction.

From Dun & Bradstreet Canada Limited/Limitée, Key Business Ratios, 1989.

With the desired income known, only three statistics are necessary to enable the planner to make a complete projected income statement. These three statistics are

1   The average merchandise (inventory) turnover for this type of business
2   The average markup (gross margin)
3   Profits as a percentage of sales

Merchandise turnover is the number of times the average inventory is sold each year. If a firm carries an inventory of $15,000 and has a cost of goods sold of $60,000, the merchandise turnover is four times per year. *Cost of goods sold* (more details can be found in our review of accounting statements in Chapter 10) is the price paid for the merchandise purchased and sold. Merchandise turnover is computed by dividing the cost of goods sold by the average inventory carried in stock. For this example, the computation is as follows:

$$\frac{\text{Cost of goods sold}}{\text{Average inventory}} = \frac{\$60,000}{\$15,000} = 4 \text{ (the merchandise turnover)}$$

Inventories carried and their adequacy and inadequacy are one of the truly dynamic subjects in management. They will be referred to many times throughout this text and discussed in detail in a later chapter.

The *average markup* is the dollar difference between the cost of goods sold and sales, expressed as a percentage of sales. In dollar amounts, the markup provides the gross margin. If sales are $100,000 and cost of goods sold is $60,000, the gross margin is $40,000. Expressed as a percentage of sales, we observe that the markup is 40 per cent. It is computed by dividing gross margin by sales. In this example, the computation is as follows:

$$\frac{\text{Gross margin}}{\text{Sales}} = \frac{\$40,000}{\$100,000} \times 100 = 40\% \text{ (markup)}$$

Profits as a percentage of sales means just that. New firm planners want to find out what percentage of the sales dollar remains in the company as profits in their line of business. Existing operators want this figure to compare their firm's average with the averages of other similar firms. The arithmetical computation is to divide average profits by the sales volume, as follows:

$$\frac{\text{Net profits}}{\text{Sales}} = \frac{\$15,000}{\$100,000} \times 100 = 15\% \text{ (profits as a percentage of sales)}$$

This percentage can be figured on the basis of profits either before federal income taxes or after applicable income taxes have been deducted. It is important for planners to know which basis they are using.

The more searching you do for figures, the better your planning will be. Local or regional averages are generally more applicable than national averages. You may find three figures from three different sources for average merchandise turnover. You must then decide which are most applicable to our area. Without specific factors to support one or the other, it may be best to average the three for planning purposes. Similar considerations should be applied to the markup and profits as a percentage of sales figures.

BUILDING A PROJECTED INCOME STATEMENT

With only these three statistics and our desired profit, we may now proceed to construct a projected income statement for a planned retail firm. The new student should follow each step and each calculation carefully.

For our illustration of this process, let us assume that the carefully gathered and adopted figures for these three items are as follows:

Profits as a percentage of sales: 12 per cent

Merchandise turnover: four times per year

Markup: 35 per cent of sales

Desired profit: $15,000 (including salary and return on investment)

The key parts of an income statement are as shown in Table 7-1. Actual figures for the above situation have been inserted with each entry numbered in parentheses (1), (2), etc., so that the explanatory comments following the table may be traced. Detailed information can be found in Chapter 10.

TABLE 7-1

JONES HARDWARE COMPANY
PROJECTED INCOME STATEMENT
YEAR BEGINNING JANUARY 1, 199–

Sales		$125,000.00 (2)
Cost of goods sold:		
Beginning inventory, Jan. 1	$ 20,312.50 (5)	
Purchases during the year	81,250.00 (7)	
Goods available for sale	$101,562.50 (6)	
Less ending inventory, Dec. 31	20,312.50 (5)	
Cost of goods sold		81,250.00 (4)
Gross margin		$ 43,750.00 (3)
Operating expenses		28,750.00 (8)
Net profit from operations		$ 15,000.00 (1)

All the figures on this projected income statement have been computed from only the four facts previously determined. The statement has been completed from the bottom up and not from the top down. The numbers in parentheses indicate the order in which they were inserted. Their explanation follows:

(1) The desired profit is $15,000. This is the goal desired by the planner. We therefore insert this figure first on the last line.

(2) We have found that profits average 12 per cent of sales, so we must find the amount of which $15,000 (profits) is 12 per cent. We divide $15,000 by 12 to find 1 per cent ($1,250) and multiply by 100 to find 100 per cent of sales. We can now insert $125,000, our necessary sales volume.

(3) We have determined in our search of statistics that markup averages 35 per cent of sales. Accordingly, we find 35 per cent of our $125,000 sales and insert this figure as our gross margin ($43,750).

(4) Gross margin is the difference between what we paid for the merchandise (our cost) and what we sold it for. Therefore, if we subtract the gross margin ($43,750) from the sales ($125,000), it must tell us the cost of goods sold. Accordingly, we insert this figure on the projected income statement ($81,250).

(5) We have determined that the desired merchandise turnover is four times per year. This means that if the cost of goods sold is $81,250, it represents four times the average inventory that must be carried in stock to produce the sales volume we have indicated. Therefore, $81,250 divided by four gives us $20,312.50 as the average inventory necessary to support our sales volume. This figure is inserted on the statement for both our beginning and our ending inventory. If enlarged inventories are contemplated, adjustments can be made. For present purposes, we will assume that the inventory will remain at the same level.

(6) The cost of goods sold plus the inventory on hand at the end of the year must total the value of all the merchandise that has been available for sale during the year. Therefore, we add the cost of goods sold ($81,250) and the ending inventory ($20,312.50) to arrive at goods available for sale ($101,562.50).

(7) If $101,562.50 of goods were available during the year but only $20,312.50 were on hand in the beginning inventory, the difference must represent the merchandise purchased during the year. Therefore, we subtract the beginning inventory of $20,312.50 from goods available of $101,562.50 to arrive at purchases of $81,250.

(8) If gross margin is $43,750 and net profit from operations is $15,000, the difference must be the total of the operating expenses during the year. By subtracting the net profit from the gross margin, we have the total operating expenses of $28,750.

We have now completed a first-phase projected income statement. Operating expenses will have to be detailed at a later date. They will again be based upon available statistics on how much should be paid for rent, salaries, supplies, and other expenses. These amounts will each be computed as a percentage of sales. The comparable figures are easily available from the same source we have previously noted. Most reports will express these expenses as a percentage of sales.

This projected income statement tells the planners that if they are to realize the objective of $15,000 net profit, they will have to produce a sales volume of $125,000, maintain a merchandise inventory of $20,312.50, turn the inventory over four times during the year, and maintain an average markup of 35 per cent on their entire sales volume.

SPECIAL ASPECTS OF SERVICE FIRM PLANNING

We have previously noted that a purely service firm that does not carry an inventory of merchandise for resale to its customers will not have a cost of goods sold section on its income statement. (See Table 10-3.) The income section of the statement will reflect the total dollars derived from sales of a service rather than from sales of a physical product. The operating expense section of the statement will include all expenses incurred, including any supplies used in rendering the firm's service.

Some service firms may also have sales of products—such as a TV repair shop that also sells new television sets. In such cases, they should preferably separate sales income into service fees and product sales, have a special cost of goods sold section for the new product sales, and assign operating expenses to each phase of the operations as possible. Most helpful for proprietors of such firms is to develop income statements in separate columns, one for retail sales and one for service operations, and then total the two across the sheet for a summary of total operations. Each phase of the business can then be closely analyzed to determine its profitability.

SPECIAL ASPECTS OF MANUFACTURING FIRM PLANNING

The same type of statistics to which we have previously referred are also abundantly available for planners of new factory operations that produce their final products from raw materials. Financial statements for factory firms, however, have distinct features that are not part of retail firm statements. Some of these are:

T A B L E 7 - 2

BALANCE SHEET
GOMEZ AUTO BODY MANUFACTURING COMPANY
JANUARY 1, 199–

ASSETS

Current assets:			
Cash		$ 6,000	
Notes receivable		4,200	
Marketable securities		15,800	
Inventories:			
Raw materials	$ 25,000		
Goods in process	40,000		
Finished goods	48,000	113,000	
Prepaid assets		1,000	
Total current assets		$140,000	
Fixed assets:			
Land		$ 45,000	
Plant buildings	$165,000		
Machinery and equipment	80,000		
	$245,000		
Less depreciation	105,000	140,000	
Total fixed assets		185,000	
Total assets		$325,000	

LIABILITIES

Current liabilities:		
Accounts payable	$ 40,000	
Notes payable	20,000	
Accrued taxes payable	5,000	
Total current liabilities		$ 65,000
Fixed liabilities:		
Contracts payable		35,000
Total liabilities		$100,000

SHAREHOLDERS' EQUITY

Capital shares outstanding:		
Preference share	$ 80,000	
Common stock	100,000	
Retained earnings	45,000	
Total shareholders' equity		$225,000
Total liabilities and shareholders' equity		$325,000

1   The merchandise inventory figure on the balance sheet of a factory is not one figure representing total inventory on hand. Instead, it is broken down into raw materials, goods in process, and finished goods. (See Table 7-2.)

    This means that when one is planning a factory operation, provision must be made not only for buying the original raw materials but also for carrying the investment in goods in process (half-finished goods) and the finished goods until they are sold. That is why the total inventory investment of a small factory is usually a higher percentage of total current assets than in most other types of firms. Average statistics are available to help the new factory planner determine the required investment.

    Accounting is a bit more involved for factory operations because of the necessity of keeping track of the value of goods in process and total cost of the finished goods. This involves cost accounting procedures to add the labour expenses and overhead costs to raw materials placed in production to find the value of the unfinished products and the value of the products finished in the factory and placed in inventory for sale.

2   The income statement for a factory will show the cost of goods manufactured and sold, rather than merely a beginning inventory, plus purchases, less ending inventory, to find cost of goods sold, as is done for a retailing firm. The total cost of goods manufactured is preferably shown as a separate statement. (See Tables 7-3 and 7-4.)

This again is because the factory uses raw materials, expends labour and overhead on them, has products in all stages of manufacture in its inventories at a given time, and must calculate the total costs of its completed products.

Some factories produce products to order only, rather than producing for inventory stock on hand. This enables them to minimize the investment in materials and assures that all goods finished are sold as soon as they are ready for delivery.

The examples of a balance sheet, an income statement, and a statement of cost of goods manufactured for a small factory shown in Tables 7-2, 7-3, and 7-4 illustrate the preceding comments.

We turn now to the market survey in the desired income approach to planning—Step 2 in Chapter 9—to find out if the necessary sales can reasonably be achieved in the market you plan to serve. It is useless to further refine your financial planning unless that volume of sales can be achieved. When you know the results of your market survey are favourable, you can proceed to determine the assets required for the business and how they will be provided.

TABLE 7-3

THE KELLY MANUFACTURING COMPANY
INCOME STATEMENT
FOR YEAR ENDED DECEMBER 31, 199–

Sales		$2,150,000
Less cost of goods manufactured and sold		1,450,000
Gross margin on sales		$ 700,000
Operating expenses:		
Marketing expenses (listed in detail)	$350,000	
Administrative expenses (listed in detail)	175,000	
Total operating expenses		525,000
Profit from operations before taxes		$ 175,000

TABLE 7-4

SMUCKER MANUFACTURING COMPANY
STATEMENT OF COST OF GOODS MANUFACTURED
YEAR ENDED DECEMBER 31, 199–

Direct materials:		
Raw materials inventory January 1	$100,000	
Plus purchases during year	65,000	
Materials available during year	$165,000	
Less inventory December 31	40,000	
Direct materials used during year		$125,000
Direct labour expenses for year		265,000
Factory overhead		
(All factory overhead expenses would be listed in detail: indirect labour; power, heat, and light; salaries; factory supplies; depreciation; repairs and maintenance; patent expenses and insurance; and so on.)		80,000
Total manufacturing costs		$470,000
Add work in process January 1		45,000
		$515,000
Less work in process December 31		65,000
Cost of goods manufactured during the year		$450,000

QUESTIONS FOR CLASS DISCUSSION

1   How much would you plan on as your profits before taxes and as a return on your investment if you started a new small firm today?

2   What does *the desired income approach to planning* mean to you? Do you agree with it? Why?

3   Where can people who plan new firms find some statistics to guide their planning?

4   Where would you look for industry statistics if you were planning a new hardware store?

5   What are the key items of statistics needed to make a projected income statement?

6   Why would it be desirable to have key statistics, like the current ratio, broken down into the upper quartile, median, and lower quartile? In which quartile would you want your firm to be?

7   What is meant by the merchandise turnover? How is it computed?

8   What is *average markup*? Can it be expressed both in dollars and as a percentage of sales? Give examples.

9   Why is it important to know whether profits as a percentage of sales are computed on profits before or after income taxes?

10   If you know goods available for sale and the beginning inventory, how do you find purchases?

11   If you know cost of goods sold and merchandise turnover, how do you find the average inventory?

Projects for Home Assignment and/or Class Discussion

1   Explain what is meant by the statement that "today's students have one great advantage over their grandparents in planning new business firms."

2   How can today's planners effectively use industry statistics in planning? How do you account for the fact that different sources of statistics vary in their averages?

3   Write a brief explanation of the meaning and importance of merchandise turnover.

REFERENCES FOR FURTHER READING

Archer, M., *An Introduction to Canadian Business*, 5th ed., McGraw-Hill Ryerson Ltd., Toronto, 1986, Chapter 12.

Tate Jr., C.E., L.C. Megginson, C.R. Scott Jr., and L.R. Trueblood, *Successful Small Business Management*, 3rd ed., Business Publications, Inc., Plano, Texas, 1985, Chapter 21.

Minding Your Own Business, Federal Business Development Bank, Montreal, 1982, Volume 1, Chapters 1 and 2.

3

FINANCIAL PLANNING AND FINANCING THE NEW FIRM

8

Choosing a Legal Form of Organization

LEARNING OBJECTIVES

After reading this chapter, you will be able to:

1. **U**nderstand the importance of selecting the proper legal form of organization for a given firm
2. **U**nderstand the advantages and possible disadvantages of the sole proprietorship form of organization
3. **C**ompare the advantages and disadvantages of being a partnership
4. **F**orm a corporation and recognize why or why not this form of organization is appropriate for many firms
5. **U**nderstand the differing income tax rates that apply to sole proprietorships and partnerships as compared to corporations

New firm planners should do some serious thinking about what legal form to choose for the new firm. This means determining what the status of the business will be in the eyes of the law. The choice has very important consequences.

More than 99 per cent of the more than one million businesses in Canada are organized legally as (1) sole proprietorships, (2) partnerships, or (3) corporations. It is our intention here to evaluate the characteristics, advantages, and disadvantages of these three legal forms. Other legal forms, such as joint ventures or investment trusts, are rarely used and not considered here.

When confronted with the choice of a sole proprietorship, a partnership, or a corporation, too many students and small firm planners and operators mistakenly believe that the corporation is intended only for very large firms. All three of these legal forms are available to small firms. Different factors may affect the choice in a particular case. In all cases, all three forms should be looked at carefully. Some of the items that affect the decision include plans for expansion, product or service being sold, needs for raising capital now and in subsequent years, liability characteristics of the planned firm, the proprietor's available investment funds, need for continued life of the firm, alternatives for bringing desired people into the firm, and legal requirements of the particular locality.

We can note that of the total number of business firms in Canada, approximately 60 per cent are proprietorships that do about 30 per cent of the total sales volume; approximately 12 per cent are partnerships doing about 10 per cent of the total sales volume; and approximately 30 per cent are corporations doing more than 60 per cent of the total sales volume in the country. It is these types of statistics that encourage the erroneous belief that the proprietorship is the almost exclusive choice of legal form for small firms. The data do not reveal to the casual observer the reasons why the larger firms have chosen the corporate form. Business prudence should include an understanding of the options.

THE SOLE PROPRIETORSHIP

A sole proprietorship is a business owned and operated by one person. The owner and the business are synonymous in the eyes of the law. All assets in the firm are owned by the proprietor, subject only to the liabilities incurred in its establishment and operation. The proprietor is solely responsible for its debts and any losses incurred, assumes all its risks, provides most of its capital, and provides its total management. The only requirement for its establishment is that the owner obtain any licences required in the municipality and start operations.

This simplicity in establishment has probably accounted for the popularity of this legal form of operation. This choice may represent an oversight of other factors that would indicate the desirability of another legal form.

Advantages of the Sole Proprietorship

The literature on business asserts that the proprietorship form has several advantages, such as:

1   Simplicity of organization
2   Owner's freedom to make all decisions
3   Owner's enjoyment of all profits
4   Minimum legal restrictions
5   Ease of discontinuance
6   Tax advantages

These alleged advantages should be carefully reviewed to distinguish between mere characteristics and true management advantages. Some thoughts in this regard are as follows:

1 Simplicity of Organization   If the new firm owners choose a legal form of organization only because of its simplicity, they probably demonstrate that they lack overall business competence and a thorough knowledge of legal forms, and that they are the type of owners who always look for the easiest way to make decisions. Simplicity of organization is truly a characteristic of the proprietorship, but no inherent management advantages are to be noted because of this simplicity.

2 and 3 Owner's Freedom to Make All Decisions and Enjoy All Profits   To allege that one advantage of the proprietorship is that the owner is free to make all the decisions and to receive all the profits completely ignores the facts of a close corporation (explained later in this chapter). If these same business people have their businesses incorporated for 100 shares of common stock and they decide to give one share to their spouses, one share to a son or daughter, and retain ninety-eight shares in their name, who then makes all the decisions? Who then receives all the profits? Surely the owner has the same authority as if the firm were a proprietorship. So again, these alleged advantages become merely nonexclusive characteristics of a proprietorship.

4 Minimum Legal Restrictions   This factor, in the sense of fewer reports to be filed with government agencies, no paid-up capital taxes to be paid, and no charter restrictions on operations, can be an advantage from the standpoint of time and expenses involved. Whether or not this advantage would dominate in the final selection remains to be seen after the total business picture has been reviewed.

5 Ease of Discontinuance   This is truly a characteristic of the proprietorship. To discontinue a proprietorship means essentially closing the front door. When we recognize, however, that sound business firms are not organized with the thought of discontinuing them, we must question whether this is truly an advantage of this particular form. Our concern is not the establishment of the Mom and Pop type of firms but solid business firms that may start small but have the potential for growth, good profits, and a good future for the owner. These objectives should be kept in mind as we choose our legal form of organization.

6 Tax Advantages   Alleging tax advantages as a bonus of the proprietorship form of legal organization defies the fact that as taxable income increases, the rate on individual income is higher than on corporate taxable income or total taxes on the divided income of a partnership. Total federal and provincial income taxes should be a prime consideration in the choice of any legal form. The government expects business people to practise tax avoidance rather than tax evasion, and the choice of a legal form may be of assistance in this regard. Examples of various taxable income levels and the applicable income taxes for the different legal forms of organization are presented in a later section of this chapter.

Disadvantages of the Sole Proprietorship

The literature on business also describes the various disadvantages of the proprietorship as follows:

1   Owner's possible lack of ability and experience
2   Limited opportunity for employees
3   Difficulty in raising capital
4   Limited life of the firm
5   Unlimited liability of proprietor

A brief evaluation of these items follows.

1 The Owner's Lack of Ability and Experience   The owner may truly lack these qualifications. It is to guard against this possibility that preownership experience is recommended for those planning to own their own firms. Sound college courses in management are available to college students. Participation in management development courses can be tremendously helpful. Those without formal study in management can learn much from working for other firms in the same line of business. Testing one's own competence through studies of good business texts should be a prelude to investing in and opening a new firm. Only when owners feel that they know a great deal about the particular firm they propose should they proceed. It should be pointed out, however, that this feature of the owner's capability is not inherent in the legal form of organization chosen. Lack of ability and experience can ruin a partnership or a corporation just as easily as it can a proprietorship.

2 Limited Opportunity for Employees   This point has been overdone as a disadvantage of the proprietorship. Aggressive, capable employees may indeed desire more rewards faster than the firm can provide them. You can indeed promote some people only so far, and the best thing you can do for them is to promote them out the front door. But let us realize that if the same firm is a partnership or a small firm corporation, the employees' environment, potential rewards, and promotions are the same. Small firms generally face the problem of keeping good employees. All large firms face this problem. Also, probably a refreshing thought in this regard is that small firms have not fully utilized profit sharing, bonuses, or a share in the ownership of the firm in order to keep key people on the payroll. Possibilities of share ownership in a corporation add to these benefits. Good employees are a firm's most valuable asset. The problem of obtaining and keeping them is not solved merely through the choice of a legal form. Personnel policies are discussed in Chapter 18.

3 Difficulty in Raising Capital   This can be a problem. On the average, two people have more capital then one. It follows that, on the average, two people would have more to invest in providing the capital needs of a new small business. Not all firms have this problem, however. If it does exist and the planner does not wish to share ownership of the firm, this would restrict the alternatives in raising adequate capital. When the planner has seriously faced the problem of building a sound financial structure for the firm, its investment needs can be compared with available funds and a decision can be made. If the assets are adequate, the planner will have no disadvantage due merely to the difficulty in raising capital.

4 Limited Life of the Firm   Discussions of this feature of legal forms are usually restricted to the partnership form of organization, but it also applies to proprietorships. What is involved is the matter of legal discontinuance of the firm. Untimely, unanticipated, or unplanned removal of the proprietor from operation of the business may have ramifications for creditors of the firm. Restrictions on credit granted may be founded in this matter of limited life. An owner's record for stability, honesty, and capability can largely overcome this practical problem. When these are unknown, as in the case of a new firm, it may have some application.

5 Unlimited Liability   By far the greatest disadvantage of the proprietorship is its inescapable feature of *unlimited liability*. This disadvantage is one that applies directly to the owners. It means that, even though they believe that they have invested only part of their total capital in the business, they are liable to the full extent of their total assets for the liabilities of the firm. A damaging lawsuit lost, a judgement for injuries suffered by a customer on the premises, or a serious accident involving injuries to outside persons are some of the things that can create liabilities far beyond anything anticipated when the firm was planned. It is this feature of the proprietorship that causes many owners, when aware of unlimited liability, to put their homes in their spouses' names in order to keep the home from being available to pay such claims. In light of recent changes in many provincial family law legislation, the legal owner may not be relevant due to the requirement of equal split of assets on divorce. The owner's savings accounts, investments, and any other assets are liable in these cases. As we noted earlier, in the proprietorship legal form the owner and the business are synonymous, and all assets, not just those the owner thinks are invested in the firm, are liable to pay its debts. Insurance protection can be provided, of course, and this matter will be discussed in a later chapter.

THE PARTNERSHIP

A partnership is usually defined as an association of two or more persons to carry on as co-owners of a business for profit. Partnerships are based upon a partnership agreement. The partnership agreement should always be in writing, even though this is not a legal requirement. It should cover all areas of possible disagreement among the partners. It should define the authority and the rights and duties of each partner, and the limits to such authority. It should include an agreement on how profits and losses are to be divided. Their treatment need not be the same. In the absence of an agreement to the contrary, profits and losses are divided equally among all partners. Partners may make special arrangements to pay members of the firm for services rendered, interest on capital investment, time spent, or advance drawings before the balance of profits is to be divided in an agreed ratio.

Many successful partnership firms have been dissolved because of serious disagreements between original partners that were not anticipated in the partnership agreement. Thoroughness in this matter cannot be overemphasized.

Advantages of the Partnership

The following advantages of the partnership form of organization are usually cited in business books:

1   Ease of organization
2   Combined talents, judgements, and skills
3   Larger capital available to the firm
4   Maximization of personal interest in the firm
5   Definite legal status of the firm
6   Tax advantages

With the benefit of our previous discussion of the proprietorship, we can quickly evaluate these alleged advantages: ease of organization should not be a management consideration in starting a new firm; greater financial potential is true only in average terms; personal interest of partners should be no greater than if each had shares in a corporate form of organization; and definite legal status can be important to creditors. In most income brackets, a group of partners would pay less in total income taxes than the owner(s) would under either of the other chief legal forms.

Advantages of potential substance, then, as compared with the proprietorship, seem to be possibly greater capital available, generally less income tax on the same net profits, and a positive legal status. As compared with the corporation, only the tax consideration would remain as a potential advantage.

Disadvantages of the Partnership

The partnership has some very real disadvantages, which can be serious to well-meaning people who start their firms in good faith. Four disadvantages merit brief discussion.

1 Unlimited liability
2 Limited life
3 Divided authority
4 Danger of disagreement

1 Unlimited Liability   Just as this condition applied to the proprietorship, it is even more serious in the partnership. Not only is a partner liable for debts he or she contracts for the firm, but a partner is also responsible to the full extent of his or her resources for debts contracted by the other partners, unless the form of partnership specifically limits liability as in the case of a *limited partner*.

2 Limited Life   Any change whatsoever in the list of general partners automatically ends the life of the existing partnership, and a new legal entity must be created by the remaining partners. Admission of a new partner, death of an existing partner, and withdrawal of any general partner are cases in point. Restatement of all assets and readmission of all liabilities and individual capital accounts are part of the process. This is also known as *mandatory dissolution*. The limited life provision, however, can be overridden by a specific partnership agreement.

3 Divided Authority   It is one thing for a good factory manager and a good salesperson to combine their talents in a partnership. Each can have clearly defined areas of operation. Other areas, however, such as policy for the total firm, financing plans, personnel management, and ideas on expansion, can create divided authority and delay decisions for the firm. Some activities always seem to provide possibilities of conflicting authority.

4 Danger of Disagreement   The ever-present possibility of a disagreement between the partners can be extremely serious. Even though a very thorough partnership agreement is written, clauses are subject to various interpretations, some partners may willfully exceed clearly defined authority, and discontent can develop between the partners. Only honest and capable people of great mutual respect should engage in partnerships.

Types of Partners

Partnerships are usually either *general partnerships* or *limited partnerships*. A general partnership is one in which each partner carries the unlimited liability for the firm's debts. A limited partnership is one in which some partners may have their liability limited to the extent of their investment. A firm must have at least one general partner (active partner) who carries the unlimited liability obligation. Withdrawal of a limited partner does not dissolve the partnership as withdrawal of a general partner will do. Limited partnership agreements must usually be filed with a government official. Without notice as to the acceptance of a limited partner, all partners are considered to be general.

There are many other special types of partners that new firm planners may wish to investigate. *Secret partners* are those who play an active role in the business but are not identified to the public as partners. *Silent partners* are those who are not active in operations but share in the profits. *Dormant partners* are not active and are not known to the public. An *ostensible partner* is one who lends his or her name and credit to the firm, but who has no financial interest in the business. Special circumstances may make it necessary to choose these types of partners, but their use is not normally recommended. It must be remembered that while these special classes of partners differ in their relationship to one another, they are all equally liable to the public for partnership debts and liabilities. The limited partnership, on the other hand, enables many new firm planners to obtain capital that might otherwise not have been available. In most such cases we have reviewed, the corporate form of organization would have served everyone's purpose in a superior manner.

THE CORPORATION

Just as the problems of size and need for acquiring more capital motivated the creation of the partnership rather than the proprietorship, they also motivated the next step to the modern corporation as a legal form of organization. The second step was also made necessary by the problems of unlimited liability and limited life that characterized the partnership. A developing industrial world needed a legal form of organization that would provide limited liability for owners and perpetual life for the business firm. Accordingly, in 1819 in the famous Dartmouth College case, Justice John Marshall gave the first legal recognition to a new type of business organization, which was to become known as the corporation. He defined it as "an artificial being, invisible, intangible, and existing only in contemplation of law." Its ownership would be divided into shares.

Though the corporate form of organization was originated in this background, it was never contemplated to be used only by giant firms. Its advantages and disadvantages have always been equally available to small firms as well.

How to Organize a Corporation

In Canada, there are eleven general *Companies Acts*, one for incorporation under *federal law* and one each for incorporation under *provincial law*. A federal company incorporated under the *Canada Business Corporations Act* may carry on its business in all provinces as of right; no licence is required for a federal company in Ontario, Quebec, and New Brunswick, although the other provinces impose a registration requirement. The *Companies Acts* of the provinces vary according to history and local requirements; however, in the main they are comparable to the general legislation under which federal companies are incorporated. If a provincially incorporated company wishes to conduct business in other provinces, as an "extra-provincial" company, it will have to register (obtain a licence) in those provinces. In the provinces of Ontario and Quebec, incorporation in either one allows the company to operate in the other. The decision regarding the jurisdiction (place) of incorporation will generally depend on factors such as the ease of incorporation, reporting requirements, fees payable, and the like. For small companies it is advisable to incorporate in the province where the company's business is conducted and where the principals normally reside.

The actual incorporation is done by filing *Articles of Incorporation* (Memorandum of Association) signed by the subscribers and paying the applicable fee. This sets out such information as the name of the company, the location of its head office, and the objects for which the company is formed, and it provides details regarding directors, the authorized capital, and the shares that the subscribers to the Memorandum agree to take. This will, then, become the charter of the company. Upon approval, the Registrar of Companies approves the application, issues a certificate of incorporation (in some provinces this may be called the granting of Letters Patent), and publishes a notice of incorporation in the provincial (or federal) "Gazette."

The selection and registration of a distinctive corporate name is an important step in the process of incorporation. The corporate name must convey the information that the firm has the protection of limited liability for its members. It is required that the words "Limited," "Incorporated," or "Corporation," or the abbreviations "Ltd.," "Inc.," or "Corp.," be the last word of the company's name. Names liable to conflict with another existing business organization, whether incorporated or not, are not acceptable.

It is permissible for a company to have a bilingual name, that is, a name in an English and a French form. The practice is to separate the English and French forms with a hyphen; for example "XYZ OF CANADA LIMITED - XYZ DU CANADA LIMITÉE."

Total incorporation costs vary from $800 to $1,000 depending on location and the complexity of the situation. Although the use and counsel of a lawyer is generally advisable, a small business person can actually do the incorporation personally and save several hundreds of dollars in legal fees. There are publications available in most bookstores providing step-by-step instructions and guidance regarding the prcedures involved.

Types of Corporations' Shares

The authorized capital of a corporation is divided into shares with par value or without par value or both, and may consist of shares of more than one class (type).

Most small firms have only one class of shares called *common shares*. If the corporation is federally incorporated, these must be without nominal or par value. There are other classes of shares that have special preferences, rights, conditions, and restrictions attached thereto. *Preference shares* have a priority over the classes of shares as to the payment of dividends. Stated preference shares—such as 8 per cent preference—must receive dividends before any dividends may be declared on the common shares. *Cumulative preference* means that the preference share must receive its dividends for any years in which no dividends were paid before the common may receive dividends. *Participating preference* means that the preference shares must share in any further dividends after the common have received a specified maximum dividend. *Redeemable* means that the corporation may purchase or redeem the shares upon the demand of the corporation, or that the corporation is required to purchase or redeem such shares at a specified time or upon the demand of a shareholder. Holders of *convertible shares* have the privilege of converting their shares, under specified conditions, into another class of shares.

Advantages of the Corporation

After discussing the operation of the other forms of organization, there is little to argue with in the claimed advantages of the corporation, which are as follows:

1   Limited liability to shareholders
2   Perpetual life
3   Ease of transferring ownership
4   Ease of expansion
5   Applicability to all sizes of firms

1 *Limited Liability to Shareholders*   Rather than risk their entire assets to the debts of the business, the new firm owners or investors buy shares at a given price, and this investment is the total liability to which they can be subjected. Only those assets that a small firm planner turns over to the firm in exchange for shares become corporate property. Total corporate liability is the assets listed on its balance sheet. No longer need the owners of a small corporation fear the unexpected judgement against them as a threat to their other assets. It should be noted, however, that banks and other lenders may (and often do!) require the personal guarantees of the shareholder(s) for corporate debt. This is especially common for small corporations.

2 *Perpetual Life*   If all the shareholders of a given corporation died on the same day, the business would go on as a legal entity. Shares would pass to the heirs of the original owners and they would inherit a going concern.

3 *Ease of Transferring Ownership*   Shareholders can sell their shares whenever they want to, provided they can find a buyer. Formal transfer of share certificate titles is normally handled by a fiduciary agent, usually a trust company, that will issue a new certificate in the name of the new owner of the shares. Operations of the company are not affected by this transfer.

4 Ease of Expansion of the Company   Although additional sale of shares is not the only way to raise capital for expansion, it is usually easier to sell additional shares when expansion is contemplated. Many corporations, large and small, will receive permission from the appropriate authorities to create and to sell more shares than originally planned for sale. The balance is held as "authorized but not issued" shares. It should appear on the balance sheet in the net worth section for informational purposes. If all authorized shares have been sold, a corporation may request permission to sell additional shares when an expansion is contemplated.

5 Applicability to Both Large and Small Firms   Truly an advantage of the corporate legal form is its versatility. Regulations and charter requirements are the same for small or large corporations.

Other advantages often claimed for the corporation, such as that it permits employee profit sharing and encourages efficiency in management, must be termed as possible but not exclusive characteristics. Profit sharing is possible other than through shares in any legal form of organization. Efficiency in management is not guaranteed to any firm because of its legal form. This is the responsibility of management in all cases.

Disadvantages of the Corporation

The chief disadvantages are:

1   Government regulation
2   Expense of organization
3   Capital tax

1 Government Regulation   All good things demand some sacrifice. In the case of the corporation, the chief sacrifice is the necessary acceptance of government regulation. This begins with the necessity of obtaining a charter from the federal government or from the home province of the corporation. For small firms operating in only one province, it is recommended that the charter be obtained in that province.

2 Expense of Organization   There is an expense in organizing a corporation. The use of an attorney is to be recommended when applying for a charter. Total expenses for this process range from $800 to $1,200 in most cases. Requirements for the charter include specifying the business activity in which the firm will engage, types of shares it desires to issue, and quantities of each to be authorized.

3 Capital Tax   The province in which the firm is incorporated may levy an annual capital share tax on paid-up capital.

The activities of the corporation will be restricted to those specified in the charter. For instance, a small firm authorized to engage in the men's clothing business cannot open a grocery store unless the terms of the charter are broad enough and/or so specify. The sometimes cited advantages of impersonal management of a corporation need not apply to small firms using the advantages of the corporate form of legal organization.

DECIDING ON THE LEGAL FORM FOR THE NEW FIRM

How, then, will the new planners decide upon their legal form of organization? As previously mentioned, they will consider the importance of unlimited liability, the protections available through public liability insurance, their expansion plans, the nature of the product, dangers inherent in the service or product, and the relative incidence of risks in normal operations that might provoke lawsuits and judgements against them. Through the potential of preference shares, a corporation can attract investors who prefer dividends to increased market price. Preference shares do not normally carry voting power, and the planner is able to keep control of the company by retaining 51 per cent of the voting common shares. It is the authors' view that far too many small firms have neglected the use of the corporate form. Its protections and potentials should be carefully considered by any new firms that plan to grow large and profitable.

INCOME TAXES AND LEGAL FORMS OF ORGANIZATION

Students have often heard that tax considerations play an important part in most business decisions. The choice of a legal form of organization can be one of those decisions with significant tax consequences. It is never too early for college students to get an idea of the taxes to which they will be subjected as business owners or as salary earners. The tax area is an ever-changing environment; one must obtain up-to-date advice when making decisions about incorporation, dividends, etc.

There are three levels of taxation in Canada: federal, provincial, and municipal. The federal government levies both direct and indirect taxes, the most important of which are the corporate, personal income taxes, and, until the end of 1990, the manufacturer's sales tax. Effective January 1, 1991, the manufacturer's sales tax (13.5 per cent) was replaced with the Goods and Services Tax (GST) at the rate of 7 per cent. The GST is modeled on European-style value-added tax and is taxing most purchases of goods and services. More detailed information on how the GST operates will be presented in Chapter 23.

The provincial governments levy direct taxes, such as income tax, retail sales tax, special taxes on specific primary industries (mining, logging), and, in some provinces, paid-up capital taxes. Municipalities function under the guidance of provincial legislation and impose direct taxes on real estate, water consumption, and places of business. Income taxes imposed by the provinces are collected by the federal government, except in the cases of corporate taxes imposed by the provinces of Quebec, Alberta, and Ontario and personal income tax imposed by Quebec.

Because provincial and local taxes vary, we will concentrate here only on federal income taxes currently in effect.

Generally speaking, all companies resident in Canada are liable to federal income tax. The tax is applied upon income received or receivable during the taxation year from all sources inside or outside of Canada, less certain deductions permitted by the *Income Tax Act*.

There is no one form of legal organization that claims the best advantage in all instances. The applicable federal income tax is affected by the amount, the distribution, and the source of net taxable income involved in any business. Income tax rates for proprietorships and partnerships are progressive—the higher the income bracket, the higher the tax rate. The rates are 17 per cent on up to $28,275 and 29 per cent on over $56,550. Of course, provincial taxes are additional (see Tables 8-1, 8-2, and 8-3). For corporations, the federal *Income Tax Act* contains a number of special income tax rate adjustments that apply to special types of income. The two most significant ones are the Small Business Deduction and the Manufacturing and Processing Deduction.

TABLE 8-1

NET TAXABLE INCOME LEVELS NECESSARY TO REACH CERTAIN TAX RATE AVERAGE FOR FEDERAL INCOME TAXES IN 1990

FOR SINGLE PROPRIETORS FILING INDIVIDUAL RETURNS		PARTNERSHIPS	CORPORATIONS
$0–28,275	17%	The income levels remain the same, but each partner pays income tax only on his/her share of the firm's profits as determined by the profit-and-loss sharing ratio.	Income eligible for the small business deduction: 12%
$28,276–56,550	26%		Income not eligible for the small business deduction but eligible for the manufacturing and processing deduction: 24% (1991: 24%, 1992: 23%)
$56,551+	29%		Income not eligible for the small business deduction nor for the manufacturing and processing deduction: 28%

Source: G.G. Cunningham & Associates, North York, Ontario.

TABLE 8-2

SAMPLES OF TOTAL INCOME TAXES PAID ON INCOME BY DIFFERENT LEGAL FORMS OF ORGANIZATION IN ONTARIO IN 1990

NET TAXABLE INCOME	SINGLE PROPRIETOR	TWO-PERSON PARTNERSHIP	CORPORATIONS*	
			(1)	*(2)*
$ 20,000	$ 4,267	$ 2,520	$ 4,568	$ 8,868
40,000	11,595	8,534	11,179	17,736
70,000	24,554	19,082	24,341	34,358
100,000	38,522	31,406	38,356	53,202

(1) Income not eligible for the manufacturing and processing deduction but eligible for the small business deduction.

(2) Income not eligible for the small business deduction and not eligible for the manufacturing and processing deduction.

* The figures shown include the tax paid by the corporation and the tax that would have to be paid by the individual shareholder if all of the after-tax corporate earnings were paid out to the sole shareholder as dividend.

Source: G.G. Cunningham & Associates, North York, Ontario.

TABLE 8-3

SAMPLES OF TOTAL INCOME TAXES CURRENTLY (1990) PAID ON INCOME OF $40,000 BY CORPORATIONS ELIGIBLE FOR SMALL BUSINESS DEDUCTION IN DIFFERENT PROVINCES

PROVINCE	TAXES PAID	PROVINCE	TAXES PAID
Alberta	$7,238	Ontario	9,136
British Columbia	8,736	Prince Edward Island	9,136
Manitoba	9,136	Quebec	6,601
New Brunswick	8,736	Saskatchewan	9,136
Newfoundland	9,136	Yukon	7,136
Nova Scotia	9,136	Northwest Territories	9,136

Canadian-controlled private corporations enjoy a 16 percentage point tax rate reduction from the top basic rate of 38 per cent (28 per cent after the provincial abatement for income earned in Canada) on active business income of up to $200,000 annually. Any income in excess of the small business limits is taxed at the top corporate rate. When planning the amount and timing of salaries, bonuses, hirings of additional staff, and other reasonable expenses that may be used, within reasonable limits, to reduce business income, particular attention should be given to eligibility for the Small Business Deduction. Similar to the federal incentive, some provinces also have a special, lower, small business tax rate applicable to small business income. In addition, some provinces are offering a temporary tax holiday for newly incorporated businesses not related to any other corporation!

All corporations resident in Canada not entitled to the Small Business Deduction are entitled to a reduced rate of tax on their profits derived from manufacturing and processing. This reduction amounts to 3 per cent in 1990 and up to 5 per cent after 1991. There are complex rules and calculations required to determine the amount of the manufacturing and processing profits as compared to profits arising from other corporate activities, such as selling and distribution. A corporate surtax of 3 per cent of the federal taxes payable is applied for 1990.

Let us clearly understand that we are talking about tax rates on *net taxable income* and what the term means. Net taxable income is the remaining income after all legitimate deductions have been taken. Charitable, educational, and dependent deductions, for example, are subtracted from gross income earned to arrive at net taxable income.

There is one very important difference between legal forms of organization in computing the taxable income of the firm. In proprietorships and partnerships, any withdrawals of cash by the owners during the year are considered as withdrawals of capital for tax purposes, even though the owners may consider them as regular salaries for themselves. In closing the books at the end of the year, such amounts are charges to their capital account balances and may not be recorded as operating expenses of the business. Proprietors and partners pay income taxes on the total profit shown on the income statement irrespective of any withdrawals made during the year. It will be recognized from our definition of proprietorships and partnerships that they are not taxable units at law but are part of the owners' personal identities as taxpayers. It is the individual in a proprietorship and the partners in a partnership who pay the taxes—not the firm.

This is quite different from the corporation. By definition, the corporation is an artificial being (person) at law. It is, therefore, recognized as a separate unit for tax purposes. Small firm owners who operate as corporations can charge reasonable salaries to the business, and these become operating expenses of the firm. Such salaries are accordingly deducted before arriving at net taxable income for the corporation. It is the remaining income that is taxed at the various corporate rates explained earlier. The owner of the small corporation then files a separate individual tax return and pays individual rates on the salary withdrawn and charged to the corporation.

It is this situation that gives rise to the much quoted and often misunderstood "double taxation," which is attributed to corporations. The owners pay personal income taxes on their salaries, which is a deductible operating expense to the corporation. They also pay individual income tax rates on any dividends declared on the stock of the corporation, which they own. Dividends paid by a corporation are not a deductible expense to the corporation, but are considered a distribution of remaining profits.

A reasonable salary paid to a spouse and/or children employed in an incorporated or unincorporated business may be claimed as business expenses if they are legitimately employed in the business. This can be used as a means of helping children work their way through college at less expense than giving them nondeductible gifts.

Choice of fiscal year-end is also important for many proprietors in the start-up stages. The *Income Tax Act* allows taxpayers to choose fiscal year-ends other than calendar year-ends for their businesses, and this measure can be used to defer the payment of income taxes. Thus, if a business is started on June 1, 1990, the proprietor can choose a fiscal year-end at, say, January 31, 1991. Consequently, income tax for the period June 1 to December 31, 1990, instead of being payable on April 30, 1991, has been deferred a full year to April 30, 1992. In the case of a firm with start-up losses, however, a calendar year-end may be preferable.

A close study of Tables 8-1, 8-2, and 8-3 will reveal valuable information for decision making by new small firm owners. For example, they may minimize total income taxes by drawing salaries close to the amount where individual income tax rates equal the corporate rate. They may find it desirable to qualify members of their families as salaried employees (which means they must render service to the company) or as bona fide partners, so they share the profits equitably in a profit-and-loss sharing ratio. Thus, they will reduce total taxes on the firm. This is not a suggestion to risk fraudulent practices but merely to practise legal tax avoidance, which the government allows all citizens to do. Students are often amazed to discover the rates of federal income taxes paid by business firms. Therefore, it is good to realize the extent to which business firms do contribute to maintaining government and social services. New respect for parents' business ability can also result.

Business income earned and distributed by a small business will bear approximately the same total tax as if the income has been earned directly by the individual shareholder. This result is achieved because the corporate tax on earnings will approximately equal the dividend tax credit that individual shareholders claim. However, for example, if the business earns $100,000 and the owner requires only $60,000 for his or her living expenses, the proprietor will pay full personal income taxes on the $100,000. That is, the federal income tax on the $40,000 (over the $60,000 needed) will be at a rate of 29 per cent. Whereas the corporation would pay federal tax on the $40,000 at a rate of 29 per cent: This works out to be at a rate of only 12 per cent on the $100,000, effectively allowing a deferment of 17 per cent of federal taxes until the corporation is wound up or the shareholder chooses to withdraw funds from retained earnings. The overall deferment actually will be over 17 per cent, since provincial taxes are deferred likewise.

The decision to incorporate or not to incorporate, from a taxation point of view, clearly depends on the income level of the business and the owner's cash requirements. There are, of course, other considerations (liabilities, ease of transfer of ownership, etc.), as discussed earlier.

Although there are no tax benefits, small business owners often, by necessity, defer salaries (their own and their employees') because there is not enough cash available. This is called *accrual*. These deferred (accrued) salaries or bonuses and the tax thereon must be paid within 180 days. In order to conserve cash, it is still possible to convert the salaries into a loan to the business, but the tax must be paid as if the salaries or bonuses were actually received.

QUESTIONS FOR CLASS DISCUSSION

1   Why would a small business proprietor ever consent to being a general partner and allow a partner to be a limited partner?

2   Evaluate "ease of discontinuance" as an advantage of the proprietorship form of legal organization.

3   Is the owner of a small corporation as "free to make all the decisions" as a single proprietor? Explain.

4   What are the legal requirements for starting a business as a proprietorship?

5   Is "limited opportunity for employees" an exclusive problem for small firms? How does this problem affect large firms?

6   What does the term *limited liability* really mean to holders of shares of a corporation?

7   Can lack of ability and experience in small firm owners be corrected solely by their adopting another legal form of organization for the business?

8   What is a partnership agreement? What should it include?

9   At what level of net taxable income does a Canadian citizen reach the 26 per cent federal income tax level? 29 per cent? 17 per cent?

10 What are the federal and provincial income tax rates on corporations eligible for small business deduction?

11 What factors in a business would suggest to you that limited liability should be in effect?

12 How could expansion plans affect the choice of a legal form of organization?

Projects for Home Assignment and/or Class Discussion

1   Write a short paper explaining why the authors believe that more small firms should be incorporated. Do you agree?

2   Demonstrate in writing your understanding of what the term *unlimited liability* means to owners of small firms.

3   Compute the federal income tax on a small manufacturing corporation that made $75,000 net profit last year. Compare your answer with the tax paid on the same profit by a single proprietor.

4   See if you can obtain an actual partnership agreement or a corporate charter and then list the important features of each. Ask your instructor to review its provisions with the class.

REFERENCES FOR FURTHER READING

Archer, M., *An Introduction to Canadian Business*, 5th ed., McGraw-Hill Ryerson Ltd., Toronto, 1986, Chapters 2 and 3.

Cunningham, G., *Buy Yourself A Job & Be Your Own Boss*, McGraw-Hill Ryerson Ltd., 1990, Chapter 3.

Georgas, M.S., *Federal Incorporation & Business Guide*, 5th ed., International Self-Counsel Press, North Vancouver, B.C., 1986.

Iacobucci, F., M.L. Pilkington, and J.R.S. Prichard, *Canadian Business Corporations*, Canada Law Book Company Limited, Toronto, 1977.

Kao, R.W.Y., *Small Business Management: A Strategic Emphasis*, 2nd ed., Holt, Rinehart and Winston of Canada, Ltd., Toronto, 1984, Chapter 6.

Tate Jr., C.E., L.C. Megginson, C.R. Scott Jr., and L.R. Trueblood, *Successful Small Business Management*, 3rd ed., Business Publications, Inc., Plano, Texas, 1985, Chapter 19.

Anger's Digest of Canada Law, 20th ed., Canada Law Book Inc., Toronto, 1987.

Canada Corporations Law Reporter, CCH Canadian Limited, Toronto. A loose-leaf system of Statute Law, explanations, and forms with respect to federal and provincial laws related to companies.

• •

9

Surveying the Market to Be Served: Finding Its Limits, Its Nature, and Its Sales Potential

LEARNING OBJECTIVES

After reading this chapter, you will be able to:

1. **E**xplain the importance of the total marketing concept and how it is used by the business planner

2. **I**dentify the target customers, their buying habits, and what it takes to get them to buy the firm's product or service

3. **U**nderstand the objectives of market surveys in determining the needs and wants of the target customers and identifying how many of them exist in the market area

4. **U**nderstand the importance of determining trends of customers buying preferences and how to deal with changes in the market
5. **U**se market survey information to make adjustments to business plans

It often comes as a severe shock to new small firm planners when they are told they should study their market carefully before investing. Why? Such surveys will show the planner much about where customers will come from and the nature of the people in that market, so he or she can determine whether they will be prospective customers for the proposed firm. Most important, this kind of survey will give the planner some idea of a reasonably attainable sales potential if a good merchandising job is done by the firm.

When a new firm is started without a fairly accurate idea of the sales potential, poor planning is in evidence. Such neglect may easily place the future of the firm in jeopardy from the beginning. With luck, the firm may succeed anyhow, but it is much better to first study the market thoroughly and then to build the firm to fit that market.

Few aspects of total business management have improved as much in recent years as accuracy in making market surveys. Planners may employ an outside firm to study their suggested market; advertising firms and market research firms often specialize in such surveys. The abundance of data available for use in these surveys is amazing. Some sources are listed later in this chapter. The cost of having market surveys made for a newly planned firm will vary from city to city and with degree of detail requested. Costs of $2,100 to $5,000 are common for small firms.

If new firm planners themselves cannot undertake the survey, any costs they pay for a good market survey may be the best investment they can make. If the survey shows that the desired or required sales potential does not exist in the market, their expenditures for the survey will protect them from losing their contemplated investment in a firm that cannot produce profitable results. If it should demonstrate that potential sales volume exceeds that required to produce desired minimum profits, they can adjust their planning to support this larger volume and larger profits.

THE OBJECTIVE OF A MARKET SURVEY

Stated most simply, the objective of a market survey is to determine a reasonably attainable sales volume in a specific market area for a specific type of business. This means finding out how many potential consumers of the planned merchandise or service there are in this market, and how many of them can reasonably be expected to become customers of the firm under consideration.

The thoroughness of a market survey will vary under different conditions. The survey is essential for stores that plan to develop much of their own customer traffic. If sales are to depend on the firm's merchandising policies, sales promotion efforts, special services, or uniqueness, a particularly thorough market survey should be made in advance. Firms that plan to rely on the established customer flow already generated by other businesses in the area may follow less thorough procedures. The latter types of firms have often been described as "parasite stores," meaning that their location has been dictated by the existing firms in the area that have already attracted a substantial traffic flow which the new firm will tap for its own sales. Examples of small firms in this category are a restaurant in an office-tower lobby, a dress shop next to a large department store, an office-building tobacco shop, or a drugstore in an airline terminal. In these cases, the amount and nature of the traffic and its sales potential are pretty well established. Such firms may still, however, engage in various types of sales promotion activities to increase total income within that traffic.

Our chief concern here is with the types of firms that must rely heavily on a market survey to help them build much of their customer traffic.

WHAT IS A MARKET?

The market or trading area for a particular firm is the area that it seeks to serve with its products or services. From the buyer's point of view, it is the area within which the buyer knows he or she can find desired goods and services at desirable prices. The definition of a market, or trading area, from the buyer's and the seller's view, may not be the same. Sellers may desire to expand their markets beyond the limits that are normally recognized by buyers. Experience will tell merchants the proper limits of their trading areas if they have the means of measuring the sources of sales. Market areas may change with the development of new shopping centres in adjacent areas. At any given time, a market has its limits set by the area within which the firm can economically sell its goods or services.

PROCEDURE FOR MAKING A MARKET SURVEY

We know that the objective of the market survey is to determine a reasonable sales forecast. How is this accomplished? The procedure will vary from factory to wholesaler to retailer. In all cases, however, it will seek to determine the number of customers in the market area who may become customers for the planned business. For retailing, the steps should include the following:

1 Determine the limits of the market or trading area.
2 Study the population within this area to determine its potential sales characteristics.

3   Determine the purchasing power of the area.

4   Determine the present sales volume of the type of goods or services you propose to offer.

5   Estimate what proportion of the total sales volume you can reasonably obtain.

Each of these steps involves special considerations that deserve discussion here.

1 Determining Limits of the Market Area   Firms in downtown locations, especially those in the central business districts of large cities, tend to draw customers from a wider market area than those in suburban or small city locations. This is so because customers come from wider areas to shop at the larger department stores or widely publicized shops, and they also come into the urban area for specialized services such as medical care. Downtown locations therefore often face much more competition than suburban or small city locations. The decline of public transportation systems in most cities has been accompanied, in many areas, by an increase in the number of freeways and express highways, so potential customers still go downtown despite increased suburban and small-city shopping centres. But partly because of decreasing public transportation, the number of suburban shopping centres has increased. The conclusion is, however, that for small firms, the market limits in urban locations are generally the same as for larger firms.

Interestingly, even a large department store reports that it measures its market area in terms of ease of access. This access is measured in five-minute, ten-minute, fifteen- and twenty-minute drives from its location in the central business district. Whenever travel obstacles, such as bridges, narrow streets, or congested areas, are encountered, the area beyond is considered less significant as part of the market area to be served. Cities bordering on a river, such as Winnipeg, find that their market area may be limited by that factor. Railroad yards, cemeteries, and other traffic obstacles can have similar effects on a given market area.

It is worth noting here that in the late 1980s extremely large shopping malls were introduced in Canada. The West Edmonton Mall, conceived and built by the Ghermezian brothers, immigrant entrepreneurs, is some eight city blocks long and has over 900 stores. It provides a total shopping, recreational, and entertainment environment. Of course, these gigantic malls are drawing on a significantly larger area than the traditional shopping centres.

In suburban and small-city locations, the market area is determined more by the neighbouring population and its characteristics, the nature of other stores in the area, and parking facilities. Ease of access and location, size, and quality characteristics of the firm are also important. Although many shoppers visit more than one shopping centre, they generally tend to patronize the nearest centre if it satisfies their needs.

A popular method of measuring market areas for small firms in suburban and small-city areas is, therefore, to draw a map of their area and plot the location of competitors. By measuring the distance in each direction from closest competitors, small firm proprietors may establish an area in which, other things being equal, they should be thought of first by most shoppers. This assumes, of course, that the firm's existence is well known.

Adequacy of market area for a new small firm can be measured according to approximately how many people are necessary to support an average firm in this line of business. A composite of some of the best market research in this area shows, for example, that 600 people are needed to support one grocery store. See Table 13-1 for population requirements estimated to support one store in several other types of business. If a town of 10 000 population has ten grocery stores, or an average of one grocery for every 1000 people, the figures would suggest that the local population could support another grocery. Grocery retailers normally serve only their immediate neighbour-hoods and the limits of their market area are almost determined by that neighbourhood.

The factor of economical limits to a market area is most applicable when such elements as delivery expense are involved. It just does not pay to deliver in remote areas when the time and expense required are prohibitive.

Recognition of primary areas (where the firm has distinct advantages) as against secondary areas (where some trade is still possible) has less significance for the typical small firm than for larger ones.

2 Studying the Population Within the Market Area   What does the market researcher look for in studying population to make a market survey? Its *size* is important—but size does not guarantee that the population has sufficient numbers of the type of customers sought. The *trend* of the total population is important. Growing populations are usually better markets than stable or declining populations. For many market surveys, the population should be translated into *number of households* in order to make a more meaningful survey. The *part-time* nature of the population is very significant, especially in resort towns.

After the size of the population is determined, a study of its characteristics may be even more important to the new firm planner.

A first classification of vital statistics relative to the population would include determining its composition by sex, age, income, occupation, marital status, average family size, race, religion, and average educational level. These characteristics vary sharply from city to city. Victoria, B.C., is not a likely market for too many baby clothes stores. College towns are usually good markets for young people's clothing. Bookstores do better where the educational level is high. A market survey for a particular type of business looks for those characteristics that make demand for its products or services likely.

Behavioural characteristics of the population are also very important. Do people buy the subject products weekly, monthly, on impulse or after shopping, in certain seasons or regularly? Is the usual objective in buying these products their obvious usefulness or their ability to satisfy psychological desires, or do they have special uses of significant quantity? Who makes the purchasing decision? Who makes the purchase? Who uses the product? Are the people brand-conscious or price-conscious? Is the population responsive to good promotion and advertising?

It should be obvious that the more planners know about the population and its characteristics, the better sales forecast they can make.

3 Determining Total Purchasing Power of the Market Area   The next step in a thorough market survey is to determine the total purchasing power of the market area. The average income, found in studying population characteristics, is most helpful here. Occupations carry certain income ranges and can assist in determining total purchasing power. Other sources of key data are listed later in this chapter.

4 Determining Present Sales Volume in the Line of Business   Students may be amazed to find that even statistics for the present sales volume can be obtained. The market surveyor not only wants to know the total sales in a particular line, but also desires to estimate how the present sales volume is divided among the local firms engaged in this line. Average consumer expenditures in any given line are available. See the sources listed later in this chapter.

5 Determining What Proportion of Sales Volume You Can Obtain   It should be recognized in approaching this final objective of the survey that one new firm has little effect either on the total purchasing power in a market area or on the distribution of consumer expenditures. Until the new firm becomes better established, it must rely upon capturing a portion of the existing sales volume in that market area. Its initial merchandising and promotional activities will be directed toward that objective. Important attention, however, may be given to what additional demand may be created by promotion. This is especially important for new products.

This initial sales forecast will be governed by whether or not the market area is saturated with similar stores or has less than the normal number of competitors. Substantial knowledge on this matter will have been gathered in Step 4.

Barring special circumstances, a market survey will determine whether the new firm can obtain a proportionate share of the total sales in this line in the market surveyed. This means that if five competitors are now dividing $500,000 of sales in the market, entrance of the new firm should make it six firms dividing $500,000 of sales. Anticipated growth in population can be reflected in the forecast. Merchandising policies should be directed to the set objective. Promotion activities of all types should be consistent with this objective. The new small firm has in its favour the fact that it is closer to customers within a certain area, the discontent of potential customers with existing firms, the promotion of its opening, and the accompanying opportunity to make permanent customers of the first visitors; and it can have a set of services that have been planned to meet the competition. New small firms may have other advantages, such as established contacts or contracts for substantial sales, exclusive distributorships for highly desired merchandise, well-known persons in their employ who bring customers, handier parking facilities, or price lines or lines of merchandise not offered by the competition. All these factors should be taken into account as the final sales forecast is determined.

This forecast of potential sales can then be used as the foundation of a budgeted income statement for the coming year. It is this statement that provides the basis for all budgeting and policy making.

It must be quickly recognized here that neglect of good market surveys has been a feature of too many newly planned small firms. This is probably due to lack of familiarity with the sources of dependable market data, which are easily available, and/or lack of knowledge of how to use analytical procedures. For these reasons, the next section of this chapter is devoted to sources of data for making market surveys.

In market research, data collection tends to consume the most time and effort. There are two principal kinds of sources: (a) primary sources—data gathered for the first time, typically collected personally by the researcher; and (b) secondary sources—data already assembled and reported on.

"PEOPLE SURVEYS" FOR COLLECTING MARKET INFORMATION

One effective method for gathering market information is the use of "people surveys," which are made by surveying the population who live in a designated market area. Such surveys can rarely attempt to reach all persons in the area; instead the market researchers select a representative group of persons to be contacted. Even the highly important national television ratings, for example, involve the use of only about 1200 homes. The selected group becomes known as *the sample*. Care in choosing a true cross section of people represented in the sample will greatly affect its accuracy and reliability.

Small firm planners may use three different types of people interviews:

1 Telephone surveys
2 Mail surveys
3 Personal interviews

The techniques in formulating questions for each of these types of interviews vary. Specific questions that will provide pertinent answers that can then be analyzed should be built into each type of interview questionnaire. Each type of interview has characteristics that can be summarized as follows:

1 Telephone Surveys This type of interview offers the advantage of economy and speed in the collection of desired data. To be effective, telephone surveys demand short, clear, and easily understood questions. A sound questionnaire, a truly representative sample group, and courteous telephone interviewers are the only requirements for gathering the key data, which are then analyzed.

2 Mail Surveys   Using the mail to gather basic data is more expensive than telephone interviews but still much less expensive than personal interviews, especially when a large market area is being studied. The rate of return is the key to whether or not it is successful. Today, a 20 per cent return on such mail surveys is considered excellent. Experience has shown that the shorter the interview sheet, the higher the rate of return.

3 Personal Interviews   Personal interviews require much more time than other types and, accordingly, are the most expensive kind of survey to conduct. But when a broad section of opinion is being sought they are usually considered the most reliable. They enable the interviewer to interpret questions, to explore the respondents' opinions, and to identify areas of information that although not anticipated may be valuable in the final analysis of data collected.

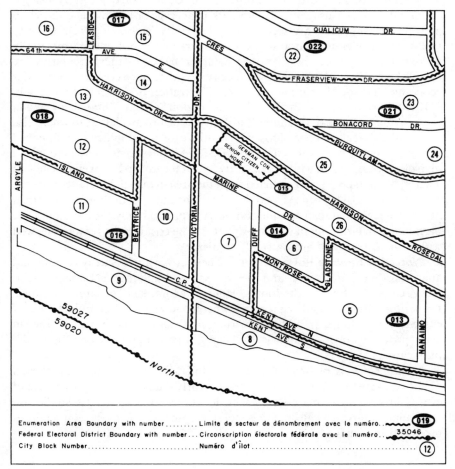

F I G U R E   9 - 1 • Census Tracts/Enumeration area map.

Source: Series G81-13, 1984 Census of Canada, Statistics Canada.

OTHER BASIC SOURCES OF DATA FOR MAKING MARKET SURVEYS

1 Canadian Census   An excellent source of geographical market and population data is the Canadian census conducted by Statistics Canada for the years ending in 1 and 6. Much of the desired information about population breakdown statistics with respect to age, sex, race, income, educational level, occupation, etc. can be found in census reports.

The two basic geographical units of census data that offer the highest potential for market analysis and the development of marketing strategy are those related to census tracts and enumeration areas.

Enumeration areas (EA) are the building blocks of the whole census. An EA is the section of a city or town or of the rural countryside covered by a single enumerator, or census taker. It represents an average of 150 households or 500 persons. Census tracts are sections of a large city, embracing from three to twelve or more enumeration areas. Census tracts are not created by simply aggregating a number of EAs into a larger package; the boundaries are established to include groups of adjacent EAs that have common or similar economic and social characteristics. An illustration is shown in Figure 9-1.

It should be noted that the Data Dissemination Section of Statistics Canada can provide a service of unlimited flexibility—one not available anywhere else in the world—called geocoding, which utilizes a geographically referenced data storage and retrieval system (GRDSR). All one needs to do is to take a map of a given city and with a pen outline the exact area to be covered. Then, in a letter, list the specific data needed from the area in question to determine the best prospects. The census people will translate the outline map into a numerical code that instructs the computer to pull out only the data that have been requested for only the area designated. The cost is most reasonable, well within the capacity of even a small retailer.

2 Statistics Canada Publications   These cover a wide array of data and analyses. (See Figures 9-2 and 9-3 for samples.) Statistics Canada maintains regional offices at St. John's, Halifax, Montreal, Toronto, Winnipeg, Edmonton, Regina, and Vancouver where one can find complete files of current publications. In addition, certain libraries located in major cities in every province are designated as "full depository" and receive one copy of all publications.

3 Annual Census of Manufacturers   In addition to census data referred to above, Statistics Canada also provides yearly data on such topics as size of establishment, operating costs, wages, locations, etc., as well as studies on particular industries. It includes total shipments of most commodities produced in Canada.

TABLE 3-49. Small Businesses – Selected Operating Results and Balance Sheet Items, by Size and Industry, 1986 – Continued

TABLEAU 3-49. Petites entreprises – Certains résultats d'exploitation et postes du bilan, selon la tranche de recettes et la branche d'activité économique, 1986 – suite

Industry group and financial characteristics		Revenue group – Tranche de recettes			
			$10,000 -	$100,000 -	$500,000 -	$2,000,000 -
Groupe d'activité économique et caractéristiques financières	Total	$99,999	$499,999	$1,999,999	$5,000,000

number – nombre

Mining industries – Industries des mines

| Businesses reporting – Entreprises déclarantes | 6,063 | 2,819 | 1,748 | 1,165 | 331 |

thousands of dollars – milliers de dollars

Operating results – Résultats d'exploitation:

	Total	$10,000-$99,999	$100,000-$499,999	$500,000-$1,999,999	$2,000,000-$5,000,000
Revenues – Recettes	2,693,984	125,114	425,922	1,119,800	1,023,147
Wages and salaries – Salaires et traitements	636,112	21,653	101,576	296,955	215,929
Incorporated – Constituées en société	627,494	19,000	97,188	295,377	215,929
Unincorporated – Non constituées en société	8,618	2,653	4,388	1,578	–
Depreciation – Amortissement	341,303	13,214	42,192	142,408	143,488
Other expenses – Autres frais	1,837,109	74,052	215,818	655,653	891,586
Net profit (loss) – Profit (perte) net(te)	-120,540	16,195	66,336	24,785	-227,856
Incorporated – Constituées en société	-134,590	7,141	61,831	24,295	-227,856
Unincorporated – Non constituées en société	14,050	9,054	4,506	490	–

Balance sheet – Bilan:

Assets – Actif	5,891,959	460,000	1,049,294	1,744,482	2,638,183
Liabilities – Passif	2,918,792	206,688	458,257	844,039	1,409,808
Equity – Avoir	2,973,167	253,312	591,037	900,443	1,228,375
Income generated – Revenus générés:	856,875	51,062	210,104	464,147	131,561

number – nombre

Manufacturing industries – Industries manufacturières

| Businesses reporting – Entreprises déclarantes | 53,035 | 19,516 | 18,879 | 10,028 | 4,612 |

thousands of dollars – milliers de dollars

Operating results – Résultats d'exploitation:

	Total	$10,000-$99,999	$100,000-$499,999	$500,000-$1,999,999	$2,000,000-$5,000,000
Revenues – Recettes	30,045,723	852,045	4,425,477	10,296,678	14,471,523
Wages and salaries – Salaires et traitements	7,633,299	180,964	1,348,522	2,764,883	3,338,931
Incorporated – Constituées en société	7,484,394	138,586	1,263,425	2,745,463	3,336,921
Unincorporated – Non constituées en société	148,905	42,378	85,097	19,421	2,010
Depreciation – Amortissement	788,580	37,472	147,004	277,427	326,677
Other expenses – Autres frais	20,220,866	588,213	2,748,832	6,732,231	10,151,589
Net profit (loss) – Profit (perte) net(te)	1,402,978	45,397	181,119	522,135	654,326
Incorporated – Constituées en société	1,260,397	-33,716	126,190	514,476	653,448
Unincorporated – Non constituées en société	142,580	79,113	54,929	7,660	878

Balance sheet – Bilan:

Assets – Actif	17,732,842	793,841	2,774,693	5,794,738	8,369,570
Liabilities – Passif	11,665,312	517,285	1,915,160	3,710,428	5,522,439
Equity – Avoir	6,067,530	276,556	859,533	2,084,310	2,847,131
Income generated – Revenus générés:	9,824,857	263,832	1,676,645	3,564,446	4,319,933

See Sources and Notes at the end of this table.
Voir sources et notes à la fin de ce tableau.

FIGURE 9-2•

Source: Statistics Canada, *Market Research Handbook, 1990,* Cat. No. 63-224. Reproduced with the permission of the Minister of Supply and Services Canada, 1990.

TABLE 5. Summary and Selective Detailed Family Expenditure by City,
Canada, 1986 – Continued

All Families and Unattached Individuals

| | | Atlantic Provinces – Provinces de l'Atlantique | | | | | | | | | | Québec | |
| | | St. John's (Nfld.) St. John's (T.-N.) | | Charlottetown-Summerside | | Halifax | | St. John (N.B.) St. John (N.-B.) | | Other cities 30,000 + Autres villes de 30,000 + | | Québec | |
		Av. per fam. Moy. par fam.	% rptg. % décl.	Av. per fam. Moy. par fam.	% rptg. % décl.	Av. per fam. Moy. par fam.	% rptg. % décl.	Av. per fam. Moy. par fam.	% rptg. % décl.	Av. per fam. Moy. par fam.	% rptg. % décl.	Av. per fam. Moy. par fam.	% rptg. % décl.
2200-2283	**Household operation**	**1553**	**100.0**	**1243**	**99.7**	**1596**	**100.0**	**1570**	**100.0**	**1574**	**98.9**	**1347**	**99.7**
2200-2205	Communications	464	99.5	457	98.6	542	100.0	472	99.2	493	98.1	377	99.3
2200-2204	Telephone	436	98.6	432	98.6	500	99.7	436	99.2	460	97.3	342	99.3
2201-2204	Telephone services	432	98.6	429	98.6	495	99.7	432	99.2	457	97.3	335	99.3
2202	Basic charge	200	98.2	164	96.0	192	99.6	167	99.4	179	94.8	169	98.6
2204	Long distance toll charges	222	82.2	258	89.2	294	93.3	254	87.1	273	87.3	157	85.2
2210-2213	Child care	224	18.7	175	17.3	237	16.9	213	19.9	252	25.6	284	19.8
2230-2234	Pet expenses	145	43.3	96	40.5	145	49.9	194	57.8	148	52.2	82	38.9
2240-2250	Household cleaning supplies	260	99.8	189	97.7	217	99.5	223	95.8	258	98.9	187	99.3
2260-2268	Paper, plastic & foil household supplies	280	100.0	193	98.0	241	99.7	236	97.7	254	98.9	207	99.7
2300-2498	**Household furnishings and equipment**	**1241**	**94.3**	**741**	**90.2**	**1176**	**96.2**	**1152**	**95.1**	**1136**	**93.3**	**1065**	**91.3**
2300-2344	Household furnishings	641	86.7	378	80.4	589	85.6	563	83.2	555	78.9	540	78.5
2300-2318	Furniture	414	52.8	249	44.1	379	61.6	401	54.6	296	45.4	294	39.1
2320-2329	Household textiles & related materials	164	77.4	93	71.8	130	76.7	124	73.7	135	71.3	146	69.7
2360-2483	Household equipment	574	91.0	326	85.8	502	93.4	543	91.2	523	89.3	480	85.0
2360-2403	Household appliances	331	65.2	153	52.9	253	64.4	281	63.6	279	57.9	230	52.8
2490-2498	Services related to furnishings & equipment	26	33.1	37	33.0	86	56.4	47	47.7	58	44.3	45	33.1
2500-2879	**Clothing**	**2465**	**99.4**	**1681**	**99.7**	**2051**	**99.7**	**1702**	**99.4**	**1982**	**98.6**	**2461**	**100.0**
2500-2583	Women's wear (14 years & over)	1267	92.9	764	86.0	1058	89.5	849	83.6	978	89.5	1244	89.8
2590-2663	Girl's wear (4-13 years)	179	25.3	102	17.5	90	15.1	95	17.6	148	23.0	140	18.3
2670-2753	Men's wear (14 years & over)	721	82.1	560	73.5	580	79.4	501	77.8	569	79.6	720	73.4
2760-2813	Boy's wear (4-13 years)	117	24.0	67	19.3	77	18.9	74	16.9	96	18.9	102	17.2
2820-2850	Infants' wear (under 4 years)	40	13.5	19	10.6	30	13.1	28	14.5	41	14.9	53	13.1
2860-2879	Clothing material, notions & services	142	81.1	168	94.1	217	92.4	155	93.2	150	84.7	202	93.7
2870-2879	Clothing services	100	77.1	138	89.0	159	89.9	103	84.6	92	80.6	131	87.3
2872-2874	Laundry & dry-cleaning	79	73.7	112	86.5	128	83.7	80	81.1	70	75.3	82	81.3
2900-2965	**Transportation**	**4122**	**98.2**	**3574**	**98.0**	**4956**	**99.2**	**4146**	**98.9**	**3802**	**95.3**	**4189**	**97.0**
2900-2946	Private transportation	3728	86.2	3267	77.1	4461	85.4	3829	84.2	3581	80.1	3896	82.9
2900-2904	Purchase of automobiles & trucks	1669	27.3	1730	29.0	2535	31.9	1711	25.9	1610	24.4	1855	24.4
2930-2946	Operation of automobiles & trucks	1996	85.8	1483	76.8	1829	82.9	2049	82.4	1821	79.1	1938	82.9
2930	Automotive fuels	1078	84.1	785	73.6	912	77.2	1042	79.0	967	77.5	901	75.1
2935-2939	Maintenance & repair jobs	197	72.8	238	67.8	282	69.3	273	72.1	258	72.3	297	70.2
2944	Private & public insurance premiums	447	82.8	291	73.4	355	76.4	442	78.2	376	76.2	431	75.1
2950-2965	Public transportation	394	67.4	306	84.7	495	85.0	317	82.9	220	67.2	293	71.4
2950-2954	Local & commuter transportation	133	50.9	105	70.9	161	77.1	107	61.7	70	51.6	183	66.6
2960-2965	Intercity transportation	261	33.9	202	48.7	334	52.9	210	46.5	150	38.7	110	27.0
2961	Air	219	25.6	155	22.3	278	31.1	171	22.1	115	16.0		
3000-3063	**Health care**	**582**	**96.0**	**541**	**98.4**	**530**	**97.0**	**473**	**97.2**	**573**	**93.0**	**730**	**96.2**
3000-3053	Direct costs to family	405	94.7	353	96.8	360	95.8	288	94.4	393	90.2	497	95.1
3001-3002	Medicinal & pharmaceutical products	125	87.2	155	91.9	121	91.0	91	90.4	95	83.2	121	88.8
3040-3042	Photographic vehicles & outboard motors	120	55.4	92	57.8	144	55.0	94	41.7	199	51.2	168	56.1
3060-3063	Health insurance premiums	176	59.4	188	61.5	170	60.3	185	60.3	180	57.4	232	50.1
3060	Public hospital & medical plans												
3061-3063	Private health care plans	174	58.2	188	61.5	170	60.3	184	59.9	179	57.4	232	50.1
3100-3153	**Personal care**	**778**	**99.6**	**598**	**100.0**	**665**	**99.7**	**618**	**100.0**	**639**	**99.4**	**682**	**100.0**
3100-3140	Personal care supplies & equipment	521	99.6	369	100.0	426	99.7	398	99.0	410	99.1	406	100.0
3100-3114	Toilet preparations & cosmetics	304	99.6	218	98.9	247	99.1	220	97.6	222	98.5	248	98.8
3150-3153	Personal care services	258	93.9	229	92.6	238	91.5	220	90.6	229	95.0	276	93.5
3200-3370	**Recreation**	**1398**	**93.8**	**1185**	**96.1**	**1731**	**98.4**	**1631**	**98.3**	**1450**	**94.0**	**1896**	**95.1**
3200-3271	Recreation equipment & associated services	390	78.2	315	75.4	411	86.3	392	81.3	453	78.4	435	78.8
3210-3229	Toys, games & hobby equipment	156	57.0	121	47.7	133	60.6	141	63.4	193	59.7	170	56.5
3230-3256	Photographic goods & services	112	61.7	75	55.2	123	73.5	108	68.2	105	62.9	93	63.2
3280-3298	Recreation vehicles & outboard motors	159	27.4	115	25.1	218	36.0	320	37.7	157	31.8	501	28.9
3280-3289	Purchase of recreation vehicles	117	19.1	75	17.6	144	24.1	241	22.8	73	21.3	440	19.7
3301-3319	Home entertainment equipment & services	395	77.1	269	72.9	434	80.8	393	83.9	382	77.0	234	73.6
3320-3370	Recreation services	455	93.9	486	94.2	668	94.4	526	94.8	458	86.8	637	90.6
3320-3325	Spectator entertainment performances	205	96.8	224	91.0	240	90.7	217	91.7	180	80.0	234	86.4
3330-3350	Use of recreation facilities	98	45.8	151	65.5	190	70.9	174	68.4	167	57.7	153	62.3
3360-3361	Package travel tours											235	15.5

F I G U R E   9 - 3 •

Source: Statistics Canada, *Family Expenditure in Canada, 1986,* Cat. No. 62-555.

4 The Financial Post Canadian Markets   This annual publication by Maclean Hunter is considered indispensable by professional market research people. It is an excellent handbook of marketing facts; it contains consumer market data, a national industrial survey, and a bibliography of published market research studies. It has an exclusive guide to buying power and gives area ratings by income, by retail sales, and by market growth rates. (Samples are shown in Figures 9-4 and 9-5.)

TABLE 5. Summary and Selective Detailed Family Expenditure by City,
Canada, 1986 – Continued

All Families and Unattached Individuals

| | | Atlantic Provinces – Provinces de l'Atlantique | | | | | | | | | | Québec | |
| | | St. John's (Nfld.) / St. John's (T.-N.) | | Charlottetown-Summerside | | Halifax | | St. John (N.B.) / St. John (N.-B.) | | Other cities 30,000 + / Autres villes de 30,000 + | | Québec | |
		Av. per fam. / Moy. par fam.	% rptg. / % décl.	Av. per fam. / Moy. par fam.	% rptg. / % décl.	Av. per fam. / Moy. par fam.	% rptg. / % décl.	Av. per fam. / Moy. par fam.	% rptg. / % décl.	Av. per fam. / Moy. par fam.	% rptg. / % décl.	Av. per fam. / Moy. par fam.	% rptg. / % décl.
3380-3386	Reading materials & other printed matter	186	95.4	167	93.6	217	94.9	175	93.7	186	92.3	230	92.4
3390-3400	Education	488	52.2	153	36.3	420	52.8	265	46.9	326	48.5	324	51.3
3396-3398	Tuition fees	309	21.8	103	13.4	283	27.0	170	19.2	209	14.4	176	31.5
3500-3515	Tobacco products & alcoholic beverages	1366	93.4	1004	82.3	1223	90.3	894	85.6	939	87.0	1061	94.0
3500-3503	Tobacco products & smokers' supplies	572	55.6	533	55.3	599	58.0	476	54.5	565	59.2	486	51.7
3502	Cigarettes	479	43.0	499	51.0	562	53.8	406	43.4	504	47.7	436	45.3
3510-3515	Alcoholic beverages	793	89.0	471	72.5	624	83.2	418	72.7	374	73.0	575	88.7
3510-3512	Served on licensed premises	226	54.1	211	54.4	256	60.6	150	46.6	88	39.5	150	60.0
3513-3515	Purchased from stores	567	88.0	260	66.8	368	81.4	268	70.9	287	71.1	425	87.7
3600-3612	Miscellaneous	831	89.9	695	88.4	1118	96.3	891	94.4	906	90.0	753	93.9
3600	Interest on personal loans	421	61.9	316	47.0	554	63.8	386	56.1	485	60.6	232	40.1
3605	Dues to unions & professional associations	145	43.9	80	27.8	166	41.3	128	38.8	136	38.0	209	47.4
3607	Government-run pool & lottery tickets	75	51.5	94	52.9	123	74.0	157	70.9	92	62.7	126	75.2
3700-370J	Personal taxes	5872	92.7	4677	87.2	7321	88.2	5497	83.1	5122	83.8	7220	88.3
3710-3716	Security	1753	83.2	1362	74.4	1956	84.5	1533	75.3	1603	73.9	1729	85.1
3710	Life insurance premiums	224	39.0	170	39.4	306	55.1	305	54.8	235	45.8	316	64.5
3713	Unemployment insurance payments	510	80.5	391	71.1	519	77.6	419	67.5	414	68.5	442	73.7
3714-3716	Retirement & pension fund payments	1007	82.0	799	72.6	1115	80.6	808	67.9	953	69.5	964	78.1
3714	Canada & Quebec pension plan	410	82.0	291	72.3	400	80.6	311	67.9	310	68.8	357	77.8
3715	Other government	455	29.5	343	20.1	612	34.1	214	12.2	372	16.6	384	22.0
3716	Other (excl. RRSP)	142	13.4	165	13.0	103	10.1	284	23.1	272	15.1	223	16.9
3720-3724	Gifts and contributions	749	89.6	785	91.9	1369	96.6	1566	93.9	1832	96.1	542	81.1
3720-3722	Persons outside spending unit	539	79.8	536	85.1	1103	91.0	1218	89.0	650	92.4	452	64.8
3720-3721	Money gifts and contributions	210	33.8	220	29.1	595	40.1	740	41.5	278	50.2	294	28.5
3722	Other gifts eg. flowers, clothing, toys	328	69.3	316	72.2	508	81.0	478	78.8	371	79.2	157	52.0
3723-3724	Charitable organizations	210	75.2	249	78.3	266	84.6	348	81.4	1182	86.7	90	64.6
3723	Religious organizations	171	60.1	162	54.6	178	52.0	258	58.6	1049	65.2	38	34.4
3724	Other charitable organizations	39	61.3	87	71.8	88	74.0	90	73.3	133	79.0	52	53.8
1000-3612	Total current consumption	26296	100.0	20802	100.0	26512	100.0	22971	100.0	23433	100.0	25076	100.0
1000-3724	Total expenditure	34671	100.0	27625	100.0	37158	100.0	31566	100.0	31990	100.0	34568	100.0
3800-3855	Total value of items not purchased	402	77.5	371	77.3	576	84.6	553	83.5	539	88.5	284	55.5
3800-3830	Value of food not purchased			18	13.4	45	17.9	25	16.4	28	13.9	33	12.1
3850-3855	Value of gifts received	383	76.7	354	75.3	531	80.9	528	81.1	511	86.9	246	52.8
	Selected items in net change in assets:												
3900	Registered retirement savings plans	303	21.3	363	22.2	302	27.1	476	23.1	156	14.7	593	26.5
3901	Change in principal of mortgage on home	-724	39.4	-140	22.3	-1640	33.0	-1126	37.5	-832	38.2	-986	36.7
3902-3904	Additions, renovations etc. to home	778	32.1	507	16.0	594	26.2	650	30.4	830	28.2	635	25.9

F I G U R E   9 - 3 • (continued)

5 Sales & Marketing Management Magazine   Once each year (usually in August) it publishes its "Survey of Buying Power" issue, which contains information on total population, households, breakdown of retail sales, and total purchasing dollars represented in each city and county in every state of the United States. (An illustration is shown in Figure 9-6.) With the increasing emphasis on "free trade," or "freer trade," with the United States, this excellent American source can provide very valuable information to Canadian businesses contemplating entering this vast market.

6 Consumer Attitudes & Buying Intentions   Published by The Conference Board of Canada, this quarterly publication examines attitudes of a cross section of Canadian population toward economic conditions and gathers information about buying intentions in the next six months. (See Figure 9-7 for an illustration.)

Estevan
C

Income:
11% Above National Average

Pers'l Income, 1990	$188,219,800
% Canadian Total	0.04
Per Capita	$18,200

Population:

June 1, 1990	10,300
% Canadian Total	0.04
% Change, '81-'90	12.63
Average Annual Growth Rate	1.33%

Market:
7% Above National Average

Retail Sales, 1990	$78,560,000
% Canadian Total	0.04
Per Capita	$7,600

In census division 1.

POPULATION

1986 Census:

Total		10,160
Male		5,110
Female		5,050

Age Groups:	Male	Female
Under 4	455	455
5-9	415	410
10-14	365	320
15-19	345	350
20-24	550	500
25-29	580	505
30-34	465	410
35-39	320	270
40-44	265	235
45-49	195	225
50-54	205	200
55-59	210	205
60-64	180	200
65-69	170	200
70-74	150	230
75 +	245	335

MARITAL STATUS

1986 Census: (Age 15+)

Single (never married)	1,860
Married (incl. sep.)	5,110
Widowed	605
Divorced	180

MOTHER TONGUE

	1986 Census	% Total
English	9,010	88.7
French	155	1.5
German	345	3.4
Ukrainian	130	1.3
Other	520	5.1

HOUSING

1986 Census:

Occupied Private Dwellings, Total	3,745
Owned	2,525
Rented	1,220
Single detached	2,520
Movable dwellings	225
Other dwellings	995

FAMILIES

1986 Census:

Families in private households, total	2,645
Husband-wife families	2,420
Lone-parent families	225
Ave. no. persons per family	3.2
Ave. no. children per family	1.3

COMMUNITY NEWSPAPER(S)

	1989 Total Circulation
Estevan Mercury	4,820
Estevan This Week	9,150

PRIVATE HOUSEHOLDS

1986 Census:

Priv. households, total	3,745
Pop. in private households	9,960
Ave. no. per household	2.7

INCOME

1986 Census:

Average employment income: $

Male	34,356
Female	19,595
Ave. census family income	45,630
Ave. household income	38,839

LEVEL OF SCHOOLING

1986 Census:

Population, 15 years +	7,530
Less than Grade 9	1,195
Grades 9 - 13	3,695
Trades/non-university	1,695
University, without degree	580
University degree	355

LABOR FORCE

1986 Census:

Males:

In the labor force	3,020
Employed	2,865
Not in labor force	735
Participation rate:	80.40
15-24 years	84.60
25 years +	78.72

Females:

In the labor force	2,015
Employed	1,815
Not in labor force	1,750
Participation rate:	53.40
15-24 years	71.00
25 years +	48.38

VITAL STATISTICS

	1987
Births	202
Deaths	81
Natural Increase	121
Marriages	98

AVERAGE HOUSEHOLD EXPENDITURES

	1989
Food	$6,276
Shelter	$6,911
Clothing	$2,755
Transportation	$6,204
Health & Pers. Care	$1,674
Recr'n, Read'g, & Education	$2,983
Taxes & Securities	$9,503
Other	$7,725
Total Expenditures	$44,031

OCCUPATIONS BY MAJOR GROUPS

1986 Census:

	Male	Female
All occupations	3,015	1,975
Managerial & Admin	330	140
Teaching	45	90
Health	35	205
Technical, Social, Religion, & Art	150	50
Clerical	110	630
Sales	265	275
Service	195	455
Primary	400	30
Processing	55	0
Fab. & Repair	325	15
Construction	485	10
Transport	185	30
Other	415	25

MANUFACTURING INDUSTRIES

	1985	1980
Plants	16	14
Employees	270	157
	$000	
Salaries, wages	6,422	2,405
Mfg. cost	14,226	6,601
Mfg. shipments, value	24,167	10,753
Total value added	10,577	4,104

NEW VEHICLE REGISTRATIONS

	1988
Cars, domestic	227
Cars, imported	27
Small trucks, domestic	191
Small trucks, imported	7
Medium & heavy trucks	17

TAXATION

	1987
Total returns, no.	7,460
Total inc., $000	168,065
Total tax, $000	35,072
Total taxable returns, no.	5,950
Average inc., $	22,529
Average tax, $	5,894

RADIO STATION(S)

	1989 Power
CJSL	10,000w

HOMES BUILT

	1988	1987	1986
No.	108	131	n.a.

BUILDING PERMITS

	1988	1987	1986
		$000	
Value	12,017	12,955	14,969

FIGURE 9-4 •

Source: *The Financial Post Canadian Markets, 1990.*

Retail Sales, 1990

(Sales in $ millions)
By Class of Business
(1) By Province, Economic Region and Census Division

	Total Sales		Food Stores		Motor Vehicle Dealers		Service Stations		Clothing & Shoe Stores		Hardware Stores		Furniture, Appliances, TV & Radio	
	($M) Sales	% of Cdn Total	($M) Sales	% of Cdn Total	($M) Sales	% of Cdn Total	($M) Sales	% of Cdn Total	($M) Sales	% of Cdn Total	($M) Sales	% of Cdn Total	($M) Sales	% of Cdn Total
CANADA	188,254.6	100.00	44,650.3	100.00	42,293.7	100.00	14,506.0	100.00	10,350.6	100.00	2,077.9	100.00	5,068.3	100.00
NEWFOUNDLAND	3,497.5	1.86	959.9	2.15	649.2	1.53	367.1	2.53	181.9	1.76	32.3	1.55	88.9	1.75
Avalon Peninsula	1,738.0	0.92	435.7	0.98	311.7	0.74	166.4	1.15	87.8	0.85	15.0	0.72	37.7	0.74
Division No. 1	1,738.0	0.92	435.7	0.98	311.7	0.74	166.4	1.15	87.8	0.85	15.0	0.72	37.7	0.74
South Coast-Burin Peninsula	282.3	0.15	94.0	0.21	53.5	0.13	35.4	0.24	16.0	0.15	3.0	0.14	9.6	0.19
Division No. 2	152.0	0.08	49.7	0.11	30.2	0.07	19.3	0.13	8.5	0.08	1.6	0.07	4.8	0.10
Division No. 3	130.3	0.07	44.3	0.10	23.3	0.06	16.2	0.11	7.5	0.07	1.4	0.07	4.8	0.09
Notre Dame Bay-Bonavista Bay	731.6	0.39	221.2	0.50	142.1	0.34	85.4	0.59	39.2	0.38	7.3	0.35	19.5	0.38
Division No. 6	276.4	0.15	68.6	0.15	55.6	0.13	28.1	0.19	13.1	0.13	2.4	0.12	5.7	0.11
Division No. 7	210.1	0.11	70.5	0.16	40.4	0.10	27.1	0.19	12.0	0.12	2.2	0.11	5.5	0.11
Division No. 8	245.1	0.13	82.2	0.18	46.2	0.11	30.1	0.21	14.0	0.14	2.6	0.13	8.2	0.16
West Coast-Labrador	745.6	0.40	209.0	0.47	141.9	0.34	79.8	0.55	38.9	0.38	7.1	0.34	22.1	0.44
Division No. 4	133.9	0.07	40.9	0.09	28.0	0.07	14.9	0.10	7.5	0.07	1.4	0.07	4.2	0.08
Division No. 5	286.5	0.15	75.0	0.17	54.2	0.13	28.8	0.20	14.4	0.14	2.5	0.12	6.7	0.13
Division No. 9	135.1	0.07	43.3	0.10	24.1	0.06	16.0	0.11	7.5	0.07	1.4	0.07	5.7	0.11
Division No. 10	190.1	0.10	49.7	0.11	35.6	0.08	20.1	0.14	9.5	0.09	1.8	0.08	5.5	0.11
PRINCE EDWARD ISLAND	798.5	0.42	153.6	0.34	181.5	0.43	47.3	0.33	30.8	0.30	10.6	0.51	13.5	0.27
Prince Edward Island	798.5	0.42	153.6	0.34	181.5	0.43	47.3	0.33	30.8	0.30	10.6	0.51	13.5	0.27
Kings County	111.8	0.06	25.0	0.06	24.8	0.06	7.9	0.05	4.7	0.05	1.6	0.08	2.0	0.04
Queens County	427.4	0.23	74.7	0.17	97.2	0.23	22.2	0.15	15.6	0.15	5.3	0.26	6.6	0.13
Prince County	259.3	0.14	53.9	0.12	59.5	0.14	17.2	0.12	10.4	0.10	3.6	0.17	4.9	0.10
NOVA SCOTIA	6,382.4	3.39	1,630.3	3.65	1,346.8	3.18	576.7	3.98	275.5	2.66	59.6	2.87	101.7	2.01
Cape Breton	1,017.4	0.54	275.1	0.62	240.6	0.57	98.3	0.68	43.5	0.42	10.0	0.48	16.2	0.32
Inverness County	133.7	0.07	39.5	0.09	27.0	0.06	14.8	0.10	6.1	0.06	1.4	0.07	2.5	0.05
Richmond County	65.8	0.03	21.1	0.05	12.8	0.03	7.8	0.05	3.1	0.03	0.7	0.03	1.1	0.02
Cape Breton County	766.0	0.41	198.7	0.44	189.7	0.45	69.7	0.48	31.9	0.31	7.3	0.35	11.7	0.23
Victoria County	51.9	0.03	15.8	0.04	11.0	0.03	5.9	0.04	2.4	0.02	0.5	0.03	0.9	0.02
North Shore (Nova Scotia)	1,056.7	0.56	291.8	0.65	237.5	0.56	105.3	0.73	45.2	0.44	10.4	0.50	16.8	0.33
Colchester County	317.5	0.17	82.4	0.18	74.6	0.18	28.2	0.19	13.6	0.13	3.0	0.15	4.8	0.10
Cumberland County	217.1	0.12	63.0	0.14	42.3	0.10	24.4	0.17	8.9	0.09	2.2	0.11	3.5	0.07
Pictou County	334.1	0.18	90.3	0.20	79.9	0.19	31.5	0.22	13.9	0.13	3.3	0.16	5.2	0.10
Guysborough County	69.4	0.04	23.7	0.05	14.7	0.03	8.5	0.06	3.4	0.03	0.8	0.04	1.2	0.02

FIGURE   9-5•

Source: *The Financial Post Canadian Markets, 1990.*

Vermont

POPULATION—12/31/89

S&MM ESTIMATES

METRO AREA County City	Total Population (Thousands)	% Of U.S.	Median Age Of Pop.	% of Population by Age Group 18-24 Years	25-34 Years	35-49 Years	50 & Over	Households (Thousands)
BURLINGTON	136.6	.0547	29.8	15.6	19.5	21.0	18.9	50.8
Chittenden	131.4	.0526	29.7	15.9	19.4	21.0	18.7	48.9
• Burlington	38.9	.0156	28.3	26.0	17.5	15.0	23.3	15.1
Grand Isle	5.2	.0021	33.3	8.0	18.4	20.9	25.9	1.9
SUBURBAN TOTAL	97.7	.0391	30.3	11.5	20.2	23.4	17.2	35.7
OTHER COUNTIES								
Addison	32.0	.0128	30.5	13.0	18.5	19.5	22.2	11.4
Bennington	36.1	.0145	34.5	9.7	16.0	20.4	28.8	14.4
Caledonia	28.6	.0114	33.0	9.6	17.2	19.2	27.4	11.0
Essex	7.2	.0029	33.8	8.3	16.0	20.4	27.7	2.7
Franklin	38.1	.0152	32.0	8.7	17.3	19.8	24.9	13.7
Lamoille	18.7	.0075	31.3	11.6	19.8	20.0	22.6	7.3
Orange	25.3	.0101	32.4	9.6	18.0	20.0	25.4	9.4
Orleans	24.6	.0099	33.0	8.3	16.8	19.4	27.3	9.1
Rutland	62.6	.0250	33.7	10.5	17.4	19.7	28.1	24.1
Washington	55.6	.0223	33.2	10.4	17.8	20.7	26.2	21.8
Windham	40.1	.0160	33.7	8.9	19.3	19.8	27.8	16.6
Windsor	56.7	.0227	34.9	8.3	17.7	20.9	28.9	23.1
TOTAL METRO COUNTIES	136.6	.0547	29.8	15.6	19.5	21.0	18.9	50.8
TOTAL STATE	562.2	.2250	32.3	11.2	18.2	20.3	24.8	215.4

RETAIL SALES BY STORE GROUP—1989

Total Retail Sales ($000)	Food ($000)	Eating & Drinking Places ($000)	General Mdse. ($000)	Furniture/ Furnish/ Appliance ($000)	Auto-motive ($000)	Drug ($000)
1,256,207	273,293	146,152	117,809	66,389	230,375	30,259
1,237,298	271,704	144,214	116,289	66,201	222,992	30,071
372,697	56,687	56,997	62,146	16,025	22,798	9,445
18,909	1,589	1,938	1,520	188	7,383	188
883,510	216,606	89,155	55,663	50,364	207,577	20,814
204,370	44,390	18,380	12,656	3,004	55,729	7,200
448,530	79,641	38,788	22,010	19,702	84,094	10,079
186,128	46,055	15,131	14,694	8,115	45,393	5,042
11,040	3,086	2,643	30	127	1,053	11
269,154	73,428	16,312	15,317	10,749	69,398	7,999
144,464	40,802	20,129	9,562	3,826	12,076	5,803
132,424	37,928	12,771	2,784	2,146	17,428	3,875
171,998	42,494	12,047	16,358	4,572	48,298	5,724
586,125	121,007	62,463	44,116	23,554	141,689	15,807
474,039	95,801	39,644	33,112	24,035	117,077	10,878
444,869	92,017	45,767	20,265	23,485	84,012	10,906
399,685	87,244	43,548	13,634	14,692	122,704	5,898
1,256,207	273,293	146,152	117,809	66,389	230,375	30,259
4,729,033	1,037,186	473,775	322,347	204,396	1,029,326	119,481

EFFECTIVE BUYING INCOME—1989

METRO AREA County City	Total EBI ($000)	Median Hsld. EBI	% of Hsls. by EBI Group: (A) $10,000-$19,999	(B) $20,000-$34,999	(C) $35,000-$49,999	(D) $50,000 & Over	Buying Power Index
BURLINGTON	1,944,335	29,307	19.8	26.9	18.1	22.6	.0625
Chittenden	1,879,083	29,424	19.6	26.8	18.1	22.8	.0607
• Burlington	500,912	22,595	25.1	26.8	12.8	15.7	.0172
Grand Isle	65,252	27,050	22.4	29.9	17.6	17.3	.0018
SUBURBAN TOTAL	1,443,423	32,526	17.5	26.9	20.4	25.5	.0453
OTHER COUNTIES							
Addison	373,888	25,004	23.9	31.5	16.2	14.2	.0118
Bennington	479,530	24,850	24.5	31.4	16.0	14.4	.0180
Caledonia	288,067	20,058	29.4	30.6	12.3	7.3	.0099
Essex	68,435	20,130	31.8	32.5	12.1	5.7	.0018

EFFECTIVE BUYING INCOME—1989

METRO AREA County City	Total EBI ($000)	Median Hsld. EBI	% of Hsls. by EBI Group: (A) $10,000-$19,999	(B) $20,000-$34,999	(C) $35,000-$49,999	(D) $50,000 & Over	Buying Power Index
Franklin	404,056	22,622	25.6	29.1	15.6	11.3	.0139
Lamoille	214,852	22,897	25.4	32.8	13.6	10.0	.0072
Orange	292,937	23,903	26.7	31.9	15.9	11.7	.0088
Orleans	233,680	19,286	31.1	30.1	10.3	7.6	.0085
Rutland	747,374	24,166	25.0	30.7	16.5	11.9	.0266
Washington	657,921	22,980	26.1	30.4	15.4	11.5	.0227
Windham	540,464	24,283	25.5	28.8	15.8	14.4	.0191
Windsor	685,933	23,022	25.7	31.8	14.6	10.9	.0221
TOTAL METRO COUNTIES	1,944,335	29,307	19.8	26.9	18.1	22.6	.0625
TOTAL STATE	6,931,472	24,343	24.6	29.8	15.8	14.1	.2329

Virginia

POPULATION—12/31/89

S&MM ESTIMATES

METRO AREA County City	Total Population (Thousands)	% Of U.S.	Median Age Of Pop.	% of Population by Age Group 18-24 Years	25-34 Years	35-49 Years	50 & Over	Households (Thousands)
CHARLOTTESVILLE	128.0	.0511	31.0	16.8	19.8	19.8	22.2	49.2
Albemarle	65.1	.0260	30.4	17.4	19.9	21.1	19.7	24.7
Charlottesville city	41.2	.0165	30.9	20.3	20.0	16.7	25.1	16.8
• Charlottesville	41.2	.0165	30.9	20.3	20.0	16.7	25.1	16.8
Fluvanna	12.2	.0048	33.7	8.9	16.5	21.4	26.5	4.4
Greene	9.5	.0038	32.1	8.4	20.5	22.7	21.3	3.3
SUBURBAN TOTAL	86.8	.0346	31.0	15.2	19.5	21.3	20.8	32.4
DANVILLE	111.2	.0445	35.1	9.6	16.1	20.7	29.4	40.7
Danville city	44.9	.0180	37.6	9.6	15.3	19.2	34.3	17.7
• Danville	44.9	.0180	37.6	9.6	15.3	19.2	34.3	17.7
Pittsylvania	66.3	.0265	33.7	9.5	16.7	21.7	26.1	23.0
SUBURBAN TOTAL	66.3	.0265	33.7	9.5	16.7	21.7	26.1	23.0

RETAIL SALES BY STORE GROUP—1989

Total Retail Sales ($000)	Food ($000)	Eating & Drinking Places ($000)	General Mdse. ($000)	Furniture/ Furnish/ Appliance ($000)	Auto-motive ($000)	Drug ($000)
1,063,350	227,625	93,575	116,395	57,462	199,772	33,482
194,281	35,354	14,248	48,641	5,562	13,703	2,362
831,404	178,335	77,227	66,930	51,264	180,304	30,593
831,404	178,335	77,227	66,930	51,264	180,304	30,593
17,091	7,258	783	108	148	2,647	103
20,574	6,678	1,317	716	488	3,118	424
231,946	49,290	16,348	49,465	6,198	19,468	2,889
648,638	159,647	61,454	87,518	30,353	134,417	32,155
546,612	127,331	51,850	81,779	27,768	118,004	26,120
546,612	127,331	51,850	81,779	27,768	118,004	26,120
102,026	32,316	9,604	5,739	2,585	16,413	6,035
102,026	32,316	9,604	5,739	2,585	16,413	6,035

FIGURE 9-6•

Reprinted by permission of *Sales & Marketing Magazine.* Copyright August 1990, Survey of Buying Power.

F I G U R E   9 - 7

INDEX OF CONSUMER ATTITUDES
Seasonally Adjusted (1961=100)

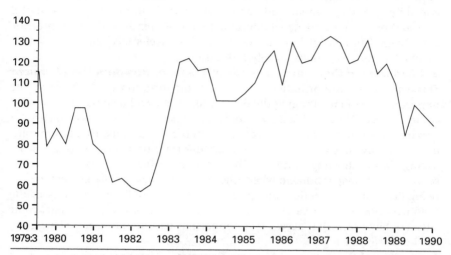

Source: Adapted from the Conference Board of Canada.

		1989				1990
	Q1	*Q2*	*Q3*	*Q4*	*YEAR*	*Q1*
***CCI*[1]**						
Canada	107.95	84.07	99.59	95.61	96.80	90.16
Atlantic	122.65	76.32	96.27	90.24	96.37	72.17
Quebec	107.29	92.47	109.02	103.94	103.18	102.14
Ontario	106.82	83.85	89.85	86.56	91.77	83.38
Prairies	101.70	71.21	97.61	84.04	88.64	87.09
British Columbia	111.27	85.55	117.64	127.29	110.44	119.41
***MAJOR PURCHASE*[2]**						
Canada	32.85	25.04	35.97	40.42	33.57	33.12
Atlantic	36.01	27.61	34.52	39.19	34.33	24.72
Quebec	27.38	23.78	31.26	35.63	29.51	30.73
Ontario	34.57	28.65	32.90	37.39	33.38	37.18
Prairies	35.97	19.04	43.20	38.90	34.28	32.63
British Columbia	36.30	26.96	45.69	48.80	39.44	40.19

[1] CCI is the Index of Consumer Attitudes—Seasonally adjusted.
[2] Major Purchase refers to the number of people responding "good" to the following
question: Do you think that right now is a good time or a bad time for the average person
to make a major outlay for things such as a home or a car or some other major item?

Source: *Survey of Consumer Attitudes and Buying Intentions, Winter, 1990.* The Conference Board of
Canada.

7 Trade Sources Many business, trade, and professional associations issue regular reports on total sales volume, costs, operating data, and other relative data in their particular fields, which can assist the new firm planner. Numerous trade and technical periodicals devote one issue per year to a listing of products and suppliers as a guide to buyers. The bulletins and newsletters issued by several Canadian banks and financial institutions can provide useful information on current economic and financial trends and developments. Handbooks, Industrial Directories, City Cross-Reference Directories, and Media Directories usually supply a wealth of information.

8 Chambers of Commerce, Boards of Trade, or Business Development Departments Major cities have these organizations, which have the important job of encouraging the development of new business firms in their communities. They will gladly supply all types of information regarding population studies, income characteristics of the community, trends, payrolls, industrial development, and so on. Such information is usually free for the asking. Maps showing major trading areas are often available from these sources. Such maps indicate where the major business of the subject area is being done and thus reflect buying habits of the population. A study of the road network of any area gives information on ease of access to a particular site. We have seen that access is an important consideration in determining market area limits.

9 Provincial Government Market Surveys These are prepared in most provinces by the appropriate departments, such as, for example, Ministry of Industry, Trade and Technology (MITT) in both Ontario and Manitoba. They usually cover all aspects of the provincial economy and provide comparative statistics and market data.

10 Faculties and Departments of Business, Management, and Economic Research at Universities These organizations are usually fortified with many market studies. Published reports are available to the public.

11 Market Research and Advertising Firms Many of these firms offer their professional services in making complete market surveys. They also, however, have reports covering special market areas, which in many instances may be procured. Often one can obtain multi-client reports at a very reasonable cost.

READJUSTING THE PROJECTED INCOME STATEMENT TO REFLECT RESULTS OF THE MARKET SURVEY

In Chapter 10 we will construct a projected income statement based upon average firm statistics and the desired profit. Our chief objective there is to find what volume of sales will be necessary to produce the desired profit. In that process we will see that $125,000 of sales is required if the small firm planner has the average merchandise turnover, average markup, and profits as a percentage of sales in order to achieve the desired profit of $15,000.

If our market survey shows that we can reasonably expect a sales volume of $200,000, for example, we can refine that projected income statement to reflect this sales volume; thus, we can convert that statement into a budgeted income statement for the first year of operation. This can be done by applying the same standard statistics to the newly determined expected sales volume. In Chapter 7 we found those statistics to show profits as 12 per cent of sales, merchandise turnover four times per year, and markups as 35 per cent of sales. With the increased sales volume, we would naturally expect the profits to exceed the $15,000 previously planned for. As we apply these figures against the new sales volume, the profit becomes $24,000 (12 per cent of $200,000), gross margin becomes $70,000 (35 per cent of $200,000), cost of goods sold becomes $130,000 ($200,000 less $70,000), and average inventory increases to $32,500 ($130,000 divided by turnover of four times per year). Operating expenses will increase from the $28,750 for a volume of $125,000 to $46,000, the difference between a gross margin of $70,000 and a net profit of $24,000. Individual expenses will increase at the same percentages of the increased sales volume.

To clarify this process, we can compare the projected income statement from Chapter 10 with the refined budgeted income statement, which now reflects the results of the market survey. This comparison is shown in adjacent columns in Table 9-1.

TABLE 9-1

JONES HARDWARE COMPANY
COMPARISON OF PROJECTED AND BUDGETED INCOME STATEMENTS THAT REFLECTS MARKET SURVEY

	PROJECTED STATEMENT BASED ON INCOME NEEDS TO MAKE DESIRED PROFIT	*BUDGETED STATEMENT BASED ON SALES VOLUME AS PER MARKET SURVEY*
Sales	$125,000.00	$200,000.00
Cost of goods sold:		
Beginning inventory, Jan. 1	20,312.50	32,500.00
Plus purchases during year	81,250.00	130,000.00
Goods available for sale	$101,562.50	$162,500.00
Less ending inventory, Dec. 31	20,312.50	32,500.00
Cost of goods sold	$ 81,250.00	$130,000.00
Gross margin	$ 43,750.00	$ 70,000.00
Operating expenses (total)	28,750.00	46,000.00
Net profit from operations	$ 15,000.00	$ 24,000.00

The right-hand column, based on a reasonable sales forecast of $200,000, now becomes the basis of all budgeting for the new firm. It is now appropriate to detail each operating expense in dollar amounts, based on industry statistics showing what percentage of sales should be spent on each operating expense. Reference to our basic sources of statistics, cited in Chapter 10, may be necessary. These will tell us the percentage of sales that should be spent on rent, employee salaries, average owner salaries, bad-debts expense, depreciation, advertising, and miscellaneous expenses. Precise expense accounts will, of course, vary with the particular type of business being planned. We know now from our budgeted income statement that a total of $46,000 is appropriate for total operating expenses. We must divide this total into the individual expense accounts that make up this total.

DETAILING THE OPERATING EXPENSES

Our budgeted income statement is based on an average markup of 35 per cent, which provides the gross margin of $70,000. Our net profit from operations is 12 per cent of sales, or $24,000. The difference between these two amounts, $46,000, is listed on the statement as operating expenses. This means that 23 per cent of sales (this $46,000) must cover all our operating expenses if we are to arrive at the profits of $24,000 as planned.

The same statistical sources used in Chapter 7 will provide typical breakdowns of operating expenses for our type of business. Modest variations will be found, depending upon the precise type or size of the store under consideration.

A typical set of operating expenses, expressed as a percentage of sales, for an average hardware store can be found as follows:

Rent, 4 per cent

Employee salaries, 8 per cent

Advertising, 1 per cent

Bad debts, 1 per cent

Delivery expense, 2 per cent

Depreciation, 1 per cent

Supplies, 1 per cent

Miscellaneous expenses, 5 per cent

These expenses total 23 per cent of sales, as per our budgeted income statement. This is not the normal case. All new planners must study their expense structures to ascertain the appropriateness of the individual expense to their particular firms. Perhaps in our case delivery service is not contemplated. Perhaps the owner plans a greater expense for employee salaries.

The important thing in planning in this case is that the total operating expenses not exceed 23 per cent of sales if the firm is to stay on schedule, as per the budgeted income statement.

If we assume that the above percentages are acceptable to our planning for the Jones Hardware Company, we then convert the percentages into dollar amounts. These would be as follows:

Rent, $8,000

Employee salaries, $16,000

Advertising, $2,000

Bad debts, $2,000

Delivery expense $4,000

Depreciation, $2,000

Supplies, $2,000

Miscellaneous expenses, $10,000

Since the generous amount left for miscellaneous expenses may seem excessive to the uninitiated, we should emphasize here that there are always unanticipated expenses in any business. It is usually wise to abide by the suggestions of standard statistics in this regard.

We have now examined every detail in planning income, margins, inventories, and expenses for the new firm. The complete budgeted income statement, completed in Chapter 10, can serve as a schedule against which to check our operations each month or at other periods. Conformance to that schedule will ensure that the planned results will become fact. The finalized budgeted income statement is shown in Table 9-2.

TABLE 9-2

JONES HARDWARE COMPANY
BUDGETED INCOME STATEMENT
FIRST YEAR OF OPERATIONS

Net sales		$200,000
Cost of goods sold:		
Beginning inventory, January 1	$ 32,500	
Purchases	130,000	
Goods available for sale	$162,500	
Ending inventory, December 31	32,500	
Cost of goods sold		130,000
Gross margin		$ 70,000
Operating expenses:		
Rent	$ 8,000	
Employee salaries	16,000	
Advertising	2,000	
Bad-debts expense	2,000	
Delivery expense	4,000	
Depreciation	2,000	
Supplies	2,000	
Miscellaneous expenses	10,000	
Total operating expenses		46,000
Net profit from operations		$ 24,000

As we take a look back at what we have accomplished in our planning to this point, we will recall that we planned to have a profit expectancy of $15,000 on our projected income statement to cover the owner's time and return on the investment. Because our market survey showed a higher than minimum sales volume attainable, we now have a planned profit of $24,000 on our budgeted income statement. It is always good news in planning to find that we can achieve more than planned minimums of sales and profits.

But even in our continuing study for Mr. Jones, we should not assume that he will become rich overnight. That $24,000 net profit from operations represents profits before federal income taxes are applied. If he has incorporated the business, his federal income taxes will be less at most levels of profits. If he is operating as a proprietorship, his federal income taxes will be higher at most levels of profits. Possible surtaxes may be in effect in the first year of operation as well. The matter of legal forms of organization and applicable income taxes was explored in Chapter 8.

We can be satisfied with our planning since we have found that our desired profit is more than attainable. Our sales volume seems reachable with good merchandising. With good management we should achieve our objectives.

Our attention can now turn to the next step in planning—providing a financial structure for the firm. This will be covered in Chapter 12.

QUESTIONS FOR CLASS DISCUSSION

1 What is a market survey? What is its objective?
2 What kinds of firms should make especially thorough market surveys? Why?
3 What is a parasite firm?
4 How can inaccessibility limit a market area? Give examples.
5 Why is a study of population characteristics important in making a good market survey?
6 Do you agree that the urban small firm gets business from a wider area than its immediate neighbourhood? Explain.
7 How can new firm planners find the total purchases in their counties for a particular line of goods?
8 Compare telephone surveys, mail surveys, and personal interviews for cost, coverage, and effectiveness.
9 What services do *Sales & Marketing Management Magazine* and *The Financial Post Canadian Markets* provide for new firm planners and for established retail firms?
10 Do you think a professional market survey is worth $1,000? What advantages would such a report have, even if it shows that the planned firm should not be established?

11 Do you feel competent to make a market survey now?

12 How would you compare the projected income statement prepared in Chapter 7 with the budgeted income statement that is prepared after the results of the market survey are known?

Projects for Home Assignment and/or Class Discussion

1 Explain how you would proceed if you planned to make your own market survey for a new independent grocery in your hometown.

2 Prepare sample questions you would include in a telephone survey, a mailing survey, and a personal interview. Explain how they would differ.

3 See if you or your instructor can obtain a census tract and/or trading area map of the local town or district. Study it and determine the key items revealed on each.

REFERENCES FOR FURTHER READING

Archer, M., *An Introduction to Canadian Business*, 5th ed., McGraw-Hill Ryerson Ltd., Toronto, 1986, Chapter 9.

Beckman, M.D., W.S. Good, and R.G. Wyckham, *Small Business Management*, John Wiley & Sons Canada Ltd., Toronto, 1982, Chapter 9.

Byers, Gerald L. and Harry E. Teckert, *Marketing For Small Business*, Financial Post/Macmillan Company of Canada Ltd., Toronto, 1980.

Cunningham, G., *Buy Yourself A Job & Be Your Own Boss*, McGraw-Hill Ryerson Ltd., 1990, Chapter 5.

Darmon, Rene Y., Michele Laroche, and John V. Petrof, *Marketing in Canada: Management Perspective*, 3rd ed., McGraw-Hill Ryerson Ltd., Scarborough, Ontario, 1989.

Kao, R.W.Y., *Small Business Management: A Strategic Emphasis*, Holt, Rinehart and Winston of Canada Ltd., Toronto, 1981, Chapter 8.

Knight, R.M., *Small Business Management in Canada*, McGraw-Hill Ryerson Ltd., Toronto, 1981, Chapter 6.

Sommers, M.S., J. Barnes, W.J. Stanton, and C. Futrell, *Fundamentals of Marketing*, 5th Canadian Edition, McGraw-Hill Ryerson Ltd., Scarborough, Ontario, 1989.

Tate Jr., C.E., L.C. Megginson, C.R. Scott Jr., and L.R. Trueblood, *Successful Small Business Management*, 3rd ed., Business Publications Inc., Plano, Texas, 1985, Chapters 15 and 16.

"Market Planning," *Your Business Matters*, The Royal Bank of Canada, 1979.

Understanding the Basic Financial Statements from a Management Viewpoint

LEARNING OBJECTIVES

After reading this chapter, you will be able to:

1. **U**nderstand the importance of formal financial statements
2. **K**now the balance sheet formula and identify its sections
3. **C**alculate some important ratios and formulas that relate to the balance sheet
4. **K**now how the income statement is constructed and identify its major sections

This matter of understanding financial statements is so important that we will preface our entire investigation of management fundamentals by clarifying for nonaccounting students and new small firm planners the relationships between the two basic financial statements, as well as their meaning and composition. Thorough competence in managing any business demands this knowledge, which necessarily reflects the results of operations and the present financial position of the firm. Management decisions must be weighed in terms of their effect on these statements. It is not enough to wait for weeks or even months after the close of a fiscal period to have an accountant prepare the results of operation and advise the firm of its current financial position. Formal statements and tax returns may be delayed this way, but the owners need current information at all times.

Two basic financial statements and a cash flow analysis will be considered in this chapter. The *balance sheet* and the *income statement* are the two financial statements that should be considered first.

THE BALANCE SHEET

The balance sheet shows the assets, liabilities, and owner's net worth in a business *as at a given date. Assets* are the things owned by the business, including both physical things and claims against others. *Liabilities* are the amounts owed to others, the creditors of the firm. *Net worth* is the owner's claim to the assets after liabilities are accounted for.

Accounting has a basic equation that says *assets minus liabilities equals net worth.* In simplest terms, this means that what the business owns, less what it owes to creditors, equals its net worth. If liabilities exceed assets, the net worth is a minus quantity. Profits made in each fiscal period increase net worth as they are carried from the income statement to the balance sheet. See Table 10-1 for an example of a balance sheet for a very small firm. Note again that the balance sheet is a *point-of-time* statement, like a "snapshot" of the business at a given time.

THE INCOME STATEMENT

The *income statement* shows the income received and the expenses incurred *over a period of time.* Using a photographic analogy again, it is like a motion picture: it has a beginning and an end. Income statements are usually issued for a year's operations, but interim statements may also be made for a month, a quarter, or a half-year. Some firms have daily or weekly income statements. Even though formal income statements may be issued only once a year, the proprietor should know for shorter periods whether the income has exceeded the expenses and by how much.

TABLE 10-1

ABC COMPANY
BALANCE SHEET
AS AT DECEMBER 31, 199—

ASSETS

Current assets:			
Cash		$1,780	
Accounts receivable		3,100	
Merchandise inventory		4,500	
Prepaid expenses		760	
Total current assets			$10,190
Fixed assets:			
Store equipment	$4,200		
Less accumulated depreciation	900	$3,300	
Office equipment	$2,000		
Less accumulated depreciation	500	1,500	
Delivery truck	$3,000		
Less accumulated depreciation	1,000	2,000	
Total fixed assets			6,800
Total assets			$16,990

LIABILITIES

Current liabilities:			
Accounts payable		$1,500	
Notes payable		1,000	
Contracts payable		2,000	
Total current liabilities			$4,500
Fixed liabilities:			
Contracts payable		$2,000	
Long-term note payable		1,000	
Total fixed liabilities			$3,000
Total liabilities			$ 7,500

NET WORTH (OWNER'S EQUITY)

J. Jones, proprietorship			9,490
Total liabilities plus net worth			$16,990

Income received (sales) comes essentially from the sales of the merchandise or service that the business is formed to sell. Expenses incurred are the expired costs that have been incurred during the same period of time.

The income statement for firms with an inventory to sell has three basic parts: the *income received*, the *cost of goods sold* during the period, and the *operating expenses* incurred during the same period. The difference between sales income and cost of goods sold is known as the *gross margin*. When the operating expenses are subtracted from the gross margin, we arrive at net profit from operations.

Service firms, such as banks, insurance companies, laundries, consulting firms, ticket agencies, or repair services, which do not carry an inventory of merchandise for sale, will not have a cost of goods sold section on their income statement. Their statements will show total income from all sources and then deduct operating expenses, which may be classified in various ways. Larger firms usually separate these expenses into administrative and selling expenses.

All accounts that record income and expenses during the fiscal period are summarized at the end of each period. The income and expense accounts are then closed, and the resulting profit or loss is transferred to the owner's net worth account. This is in contrast to balance sheet accounts, which remain open in the ledger until the particular asset is disposed of, the liability is paid off, or a change is made in the ownership. An example of an income statement is shown in Table 10-2 on page 168.

Now we should return to the example of the balance sheet statement shown in Table 10-1.

RELATIONSHIPS WITHIN THE BALANCE SHEET

First note that the total assets ($16,990) minus the total liabilities ($7,500) equal the owner's net worth or proprietorship ($9,490). This is the fundamental accounting equation:

$$\text{Assets} - \text{Liabilities} = \text{Proprietorship (Owner's Equity)}$$

Every asset, liability, and net worth account is presented on the balance sheet.

RATIO ANALYSIS

Ratio analysis is a means of extracting information from financial statements. This information is taken by the user to satisfy certain objectives. Different users, however, have different needs. The small business person may be interested in various measures of profitability, whereas a creditor may be more interested in measures of liquidity or solvency. For the purpose of this book the following three measures are considered relevant:

1 Tests of liquidity
2 Tests of solvency and
3 Tests of profitability

We will now discuss each test in turn.

Tests of Liquidity

Liquidity is a term used to describe a given company's capacity to meet current obligations. In essence, it represents the cycle whereby assets are converted to cash, which in turn is used to satisfy outstanding liabilities. In the process, revenue is generated.

Current Ratio

Note that the assets are divided into *current assets* and *fixed assets*. This distinction is not necessary to make the books balance but is made for management reasons. The relationship between *current assets* and *current liabilities* is a prime measure of liquidity of any firm. *Liquidity* is the measure of ability to pay debts as they become due.

Current assets are those that are in the form of cash or will convert into cash within one year. Current liabilities are those debts that will be due within one year. The relationship between current assets and current liabilities is called the *current ratio*. Sound financing demands that this ratio be at least 2 to 1. The current ratio is found by dividing the current assets by the current liabilities:

$$\text{Current Ratio} = \frac{\text{Current Assets}}{\text{Current Liabilities}} = \frac{\$10,190}{\$4,500} = 2.26$$

The ABC Company, therefore, has a current ratio of 2.26 to 1 and is safely within the sound rule of a 2 to 1 current ratio.

The current assets should be analyzed to see that they do in fact qualify as assets that will convert into cash within ninety days. A merchandise turnover of three times per year, or once every four months, indicates that the entire inventory amount will not convert into cash within the required period. Your banker will reduce your current ratio when such circumstances exist.

Quick Ratio

The *quick ratio* is also known as the acid test of liquidity. It is the relationship between only the most liquid assets (cash and accounts receivable) and the total of the current liabilities. The conservative rule is that this ratio should be at least 1 to 1. In other words, cash plus receivables should equal or exceed the current liabilities.

$$\text{Quick Ratio} = \frac{\text{Cash Plus Receivables}}{\text{Current Liabilities}}$$

$$= \frac{\$1,780 + \$3,100}{\$4,500}$$

$$= \frac{\$4,880}{\$4,500}$$

$$= 1.08$$

Thus, the ABC Company meets this test of liquidity because the company's quick ratio of 1.08 exceeds the minimum of the conservative rule. The quick ratio combined with the current ratio of 2.26 indicates that the present liquidity of the company is good.

Working Capital

Working capital is the difference between current assets and current liabilities expressed in dollars. On the balance sheet of the ABC Company we see total current assets of $10,190 and current liabilities of $4,500. Working capital is therefore $5,690 ($10,190 − $4,500). In normal operations involving daily sales receipts, buying more merchandise, meeting payrolls and other expenses, and making payments due on current liabilities, it is the net working capital that provides the ability to meet all obligations as they become due. The measurement of adequate cash on hand, as discussed later, is a valuable supplement in determining the adequacy of working capital.

Tests of Solvency

As we have already seen, liquidity measures a company's ability to satisfy or service debt instruments and/or current liabilities. In a sense, liquidity is a subset of a larger one. That is, solvency measures a company's ability to satisfy all debt, both short term (current) and long term. It is therefore evident that the two categories of measurement are related, each serving different users.

Times Interest Earned Ratio

This ratio is used as an indicator by longer term debt holders to determine whether the company's financial health is strong enough to continue servicing their debt obligations. The information is taken from the income statement on page 168.

$$\text{Times Interest Earned} = \frac{\text{Net Profit from Operations} + \text{Interest Expense}}{\text{Interest Expense}}$$

$$= \frac{\$25,000 + \$2,000}{\$2,000}$$

$$= 13.5 \text{ times}$$

Net Profit from Operations plus Interest Expense is called Earnings Before Interest and Taxes (EBIT).

Debt-Equity Ratio

This ratio expresses what contributions were made to acquire assets and by whom. Hence, the larger the portion provided by the owner(s), the less risk is available to be assumed by the creditors. Three ranges of debt-equity exist:

1   Where the ratio is less than one, there is the lowest level of risk
2   Where the ratio is equal to one, there is a moderate risk
3   Where the ratio is greater than one, risk is at its highest level

Therefore, as the ratio increases in value, so too does risk.

$$\text{Debt-Equity Ratio} = \frac{\text{Total Liabilities}}{\text{Total Owner's Equity}}$$
$$= \frac{\$7,500}{\$9,490}$$
$$= 0.79$$

Proprietorship Ratio

This ratio is closely related to the debt-equity ratio. The emphasis here, however, is on what investment the proprietor actually has in his or her own company. Generally expressed as a percentage, the *proprietorship ratio*, or owner's equity ratio, is the relationship between the owner's investment in the firm and the total assets being used in the business. It is computed by dividing the owner's investment by the total assets. For the ABC Company we see that the owner's investment (the equity in the assets) is $9,490. Total assets used in the business are valued at $16,990.

$$\text{Proprietorship Ratio} = \frac{\text{Owner's Investment}}{\text{Total Assets}}$$
$$= \frac{\$9,490}{\$16,990}$$
$$= 56\%$$

The proprietorship ratio can be expressed as a ratio of owner investment to total assets or as a percentage of those total assets. In this case, proprietorship is 56 per cent of total investment in the firm or a ratio of 0.56 to 1.00. This proprietorship ratio is safely above the conservative minimum of 50 per cent.

Tests of Profitability

The above ratios are important because the proprietor must be able to understand the viewpoint of those he or she deals with, especially in obtaining debt and in accruing liabilities. However, the small business owner should always be more focused on the total picture. That is, primary interest should be directed towards long-run survival. In order to satisfy this primary concern, some level of profitability is necessary to ensure an adequate return on the owner's investment (ROI). Tests of profitability are designed to accomplish this. As done in the Times Interest Earned Ratio, information is extracted from the income statement.

Return on Sales—ROS

This ratio is a broad one that gives one a feel for the overall performance in any given period. Because of its wide and encompassing nature, the ratio should be used with caution. For example, where an extraordinary gain is realized (an addition to income that is not ordinary in the business sense), the ratio might be artificially high. Common examples include proceeds from an insurance claim or an award from an outstanding litigation hearing.

$$\text{Return on Sales} = \frac{\text{Net Income}}{\text{Net Sales}}$$
$$= \frac{\$25,000}{\$100,000}$$
$$= 25\%$$

Return on Total Assets

This measure is an indicator of the productivity or relative efficiency of assets. Since assets perform equally well whether financed by the owner or through borrowed money, the return on assets should be calculated *before* deducting the interest expense. This measure indicates to the proprietor whether or not he or she has chosen the best alternative available for the use of his or her assets.

$$\text{Return on Total Assets} = \frac{\text{EBIT}}{\text{Average Total Assets}}$$
$$= \frac{\$28,000}{\$16,990}$$
$$= 1.65$$
$$= 165\%$$

Return on Owner's Equity

This ratio is an important indicator of profitability because it suggests how well the company is performing with the proprietor's investment.

$$\text{Return on Owner's Equity} = \frac{\text{Net Income}}{\text{Average Owner's Equity}}$$
$$= \frac{\$25,000}{\$9,490}$$
$$= 2.63$$
$$= 263\%$$

There are many other ratios utilized in the analysis of business firm operations. Most small firms that maintain adequate current ratios, quick ratios, working capital, proper inventories, and a 50 per cent proprietorship ratio will maintain a sound financial structure.

Note to Ratio Analysis

Ratio analysis is very helpful in the analysis of a company when comparing the company to industry standards and to other similar companies. They are also very useful in providing comparison data to the company itself with respect to past performance, projected future performance, and present actual performance. Such analyses are indispensible for the small business owner. However, a word or two of warning are critical here. Ratios should not be used as absolute indicators of various performance measures for a number of reasons. Primarily, those ratios can be significantly misleading when special quirks arise as described in the Return on Sales example. Moreover, this effect can be extended to a comparison with other companies that have similarly faced special circumstances. Finally, one should be very careful in using the ratios by always attempting to examine those input factors to determine the ratio. Only under such discretion can these ratios be used effectively.

CASH FLOW ANALYSIS

The above analysis of the financial statements is critical in understanding any company's performance or direction. However, the small business owner may find the statements of no use in the day-to-day operations. The financial statements suit this purpose well in that they create a focus of the macro (major) occurrences over any given period of time. This is often no consolation to the small business owner who looks to the projected income statement for the period only to discover that he or she will make money this period, but tomorrow three deliveries are due COD (cash on delivery) and a negligible amount of cash is in the till and bank account. It is quite feasible that he or she will indeed make money during this period, but the timing of the revenues and expenses are clearly not synchronized. *Cash flow analysis* is the answer and shall be discussed here.

Cash flow analysis is very simple, yet is often overlooked as being a tool of management. In general, small businesses are often cash hungry. This might be due to rapid growth or to poor cash management. In the following, a system of cash management will be set forth that is both simple and very useful.

The primary tool of the system is a *journal*. The system operates as follows:

1   On a daily basis the owner or designated employee enters all transactions in the journal that will have an effect on cash today or in the future. Let us take an example, one that can be followed through. Assume we are in the service sector providing bicycle repairs as our primary source of revenue, and let us further assume that we also sell bicycle parts. We begin by matching a cash flow period to a period that will be covered by one income statement. For simplicity, we assume that today's date is January 1, 1991, and that the income statement for the next period will cover the period beginning January 1, 1991, and ending January 31, 1991. The journal should then be set up to cover 31 days.

2   Our transactions today, day one, are: (a) one bicycle was brought in for repairs that will cost the bicycle owner $35 (parts and labour included). The bicycle will be ready in two days (day three); (b) one bicycle is brought in that requires a tune-up and derailer adjustments, which will cost the bicycle owner $50 (parts and labour included). This bicycle will be ready tomorrow (day two).

3   To this point we have seen examples of potential revenues flowing in from our normal business operations. The next step is to total the cash effect of each day of operation. For simplicity's sake we assume that we generated no revenue on day one but we have a cash balance of $45. If no other transactions occur, this will mean that in day two the end of the day cash balance will be $95 and, similarly, in day three the cash balance will be $130.

4   The final step in the cash management process is to plan expenditures so that a negative cash balance is never attempted. Returning to our bicycle repair shop scenario, assume that the second bicycle, which was to be ready for day two, is in need of a new derailer, which costs us $35; but if two derailers are purchased the total cost is $55. By purchasing two derailers we could save just over 20 per cent, which would increase our margin of profit for this job. This would also mean that we cannot take delivery of the derailers until day two because today's cash balance is only $45, as evidenced in our journal.

This kind of cash management seems rather simplistic on the surface. However, when transactions are numerous on a daily basis and the cash balances are in the hundreds of dollars, the proprietor cannot expect to remember all of the transactions and the timing of the cash flows (both revenues and expenditures). Under these circumstances the daily cash journal is an indispensable tool of management.

The cash journal is at the extreme simple level of cash management. At the other end of the spectrum is the income statement. It is usually the case that the final cash balance in the cash journal at the end of the period (in our example, January 31, 1991) does not coincide with the net profit. To reconcile the difference, we make use of a cash flow statement. This statement is identical to the income statement in format and appearance but has the key difference of excluding noncash items. Examples of noncash items are: depreciation, accruals of expenses, and deferrals. The cash statement is very similar to the cash income statement. Differences do exist; however, they are beyond the scope of this discussion. The message here is that one can extrapolate from the projected income statement to budget for that period's expenditures. In our example from ABC Company, noncash charges (depreciation) total $1,700. Therefore, the actual cash from operations would amount to $25,000 + $1,700 = $26,700. In this example the difference might be considered negligible. However, circumstances could easily arise where the small business owner would derive a great deal of comfort in knowing that an additional $1,700 were available in some given period.

TRADING ON EQUITY

In connection with owner investment, we should become familiar with the phrase *trading on equity*. This phrase refers to the relationship between *creditor capital* (liabilities) in the business and *owner capital. Trading on too thin an equity* is a term used to describe owners who have too little of their own money invested compared with the creditor capital (liabilities) used to finance the business. A proprietorship ratio of 50 per cent indicates that the owner or owners have invested half the value of the total assets used in the business. When this ratio falls below 50 per cent, the outside creditors are supplying more of the firm's total capital needs than the owners are. This indicates, in most cases, that further capital or credit will be more difficult to obtain either from current loans, sale of securities, or other investors. Such owners are truly trading on too thin an equity and probably need more investment capital of their own.

An example of trading on too thin an equity would be the owner of a dress shop that needs $60,000 in total assets. The owner raises $50,000 of that total with credit from merchandise suppliers, short-term loans from friends, and a ninety-day bank loan. All these debts are current liabilities. The owner's investment on the opening day balance sheet is only $10,000. That balance sheet shows total assets of $60,000, current liabilities of $50,000, and proprietorship of $10,000. The resulting proprietorship ratio is 16⅔ per cent ($10,000 divided by $60,000), which is far short of the recommended 50 per cent. It will be most difficult to obtain further credit of any kind. The pressing debts make the business less able to weather any kind of a serious drop in profits.

The reason that creditors look to the proprietorship ratio is to see how much of the total risk is being borne by the owners of the firm. The owners' incentive to stick with the firm in less prosperous times is often influenced by the extent of their investment. When they have only a small part of the total investment, the temptation to "leave a sinking ship" is great. If that happens, the creditors stand to incur serious losses.

We should also note here that *all shareholders are owners.* Both preference and common shareholder investments count as owner capital in computing the proprietorship ratio. *Bondholders are creditors.* Their investment is listed on the balance sheet as fixed liabilities. The total face value of all bonds outstanding is counted as creditor capital in computing the proprietorship ratio. We will look at this matter more closely in Chapter 11 when we discuss financing sources for small firms.

It is recognized, of course, that there are special types of business firms in which variations from the ideal ratio rules advocated here can be justified. Public utilities are a notable example. Unless positive evidence is available to justify exceptions, however, the new firm planner will do well to abide by these conservative rules of financial soundness in making plans for the new firm.

In summary, our analysis of the ABC Company's balance sheet shows a healthy financial structure. Its current ratio, quick ratio, and proprietorship ratio all exceed the minimums dictated by sound financing principles. Its working capital seems to be adequate. Before sitting back, however, the owner should check these ratios against the available statistics for the most efficient firms in the same line of business. Sources of such data are discussed in Chapter 7.

Now we turn to an analysis of the income statement, an example of which is shown in Table 10-2.

ANALYSIS OF THE INCOME STATEMENT

Note first that the period of the ABC Company income statement shown in Table 10-2 is one year, ending December 31, 199–. As a period-of-time statement, a proper title necessitates that two dates be stated or determinable. "Year ended December 31, 199–" is the standard form for the statement. Parenthetically, let us note here that the calendar year is not necessarily the best fiscal period (annual accounting and tax period) for all businesses. More and more firms are using the date of actually starting the business as the beginning of an annual fiscal period, or some other date in the year that more closely represents a complete cycle in annual operations. This is particularly true of firms that have a high degree of seasonal variation in their income.

The ABC Company income statement emphasizes the basic parts previously described. The firm earned $25,000 profit from operations. It had net sales of $100,000, of which $40,000 was paid for the merchandise that was sold and $60,000 was its gross margin. It paid out $35,000 in operating expenses, and thus had $25,000 profit from operations remaining in the business. The experienced student or business person will judge this a highly successful business on the basis of these facts. Not many firms operate on a markup of 60 per cent of sales price. Two qualifying factors must be kept in mind, however. First, the $25,000 represents both salary and return on investment for Mr. Jones, the owner. Second, the $25,000 profit from operations is before federal and provincial income taxes on profits have been paid. The shocking truths concerning this will be discussed later. We can be sure at this point that the proprietor with three children will not be living in great luxury if this firm is the family's sole source of income.

TABLE 10-2

ABC COMPANY
INCOME STATEMENT
YEAR ENDED DECEMBER 31, 199—

Sales		$100,000
Cost of goods sold:		
Beginning inventory Jan. 1	$10,000	
Purchases during year	40,000	
Goods available for sale	$50,000	
Less ending inventory Dec. 31	10,000	
Cost of goods sold		40,000
Gross margin		$ 60,000
Operating expenses:		
Rent	$ 6,000	
Salaries to employees	15,000	
Supplies used	2,000	
Advertising and promotion	1,000	
Insurance expense	1,000	
Delivery expense	2,000	
Depreciation expense	1,700	
Bad debts	1,000	
Local taxes paid	1,000	
Utilities expense	300	
Interest expense	2,000	
Miscellaneous expenses	2,000	
Total operating expenses		35,000
Net profit from operations		$ 25,000

An attractive profit does not mean that the income statement should not have regular analysis by the proprietors. As they review their year's operation, they should ask themselves at least the following questions:

1 Is our markup high or low compared with successful firms in this type of business?
2 Is our consequent cost of goods sold high or low?
3 Is our inventory adequate for the sales volume that the business produced? Did we lose sales because of stockouts? Is our inventory inadequate for the sales volume? Is our inventory too large? Are excess inventories costing too much?
4 Is our total overhead in line with the most efficient firms of this type? Is our occupancy charge (rent) the proper percentage of sales? How about our other expenses?

TABLE 10-3

BILL'S HOME LAUNDRY & DRY CLEANING
INCOME STATEMENT
YEAR ENDED FEBRUARY 28, 199–

Income:		
From laundry operations	$125,000	
From dry cleaning	65,000	
From repairs and miscellaneous	10,000	
Total income		$200,000
Operating expenses:		
Variable expenses:		
Employee wages	$98,000	
Delivery expenses	4,000	
Operating supplies	18,000	
Repairs and maintenance	3,000	
Administrative and legal	1,000	
Advertising	1,500	
Bad debt expense	300	
Miscellaneous expenses	4,200	
Total variable expenses		$130,000
Fixed expenses:		
Rent	$ 6,000	
Utilities	8,500	
Insurance	4,000	
Taxes and licences	2,500	
Depreciation	9,000	
Total fixed expenses		$ 30,000
Total operating expenses		160,000
Net profit from operations		$ 40,000

Typical income statement for a service type business that does not carry an inventory of merchandise for sale. Note that this income statement does not have a cost of goods sold section.

As we saw in Chapter 7, the availability of abundant trade statistics will give the proprietors comparative data with which to find answers to these questions. Studying their operations will usually reveal special strengths of their firm and areas that need improvement. For example, they may find that their merchandise turnover was four times per year but that the most successful firms operate with a turnover of five times per year while maintaining the same margins. They should satisfy themselves as to why other firms have this turnover and pursue the possibilities of improving their own operation. They may find that successful firms operate with a smaller loss on bad debts. If so, this should cause them to question their whole credit-account policy. Similar analysis should be made of all key items of the balance sheet and the income statement. When used in this way, the basic accounting statements become tools for management to use for decision making and not merely dreary accounts of what happened in the last fiscal period.

An income statement for *service firms* that do not carry an inventory of merchandise for sale will not have a cost of goods sold section. They will show total income from services or fees and then deduct the operating expenses to arrive at net profit from operations. See Table 10-3 for illustration.

TABLE 10-4

THE FIVE KINDS OF ACCOUNTS: DEFINITION AND STATEMENT APPEARANCE OF EACH

These accounts appear on the balance sheet (a point-of-time statement)	1. Assets—things owned 2. Liabilities—amounts owed 3. Net worth—owner's investment
These accounts appear on the income statement (a period-of-time statement)	4. Income—sales revenue 5. Expense—expired costs

TABLE 10-5

THE FIVE KINDS OF ACCOUNTS: HOW INCREASES AND DECREASES ARE MADE FOR EACH

ACCOUNTS	*INCREASES*	*DECREASES*
1. Assets	Debits	Credits
2. Liabilities	Credits	Debits
3. Net worth	Credits	Debits
4. Income	Credits	Debits
5. Expense	Debits	Credits

Income statements for *manufacturing firms*, their cost of goods manufactured statements and balance sheets, are illustrated in Chapter 7. See Tables 7-2, 7-3, and 7-4.

Tables 10-4 and 10-5 summarize much of what has been discussed. They will serve as a useful guide for students having their first introduction to the preparation and use of accounting statements and their value to management. For people who are already proprietors, they will be a useful refresher.

Table 10-4 shows that there are only five different kinds of accounts used in the most sophisticated accounting systems. It defines the accounts and shows on which of the two basic statements they appear. Students should note again the difference between a *point-of-time* and a *period-of-time* statement. Table 10-5 shows how each of these accounts is increased or decreased in the operation of a double-entry bookkeeping system. Most new students are surprised to learn that there is nothing sacred in the terms *debit* and *credit*. They could as easily be called left and right, port and starboard, or gee and haw. In Chapter 23 we will study how to install a simplified journal-ledger accounting system that will adequately serve most small firms.

QUESTIONS FOR CLASS DISCUSSION

1 Where is the owner's investment plus any accumulated profits shown in the basic financial statement?

2 How can you justify showing "Accounts Receivable" as an asset on the balance sheet?

3 What is the chief difference between a balance sheet and an income statement? Explain.

4 How is the profit for a fiscal period transferred from the income statement accounts to the owner's net worth account?

5 Do the terms *debit* and *credit* mean anything different from *left* and *right*?

6 Are all accounts increased with debits?

7 What are the five different kinds of accounts?

8 What does each of the five kinds of accounts represent?

9 What is the difference between current assets and fixed assets?

10 What is the current ratio? What is the conservative rule as to a minimum limit on this ratio?

11 Is the quick ratio different from the current ratio? How?

12 Describe two ratios that test profitability. When should one be cautious about using such ratios?

13 When a business is said to be trading on too thin an equity, what is meant?

14 Do you agree that total assets represent the total capital employed in the business? If so, how is this capital provided?

15   What is the working capital of any business?

16   When business owners analyze their income statement, what facts and comparisons should they consider?

17   What do we mean when we say that the net worth, or proprietorship account, represents the owner's claim to the assets?

18   When a firm sells merchandise for cash, what account is credited and what account is debited?

Projects for Home Assignment and/or Class Discussion

1   The current ratio is often referred to as the firm's test of liquidity. Explain in a short paper how the current ratio is truly such a test and how it assures the ability to pay current bills as they become due.

2   "Trading on too thin an equity" means that the creditors have more investment in the firm than the owners.
   a Explain in a short essay how such a condition can affect the success of the business.
   b Prepare a balance sheet for a small firm that illustrates a condition of trading on too thin an equity.

3   Make up your own example of an income statement for a service business and for a retail business. Explain their basic difference.

4   See if you can obtain a balance sheet of an existing business firm and compare it with the samples in the text.

REFERENCES FOR FURTHER READING

Archer, M., *An Introduction to Canadian Business*, 5th ed., McGraw-Hill Ryerson Ltd., Toronto, 1986, Chapter 17.

Beckman, M.D., W.S. Good, and R.G. Wyckham, *Small Business Management*, John Wiley & Sons Canada Ltd., Toronto, 1982, Chapter 10.

Cunningham, G., *Buy Yourself A Job & Be Your Own Boss*, McGraw-Hill Ryerson Ltd., 1990, Chapter 10.

Kao, R.W.Y., *Small Business Management: A Strategic Emphasis*, 2nd ed., Holt, Rinehart and Winston of Canada Ltd., Toronto, 1984, Chapter 9.

Langhout, J., *Analysis and Interpretation of Canadian Financial Statements*, University Press of Canada, St. John's, Newfoundland, 1972.

Meigs, W.B., R.F. Meigs, and W.P. Lam, *Accounting: The Basis for Business Decisions*, 6th Canadian Edition, McGraw-Hill Ryerson Ltd., Toronto, 1991, Chapters 1 and 2.

Tate Jr., C.E., L.C. Megginson, C.R. Scott Jr., and L.R. Trueblood, *Successful Small Business Management*, 3rd ed., Business Publications, Inc., Plano, Texas, 1985, Chapter 19.

"Financial Reporting and Analysis–the Independent Business Way," *Your Business Matters*, The Royal Bank of Canada, 1986.

"How to Read Financial Statements," The Canadian Securities Institute, Toronto, 1985.

11

Sources of Financing for New Small Firms

LEARNING OBJECTIVES

After reading this chapter, you will be able to:

1. **E**xplain the concept of capital and how entrepreneurs use it in small business
2. **I**dentify both personal and other sources of funds for small firm financing
3. **K**now why it is important to have adequate capital as a new entrepreneur
4. **C**ontrast options for financing the small firm—using funds borrowed from others or getting funds by selling a part of the ownership
5. **K**now why venture capital may or may not be a good idea for the new firm

It is always sad to see a new firm with great profit potential fall by the wayside only because it was not properly financed from the beginning. And this happens too often among the thousands of new firms started in this country every year. The error comes from either not knowing the total financial needs of the firm or failing to provide for those needs in the planning stage.

No firm should ever be started without a clear and positive understanding of where its total capital needs are coming from. As we have seen in previous chapters, a very important phase of the entire planning process is to determine what assets will be needed and how they are to be provided. When the amount of the net ownership capital needed has been determined, the proprietors turn to the problem of making sure that the entire amount is available. The total sum should preferably be deposited in the company's bank account before any commitments are made by the new owners.

When several sources of capital are available, the planners must still bear in mind that all sources may not be equally desirable. Borrowed capital is shown on the balance sheet as a liability. It must be paid back at specific periods. These repayments of principal amounts are not operating expenses that are deducted on the income statement before planned profits are produced. They are payments for the provision of investment capital and are to be paid out of the profits shown on the income statement. The authors have found that failure to recognize this basic fact is the commonest cause of financial strain among small firms. It is important, therefore, to consider the repayment schedules in choosing among sources of financing.

The various types of financing available to business firms are usually classified as:

1   *Short-term capital.* This category is used to designate borrowed capital that is to be repaid within one year.
2   *Intermediate capital.* This title is applied to borrowed capital that is to be repaid in one to five years.
3   *Long-term capital.* This is capital whose repayment is arranged for more than five years in the future.

As new firm planners review the many sources of financial assistance that follow, they may find that some of these sources fall into different categories of the above listing. For example, a note payable to a commercial bank is generally considered short-term financing, but a three-year note payable to a finance company would be considered intermediate capital.

SOURCES OF FUNDS FOR SMALL FIRMS

1   Personal funds saved or inherited
2   Loans from relatives and friends
3   Trade credit (credit given by suppliers and others)
4   Loans or credit from equipment sellers

5   Mortgage loans

6   Commercial bank loans

7   *Small Business Loans Act* (SBLA) loans

8   Federal Business Development Bank loans

9   Federal and provincial development programs

10   Taking in partners

11   Selling capital shares

12   Other miscellaneous sources

Two things should be recognized when one is faced with the problem of obtaining outside capital assistance:

1   An established concern with a good record of operations usually has better access to available sources of capital than a new firm.

2   Some personal capital available for investment in the firm by the new owner is almost always essential to obtaining any type of outside assistance.

Against this background, we can investigate the possibilities of each of the sources of funds listed.

Personal Funds   Whenever potential creditors, partners, or stockholders are invited to invest in, or lend financial assistance to, a new firm, their first question is, "How much does the owner have invested?" Every business contains an element of risk, and outsiders who invest in a new firm wish to be sure that such risk is shared by the owner. We have seen that "trading on too thin an equity" means that the owner's investment is too small relative to the investment of outsiders. A financing plan that indicates that the firm is starting out on this basis does not usually invite confidence from creditors. As we will see in Chapter 12, this does not always mean that the new owners must have 50 per cent of the total capital needs to invest, but it does mean that they should likely look to other ownership capital rather than only to creditor capital in their financial plan. In any event, it is important that the would-be owners have assets of their own to invest in the firm. The closer to 50 per cent of the total capital needs that can be provided, the greater will be their independence and share of net profits.

Loans from Relatives and Friends   Although this type of borrowing to provide original investment capital is generally frowned upon by experienced business operators, it remains one of the prominent devices used in small firms' planning. Many new owners are encouraged in their enterprise by parents, relatives, or friends who offer to supply loans to the firm to get it started. Quite often, no other sources are available after normal trade credit and supplier contracts have been utilized.

It is unfortunate that many otherwise successful firms have been beset by troubles because relatives or friends interfered with the operations. Mixing family or social relationships with business can be dangerous. Many such situations might have been averted if the terms of the loans had been more clearly specified, including the rights of the lenders to insist upon making operational policy. The best way to avoid subsequent problems is to make sure that loans are made on a businesslike basis. They should be viewed as business dealings. The right of the owner to make decisions should be respected by all parties involved. Arrangements for retiring such loans, including any options for early payment, and the procedure if loans become delinquent should be clearly understood and set forth in writing. The owner should be sure such loans are properly presented on the balance sheet—payments due in one year are current liabilities; the others are fixed liabilities.

Trade Credit   Trade credit is the financial assistance available from other firms with whom the business has dealings. Most prominent are the suppliers of inventory that is constantly being replaced. We have previously noted that wholesalers who desire a retailer's business, for example, will offer generous terms for payment of invoices. Manufacturers will do the same for wholesalers whose business they desire. Financing the opening inventory usually represents one of the larger investments in a typical small firm. If a $20,000 inventory can be purchased for $10,000 down payment and the balance in thirty days, the wholesaler has virtually provided $10,000 of the required capital to open the business. The owner then has an opportunity to sell that inventory at a profit and thus to have the funds to pay off the original balance. As a record for successful operation is established, even more attractive terms may be offered on subsequent purchases. A grocer may have several such suppliers. Other firms may have only one or two major suppliers. The inducement of a sales discount for prompt payment of invoices should always tempt the owner to pay within the maximum discount period.

Loans or Credit from Equipment Sellers   This type of financial aid is often considered another form of trade credit. It does, however, have distinct characteristics. The new firm may need counters, shelves, display cases, delivery trucks, and other equipment such as air conditioning, refrigeration units, food counters. These, too, are a large investment for the new small firm and are so recognized by the major suppliers of such items. The purchases, it is hoped, are not made on a regular basis but represent a large part of the capital needed to get started. The suppliers usually offer good credit terms with a modest down payment and a contract for the balance spread over one, two, or three years.

This type of credit, when financing charges are reasonable, can be most helpful to the planner. The caution is in its overuse—remembering, again, that the principal payments must be paid out of profits anticipated. Any principal repayments of this type, too, are for the provision of capital and are not operating expenses. Too much of this type of financing can distort the current and quick ratios and upset the firm's financial liquidity. Many cases are on record where the monthly payments on such fixed assets exceed the profits earned from sales in the month.

Mortgage Loans   If the new firm planners own a commercial building, they can normally secure a mortgage on it with payments over as many as twenty years. It may be the building in which the new firm will operate. In that case, the planners will be making mortgage payments instead of rental payments to a landlord. They may wish to risk a mortgage on their homes. Even second mortgages are sometimes used, although not recommended. Mortgage loans are typically made by trust companies, credit unions, and mortgage companies. When profits are uncertain, caution is advised in committing any assets to mortgage claims. As a clear profit pattern becomes more definitely established, the use of mortgage credit becomes less risky.

Commercial Bank Loans   Historically, a line of credit at a chartered bank was designed to enable a merchant to purchase an inventory of merchandise. When the merchandise was sold at a profit, the bank was paid its loan. This situation is still followed by many banks. This use of bank credit is still the best way to establish credit with a commercial bank. Since the relaxation of bank restrictions in recent years, however, many other types of loans and financing are now available to qualified applicants. In fact, we have banks now that advertise, "If you are planning to go into business, come see us." The cold, hard facts of economic reality will be faced in such a visit, but the prospective firm owner with an otherwise sound financing plan, a reputation for integrity, and a business deemed likely to succeed may still establish some bank credit in the planning stage. Long-term loans are less generally available than short-term loans. Short-term loans are usually considered those for not more than one year. If adequate collateral is available, longer term loans may usually be obtained. Getting influential or wealthy friends to cosign notes also may be helpful.

The policies of several of the chartered banks should always be checked in the planning stage. Many small firm owners with experience have long described banks as "a place where you can borrow money when you prove that you don't need it." Some banks are earnestly trying to remove that image today. In keeping with our previously noted axiom that rewards must be commensurate with cost and risk, however, interest rates charged by banks to small firms are significantly higher than the rates charged to large firms.

Although chartered banks still dominate small business lending, credit unions and some trust companies are beginning to offer commercial loans to small businesses and it is expected that in the nineties these financial institutions will move very forcefully to compete for customers.

Small Business Loans Act (SBLA) Loans   The proprietor of a small business enterprise or one who is about to establish a new business may borrow funds under this program for the acquisition of fixed assets, modernization of premises (leasehold improvements), or the purchase of land or building necessary for the operation of the business. Working capital loans are not provided under the SBLA, nor is it possible to refinance existing debt. It is hoped, however, that eventually the SBLA will be amended to include much needed working capital financing for small enterprises. A small business, be it a proprietorship, partnership, or a limited liability company, is eligible if its actual (or estimated) gross revenue does not exceed $2 million per year and is engaged in any one of the following activities: manufacturing, wholesale or retail trade, service, transportation, construction, communication, insurance, or real estate. The maximum that a business may have outstanding under the

SBLA at any one time may not exceed $100,000, and the loan must be secured by first charge on equipment, mortgage on the premises, and sometimes additional security may be required. The loans are provided and administered by the chartered banks and other designated lending institutions, such as Credit Unions, Caisses populaires, trust companies, loan companies, insurance companies, and Alberta Treasury Branches, and are fully guaranteed by the federal government. The loans have fixed terms of repayments of the principal, typically five years, and the interest charged on these loans is fluctuating (floating) with the chartered bank's prime lending rate with an additional 1 per cent above the prime rate. In 1988 over 18 000 loans in excess of $680 million were authorized. Since inception (1961), more than 250 000 loans for about $6 billion were approved under this *Act*.

The Federal Business Development Bank (FBDB)   This is a Crown corporation that assists the growth and creation of business enterprises across Canada by providing them with financial and management services. It supplements such services available from others and it gives particular attention to the needs of smaller enterprises.

FBDB extends financial assistance to new or existing businesses of almost every type in Canada that do not have other sources of financing available to them on reasonable terms and conditions.

The qualifications for FBDB financing are that the principals of the business have sufficient investment in the business to ensure their continuing commitment and that the enterprise may reasonably be expected to be successful.

FBDB financing is available by means of loans, loan guarantees, equity financing, or leasing, or by any combination of these methods, in whatever manner best suits the particular needs of the business. Where loans are involved, they are made at interest rates that are in line with those generally available to businesses. Security is usually a first charge on fixed assets. Where equity is involved, FBDB normally takes a minority interest and is prepared to have its investment repurchased on suitable terms.

Most of the customers of the bank use FBDB funds to acquire land, buildings, or equipment. Others use them to strengthen the working capital of a business, to establish a new business, and for other purposes.

FBDB financing ranges in size from about $10,000 upwards. Most loans are $100,000 or less. Close to half of them are for $25,000 or less, and the average size of a loan is around $45,000. The amount that can be borrowed for a specific purpose depends upon the borrower's ability to satisfy the general requirements of the bank. Businesses may obtain FBDB assistance on more than one occasion if they meet its requirements. In fiscal 1990, the FBDB authorized over 5600 loans in excess of $900 million; its total portfolio is $2.8 billion to some 20 000 customers. Over the past 45 years, the FBDB has provided over $12 billion in financing to some 160 000 businesses.

In addition to its financial services, the FBDB provides for small businesses management training through an extensive series of one-day management seminars at many centres across Canada, and it develops and distributes adult education courses on small business management topics. The bank's Small Business Information Service is an enquiry and referral service available at its seventy-seven offices across the country.

CASE (Counselling Assistance for Small Enterprise) is a management counselling service wherein retired business persons act as counsellors on behalf of the bank. Its purpose is to assist owners and managers of business enterprises, particularly those of smaller size, to improve their methods of doing business. Also, it provides an opportunity for retired business people to contribute to the development of the small business community by making available a vast store of knowledge and experience. To be eligible, a business may already be established or about to engage in business in Canada. Any proprietorship, partnership, or limited company conducting virtually any type of business enterprise in Canada can apply, provided that the enterprise does not have more than seventy-five full-time employees. There is a nominal charge for this service.

Through the facilities of CASE, there is another service available: the Financial Planning Program (FPP). In FPP, the bank plays a catalytic role in the market. It puts together financial and planning packages for its customers to assist them in securing financing from private sources. In addition, the FBDB assists in financial planning with "do-it-yourself" kits and business management seminars of full-day or half-day duration. Twenty-two different business topics are covered by the seminars. Business management courses are thirty-hour courses designed by the FBDB especially for business people interested in improving their management skills, and they cover all aspects of business, including advertising, bookkeeping, personnel administration, financial management, marketing, manufacturing, and retailing.

Community Business Initiatives are the bank's newest service, developed to provide business people in smaller communities with training and counselling tailored to their needs.

Each initiative groups approximately thirty business people who meet on a monthly basis for workshops given by experts on topics chosen by the participants themselves. The project coordinator, a local business person, then visits the participants at their places of business to discuss practical applications of the issues covered in the workshop. The project calls for forty hours of group workshops and forty hours of on-site advisory time over a twelve-month period.

Federal and Provincial Development Programs   As outlined in Chapter 1, the federal government's Department of Industry, Science and Technology Canada (ISTC) has wide-ranging financial assistance programs through three organizations: Western Economic Diversification Canada (WD); the Atlantic Canada Opportunities Agency (ACOA); and ISTC itself. The WD has as its mandate broadening the economic base of western Canada. A fund to assist projects in the manufacturing and resource-based industries was established. Contributions received from this fund normally have flexible repayment terms. Most assisted projects will be in the area of new technology, product or market development, plant establishment, or industry-wide productivity improvement.

ACOA is strongly oriented towards the development of entrepreneurship and small businesses. It will not fund large projects but will attempt to develop the economic infrastructure of the Atlantic region by acting as a source of information and as an advocate within the federal system. Grants will be made to businesses that are not in farming, fish harvesting, or retail trade, which lie outside ACOA's mandate.

The Export Development Corporation (EDC) is a federally owned commercial enterprise that provides financial facilities to assist Canada's export trade. In 1989, it had assets in excess of $6.5 billion and lending, insurance, and guarantees capacities of $15 billion. EDC operates to help Canadian exporters remain competitive in world markets. It does this by providing insurance, loans, guarantees, foreign investment guarantees, and other services. Any firm, large or small, is eligible for this type of assistance. It is playing an important and increasing role in assisting Canadian exporters. In 1989, its assets totalled $6.5 billion and its lending, insurance, and guarantees capacities totalled $6 billion.

The provincial governments in every province of Canada have established development agencies or Crown corporations. Their methods of operation and levels of activity vary from province to province, but all have similar objectives—mostly to stimulate economic growth in their areas and to provide financial assistance to firms unable to secure required financing.

Taking in Partners   Despite all the cautions previously discussed, raising capital often necessitates taking one or more partners into the business. If more than one manager is not needed, the new partners may not be employed in the firm but may hold full partner status as a result of their investment in the firm. The partnership agreement (discussed in Chapter 8) is important here. Inducements can be offered to such a finance partner, but the duties, responsibilities, and authority of each partner must be clearly understood. At this point we are looking at the partnership only from the standpoint of providing a source of investment funds.

Selling Capital Shares   Aside from the technical, legal, and operational advantages of the corporate form of legal organization, its advantages as a device for raising capital are extremely significant. Many small firm owners seem to believe that the corporate form was designed only for the very large business firms. This is false. It is true that this legal form has not been as widely used as it might be. This is believed to be due to lack of knowledge of its advantages. Chapter 8 explains details of the corporation.

Consider the new firm planner who needs $100,000 in ownership capital but has only $30,000 to invest. Would it not be desirable to go to a local investment dealer as a corporation and request the sale of $50,000 of 7 per cent preference shares and $50,000 of common shares? The planner takes title to $30,000 of the voting common shares. The charter provides authorization to sell $100,000 of each type of shares. The planner can hold the unsold shares in the firm for possible future financing for expansion. The preference share is given a priority of dividends and may not have voting privilege. Usually only the common share has voting power. The planner still owns a majority of the common shares outstanding and has no problem of control. The investment

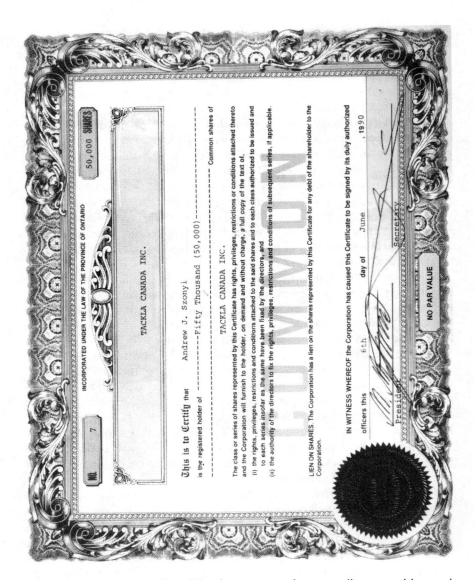

FIGURE 11-1 • Small businesses may issue creditor securities such as shares, or bonds, or promissory notes.

dealer sells the shares to customers who are probably unknown. A detailed study of the plans of the firm is contained in a prospectus, which the investment dealers will prepare. The firm planner does not have to pursue relatives or plead with friends for financial "favours," does not have to take in undesired partners to raise capital, has assured a financial plan for expansion, and has all the protections of the corporate form of organization. The investment dealer will charge for this service. The charge will be higher if the dealer guarantees the sale of the full amount, and less if the shares are sold on a "best efforts" basis. The investment dealer's fee is chargeable to organization expense and can be amortized over the succeeding five to ten years. This procedure is followed by the most informed new firm planners who desire growth. It should be investigated for appropriateness by many more. Details for forming a corporation are covered in Chapter 8.

The raising of funds described above is called "private placement" of limited share distribution. When stock market conditions are depressed, this financing route can be an important alternative to the public distribution of the company's shares—"going public."

Each province has a *Securities Act*, as well as several other laws affecting and controlling the raising of funds for business purposes from the general public. Securities Commissions in the provinces regulate public offerings of corporation securities, investigate and scrutinize the people involved in the companies' affairs, and the companies' books, and ascertain that the offering "prospectus" includes a full, true, and plain disclosure of all relevant facts—in general, to safeguard the public interest. In addition, certain rules are enforced by the various stock exchanges, by the Investment Dealers Association in Canada, and by the Broker-Dealer Association in Ontario to ensure and to maintain an ethical standard of conduct by its members. It should be noted that the public distribution of shares is an expensive source of funds for the small- or medium-sized business. A share issue will cost from $100,000 to $300,000 in legal and accounting fees and commissions; offerings of less than $2 million are just not practical any more. With public ownership there are many statutory obligations for increased disclosure of company information, regulatory reporting, and the like.

Other Miscellaneous Sources of Funds   Most of the other miscellaneous sources of funds are more available to going concerns than to persons who need financial aid for a newly planned business. If the new firm has equipment paid for through investment by the owner, if it has an inventory of merchandise that is free and clear, or if it has some accounts receivable from other sources that are being invested in the firm, loans against these can usually be obtained. *Commercial finance companies* are available in every town and most make loans against this type of collateral. Similar companies will make credit available in "floor planning" arrangements to make merchandise available. Others will purchase installment-loan contracts from the small firm owner. *Insurance companies* sometimes engage in long-term loans to substantial small business firms. These are usually secured by mortgages on real estate. *Personal finance companies* will make personal loans to small firm owners with precise repayment schedules. In the types of small firms where *factors* or *sales agents* (firms that handle all of a small business's receivables or sales) are used to handle the bulk of the firm's business, working capital is often advanced to the firm by such factors or sales agents. The textile industry is the most prominent example of this type of business activity.

Ontario, Quebec, and Nova Scotia are utilizing government incentives to private individuals to set up financial enterprises investing in small business and to private individuals or corporations investing in such enterprises. The size, financial structure, and activities of these companies are regulated by provincial law, but they remain private enterprises. In Ontario, the Small Business Development Corporations (SBDC), in Quebec, the Cooperative Development Corporation (CDC), and in Nova Scotia, the Venture Capital Corporations (VCC) operate much in the same way and are indeed a very good and likely source of funds to small businesses in these provinces.

Leasing Companies   These may be sources of funds for the acquisition of a wide variety of assets, including land and buildings, machinery and equipment, vehicles, fixtures, etc. Frequently, substantial cash may be generated by the sale and leaseback of a building owned by the business.

Venture Capital Funding   Small businesses may sometimes (albeit not too often) qualify for investment funds from venture capital firms. These companies provide equity and loan capital to potentially high-growth small companies.

When applying to a venture capital firm, it is absolutely essential to provide it with a *comprehensive business plan*. If it passes the first screening, the venture capitalist will investigate further and examine "with due diligence" the product, the technology, potential market share, competitive situation, financial requirements and projections, and, most importantly, the *competence of management*.

After the venture capitalist decides to make an investment, it usually will do so in return for part ownership in the business (common or preference shares) and/or by the provision of direct loan with share purchase options. Typically, a venture capital firm will not seek controlling interest in the business. However, it will try to protect its investment by being able to assume control if the small firm gets into financial trouble. Most chartered accounting firms, bankers, the FBDB, or financial consultants could refer a business to appropriate and suitable members of the Association of Canadian Venture Capital companies.

QUESTIONS FOR CLASS DISCUSSION

1   Why is it important for new firm planners to have some capital of their own to invest?

2   Do you think it is advisable to borrow from relatives and friends to raise capital to start a business?

3   How can loans from relatives and friends be made more businesslike?

4   What are the pros and cons of having partners in your business?

5   Are shareholders creditors or owners? Explain.

6   Are there possible dangers in borrowing too much, even if funds may be available? Explain.

7   What is the Federal Business Development Bank?

8   What is trade credit? Is it usually more expensive than bank loans?

9   Can trade credit be used in planning a new firm? How?

10   What other miscellaneous sources of funds may be used by small business firms?

11   Why do established firms have less trouble in getting outside financial assistance than newly planned firms?

12   How do equipment suppliers help provide financing for a new firm?

13   Does our government assist small firms in obtaining financing? How?

14   Do you believe that the formation of private business development companies to assist new small firms should be expanded?

Projects for Home Assignment and/or Class Discussion

1   Explain how you would distinguish between short-term, intermediate, and long-term capital if you were raising $100,000 to finance a new clothing store. Would you assure that the firm had a 50 per cent proprietorship ratio? How?

2   Explain how the investment of others can contribute to the proprietorship ratio of the firm rather than increasing the borrowed capital.

3   Can you explain the most popular forms of trade credit that would be used by a men's clothing store? Do you recommend its use?

REFERENCES FOR FURTHER READING

Archer, M., *An Introduction to Canadian Business*, 5th ed., McGraw-Hill Ryerson Ltd., Toronto, 1986, Chapters 13, 14, and 17.

Beckman, M.D., W.S. Good, and R.G. Wyckham, *Small Business Management*, John Wiley & Sons Canada Ltd., Toronto, 1982, Chapter 7.

Cunningham, G., *Buy Yourself A Job & Be Your Own Boss*, McGraw-Hill Ryerson Ltd., 1990, Chapter 6.

Kao, R.W.Y., *Small Business Management: A Strategic Emphasis*, 2nd ed., Holt, Rinehart and Winston of Canada, Ltd., Toronto, 1984, Chapters 3 and 8.

Knight, R.M., *Small Business Management in Canada*, McGraw-Hill Ryerson Ltd., Toronto, 1981, Chapter 8.

Minding Your Own Business, Federal Business Development Bank, Montreal, 1982, Volume 1, Chapters 4 and 6 and Vol. 2, Chapter 2.

. . . .

C h a p t e r

12

Determining the Assets to Be Used

LEARNING OBJECTIVES

After reading this chapter, you will be able to:
1. Identify the kinds of current and fixed assets needed to operate a business
2. Know the real dangers of underestimating assets needed to operate the business
3. Know the rules for determining the amount of cash needed before opening the doors
4. Identify the methods used to determine the necessary fixed asset capital required for the new business
5. Put together a statement of the assets to be used for the new firm
6. Know what the considerations and decisions should be for constructing an opening day balance sheet
7. Understand the methods of financing the assets needed and how to include the financing arrangements on the balance sheet

8. **D**etermine the best options for providing assets on the opening day balance sheet
9. **C**ompare the leasing of assets to the purchasing of them, including the advantages and disadvantages
10. **M**ake the necessary adjustments to the opening day balance sheet to have it conform with appropriate financial ratios

Every new firm needs various kinds of assets with which to begin operations. Cash assets are needed for working capital; cash funds are needed to invest in accounts receivable; inventories are a large asset that must be purchased. Buildings and land are expensive assets that must be acquired by purchase or rented. Supplies are assets that must be purchased. Prepaid insurance policies must be provided and premiums paid. Machinery, store fixtures and equipment, and office furniture and fixtures are other assets that must be provided for the firm. Perhaps delivery trucks need to be purchased.

One of the most common causes of financial difficulty for a new firm is the owners' failure to look seriously at the total asset requirements of the firm in the planning stage. Too many new firms open their doors literally "on a wing and a prayer," only to find that they have not anticipated or provided all the various assets needed to start operations properly. Too often the result is the necessity for then acquiring needed assets through expensive and dangerous financing or appropriating anticipated profits in advance to buy the assets that should have been provided from initial investment capital.

To avoid these dangers, the planner should analyze the firm by listing every asset the business will need. The result will be a *statement of assets to be used.* This statement can be compared to the left side (asset side) of a balance sheet.

PROCEDURE FOR DEVELOPING ASSET REQUIREMENTS

Preparing a list of all types of assets needed does not necessitate concern over their cost or how they will be provided. We can assume that cost is not a consideration at this point. In a later planning step, we will decide how to provide these assets or the services they render. In that process, we can learn much about how the business economy really works as it supplies credit, financial loans, or services under various circumstances.

The important thing at this point is that we listed every asset of every kind that the business will need. The new student will recall that assets were defined in Chapter 10 as "things owned." They can be in the form of cash, claims against others, inventories, supplies, buildings, fixtures and equipment, delivery trucks, and prepaid insurance policies. All require investment capital; all are basic assets the new firm will need.

Continuing the example of a newly planned firm, Jones Hardware Company, from Chapter 7, we have produced a budgeted income statement to serve as a guide to operations for the first year. The new firm planner must now develop a statement of assets to be used to list all the things (assets) that will be needed to operate the firm at the level indicated on the budgeted income statement.

As we have contemplated the firm's asset needs, let us assume that we have found the following assets to be essential:

Cash

Capital to carry accounts receivable

Merchandise inventory (the amount here is provided from the budgeted income statement)

Prepaid supplies

Prepaid insurance

Land and buildings

Store fixtures

Office furniture and fixtures

Delivery truck(s)

The listing of assets can be entitled a "Statement of Assets to Be Used."

We can now turn our attention to finding a dollar value to attach to each asset and/or to determining how much cash the firm should have on hand when all noncash assets have been provided. We can find out how much cash will be needed to cover our planned investment in accounts receivable. Market prices can be used to give dollar amounts to the noncash assets. Details for these calculations and conservative rules relating to them are as follows:

Cash on Hand   How much cash should the firm have on hand? The suggested conservative rule for a merchandising firm is: *Cash should equal the out-of-pocket operating expenses for the period of one turnover of the merchandise inventory.* This will seem extremely conservative for some types of firms. Unless positive reasons for relaxing the general rule are identified, however, good management demands adherence to it.

How would we find this amount for our planned firm? First, go back to the budgeted income statement (see Table 9-2) and find that total operating expenses for the first year are planned at $46,000. This figure must be divided into out-of-pocket and noncash expenditures. The out-of-pocket expenses are those paid in cash by the firm in the form of cheques written or petty cash expenditures. Noncash expenditures are those that are recorded in the expenses but do not result in the firm's actually giving up cash—such as depreciation expenses on buildings, store equipment, or office furniture and fixtures.

If $10,000 of the total year expenses of $46,000 represents noncash expenditures, the balance of $36,000 is the total of out-of-pocket expenses for the first year. This amount represents $3,000 per month ($36,000 divided by twelve). Our merchandise turnover is four times per year, or once every three months. We must therefore provide three months of out-of-pocket expenses as our cash requirement under our rule. Three times $3,000 is $9,000, which is our cash requirement for opening day.

The calculation of the cash requirement may be more easily understood this way. Merely divide the annual out-of-pocket expenses by the merchandise turnover. Thus, in our example here, the annual out-of-pocket expenses are $36,000. Divide this total by the merchandise turnover of four and we get the same $9,000 answer.

If the merchandise inventory turnover were six times per year, the cash requirement would be $6,000 ($36,000 divided by six). If the turnover were once every forty-five days (one-eighth of a 360-day business year), the cash requirement would be $4,500 ($36,000 divided by eight). These figures demonstrate the variable nature of the cash requirement and how our rule allows for this variance. The higher the inventory turnover, the lower is the requirement for cash on hand.

Service firms do not normally carry an inventory of merchandise. The conservative cash rule for service firms is: *Cash on hand should be sufficient to pay out-of-pocket expenses for three months.*

Funds to Carry Accounts Receivable   New firms which decide to sell on credit to approved customers and plan to carry the accounts receivable on their books cannot neglect the fact that they will have money invested in those accounts receivable. They may, of course, decide to sell on established credit cards only. In this way the credit card company advances the account balances to them, usually monthly, less its charge for the service. Various credit card companies have arrangements that cost the firm from 3 to 10 per cent of the amount of the sales for their service to the business firm. Such charges represent a true sales discount to the firm and must be accounted for in pricing policy. If the firm has many customers who prefer to use credit cards, this may be the most desirable method of operation. If the new firm has limited capital resources, this fact may encourage a decision to make credit sales on credit cards only. In exchange for the credit card company's charges, the firm is protected against loss on bad debts and the expenses of administering its own credit policy. It should be noted, however, that a well-managed credit policy usually has bad-debt losses that are less than the average credit-card company charges. Another alternative available to new firms is to sell for cash only. This policy defies the truism that firms selling on credit will sell more merchandise to the same customers if credit is available.

If the firm is able to carry its own accounts receivable, it can usually make the credit operation pay its own way when it charges for the credit privilege, such as in installment sales contracts or interest on monthly balances. Small firms have not exercised these possibilities nearly as much as the larger firms that have credit plans available for their customers. Details of credit policies are discussed in Chapter 27.

Financial difficulties may be encountered by the small firm that decides to carry its own receivables and is not financially prepared to tie up much of its working capital in such an asset. The proprietor who believes that all credit accounts are paid in full on the first of the following month is due for a great surprise when he or she gets into operation. The question therefore arises, "How much investment capital should be provided to carry accounts receivable?"

The conservative rule suggested here for firms planning to carry their own receivables is: *Sufficient working capital to carry 1½ to 2 times the credit sales in maximum credit period.* Applying this rule to our planned firm, we must first determine what percentage of the planned annual sales of $200,000 will be on credit. If experience and/or available statistics show that about 30 per cent of the sales are on credit, we will use $60,000. This means that credit sales average $5,000 per month. If the maximum credit period is thirty days, we should plan on 1½ to 2 times the monthly credit sales to be invested in accounts receivable by the end of the first year of operation. This means $7,500 to $10,000. The variation will be determined by the strictness of the credit-granting policy and the follow-up policies adopted on collections.

We can see from the foregoing comments why many small firms decide to absorb the credit card company charges or to discount their sales contracts with finance companies. It is indeed sad to observe a company that has a good current ratio but is unable to pay its current bills because too much cash is tied up in delinquent accounts receivable or slow-moving inventory that has not been converted into cash according to a planned schedule.

Merchandise Inventory   In the calculations for the budgeted income statement, we found that an inventory of $32,500 was necessary to support contemplated sales. We must accept this figure for the statement of assets to be used.

Prepaid Supplies and Insurance   After studying the need for supplies of various kinds and learning the insurance costs for the policies we decide we must have, we total the costs of these items. This figure becomes the dollar amount for the statement of assets to be used. We can use $1,000 for our illustration.

Land and Building   Even though we do not plan even to consider buying the land and building to be used by our firm, it is good business experience to find out what they would cost if that were our plan of operation. Landlords are not philanthropists and we would not desire that they be so. There are distinct advantages to renting as against buying, and there are also advantages to owning your own building. These considerations will be discussed later. At this time, we should get a cost estimate for the type of land and building we plan for our operation. Such an expenditure, when undertaken, is usually the largest single investment for the typical small firm.

If available land in your desired area is priced at $1,600 per front metre for a fifteen-metre lot, its cost would be $24,000. If the building you want calls for 200 square metres and construction costs are $150 per square metre, its cost would be $30,000. Such investments can be financed after a good down payment. The mistake often made, however, is believing that the mortgage principal payments are an operating expense. Such principal repayments do not come out of operating expenses but must be paid out of the net profits from operation or some new, additional investment capital must be provided to make such payments. Similar consideration must be given to providing all the fixed assets for the firm. When these are purchased on credit contracts (conditional sales contracts), the payments towards principal are not operating expenses but must also come out of the net profits or new investment capital. Many potentially successful small firms have been forced to close their doors because of this mistake in financial planning.

For the purposes here, we insert $40,000 on our statement of assets to be used as the value of land and buildings. A final decision on the matter of renting or building will be made when we make the transition to an opening day balance sheet.

Store Fixtures, Office Furniture and Fixtures   The important thing here is that as a new firm planner, we clearly understand our needs for these items. We can obtain prices from several suppliers and insert the appropriate one in the statement of assets. We will use $7,000 for our illustration – $5,000 for store fixtures and $2,000 for office furniture and fixtures.

Delivery Truck   For the purposes of this statement of assets, assume that you will purchase a delivery truck. We do not have to make the decision now about whether to use the other methods of making deliveries. Accordingly, insert $3,500 as the cost of the truck.

When we have obtained dollar amounts for all the items, we can refine our statement, as shown in Table 12-1.

TABLE 12-1

STATEMENT OF ASSETS TO BE USED

Cash	$ 9,000
Funds to finance accounts receivable	7,500
Merchandise inventory	32,500
Prepaid expenses (supplies and insurance)	1,000
Land and buildings	40,000
Store fixtures	5,000
Office furniture and fixtures	2,000
Delivery truck	3,500
Total assets required	$100,500

The new firm planners who have approximately $20,000 to invest may easily get discouraged when they see that the firm will use more than $100,000 of assets. They should not. It is good to realize that the firm will actually use the dollar amount of assets if things go as planned. It is good to appreciate how business institutions are interwoven, what credit means to the total business economy, and what alternatives there are in providing these assets for the firm. We will demonstrate that the firm can be started with the $20,000 and provide a sound capital structure when we proceed to an opening day balance sheet.

To relieve any early discouragement, we can point out several very obvious factors. First, the amount provided for investment in accounts receivable does not have to be available on opening day. The whole consideration here was to warn the new planners that they will have capital invested in these accounts during the first year. Second, new planners may quickly determine that they will rent a store space rather than build and thus eliminate a $40,000 investment. Third, credit must be considered available in providing the other assets. Good management should always take advantage of available free credit. We will look again at all these items in Chapter 27.

DEVELOPING AN OPENING DAY BALANCE SHEET

We have seen earlier in this chapter and in our study of assets which will be needed to operate the planned business that a total of $100,500 would be required to finance all these assets if they were paid for outright by the proprietor. People with abundant personal capital might be satisfied just to go ahead and buy all these things and get started. Such people often decide not even to finance the land and building that we know to be necessary. A person with a modest amount of personal assets to invest would go to the opposite extreme and use every possible assistance in the form of credit. There are options between these extremes. Some of them are:

1   Invest $100,500 and buy all the assets outright. The business would then start without liabilities of any kind.

2   Finance construction of the building and purchase of the land and plan to make the mortgage payments out of profits or other capital to be obtained later.

3   Decide to rent a store space instead of investing $40,000 in order to own your own building.

4   Decide to sell on credit only to customers who have approved credit cards.

5   Purchase the inventory with a minimum down payment and pay the balance as the merchandise is sold.

6   Finance the acquisition of store fixtures, office furniture and fixtures, and the delivery truck on available twenty-four month contracts, which are obtainable after 25 per cent down payment has been made.

7   Decide to open the doors with less than the required cash on
hand; give credit on open account, even though proper capital is
not on hand; carry the receivables on the books in the hope that
all will be collected on the first of each month; provide fewer than
the desired store fixtures in the hope that the future profits will
provide money to buy more later; leave the delivery service to a
hit-or-miss arrangement with deliveries being made in the
proprietor's personal car whenever a family member can be left in
charge of the store.

Option 7 is included only because it demonstrates the errors made altogether too often by new firms. Adopting this plan defies all the planning we
have been talking about and makes the firm immediately susceptible to the risk
of failure. Such action is not even a calculated risk. It is foolhardy action which
constitutes an invitation to failure.

Each of the other alternatives bears investigation. Final choices must be
governed by such basic considerations as:

1   We anticipate $24,000 net profit before income taxes. (We
originally planned on $15,000, but our market survey showed a
potential sales volume that would produce $24,000 profit.)

2   Unless other investment capital is known to be available (including
a possible loan from Grandma or Uncle John), we cannot let the
payment of the liabilities incurred in the provision of the assets cut
into our planned profits to the point that the proprietor's family
expenses are impaired.

3   We cannot minimize the cash and inventory needs that have been
carefully calculated in our planning.

4   It is good business to use any credit that is available without
charge.

5   Excessive interest charges should be avoided whenever possible.
The fact that interest expense is a deductible income tax item is
little solace if profits disappear and there is nothing left on which
to pay any tax.

PROCEDURE FOR DEVELOPING A BALANCE SHEET

The development of an opening day balance sheet necessitates making
decisions on how each of the assets or services is to be provided. The decisions
will vary with the individual owner. As hypothetical proprietors, we have the
following facts or constraints to assist us in making these decisions:

1   We have about $20,000 to invest.

2   We will rent an excellent building located at the desirable site
previously chosen. This will eliminate the large investment required

to purchase the building. The landlord will now have funds invested in the building. Our planner will now show rent expense on the income statement, rather than a building on the balance sheet.

3   Uncle John has indicated a willingness to loan us up to $15,000 on a five-year note with only the interest to be paid for the five years until the principal of the note becomes due. This is called a balloon note.

4   A wholesaler in our line has offered the usual terms in this type of business if they can sell us most of the inventory. These terms are 50 per cent down and 50 per cent in thirty days with no interest charge.

5   We have found a delivery truck, slightly used, which we can purchase for $2,000 with $800 down payment and monthly payments of $100 plus interest for one year.

6   We must have the new store equipment, but we find slightly used desks, files, and office machines, which are available for $1,000 cash and which will meet the needs for office furniture and fixtures.

7   The store fixtures and equipment (showcases, shelving, window displays, cash registers) can all be bought from one firm with 50 per cent down and 50 per cent due in one year.

8   We have decided to push credit card sales and reduce the open accounts receivable we carry on our books. We expect this to reduce the amount we will need for our investment in these accounts. We will accordingly keep $6,250 in our savings account, where it will earn interest until it is needed to maintain current debt payment. We will list this on our opening day balance sheet as "other bank accounts." If this $6,250 were in the form of government bonds or other readily saleable securities, we could list it as "marketable securities."

Against this background of soundly gathered information, the proprietors are now in a position to make a first draft of an opening day balance sheet and test it for financial soundness. With explanatory comments, it would look like Table 12-2.

PUTTING THE OPENING DAY BALANCE SHEET TOGETHER

Remember that our opening day balance sheet must provide for each of the assets found to be necessary for proper planning, as reflected in the statement of assets to be used that was developed in the previous chapter. Our basic decisions, or constraints, listed on the preceding page, tell us how each of those

TABLE 12-2

P.M. JONES COMPANY
OPENING DAY BALANCE SHEET
NOVEMBER 1, 199–

ASSETS

Current assets:

Cash on hand (as per calculation in statement of assets to be used)	$ 9,000	
Other bank accounts	6,250*	
Merchandise inventory	32,500	
Prepaid expenses (supplies, insurance, etc.)	1,000	
Total current assets		$48,750

Fixed assets:

Store fixtures (half cash, half credit)	$ 5,000	
Office furniture and fixtures (paid for in cash)	1,000	
Delivery truck ($800 cash, $1,200 credit)	2,000	
Total fixed assets		8,000
Total assets		$56,750

LIABILITIES

Current liabilities:

Accounts payable (due to wholesalers for balance of beginning inventory)	$16,250	
Contract payable (one-year note on store equipment)	2,500	
Notes payable (delivery truck)	1,200	
Total current liabilities		$19,950

Long-term liabilities:

Notes payable (five-year loan from Uncle John)	$15,000	
Total fixed liabilities		15,000
Total liabilities		$34,950

NET WORTH

P.M. Jones, proprietorship	21,800†
Total liabilities plus net worth	$56,750

* Funds held until needed to finance accounts receivable.
† Assets, $56,750 − Liabilities, $34,950 = Net Worth, $21,800

assets will be provided. The balance sheet lists all assets at full purchase price. Amounts owed on any of them are shown as liabilities.

We cannot compromise with proper cash on hand, so we first insert $9,000 cash on hand as a current asset. Next, we list the $6,250 as other bank accounts, which represents the funds we will hold to finance our accounts receivable. (Remember we reduced this amount from the $7,500 listed in the statement of assets to be used via a basic policy decision in our constraints in the preceding section.)

Next, we list the full value of the inventory purchased, $32,500, as merchandise inventory. But we are not paying for the entire purchase now, so we list 50 per cent of this amount as a current liability—accounts payable, $16,250. Then we can list as prepaid expenses the full value of these items (supplies and insurance—$1,000), which we pay for in full before opening day.

In the fixed asset section we can list the full purchase price of the store fixtures ($5,000), the office furniture and fixtures ($1,000), and the delivery truck ($2,000). But we received some help in providing these by incurring some liabilities to cover the balance of their purchase prices. Therefore, we must list the $2,500 contract payable on the store fixtures as a current liability and the $1,200 still owed on the delivery truck as notes payable. We were also provided with $15,000 cash by Uncle John. This is not due, except for interest, for five years, so we list that note payable as a fixed liability.

If we now total our current and fixed assets, we find that we have total assets of $56,750. Our total current and fixed liabilities are $34,950. Following our basic accounting equation that assets minus liabilities equals proprietorship, we subtract the liabilities of $34,950 from the assets of $56,750 and find that Jones' needed proprietorship is $21,800. We then insert the proprietorship account in our balance sheet for this amount and we have a completed opening day balance sheet.

As our fledgling proprietors review this first draft of a proposed opening day balance sheet, they should apply the ratio analysis, which we studied in Chapter 10. We will find that we have proposed a current ratio in excess of two to one (current assets, $48,750, divided by current liabilities, $19,950), which is good. The quick ratio proposed is substantially less than the desired one to one (cash plus receivables, $15,250, divided by current liabilities, $19,950). The reason seems to be our decision about reducing the capital necessary to finance the receivables. The proprietorship ratio is less than 50 per cent (proprietorship, $21,800, divided by total assets, $56,750). The 50 per cent minimum would require an investment of $28,375 by Jones.

If we are to strictly apply the rules we have learned about financial soundness and ratio analysis, we would go back to the drawing board and make adjustments to bring the deficient ratios into line. Possibilities which appear are:

1   Do not buy the delivery truck, thus eliminating a $2,000 truck on the asset side and a $1,200 liability. This would add the $800

down payment to cash. It would also necessitate adding the cost of a hired delivery service to the operating expenses on the income statement.

2   Request that the contract on the store fixtures be lengthened to two years, thus making half the balance due a fixed liability (amounts due more than one year hence) rather than a current liability, all of which must be paid in one year.

3   Ask Uncle John to become a partner, silent or active as he desires. Offer him 5 per cent of profits as an inducement. His note payable of $15,000 would thus be eliminated and we would have two proprietorship accounts in the net worth section of the balance sheet. Partners are co-owners, not creditors. This can be significant. You maintain control and your silent partner can be inactive and happy as you succeed. See Chapter 8 for more on this matter.

4   Incorporate the business and give Uncle John preference shares for his inducement (see Chapter 8).

If suggestions 1 and 2 plus either 3 or 4 were enacted into the financial plan, the proprietorship ratio would be well above the 50 per cent minimum, the quick ratio would be improved, and the current ratio would be even better.

Proving again that principles should be adapted rather than always adopted, we can find some justification for the balance sheet suggested in the first rough draft. Its strengths and supporting facts include a good current ratio, a rich uncle who can be available in case of pressing financial needs, a variable policy that may be applied to the present program for giving credit, and the possibility for discounting receivables via a bank loan. The availability of other funds for investment by Mr. Jones without placing a second mortgage on his home would be another strength.

When an opening day plan is finally adopted, the reader may ask, "Where is Mr. Jones' $21,800 now?" The organizing procedure begins with placing this amount and the $15,000 collected from Uncle John in a bank account in the company's name. Total deposit is $36,800. In our illustration, we have paid out $16,250 as the down payment on the merchandise inventory; we have paid out $800 as down payment on the delivery truck; we have paid out $2,500 on the store equipment and $1,000 for the office furniture; we have paid out $1,000 cash for prepaid expenses (supplies and insurance). The total of these cheques written on the bank account is $21,550. This amount, plus the $9,000 on hand in cash and the $6,250 in the savings account, totals $36,800, the total cash invested by Jones ($21,800) and by Uncle John ($15,000).

While it would be desirable for Mr. Jones to make the suggested changes in the first draft balance sheet, if the potential strengths listed do actually exist it would appear that cautious management of funds should enable him to proceed accordingly. Each proprietor must decide what exceptions to the rule

TABLE 12-3

P.M. JONES COMPANY:
LIABILITIES AND NET WORTH
AS PARTNERSHIP AND AS CORPORATION

PARTNERSHIP

LIABILITIES

Current liabilities:		
Accounts payable	$16,250	
Contract payable	2,500	
Note payable	1,200	
Total current liabilities		$19,950
Fixed liabilities		0
Total liabilities		$19,950

NET WORTH

P.M. Jones, capital	$21,800
Uncle John, capital	15,000
Total net worth	$36,800
Total liabilities	$56,750

CORPORATION

LIABILITIES

Current liabilities:		
Accounts payable	$16,250	
Contract payable	2,500	
Note payable	1,200	
Total current liabilities		$19,950
Long-term liabilities		0
Total liabilities		$19,950

NET WORTH

Preference shares outstanding	$15,000
Common shares outstanding	21,800
Total capital	$36,800
Total liabilities plus net worth	$56,750

he or she will undertake. Most important is that each knows the rules of sound financing and knows when they are in violation.

Lest we forget, we should remind ourselves that we have now produced a plan or plans for soundly financing a business that will utilize more than $100,000 of the world's limited assets with an owner investment of $21,800. Remembering that accomplishment provides an understanding of how the business economy operates.

BALANCE SHEET VARIATIONS FOR PROPRIETORSHIPS, PARTNERSHIPS, AND CORPORATIONS

The opening day balance sheet that we develop for the P.M. Jones Company, Table 12-2, shows that there is only one owner, Mr. Jones. This is a proprietorship form of legal operation. We reviewed the different legal forms of organization in Chapter 8. It is valuable here, however, to see how our opening day balance sheet would look if we had adopted the alternative of making Uncle John a partner, or if we had incorporated and sold him preference shares.

Only the right side of the balance sheet shown in Table 12-2 would have been changed in either situation. Table 12-3 shows in the first column how the right side of the balance sheet would look under the partnership suggestion. Column 2 shows how it would look as a corporation.

QUESTIONS FOR CLASS DISCUSSION

1   Why should a new firm have funds available to carry any accounts receivable it develops on the books?
2   What is meant by "going back to the drawing board" if our ratio analysis of the planned opening day balance sheet is very bad?
3   Why is it important to have a current ratio of two to one on the opening day balance sheet?
4   Why would a new business planner refuse all types of credit available?
5   What is the biggest danger in using too much credit?
6   "Payments on contracts to buy fixed assets come out of planned profits and are not operating expenses, which are deducted before profits are determined." Explain.
7   What is meant by the term *trading on too thin an equity*?
8   What does a proprietorship ratio of 50 per cent mean when measuring the soundness of the financial structure on the proposed balance sheet?

9   If the first rough draft of the proposed balance sheet fails to meet the standard ratio analysis, what should the planner do?

10 What is the error involved in ignoring high interest charges paid because "such charges are deductible for income tax purposes"?

11 Do you recall how we measured current assets? Current liabilities? Do you think these rules are too conservative?

12 In the example of the P.M. Jones Company, Mr. Jones and Uncle John invested a total of $36,800. Where is that cash now? Who provided the balance of the $56,750 of total assets now invested? Explain.

13 If a person invests in a delivery truck for a business as part of the total investment, is that truck an asset of the firm?

14 Is it possible to accurately determine in advance all the assets a business will need when it starts operations? Explain.

15 What is the conservative rule for determining how much cash a firm should have on hand? Explain the rule with an example.

16 Why is it necessary to consider whether or not sales will be made on account when evaluating total asset needs?

17 If credit sales are to be made, how much investment to carry the accounts receivable should be planned?

18 What are the pros and cons of making credit sales only on the basis of credit cards held by customers?

19 Should small business owners know the costs of the land and building even though they plan to rent? Why?

20 Can someone with only $20,000 to invest establish and control a business that requires $97,000 of assets? What are some of the alternatives?

21 What are the pros and cons of doing business with family members who help finance your new firm?

22 "Good management takes advantage of any free credit available." Do you agree? Why?

Projects for Home Assignment and/or Class Discussion

1   a How would you define a statement of assets to be used?
    b Prepare all account titles you would expect to find on a statement of assets to be used for a drugstore when the owner will own the building, will give credit to customers, which will be carried on the firm's books, will own its own truck for delivery service, and will have regular purchases of inventory products on credit.

2   How does the case requirement for service firms vary from that of a product retailer? Explain with an example of each.

3 Do you agree that firms that plan to carry their own accounts receivable should plan investment capital to do so? Explain how this can become important.

4 Explain what is meant by pointing out that every new firm planner should set up the constraints (or basic facts) that must be recognized in developing an opening day balance sheet. Give some examples.

5 Where will you find the dollar value for the merchandise inventory that is used on the opening day balance sheet?

6 Do you agree that liabilities due within one year should be classified as current liabilities on the balance sheet when only assets that convert into cash within ninety days are considered current assets? Explain your answer. Include the effects on financial liquidity of the firm if this rule is followed.

7 Explain where we would place Aunt Phoebe's investment in the original financing of the firm:
a. if her money were a five-year loan;
b. if we made her a full-fledged partner;
c. if she bought some of our capital shares.

REFERENCES FOR FURTHER READING

Cunningham, G., *Buy Yourself A Job & Be Your Own Boss*, McGraw-Hill Ryerson Ltd., 1990, Chapter 9.

Meigs, W.B., R.F. Meigs, and W.P. Lam, *Accounting: The Basis for Business Decisions*, 6th Canadian Edition, McGraw-Hill Ryerson Ltd., Toronto, 1991, Chapter 2.

Tate Jr., C.E., L.C. Megginson, C.R. Scott Jr., and L.R. Trueblood, *Successful Small Business Management*, 3rd ed., Business Publications, Inc., Plano, Texas, 1985, Chapter 19.

Minding Your Own Business, Federal Business Development Bank, Montreal, 1982, Vol. 1, Chapter 8.

"Planning and Budgeting," *Your Business Matters*, The Royal Bank of Canada, 1985.

PART

4

MARKETING
DEVELOPMENT

Location of the Firm

LEARNING OBJECTIVES

After reading this chapter, you will be able to:

1. **K**now the importance of location and site selection to business success and how to define each
2. **U**se the information compiled from the experiences of others and know where to find that information
3. **U**nderstand the factors that affect the selection of a location and site for a retail firm
4. **U**se a rating sheet to assist in comparing different sites
5. **K**now the considerations involved in selecting a location and site for a manufacturing firm, a wholesale firm, and a service firm

People in the field of real estate loudly proclaim that there are three factors that determine the value of property—either as an investment or for profitable business operations. Those three factors are:

1   Location
2   Location, and
3   Location

Business experience seems to indicate that real estate people know more about choosing proper locations for small firms than many of the small firm owners who learn belatedly what constitutes a good versus a less desirable location. Location merits some advance planning by those who would establish a new small firm. There are important guidelines, and we will review some of them here. Location is important for retailing, wholesaling, manufacturing, and service firms alike.

The subject of location is indeed a very large one. Many entire texts have been written on this one problem. At best, we can only point out some of the highlights here.

Small firm owners should distinguish between general location factors and site factors. In this sense, *location* means the region, the province, the county, or the city which represents the general market area for the planned firm. The *site* factors are the particular street, the corner, and the building within the location area. The advantages of a good location can be minimized by a poor site.

Courtesy of Chembiomed Ltd.

In the early 1980s the three fastest growing metropolitan areas in Canada were Calgary, Saskatoon, and Edmonton. This means that expanded markets were developing in these areas. In isolation, these growing markets suggest that these areas would be good places in which to establish new firms. It would be foolhardy, however, to think that there are not many other areas of the country where location of a new firm would be desirable. Moreover, not all types of firms are needed in all growing areas. We must investigate even general location factors more closely.

Small business failures often reflect complete neglect of a consideration of specific location factors. Too many small firms are established in locations because a store space happened to be available for rent. Most students can probably recall a section of their home towns that became known as the cemetery for small firms. New ones come and go every year. Business firms which otherwise would have been quite successful suffer from the start when not properly located. Some new proprietors have as the prominent factor in their choice of location such things as a desire to live in their home town, to be close to friends or relatives, to locate in a climate they prefer, to be close to a particular religious group, to be near a particular ethnic group. Others attach a certain social atmosphere to their location. In themselves, these factors may not be bad for choosing a location, but it is important that within these considerations, the proper location and proper site be chosen. Never should a particular store space be selected merely because it is available without subjecting it to some specific tests of suitability. Being well known in one's home town can be a great advantage if other considerations are in line. Knowing the population and its atmosphere, the mode of living and something of the business climate in the home town, and being known to your bankers can all be advantageous for a new proprietor if he or she chooses a location consistent with the considerations we will discuss.

If planners are not restricted by a desire to locate in a particular town or region but are looking for a location anywhere in the country, they can apply all the following general considerations.

LOCATION FACTORS FOR RETAILING

1 Industry   Study the industry of the area under consideration. Payrolls create buying power for your potential customers, and unless their permanence and growth seem probable, it is probably unwise for you to make a big investment.

The ideal location is a community with substantial permanent industry, an upward trend in community payrolls, diversified and stable industries, and a minimum of seasonality in the total activity. Seasonal business firms can be very successful. The important thing is to know the facts about the seasonal variations.

2 Population   Study the nature of the population in the area. Many students seem surprised to learn that there are many areas of our country where the population has actually decreased in recent years. Declining, stationary, or small populations do not suggest new firms for the area. Growing populations and wealthy populations desiring the goods or services you propose to offer in an expanding population area represent ideal situations. The mode of living of the community under consideration must be studied. The authors recall the proprietor of a small hardware store on the ground floor of a twenty-storey apartment building complaining about his lack of sales of garden hoses. When asked if apartment dwellers buy many garden hoses, he realized that the mode of living of most of his customers did not require many of such a product.

Study your potential market area in terms of the needs and desires of the people you want to serve. Are they home owners? Are they renters? Do they live in apartments? Are the rents high, low, or medium? Condominium owners may have a different mode of living than apartment renters. Another factor in the mode of living in a particular area is the general character of the population. Is it composed mostly of older people, a dominant religious group? Are the people native-born, mostly foreign-born, or a truly mixed group?

3 Competition   Know your competition in advance. Our free enterprise system is based upon competition. Our business history has proved that customers are best served when healthy competition prevails. Competition should not be feared. It should be known and coped with.

The two time-honoured justifications for opening a new firm in an existing line of business are (a) an expanded market and (b) presence of inefficient firms. Expanded markets are almost always the result of expanding populations. The trend of our population to the cities in recent years has provided the basis for many new firms. Much of this population growth, of course, has been in the suburbs of the larger cities. The attendant growth of sales and new firms in the suburbs has been one of the outstanding characteristics of our recent business history.

As mentioned earlier, new planners can learn a great deal about a particular area relative to its population growth and existing competition. Chambers of commerce, trade development associations, county industrial planning boards, and similar organizations can provide details about many areas. Cities are divided into census tracts or other smaller areas for various purposes. The population of each is usually recorded annually and is available at least by census years.

When the population of an area is compared with the number of competing firms, a first conclusion can be made as to whether or not the area needs another firm in this field. For example, if it takes 700 people to maintain a modern grocery store and the area now has a grocery store for every 500 people, the conclusion, on this basis, must be that this is not a good place to establish another store. The total market has not expanded. If there is only one grocery store for 1200 people, the evidence suggests this is a good location. Table 13-1 shows the size of population necessary to support various types of retail stores.

TABLE 13-1

POPULATION REQUIREMENTS FOR VARIOUS TYPES OF RETAIL STORES*

Camera and photography supplies	40 000
Drugs	2 500
Dry goods	25 000
Florist shops	7 500
Grocery stores	700
Hardware stores	5 000
Hobby shops and toy stores	25 000
Household appliances	8 500
Jewelry stores	7 500
Men's and boys' clothing	7 500
Restaurants and lunch counters	1 000
Shoe stores	6 000
Sporting goods	12 000
Stationery stores	25 000
Women's clothing	5 000

* Source: Independent study made by a group of advanced business administration students at the University of Miami. Starting from established studies, their procedure was to use data from the United States census, census of business, trade reports, and local market surveys in order to update figures for this table. Their results do not vary widely from other established studies. They emphasized in their conclusions that varying localities and conditions need study before adopting these averages.

In the former case, however, we can still consider the presence of inefficient firms. Customer reaction to existing stores, nature of stocks carried, services available, and the type of management reflected by competitors may present a situation in which a new, efficient firm would be successful despite the number of competitors now attempting to serve the same population.

Competitors should be studied in terms of their numbers, their management, how many of them are chain stores, the attractiveness of their stores, and the completeness and nature of their stocks of merchandise. If it is found that customers are dissatisfied with service, lines of merchandise, price ranges, attractiveness of stores, or other items, a basis may be found for successfully competing in that area.

4 Facilities Consider your city or town facilities. Is public transportation important to your plans, and if so, is it available with good service? Are there special problems in obtaining merchandise supplies through normal channels of distribution? Does the area have good banking facilities? Are civic associations, schools, churches, and professional services conducive to good community life and healthy business conditions? Is the local government attitude toward business encouraging or restrictive? If labour supply is important to your business, is an adequate supply available?

For manufacturers, the questions of nearness to raw materials or markets, the availability of cheap fuel, power and water, skilled labour of a special type, and financing facilities take precedence.

SITE FACTORS FOR RETAILING

Having decided upon a favourable city, or even a part of a city, in the preceding process, the planners can turn their attention to the specific site to be chosen within a generally desired location. Some of the site factors and their implications follow:

1 Parking   Does the particular site provide easy parking and access and other comforts for customers? Grandpa never worried about this factor with his general store. Hitching posts provided a place to tie the horses and were usually provided by the local government. Fields surrounded many stores and were free parking areas. Likely the most significant change in downtown retailing management in recent years has been the expense and importance of providing parking space for customers. Parking and heavy traffic in urban areas have contributed greatly to the growth of suburban shopping centres. Today parking is a fundamental part of every "save the downtown" or "bring the customers back downtown" or "revitalize the main downtown" program. An hour's free or subsidized parking is now available in many department-store lots when a purchase is made. Small firms must rely upon availability of low-cost parking or follow the same policy.

2 Surrounding Firms   What types of firms surround the site? It must be recognized that some types of business firms attract customers of one type and others attract other types. Good site choosing must consider this factor. What kinds of firms surround the site you have under consideration? Sites close to department stores are generally considered good for most types of retail stores. The general appeal of the department store to all types of customers makes this so.

Market research has provided some useful information in this regard. For example, studies have shown that men's stores should not be located next to gas stations, beauty shops, or women's apparel shops. Those who might disagree have not provided substantial evidence to support their views. Like electricity, it is more important that we know how to use research than to understand its foundation. Such neighbours just do not normally attract customers who are looking for men's clothing when visiting these shops. The innovation of clothing stores that sell both men's and women's apparel has not made sufficiently significant inroads on the principle to warrant its revocation.

3 Traffic Density   What kind of traffic is there at this site and is it adequate? Modern site analysis distinguishes between automobile and pedestrian traffic. If only automobile traffic were considered, most businesses would be located next to expressways or along main highways. Pedestrian traffic of potential customers is the key item here. Heavy automobile traffic adjacent to a suburban shopping centre can be very important, but the number of people who convert into pedestrian traffic is of even greater concern.

In urban sites, passing cars become less important. Getting these cars parked and bringing customers to the street and the store is the crucial consideration.

People traffic alone is not the most significant item in pedestrian traffic, however. Are they the type of people who are shopping for your type of merchandise? Why are they on this street at this time? Significantly, a large drug chain has staff people interview passersby on a site it is considering. With clip boards and questions, they observe, interview, and study the traffic. They ask age bracket, record sex, ask about employment, income range, objective of the trip past this site, shopping habits, interest in this type of store, etc. Their conclusion is that the site with the heaviest count of potential customers per half-hour between one and five o'clock in the afternoon and on Saturday evenings is the preferred site for the company's stores.

4 The "Going-Home" Side of the Street   Marketing research has produced the principle that the going-home side of the street is usually to be preferred to the going-to-work side of the street. This may be only a reflection of people's buying habits, but it has proved true in cases studied by advanced students. Those interested in the psychology of human conduct can form their own reasons for this principle of site choosing.

5 The Sunny Side of the Street   Market studies have also established that the sunny side of the street is less preferable for retail operations than the shady side. Our own research has found rents higher on the shady side in high-priced shopping areas. Perhaps in northern Alaska the reverse might be true because the sunshine is less frequent and may even be sought by shoppers. Merchants recognize the sunny-side-of-the-street principle by the installation of expensive awnings to combat the sun and make customers more comfortable.

Preferred Site

We must not leave this discussion with the implication that all types of retailers must be in prime, high-rent locations. Lower rents also have attractions, but they must be offset by higher advertising and promotion budgets to attract customers to the low-rent area. Some types of firms need such areas for best results. Firms that sell by mail or through travelling salespersons are obviously exempt from the considerations just discussed. Firms selling shopping merchandise should normally be close to their competitors, as we shall discuss in a later chapter. Firms concentrating on specialty goods emphasize comfort for their customers above all (see Table 13-2).

TABLE 13-2

FIRM CHARACTERISTICS THAT SUGGEST HIGH- OR LOW-RENT LOCATIONS AND FIRMS THAT USUALLY ARE IN EACH CATEGORY

CHARACTERISTICS THAT SUGGEST HIGH-RENT LOCATIONS	*ILLUSTRATIVE FIRMS*
Window displays featured	Department store
High rate of turnover	Style clothing shop
Low gross margin	Urban drugstore, bank
Appeals to transient trade	Men's shops, drugstore
Features price appeal and convenience merchandise	Discount store
Sells merchandise of high value compared to bulk	Fine jewelry store
Low overhead	Specialty tobacco and cigar store
Does little advertising	Independent hardware store

CHARACTERISTICS THAT SUGGEST LOW-RENT LOCATIONS	*ILLUSTRATIVE FIRMS*
High gross margin	Furniture store
Low merchandise turnover	Plumbing supply
Needs much space for interior displays	Automobile agency
Merchandise is low in value compared to bulk	Grain and feed store
Merchandise is essentially shopping goods	Carpet store, TV store
Has an established clientele	Neighbourhood drugstore
Does much advertising and promotion	Florist, grocery chain
Has a high overhead expense	Specialty food franchise, super service station

Site studies that have been made over many years by both government agencies and private market research groups have generally agreed that the preferred site can be associated with characteristics of the business in question. For instance, firms should generally seek low-rent locations if they have a high gross margin and low merchandise turnover, need much space of interior displays, sell merchandise that is low in value compared with bulk, sell what are considered shopping goods by most people in the area, have an established customer demand, resort to much advertising and promotion effort, or have high overhead expense. High-rent locations are more appropriate for firms that feature window displays, have a high rate of turnover, have low gross margins, appeal to transient trade, feature price appeal and convenience merchandise, sell merchandise of high value compared with bulk, have low overhead, and do little advertising.

It is unlikely that the individual firm would meet all the characteristics suggesting either a high-rent or low-rent location. The decision is usually reached in the planning stage by determining which type of location is suggested by the preponderance of characteristics represented. If the firm's characteristics imply a low-rent location on a majority of the measures, prudence recommends that such a location be given serious consideration. The many exceptions to such rules only prove the rule. Local circumstances usually account for the exceptions. A study of such a list may aid policy making in merchandising.

LOCATION FACTORS FOR MANUFACTURING

Factory locations are usually restricted to specified industrial areas of any city. Recent trends show an increase in municipal regulations in this regard. As a first consideration, the new factory planner must check the zoning laws in the area. Some industrial zones allow some types of factories and not others.

Once the available industrial zones are determined, attention is turned to the adequacy of shipping facilities, adequacy of the types of buildings available for lease or rent, and distances from factory to market and attendant shipping costs.

The factory that can be located in the central part of its total market area usually has an ideal location. This holds true for most manufacturers of consumer and industrial goods Nearness to market usually takes precedence over nearness to raw materials. Two notable exceptions are to be observed. When the manufacturing process involves (1) much waste in the processing of the product, or (2) dealing with perishable raw materials, the factory should be located close to its raw materials. An obvious example of the first situation is a saw mill, which makes finished lumber from giant logs. Shipping the logs to a mill near the final market would be wasteful and expensive. An example of the second situation is the processing of fresh fruit. Peach- and strawberry-canning factories must be near the lands where the fruit is harvested. Excessive spoilage and/or expense would result from long-distance hauling.

The speed of modern transportation systems has expanded many markets in ways not thought possible only a few short years ago. Planeloads of fresh tulips and other flowers are flown from Holland to many cities around the world. Fresh fruit from Mexico is available in Toronto as well as other markets without the benefit of freezing facilities. These instances, however, are the exception and not the rule. When considering utility versus uniqueness in consumer products, it is good to know that many people desire and can afford the products of uniqueness. The final test of any business economy, however, is the total goods and services that can be economically produced for its citizens. The average standard of living of any nation still depends on products of utility and their economical production. This truth is not intended to discourage innovations in manufacturing, distribution, and selling. It merely indicates that the greatest share of our total production is done with the objective of economical production a first consideration. The rules of experience still prevail.

LOCATION FACTORS FOR WHOLESALING

Wholesalers also are restricted by zoning laws in most cities. The objective is to be located as close to most customers as possible in a building that is suited to the type of operation planned. Good transportation facilities by rail or truck are essential for efficient reception of inventories. Local wholesalers make most deliveries by truck. When customers regularly visit the wholesaler, rather than phone in their orders, it is important that the customer area be attractive and efficient. This is not the normal situation. Most customers telephone their orders and desire speedy delivery. Emphasis should accordingly be placed on a location that makes this possible.

LOCATION FACTORS FOR SERVICE FIRMS

Locations for service firms are almost as varied as the types of firms involved. The beauty shop, the shoe repair shop, the TV repair shop do not need high-rent locations. They have become largely residential-area types of businesses. Closeness to a shopping centre is usually considered ideal. Yet there are differences, even among these service shops. Beauty shops must be attractive. Shoe repair shops have a character all of their own, which is not necessarily attractiveness. Shopping-centre promoters do not encourage this type of shop, and they are usually found in an adjacent lower-rent area. The TV repair shop is seldom seen by the customers. The chief location problem is a suitable area for doing their work. By advertising, they compensate for avoiding the high-rent districts.

Travel agencies depend upon drop-in traffic and therefore require locations on busy streets. Firms selling theatre tickets may do all their business by phone or from an upstairs office.

The most important location factor for all service firms is to know the type of customer to whom they plan to appeal. With this knowledge, choose a location and site that best fit that customer group.

QUESTIONS FOR CLASS DISCUSSION

1   What is the difference between a good location and a good site?
2   In seeking a good general location, why should the nature of the industries in the community be studied?

3   What should your attitude be toward competition when you are seeking a good location for your business?

4   What are the two most important justifications for establishing a new firm in an existing line of business?

5   Where can information be found about a community's population growth, its industry, and its community facilities?

6   Why should the planner of a new small firm consider the nature of the other stores that surround the site being considered?

7   How should the traffic at a specific site be analyzed?

8   When should a factory be close to its source of raw materials rather than its markets?

9   Why is it important to know the buying habits of potential customers when choosing a site?

10   Should a dry-cleaning business be located in a high-rent district? Why?

Projects for Home Assignment and/or Class Discussion

1   In a brief essay explain your understanding of how a more affluent society has reduced the number of people needed to support a sporting goods store.

2   How would you cope with the parking problem for your business in an urban location?

3   How would you evaluate the location of a store you like?

REFERENCES FOR FURTHER READING

Archer, M., *An Introduction to Canadian Business*, 5th ed., McGraw-Hill Ryerson Ltd., Toronto, 1986, Chapter 10.

Cunningham, G., *Buy Yourself A Job & Be Your Own Boss*, McGraw-Hill Ryerson Ltd., 1990, Chapter 5.

Kao, R.W.Y., *Small Business Management: A Strategic Emphasis*, 2nd ed., Holt, Rinehart and Winston of Canada Ltd., Toronto, 1984, Chapter 2.

· ·

14

Product Classes and Life Cycles

LEARNING OBJECTIVES

After reading this chapter, you will be able to:

1. **U**nderstand the different classes of consumer products and how each requires unique marketing attention
2. **K**now the classes of industrial products and how they are marketed
3. **U**nderstand the importance of providing quality and value to the user of services
4. **E**xamine the positioning concept as it relates to consumer products, industrial products, and services
5. **K**now the four stages of the life cycle of a product or service and how to deal with them
6. **K**now how the channels of distribution are designed to get the right products to the right customers
7. **U**nderstand how the distribution channel works in transporting, storing, and other services

8. **K**now the different types of wholesalers and retailers and how they function in the channel system
9. **U**nderstand the distribution trade-offs that can make final products more or less expensive and how to deal with them
10. **U**nderstand overall costs of distribution as they relate to the price

The particular type or types of merchandise sold by the individual firm should be reflected in the total nature of the operations.

All product can be classified into two major groups: (1) consumer goods and (2) industrial goods. Within these broad classifications, many further characteristics should be noted. We will first examine consumer goods and then turn our attention to industrial goods.

CLASSIFICATION OF CONSUMER GOODS

Consumer goods are those products purchased at retail by customers for their own use. They may be generally separated into three groups:

1 Convenience goods
2 Shopping goods
3 Specialty goods

1 Convenience Goods   Convenience goods are products that the customers desire to buy with a minimum of effort. The more convenient their purchase, the better they like it. Price is not a major factor when they seek such a product in a hurry. Customers do not search around or shop in different stores for convenience goods. Most convenience goods are purchased when the customer makes a special trip to obtain them. Other convenience goods may be purchased on impulse, perhaps in response to an attractive display. Most convenience goods are staple items of low value.

Examples of convenience goods, to most people, are tobacco, drugs, gasoline, soft drinks, newspapers, and ice cream. These are obviously items that, when wanted by customers, are wanted as quickly as possible.

2 Shopping Goods   Shopping goods are those items that most customers buy after comparing prices, fashion, quality, and service of several different sellers. Buyers *do* shop around before making a final decision on the particular item to be purchased. Most shopping goods are relatively high in value and are not bought frequently. This is why comparisons are so important to most people. Husband and wife usually consult the family budget first when considering the purchase of shopping goods. Individual buyers may place different relative values on price, fashion, quality, and service. Only when they are satisfied that they have found the best value for their situation do they make the final decision to buy.

Firms selling convenience goods should stress displays of impulse items. *Courtesy of Shoppers Drug Mart.*

Examples of shopping goods, for most people, are furniture, rugs, suits, shoes, jewelry, chinaware, automobiles, and television sets. Each can represent a substantial item in the family budget and demands close comparison before purchase.

3 Specialty Goods   Specialty goods are items that the individual buyer believes have special qualities that make him or her prefer them. They are usually items of high value. Price is not a major concern to most specialty goods customers. They usually express a preference for a particular brand and insist on this brand to the exclusion of all others.

Examples of specialty goods, for many people, are stereo sets, video tape recorders, expensive shirts, television consoles, tires, period antiques, or even brandname chocolates. People who believe that they should have only an RCA or Zenith or Mitsubishi television console, or Goodyear or Firestone radial tires, for example, will not be concerned that these goods are not available conveniently in their neighbourhoods. They will go out of their way to find a merchant in their town who carries their desired brand.

It should be observed that not all people fall into these general categories of buying habits. Cigarettes may be a shopping item for some families. People without shopping time may buy shopping goods without adequate comparison. What some customers consider specialty goods – expensive shirts, for example – may be shopping goods or even convenience goods to others. The important thing for the small firm owner is to know as much as possible about the customers' buying habits. Knowing your market is crucial in so many ways in successful business operation.

The classification of consumer goods and the examples within each classification represent what is considered the majority view of most consumers. If the firm owner finds, from study of the market, that it is in accord with these classifications, attention can be turned to the management implications for each type of consumer merchandise. Any notable exceptions found in the market can be adjusted for in merchandising policies.

MERCHANDISING GUIDES AND CONSIDERATIONS FOR DIFFERENT TYPES OF CONSUMER GOODS

The three types of consumer goods generally influence merchandising in the following ways:

1 Convenience goods
  a Less capable salespersons are needed.
  b Nearness to competitors is undesirable.
  c Store hours can usually be longer and still be profitable.
  d Variety of products in one line is not of prime importance.
  e Displays of impulse items are important.
  f Location in store is important.

2 Shopping goods
  a Location should normally be near competitors so that customers can compare goods.
  b High-rent areas are not essential.
  c More capable and higher paid sales people are necessary.
  d Ability to explain advantages of merchandise over competing products is essential.
  e Assistance to customers in value determination is important.

3 Specialty goods
  a Attractive, comfortable selling space for customers is important.
  b Advertising can cover wider areas of the city productively.
  c Efficiency in installations is important.
  d Customer services are a premium item.
  e Special sales may be less important.
  f Publicity emphasis is on location and brands more than on price.

Firms selling shopping goods need particularly well-trained and knowledgeable sales personnel. *Courtesy Government of Canada, Regional Industrial Expansion.*

INDUSTRIAL GOODS

Industrial goods are those products that are sold to other business firms, either for their own consumption or for use in their own manufacture of other products. These goods, too, are extremely varied. They may be classified as follows:

1   Raw materials: oil, grain, logs, unprocessed tobacco, wool, fresh fruits, etc.

2   Semi-manufactured goods: sheet aluminum or steel, leather, ores, pig iron, etc.

3   Parts: blades for cutting machines, automobile wheels, bearings, axe handles, etc.

4   Supplies: cleaning compounds, plastic bags, wrapping paper, fuel, office stationery, etc.

5   Machinery and equipment: all machines and equipment items used in the factory, office, or store.

Note that the same product can be both a customer good and an industrial good. The customer's purpose in buying the good will decide into which classification the particular item falls. For example, coal purchased for a factory is an industrial good, whereas coal purchased for the home is a consumer good.

Small firms do engage very much in the manufacture of many industrial goods. Individual firms may both sell their product to industrial firms and distribute them through wholesalers to retailers to consumers. The selling process is distinctly different in these two areas.

Special Features of Industrial Goods Selling

Any small firm selling to industrial users should recognize these special characteristics of industrial sales:

1   Industrial goods buyers are better informed about the products they buy. They buy products on the basis of performance and not because of advertising or emotion.

2   Many industrial goods are sold directly by the factory to the user without the use of any intermediaries.

3   There are fewer customers for individual goods, but the average sale is usually much higher.

4   Factories will often request products made to their own specifications.

5   Many industrial goods are sold with the seller providing installation and repair service.

6   Industrial goods prices are more sensitive to changing business conditions.

The implications of these characteristics for small firm manufacturers are that they must have sales people capable of demonstrating the performance of the product; they must be prepared to call on business customers rather than await buyers at the business; they must know where the potential users of the product are located (which relates to their own locations) and be prepared to offer installation and repair service either by their own staffs or through competent agents; and they must recognize the sensitive nature of industrial prices by keeping aware of business conditions.

All these factors will not apply in every case. The normal procedure in the particular line of products must be understood, however, and then the organization and services which apply must be arranged.

THE IMPORTANCE OF POSITIONING

Positioning is having potential and satisfied buyers think in a certain way about the firm's product or service. It happens in the minds of the buyers in relation to competitors' products.

For example, Ford cars are thought of as high in quality because Ford promotes the idea that "quality is job one," while the Lada car from the Soviet Union is thought of as "inexpensive." Ford's product quality and promotion methods position its products, while price positions the Lada. Both of the

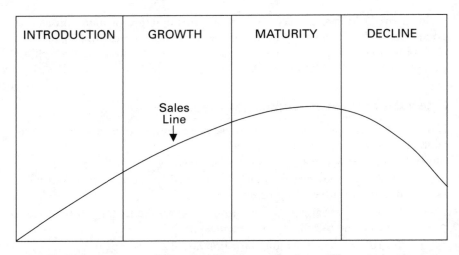

FIGURE 14-1 • Every product or service has a life cycle beginning with introduction, then to growth, to maturity, and finally to the decline stage. Good business practice attempts to extend the maturity stage by making the product or service "new and improved" to extend its life.

images exist in the minds of the buyers and in relationship to cars offered by other manufacturers.

Small business owners should identify the characteristics potential customers want and then give their product or service those attributes. This can be done by adjusting the product or service itself, improving quality, improving service, promoting differently, and by giving the customer what is wanted in a better way than the competitors. The key is to have many buyers position the small business product or service in preference to competitor's products.

LIFE CYCLES OF PRODUCTS AND SERVICES

There are four stages in the life cycle of every product or service. They are introduction, growth, maturity, and decline.

The introduction stage is where the firm promotes the demand for a new market offering. No one knows about the offering, so the selling and promotion expenses are high. During the growth stage the firm starts to make profits. However, competitors become encouraged to enter the field at this stage and price competition appears.

During the maturity stage sales increase, but eventually reach the saturation point. Price competition becomes strong; weaker firms leave the industry, while the good firms capture a larger part of the market.

Sales decline for everyone in the decline stage. Here the product or service has passed its usefulness. Black and white televisions are a good example of a product in the decline stage.

One final word about life cycle: Many products and services are able to continue the growth and maturity stages for years by adjusting the offering and promoting it differently. Many of us have bought a "new and improved" version of an old product. Just think about "Tide."

SEASONAL VARIATIONS IN SALES

Almost every business, large or small, has a very definite seasonal variation in its monthly income during the year. Stable firms such as grocery stores, for example, generally report that sales are heaviest in September, November, and December. Summer months, when schools are closed and people are off on vacation or moving to other cities, show a decline in sales. In resort towns, firms do their biggest business in the months that are vacation time for other people.

Most retailers and manufacturers do not have such a clear choice in adjusting to their seasonal variations in total income throughout the year. It is still important, however, that they know the extent of the variations. There are other things they can do in the best interests of their business firms:

* Hiring part-time employees at peak demand.
* Raw materials and finished goods inventory levels to be controlled according to the variations.
* A positive program of sales promotion for the slack periods should be considered. Perhaps special sales, attractive prices, or other ideas could increase sales in the slack months.
* Monthly break-even charts and income statements should be prepared.

In summary, all small firm owners should know their seasonal variations. When significant variations are apparent, every attempt should be made to adjust operating expenses accordingly. We have noted some of the ways this may be done.

CHANNELS OF DISTRIBUTION

Every product or service has a channel of distribution. Somehow it gets from the producer to the final user. This section deals with the process of how products, primarily, go through the channel.

Channels of distribution are "pipelines" that take the right quantities of the right products to the right location where the target customers want them at the right time. This process often requires the use of market specialists, wholesalers, and other intermediaries to ensure the customers' desires are met.

The kinds and quantities of products customers want are sometimes different than those normally produced. When this happens, channel members correct the situation by providing the wanted products in acceptable quantities and assortments.

How Distribution Channels Work

Many manufacturers sell directly to the final user, while others sell to wholesalers and other intermediaries and still others sell to retailers direct. Some wholesalers sell direct to the final consumer, others sell to other wholesalers, and still others sell to retailers. Retailers, too, often sell to other retailers and sometimes even to wholesalers, as well as final customers.

All of these techniques can work, provided the channel is managed properly and the products flow to satisfy the target customers. The key is to understand that the channel provides essential transporting, storing, and many other services which must ultimately satisfy customer needs.

Some of the activities that the channel system facilitates include the following:

1 Regrouping: activities to adjust assortments
2 Accumulating: collecting products from various producers
3 Sorting: the process of putting like qualities together
4 Assorting: putting together groups of products wanted by the target market
5 Bulk-breaking: dividing large quantities into smaller units

While these activities can be done by anyone in the channel, they are most often done by wholesalers.

DIFFERENT TYPES OF WHOLESALERS

New retailers are often confused by the various types of wholesale establishments that are available to serve their procurement needs. New wholesalers are often not sure of how their planned firms fit into the generally accepted organization of the wholesale function. The following comments should clarify the situation for both groups.

Wholesalers are generally classified as:

Full-service wholesalers (also called merchant wholesalers)

Limited-function wholesalers

Agent middlemen (also called intermediaries)

Full-service wholesalers are the most numerous in most lines of consumer goods. They usually buy their inventories directly from the manufacturers and take title to the merchandise. They store the merchandise in their own warehouses, deliver and/or assemble the products involved, and maintain a location where customers may inspect the products and place orders. They do not work on commission but rely upon their ability to sell their products at a profit to make their own operations successful. They are called *full-service wholesalers* because of the extra services they extend to their customers — such as granting credit on sales, providing delivery service, and supplying current market information.

Limited-function wholesalers provide fewer services. The list below explains how they function.

1   *Cash-and-carry wholesalers* have the same functions as a full-service wholesaler except for granting credit. Their customers pay in cash.

2   *Drop-shippers* usually sell bulky products and have them shipped directly from producer to customer.

3   *Truck wholesalers* usually will give "any time" delivery to the customer. High-service delivery of items are made from their trucks.

4   *Rack jobbers* restock many nonfood items at grocery stores on a regular basis. They usually collect for the items in cash.

5   *Mail-order wholesalers* sell out of catalogues to business and industry.

6   *Producers' cooperatives* market producers' collected products with profits going to the cooperative's customer members.

Agent middlemen are wholesalers who actually provide a procurement function for their customers. Most do not take title to the merchandise they buy or sell for their customers. They merely arrange for such sales between their customers and contacts. They usually work on commission only. Any extra services extended to their customers are the exception, not the rule. Examples of this group are *brokers*, who arrange sales for their clients without even taking title or possession of the merchandise products involved; *selling agents*, who often contract to take the entire output of a small factory and sell it wherever the market may be; and *manufacturers' agents*, who usually represent their manufacturer in only a certain specified territory and make sales of their product for delivery by the manufacturer.

Commission merchants are also usually classified as intermediaries, but they operate somewhat differently. They do not take title, but usually assume physical possession of the merchandise they are employed to sell. They often provide temporary storage until they have completed their sales. They usually provide delivery of the merchandise sold. Sometimes they grant credit to the firms to which they sell, but this is not a uniform practice. They are paid for their services by a commission on the selling prices they develop. Special arrangements with the principal they represent may add other compensation.

DIFFERENT TYPES OF RETAILERS

Retailing is getting the products to the final customers. Retailing firms identify the needs and wants of target customers and then find a way to give them the product they desire, at a price they can afford, and at the end of the distribution channel.

Customers come to retailers because of something the retailer does or has which meets their wants better than competitors. The retailer may have the best location for the customer; it may have lower prices; the convenience of shopping may be preferred; the selection, quality, variety, and service may be best. In other words, successful retailers give the customers value for their money.

Our affluent society demands costly marketing services and will support such things as spacious, air-conditioned shopping malls. *Courtesy of Cadillac Fairview.*

There are many different types of retailers in the distribution channel. Each exists because the customer prefers it to a competing firm. Some examples are:

1   High-service firms with a large or special selection of merchandise.
2   Firms with selections of merchandise and an emphasis on low prices.
3   Highly convenient offerings with few choices.
4   One-stop shopping stores containing all of the above.

High-service firms are considered speciality stores for the most part. Some department stores fit this category, too. Firms featuring low prices are supermarkets and discount houses. Vending machines and convenience stores are examples of stores with convenient offerings.

Superstores and giant department stores are examples of one-stop shopping units because they sell thousands of related and unrelated products plus provide all kinds of services like shoe repair, restaurants, ticket sales, and banking. Some of these offerings may be low-priced, mass-merchandised items, and others may be one-of-a-kind, high-cost products or services. While most of these large stores are not small businesses, many small entrepreneurs scramble their merchandise, too, in an effort to draw customers and make profits.

DISTRIBUTION TRADE-OFFS

The major trade-off for the distribution system is between the service level given and its cost. Products can be air-freighted to the consumer to provide excellent delivery times, but the cost of the final price will have to be higher than for products delivered by truck.

Another major trade-off involves storing products while waiting for orders or having many smaller, less efficient, deliveries made. Storing (warehousing) costs money, but so does delivering.

A third trade-off involves sales. If the product is not available, the customer will go somewhere else, and the sale will be lost. This trade-off is between lost sales and the cost of carrying a larger inventory.

In the final analysis, customers may be dissatisfied if the firm decides to take the low-cost distribution approach. If the firm has fewer items in stock, if they rely upon a slower form of delivery, or if the product is not available at all, customers will react by buying elsewhere.

THE TRANSPORTING FUNCTION

Getting the products to the right consumer involves selecting a physical transportation process. This function must be done on time and must get to the right location. It is a costly process that makes each product more expensive and may reduce the price competitiveness of the item.

However, it is important to point out that transporting huge shipments of British Columbia apples to Ontario may be costly, but this puts more apples on the market and ultimately reduces the cost of an apple in Toronto.

The key is determining the size of the order needed now and in a few days or weeks. Picking the optimum order quantity is important. This activity involves the concept of economies of scale. Simply stated, unit costs reduce as volume increases. Obviously, it is cheaper to ship a truckload of apples (per unit) than it is to ship one apple. All members of the channel system need to consider this.

A second consideration is how soon the products are needed. Good planning dictates using the least expensive form of transportation available that will allow for enough "lead-time" to bring the products when needed.

Products can be shipped a variety of ways. The fastest and most expensive is by air. Railroads can carry large loads, but they have some delivery limitations. Trucks are most flexible, but load size is limited. Water transportation is very inexpensive, but slow. Even pipelines can be used for some products.

Channel members must decide on the trade-off factors when they decide on the types of transportation needed for their products. The choices they make will affect the price of the products sold.

THE STORING FUNCTION

Storing or warehousing is an important channel function. It allows products to be available when needed by channel members. In many industries, producers will have products stored at many locations to service other channel members. This reduces waiting time, delivery cost, and may save sales that would be otherwise lost.

Storing, of course, costs money, which must be paid for in the price of the merchandise sold. Channel members must decide if these costs are offset by other advantages, such as having apples available all-year round, rather than just at the end of the fall harvest. Having products quickly available is another advantage, too.

Many industrial users now demand "Just in Time" delivery of product, putting the warehousing burden and cost on the supplier.

DISTRIBUTION AND PURCHASING

The key questions that small firm owners must ask themselves are: Am I buying through the established channels of distribution for this type of business? Is there another source that would give the same dependability and service? Am I getting the best prices available for comparable quality?

Most small retailers have wholesale houses available in their own locality that are eager and willing to serve them. Most consumer goods are normally distributed from manufacturer to wholesaler to retailer. In addition, there are salespeople from out-of-town suppliers who will call on the merchant to present their products. Job-lot dealers may operate in the area and have special quantities of merchandise for sale.

A basic decision the new owner must make is whether to buy only from established wholesalers who serve the area or to buy wherever needed types of merchandise are available. If the firm has a distributorship for a particular line of merchandise, the source of supply is assured as part of the distributorship arrangement.

Most small firm retailers carry similar merchandise in different price lines. Each price line may be served by a different wholesaler or distributor. Experience will soon tell the owners which are the most popular lines with their customers, and they will buy accordingly.

The inventory investment is usually the largest investment in the new small firm. Because of this, the owner must constantly be concerned with making this investment as profitable as possible. Using proper channels of distribution and being aware of trade-offs can reduce inventory and other costs. This can be done using the following strategies:

1 Determine a procedure for when to buy and how much to buy on each order.
2 Take advantage of storing and delivery by wholesalers.
3 Determine the cost of lost sales from stockouts.

The object is to have the proper merchandise available at the lowest price possible.

COST OF DISTRIBUTION

It is never too early in business education for students, small firm owners, and informed citizens to address themselves to the often-heard complaints about "the excessive costs of distribution." It is generally contended that efficiency in distribution has not kept pace with the economies of mass production. The facts bear investigation. Our best marketing studies show that up to 50 per cent of the consumer dollar goes for distribution costs and about 50 per cent for manufacturing costs. Marketing costs have increased over recent years, but only as a percentage of the retail price. In true dollar cost, marketing costs have also declined. There are definite reasons why they have not declined as much as manufacturing costs. An example of the retail cost of a popular consumer good today will illustrate the facts.

Let us consider the price of a popular line of radios or coffee makers.

It will be seen that manufacturing cost has been reduced from $20 to $12, a reduction of 40 per cent. Distribution cost has been reduced from $16 to $12, a reduction of 25 per cent. Retail price has been reduced from $36 to $24, a reduction of 33⅓ per cent.

FORMER PRICE AND ITS BREAKDOWN	*TODAY'S PRICE AND ITS BREAKDOWN*
$20 for manufacturing cost	$12 for manufacturing cost
$16 for distribution cost	$12 for distribution cost
$36 former retail price	$24 present retail price

If these percentages are seen in isolation, it would appear that distribution efficiency has not kept pace with manufacturing economies. It is this first impression that has caused most of the complaints that are heard.

Some of the ignored facts are the following:

1   Distribution costs have actually been reduced. In this example they are cut 25 per cent. New ideas in distribution are constantly being tried. Distribution markets are open to all in a free economy, and anyone who can save money can corner a large percentage of the market. Some of the new ideas that have been applied include piggyback trucks, carload rates, area distribution centres, large-size order requirements, and attractive discounts for large orders.

2   Mass-production economies necessitate wider markets in which to distribute the increased production. The wider the market served, the greater are expenses of distribution. Thus, mass production itself has added expense factors to distribution costs.

3   Consumers today have established a demand for products with high costs of distribution. As a society becomes more affluent, its increased purchasing power is reflected in a demand for more expensive consumer goods. Frozen foods entail greater distribution costs than fresh local vegetables. Imported products, which customers are demanding in rising quantities, carry extra distribution costs. Heineken is more expensive than Molson's, largely because of the distribution costs. We did not have frozen bakery goods until relatively recently. They demand refrigeration and expensive handling throughout the distribution process.

4   Some consumers, in fact an increasing percentage of them, have demanded costly marketing services. They are willing to pay for them and want them in expensive shopping centres. These services include delivery, free parking, evening shopping hours, air-conditioned stores, and sales on account. Such services are expensive and add to the total costs of distribution.

When these items have been considered, it is obvious that without great ingenuity in distribution activities, little or no reduction in distribution costs could have been achieved.

SUMMARY

Consumer goods can be classified as convenience, shopping, and speciality products. This translates into how easily they can be gotten, how easily they can be compared with competitive offerings, and how distinctive they are when compared to other products. Each class must be marketed differently.

Industrial goods are raw materials, semimanufactured products, parts, supplies, and machinery or equipment generally used to make other products. They have special marketing requirements.

A major key to services is that they must meet customer expectations. This can be done by positioning the service or product in the mind of the buyer in a positive way.

Every product has a life cycle. The introduction stage is where promoted demand is necessary to introduce the product or service. During the growth stage the firm starts to make profits, and in the maturity stage competition becomes severe. In the decline stage the product stops selling and fades away. It is important to make the growth and maturity stages last as long as possible.

Channels of distribution get the right products to the right customers. This involves the process of transporting, storing, and many other important activities and services performed by channel members. These members include the original producer, the wholesaler, and the retailer who sells to the final customer. All of these members can be in the channel, with possibly several of each, while in the case of directly marketed products, only the producer is present.

There are distribution trade-offs that affect the channel. Speed of delivery versus cost, storing versus smaller delivery, and lost sales due to stockouts versus carrying more inventory are three examples.

Finally, the overall costs of the distribution system have been reduced in the recent past as a percentage of retail price. However, these costs are still high because of wider distribution, customer demands, and the increased amount of money consumers in general have to spend.

QUESTIONS FOR CLASS DISCUSSION

1   Do you believe that less capable sales people are needed to sell convenience goods than shopping goods? Explain.

2   Why can advertising for specialty goods usually cover a wider area than for the corner drugstore?

3   When you buy a shirt or blouse, do you consider it a convenience, shopping, or specialty item? How do you distinguish between these three types of consumer goods?

4   Why should shopping goods firms generally be located in the same area in town?

5   Do you agree that factories should be located close to their markets?

6   When should a factory be located close to its source of raw materials? Why?

7   How could the same product be both an industrial good and a consumer good?

8   "Industrial goods are bought on a basis of performance and not on emotion." What does this mean to you? Give examples.

9   Are there more or fewer customers for industrial goods than for consumer goods? Explain.

10   How has an affluent society increased distribution costs?

11   Have distribution costs per unit of product really increased with the increase of mass production? Explain.

12   What could cause seasonal variations in the sales volume of a neighbourhood grocery store?

13   Are there any variations in the monthly sales of most small department stores? What could cause them?

14   How drastic do you think the seasonal variations are for a resort restaurant in a far-north village?

15   Is the fact that "we made a profit last year" a good reason to neglect study of seasonal variations? Explain.

16   What are some of the things an owner can do to aid profits when significant variations in seasonal business are normal?

Projects for Home Assignment and/or Class Discussion

1   a Prepare in one column a list of ten products that you or your family regularly purchase. In an adjacent column indicate whether you consider each a convenience good, shopping good, or specialty good.
   b Explain how different people might place some of those same products in a different category.

2   Write a short paper defending intermediaries against the charge that distribution costs have not declined as much as manufacturing costs.

REFERENCES FOR FURTHER READING

Archer, M., *An Introduction to Canadian Business*, 5th ed., McGraw-Hill Ryerson Ltd., Toronto, 1986, Chapter 10.

Sommers, M.S., J. Barnes, W.J. Stanton, and C. Futrell, *Fundamentals of Marketing*, 5th Canadian Edition, McGraw-Hill Ryerson Ltd., Scarborough, Ontario, 1989.

Tate Jr., C.E., L.C. Megginson, C.R. Scott Jr., and L.R. Trueblood, *Successful Small Business Management*, 3rd ed., Business Publications, Inc., Plano, Texas, 1985, Chapters 13 and 17.

· ·

15

Layout

LEARNING OBJECTIVES

After reading this chapter, you will be able to:

1. **K**now why layout planning must be considered a flow of people, products, materials, services, and merchandise
2. **R**ecognize the retail layout as a "selling machine"
3. **U**nderstand guidelines for good layout for retailers, based upon knowing customers' buying habits
4. **K**now the concepts and techniques necessary to deal with both shoplifting and employee theft
5. **R**ecognize the differences in layout between the wholesaler, the service firm, and the factory

The physical arrangement of the business area of a firm is known as its layout. Layouts can be good or bad and can have important effects on sales and profits. Proven established principles of layout can be applied, although these guiding principles will vary with the type of business. These principles or guidelines are different for retailers and for wholesalers, for manufacturers and for service firms. In all types of firms, however, the objective is maximum efficiency, maximum sales, and hence maximum profits. Key considerations in good layout are best discussed in terms of the general type of firm involved.

LAYOUT FOR THE RETAIL FIRM

Layout for retailers has been defined as "a selling machine." This definition, the best one the authors have heard, encompasses much of what experienced business owners include in their applications of good layout. Good layout does a great deal to maximize sales and is a vital part of the selling objective. Its basic objective is to do just that—maximize sales. How is this accomplished? The answer lies in observing and applying generally accepted rules of layout. Some of them are outlined and discussed briefly below.

Guidelines to Good Layout for Retailers

1 Customer Buying Habits   Know the buying habits of your customers. We have already noted the location of the dessert counter in a cafeteria and the prescription counter in a drugstore. These locations represent applications of knowing customers' buying habits. The hungry patrons of a cafeteria are awed by attractive displays of desserts as they enter the food line. They happily pick one quickly before even knowing what their main course will be. If they have first chosen their vegetables, main dish, and salad, they would likely have been much more reluctant to pick up the tempting dessert. Studies have shown a large decrease in dessert sales when that counter is at the end of the line rather than at its beginning.

Customers who enter a drugstore with prescriptions from their doctors in hand are not concerned with convenience in finding the prescription counter as much as they are with getting the medicine. The purchase will not be lost because they do not find the pharmacist immediately. If they have been in this particular store before, they know that prescriptions are filled at the back of the store. As they pass along attractive counters of merchandise en route to the prescription counter, they see many other kinds of products and effective displays. That is the key to layout. In making that trip through the store, customers are likely to make many impulse purchases. Impulse purchases are those which the customers never anticipated when they entered the store. Each such purchase is a credit to the application of this layout principle.

Ideal layout for most drugstores suggests the prescription counter should be at the back of the store with attractive displays of convenience and impulse merchandise along the path to the counter. *Courtesy Pharma Plus Drugmart.*

2 Merchandise Display   Display merchandise attractively. The day when all merchandise in a store was kept in closed drawers, locked showcases, or generally out of sight is long past. Customers want to find attractive displays of most items they desire to purchase. Ready comparisons are desired: comparisons of price ranges, styles, designs, or alternative products. This is all part of providing customer satisfaction. Open displays are important.

3 Customer Service   Provide good services for customers. They can include pleasant surroundings and courteous personnel in charge of opening credit accounts, competent and agreeable sales people, clean rest rooms, and convenient passageways and stairs.

4 Physical Surroundings   Make maximum use of light, ventilation, and heat. This layout guide serves the comfort of customers and employees as well.

Customer comfort aids merchandise selection. The public image of a firm can be a reflection of how well this layout principle is observed.

5 Organization of Merchandise   Display associated lines of merchandise close together. That is, products that most people tend to purchase at one time should be located at close proximity on shelves, in showcases, or on counters. Toothpaste and shaving cream are the classic examples. Shirts, blouses, and skirts are usually displayed adjacently. Customers' convenience is violated when they must travel around the store to find items they consider to be in the same group. There can be no final or all-inclusive answer on this matter because different customers associate different products in groups. Knowing your customers is a great help in this regard.

6 Visual Spaciousness   Provide a maximum view of the entire store for customers, employees, and managers. Customers prefer seeing other departments when shopping in one. Spaciousness in image is encouraged. Managers can do a better job of handling such problems as relieving crowded departments by reassigning salespersons and detecting emergencies. Employees have better morale when they are in closer contact with, or in view of, other employees.

7 Separation of Activities   Separate selling from nonselling activities. Generally, this means that such activities as the wrapping and accounting departments, credit offices, repair services, cashiers, public telephones, and customer-service counters should be located near the rear of the store. The front of any store is considered prime selling space.

8 Customer Image   Store fixtures should reflect the desired customer image. If the appeal is mainly to men, the fixtures should reflect a masculine atmosphere. For women, a more refined image with a feminine touch is appropriate. Colours and decorations are important here. This feature of layout may be frequently observed in sports shops and hair salons. When customers are equally divided between men and women, general attractiveness is foremost.

9 Utilization of Space   Know the value of your space and place merchandise accordingly. The average small retail store is ten to fifteen metres wide and from fifteen to thirty metres deep. It has several departments or displays several lines of merchandise for its customers. How should those departments be arranged? Three governing principles apply:

a   Most new shoppers turn to the right when entering a store.

b   Space in the front of the store will have more customer traffic than rear sections. Front space is, accordingly, more valuable for sales.

c   The type of merchandise offered must be considered. Convenience goods, shopping goods, and specialty goods demand different answers because buying habits vary with goods desired (see Chapter 14). It follows that allocation of space among departments should reflect these facts.

In terms of traffic and potential sales, the average floor space can be divided into specific areas. Dividing the total space into nine major sections, as in the

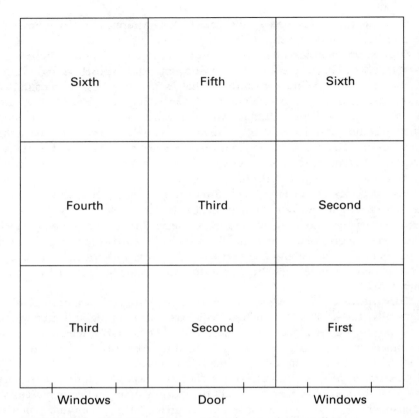

Sixth	Fifth	Sixth
Fourth	Third	Second
Third	Second	First

Windows | Door | Windows

FIGURE 15-1 • Space values in a typical retail store.

floor plans shown in Figures 15-1 and 15-2, we can attach priorities of value for first, second, third, etc. choices.

It will be noted that of the nine areas two areas are tied for second choice, two for third choice, and two for sixth choice. Only areas (1), (4), and (5) seem to be clear choices.

Whether the individual planner adopts this valuation in total or not, the important thing is to realize the general relationship of the different areas. There is no definite rule for assigning specific departments or merchandise to these areas. Some guidelines are available. They include the following:

a Impulse merchandise and other convenience goods should be located in the front areas.

b Shopping merchandise (demand goods) should be located at the rear or upstairs in the multistoreyed store.

c Nonselling departments and service departments should be in the rear.

Office Credit Department Public Telephones	Beauty Salon Rugs Drapes	Rest Rooms Will-Call Layaways
Yard Goods Knitting Supplies Major Appliances China Cutlery Fine Jewelry	Swimwear Resort Wear Children's Wear Lingerie Shoes	Men's Shop Suits Shoes Shirts Sports Ties
Better Dresses Teen's Dresses Budget Dresses	Sweaters Hosiery Ladies' Bags	Toiletries Cosmetics Jewelry Watches
Windows	Door	Windows

F I G U R E   1 5 - 2 • Possible department locations for a small department store. This plan shows space values and types of consumer goods sold.

d   It usually does not pay to move a successful department to a less valuable space in order to give a losing department a more valuable space.

e   Wide aisles for customer comfort are recommended, but creation of an occasional "obstacle course" by placing sale merchandise or other special items in an aisle may be good merchandising.

f   Make good use of available window space by placing attractive displays in them as well as on the selling floor.

LAYOUT, MERCHANDISE DISPLAYS, AND SHOPLIFTING

We have seen that a vital part of good layout is to have merchandise readily available for customers to view and compare. Many marketing tests have established that sales of particular items are much larger when the item is on an open table or open rack. At the same time, all merchants are confronted with the ever-increasing problem of shoplifting, which has attained tremendous proportions throughout the country in recent years.

These are two aspects of the shoplifting problem: stealing by employees and stealing by visitors in the store. Many millions of dollars are lost by businesses every year in each category. The problem of employee stealing demands closer control of employee activities on the premises. It is unfortunate that the necessary measures are imposed on the honest as well as the dishonest employees. Common sense dictates, however, that these procedures should be viewed in the same light as the common sense procedures against airplane hijacking. Application to all is a necessary evil to protect the innocent. If personal inconvenience for the innocent can eliminate or reduce the crime, the result must be to the benefit of all. Fidelity bonds may be purchased to insure the firm against employee thefts.

Stealing by outsiders in the store is a different matter. The laws of some provinces make it very difficult to arrest shoplifters on the premises. The firm's public image sometimes suffers, even when obviously guilty persons are prosecuted. Large expenses are incurred in maintaining security staffs within stores. Yet the crime goes on in untold millions of dollars worth of goods. Large and small firms suffer in the same manner.

Front space in a retail store is a valuable area for impulse sales. *Photo courtesy of Dan Kewley.*

Firms that acquire a reputation for prosecuting all shoplifting cases will find that the problem is reduced. Law enforcement officials recommend prosecuting as a strong deterrent to shoplifting.

Training sales people to be alert to the problem is also helpful. When people in a store are immediately welcomed with a "May I help you?" shoplifting is discouraged.

Various devices have been introduced to cope with this problem. One is the placing of metallic tags inside clothing items. These tags turn on alarm systems at all exits unless removed by the salesperson when the item is paid for or the charge slip is signed at the cash register. Other alarm systems can be provided that buzz upon disconnection of attaching cords when items are removed from open counters. The cords allow ample space and distance for complete inspection of the merchandise, but only the salesperson is to remove them, with the alarm system deactivated.

One significant conclusion has been forced upon retail firms: limits must be placed upon the customer access to some types of merchandise. Items of small bulk and relatively large value must be kept in transparent showcases or glass-doored shelves, which may be necessarily protected by lock and key. Such items as wristwatches, expensive costume jewelry, diamonds, costly cutlery, and even expensive gowns may fall into this category. Some department stores protect expensive sweaters or china in this manner. It is important that the new firm owner be aware of this problem and be prepared to cope with it, at least to keep it to a minimum. It is a sad commentary on our society that we must accept the reality of this serious problem. It is only to be hoped that improved morality may soon eliminate the problem or reduce it to a minimum. It is the honest consumers who pay the final bill for this outrageous situation.

LAYOUT FOR THE WHOLESALER

Layout considerations for a wholesaling firm are dominated by the objective of filling orders with speed and economy. This goal also emphasizes the speed and economy with which inventories are stacked in the warehouse. Emphasis must be placed on the labour costs expended in the process of storing the inventories and in filling the orders received. More than 60 per cent of total operating costs of the average wholesaler consists of labour costs; and the ability to compete depends on efficiency in controlling labour costs.

Methods that can be of assistance to wholesalers include:

1   Keeping most often demanded merchandise easily accessible.
2   Using conveyors, material-handling equipment, and overhead cranes wherever feasible.
3   Using the principle of gravity when possible. Devices based on this principle help speed order filling and inventory stocking.

Wholesalers handle many different lines of merchandise. Hence, no one rule for inventory arrangement can be suggested. Common to all wholesalers, however, is the desirability of knowing the most frequently ordered items so that application of the suggested devices may be possible.

LAYOUT FOR THE FACTORY

Factories that produce only one product, or one product at a time, have the advantage of being able to use a *continuous-production layout* – usually called a *product layout*. All operations follow the same path through the manufacturing process. Materials are received where needed in the assembly or manufacturing process, all machines are placed at the point where needed without unnecessary moving of materials or products in process, and all product comes from the assembly line at one point.

The ideal product layout calls for having raw materials delivered at the factory door nearest to where the materials go into the assembly or manufacturing line, having a continuous conveyor belt move the product in process from one station to another nearby, having any required subassemblies delivered close to the point of need, and having all finished products arrive on the same conveyor belt, even packaged and ready for delivery.

The obvious goal of all factory layout is to minimize the unproductive movement of products and materials. Possibilities for doing this are much greater in continuous-production, or product, layouts.

Factories that produce different kinds of products, or even produce products to individual orders, cannot use this arrangement for their machines and operations because the routes through the manufacturing process are different for each product manufactured. They use a *process layout* – also known as *intermittent manufacturing layout*.

Foundries and job-order printing firms are examples of factories that produce many different products, each of which may require a special sequence of machines or other operations in the process of being completed. Each product usually follows a different path through the manufacturing process. The big problem in layout here is to minimize the movement of work in process that does not add value to the final product. Having people move half-finished products in wheelbarrows from one machine to another some distance away adds nothing to the value of the finished product. Yet, much movement is often necessary to complete the orders. Another problem is that some machines may be kept busy all the time, and others are in use only part of the time. Efficient layout therefore means having the most frequently used machines in proper quantity handy for all orders.

Because of the differences in product and process layouts, costs for process layout manufacturing are usually higher than for most product layout manufacturing.

With the guiding rule of keeping unproductive movement of materials and work in process to a minimum, new firm planners should first study their production lines to see how closely they can keep them to the ideal. Keeping the production-control and production-planning personnel in close proximity to the factory production line can contribute to this overall objective.

LAYOUT FOR THE SERVICE FIRM

Service firms are so varied that little can be said of common factors shared. A barber or beautician needs an attractive shop with enough chairs to handle customers in good time, space for all the equipment used for hair treatment, and an attractive space for waiting customers and a receptionist. Many of these shops also maintain a stock of products for sale. Repair shops for major appliances are seldom seen by their customers. Customers phone the TV repair shop or the washing-machine repair shop. The machinist visits the home, does the work, and is paid. The only need is for an efficient workshop at his or her headquarters. A travel agency, if catering to transient trade, needs a well-located office with adequate counters, phone service, and comfortable places for customers to wait or to be interviewed. A firm selling only theatre tickets may operate from a home telephone or a hired desk in a business office. Others may maintain offices on a popular street if catering to drop-in traffic. A cleaning establishment needs to have its equipment arranged like a product-line factory and room to receive its customers and return finished dry cleaning. Laundries generally follow the product line in processing their services. Most of their customers may be served via delivery trucks, but counters are also usually provided to receive customers and make deliveries.

The one common factor shared by all service firms is the importance of keeping their facilities consistent with the volume and type of service they are rendering.

QUESTIONS FOR CLASS DISCUSSION

1 What action would you take against employees guilty of stealing merchandise from your business?
2 Compare a product layout (continuous production) with a process layout (intermittent layout).
3 Why is the prescription counter in a drugstore usually found at the rear of the store?
4 Can you think of any practical reasons why grocery stores often place the frozen goods close to the checkout stations?
5 How do displays of merchandise become important in layout?

6 Would you advocate open counter displays of wristwatches? If not, why not?

7 What do we mean by the relative value of space within a retail store?

8 Why shouldn't the nonselling activities be in the front of the store?

9 What are impulse goods? Where should they be located in a retail store?

10 Do you believe that window displays are an important part of total layout?

11 How would you combat the problem of shoplifting in your store?

12 What is the prime objective in layout for a wholesaler?

13 What is the difference between a product layout and a process layout?

14 "Factory layout seeks to minimize the unproductive movement of goods in process." What does this statement mean to you?

Projects for Home Assignment and/or Class Discussion

1 How have shoplifting and dishonest employees affected the problems of layout and employee policies? Do you have opinions on these subjects?

2 Explain what the statement "layout can be called a selling machine" means to you.

3 Do you agree that different parts of the same store have different "space values"? Do you agree with the space values attached to the floor plans in this chapter? Why or why not?

REFERENCES FOR FURTHER READING

Archer, M., *An Introduction to Canadian Business*, 5th ed., McGraw-Hill Ryerson Ltd., Toronto, 1986, Chapter 7.

16

Pricing Policies

LEARNING OBJECTIVES

After reading this chapter, you will be able to:
1. **U**nderstand the factors affecting individual prices
2. **I**dentify the relationship between average markup, price, and cost of merchandise to be sold
3. **R**ecognize that average markup results from merchandise being sold at different prices at different times
4. **K**now that markup must be calculated from the sales price and not from the cost of the merchandise
5. **K**now how to set initial prices using mark-on to allow for reductions from markdowns, shortages, damage, and employee discounts

FACTORS AFFECTING INDIVIDUAL PRICES

The prices that any firm can charge for its merchandise are subject to many influences. Some or all of the following considerations may apply in a particular case:

1   *Competition Act* (fair trade law)
2   Nationally advertised prices
3   Desired customer clientele
4   Competitor price policies
5   Market strategy
6   Manufacturers' suggested prices
7   Type of merchandise handled
8   Policy on loss leaders
9   Seasonal nature of sales
10 Demand factor for certain products
11 Price lining
12 Target return pricing

A word about each of these factors will introduce us to the total scene of setting prices. In addition to the *Competition Act*—a federal statute—three provinces have laws governing unfair trade practices: Ontario has the *Business Practices Act*, Alberta has the *Unfair Trade Practices Act*, and British Columbia has the *Trade Practices Act*. *Nationally advertised prices* must be recognized by small firms as at least an upper limit to the prices they place on items so advertised. *Competitor prices* on similar lines or merchandise with similar quality must be recognized when active competition exists between firms. *Market strategy* is a policy of setting prices and quality in a range not served by competitors.

Where a *special clientele* is served, its buying can be reflected in price policy. For example, if affluent people want special services and special merchandise, they are willing to pay for such service. In other cases, the desired clientele may be price-conscious people and price policy will be directed to serve them.

Manufacturers' suggested prices are designed by the manufacturers to protect the quality image of their products and protect profit margins for the individual retailer. Price policy is significantly affected by the *type of merchandise handled* by the firm, whether convenience, shopping, or specialty merchandise. This subject is pursued in detail in a later chapter. Novelties or special-interest items normally carry higher markups.

Price maintenance by a supplier is illegal, that is, a manufacturer cannot maintain fixed prices at the resale level. The rule is that a manufacturer may suggest a maximum price but may not set a minimum. An exception is when the manufacturer has evidence that the products supplied are being repeatedly used as "loss-leaders," that is, there is a *practice* of using the products as promotional (advertising) means. *Seasonal nature of sales* can affect pricing policy by making it possible to alter prices with the high and low seasons of sales volume. The *nature of overall demand* is likewise a consideration in setting individual prices. Elastic demand suggests lower prices. Specialty goods, such as luxury items and style merchandise, carry higher prices. *Price lining* is a policy of keeping merchandise in fairly well defined price ranges. Dresses at $29.95, $44.95, and $69.95 would be an example.

Target return pricing involves adding a desired percentage return on investment or a specific dollar amount return to total fixed costs in setting retail prices. The higher fixed cost total is then added to variable costs in setting prices. This method assumes a given volume in terms of units of product against which the procedure is applied. For example, a factory plans to sell 10 000 units of its product in the coming year. Fixed expenses are $150,000, variable expenses are $300,000, and it is desired to earn a profit of 10 per cent on its investment of $500,000 (or $50,000). Using the target return pricing principle, the owner would add the $150,000, the $300,000, and the $50,000 for a total of $500,000. This total is the amount that must be received in sales of 10 000 units of product in order to produce the desired return on investment. This means that the unit price would be $50 (10 000 times $50 equals $500,000).

From this maze of influences on individual prices, some always present and some justifying irregular application, there are basic considerations that take overall precedence in the determination of the price policy for the individual firm.

AVERAGE MARKUP AND INDIVIDUAL PRICES

Up to now, we have used average markup figures for our type of business in setting up the projected income statement. We have found that if a firm has sales of $100,000 and gross margin of $40,000, it has an average markup on total sales of 40 per cent. This does not mean that every item in the store was marked up 40 per cent of sales. (The principle of markup on sales, not on costs, will be explained later.) Some had more than this average markup and others undoubtedly had less than 40 per cent markup. The total year's sales probably included some loss leaders, or items which were sold below actual invoice cost. Pricing policy in total must recognize these facts—while always bearing in mind that the overall average markup must be maintained to arrive at the planned profit.

Pricing policy can be expressed diagrammatically, as in Figure 16-1.

The days when many businesses operated on a basis of a standard markup on every item in the store are long past. Almost every firm today has sales in each of the four areas shown in Figure 16-1. Dynamic pricing policy demands that owners be aware of the aggregate sales volume in each area so that overall total sales will average out to the markup necessary to provide desirable overall profits. Individual prices will reflect the many points discussed above. If loss leaders are a desirable part or necessary condition of the total merchandising plan, they must be offset by extra profit margins on other items. Loss leaders

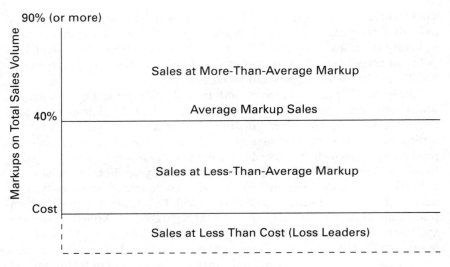

F I G U R E   1 6 - 1 • Pricing policy.

are still illegal or regulated in some provinces. Any merchandise sales in the less-than-average markup area must also be offset by sales in the above-average markup area.

Understanding this pricing policy will explain why the price of cornflakes may be $2.65 (its normal markup price) one day in a grocery, $2.25 on another day, and $2.85 on still another. Saturday specials, other sales prices, and special attractions will alter the prices of the same product from time to time. These variations are intended to attract customers who are price-conscious, yet compensate for the deficiencies in gross margin on other occasions. We can see this policy well applied in the Saturday specials of grocery stores. It should be especially noted that the prices of many of these specials are subject to a "minimum order of $10 excluding cigarettes." The idea of attracting sales by using less-than-average markup items is practised by retailers in almost every line of consumer goods. They may be used with equal effectiveness by sellers of many industrial goods.

THE NATURE AND COMPUTATION OF MARKUP

Markup represents the difference between what is paid for merchandise and the price at which it is sold to the customer. That markup, or gross margin, is the merchant's reward for rendering a social service in bringing the merchandise to the customer. The merchant has given the merchandise *place utility*. The basic justification of any profit is a reward for rendering this service.

The markup should always be computed as a percentage of the retail price, not as a percentage of the cost of merchandise. The most competent proprietor will compare sales records from period to period in terms of the percentage of sales and average markup represented for each department or type of merchandise. The total of all operating expenses, cost of goods sold, and profits must equal 100 per cent of sales. Statement analysis is always facilitated when all items on the income statement are stated as a percentage of the sales figure.

We must recall here the proprietor who insisted that the accountant was wrong in stating that there was an operating loss for the period rather than a profit. The proprietor contended that there was a profit because "markup was 25 per cent, while operating expenses were 23 per cent, including my salary, and therefore I must have a net return on investment of 2 per cent of sales." Of course, the accountant was correct; the owner's markup was based on cost and not on sales. A markup of 25 per cent of cost is equivalent to 20 per cent of sales. The firm had actually incurred a net loss from operations of 3 per cent of sales. (See Table 16-1.)

To illustrate this situation, consider merchandise costing $100. Marked up to 25 per cent of cost, the sale price would be $125 (0.25 times $100, added to $100). But operating expenses are 23 per cent of sales. This amounts to $28.75 (23 per cent times $125). Net result is a loss of $3.75 on each $125 of sales or $100 of cost of merchandise. (Markup of $25 is $3.75 less than operating expenses of $28.75.) No firm can long endure under such a condition. Obviously, this owner had to increase the markup or reduce operating expenses to get back into a profit position.

TABLES TO ASSIST IN SETTING PRICES

To ease the problem of retail pricing and still assure that markups are based on sales prices, tables have been prepared to show what percentage of cost is necessary to provide the desired percentage of sales price in the markup. A segment of such a table is shown in Table 16-1. Most office supply stores have them available.

TABLE 16-1

MARKUP EQUIVALENTS

DESIRED PERCENTAGE OF SALES	EQUIVALENT PERCENTAGE OF COST
10	11.1
13	15
15	17.7
20	25
25	33.3
30	42.9
33⅓	50
35	53.9
40	66.7
50	100

It can be seen from Table 16-1 that 20 per cent of sales, for example, is equivalent to 25 per cent of cost. If a 20 per cent markup on sales is desired and if it is easier for persons pricing merchandise, they can just take 25 per cent of the cost and add it to the cost to arrive at sales price. The important thing is to quote the markup as 20 per cent of sales price and use this figure in statement analysis.

SETTING INITIAL PRICES

Initial prices on merchandise must cover all these items:

1 Markdowns
2 Shortages
3 Damaged merchandise
4 Employee discounts
5 Operating expenses
6 Cost of goods sold
7 Profits

The new firm may not know how to estimate the volume of some of these items. Data gathered for comparable firms in the planning stage can assist in making realistic estimates. None can be neglected. It is much safer to use a generous estimate than to be short in the calculations. Operating expenses and desired profits are clearly set forth on the budgeted income statement. The other items will be reflected in a lessened net sales figure and will not normally appear in the expense accounts. It is always hoped that markdowns, shortages (like shoplifting losses), and damaged merchandise will be kept to a minimum. Employee discounts are usually desirable as a basic part of personnel policy. A popular figure used in retailing to represent the first four items listed above is 3 per cent of net sales. This will vary, of course, with different firms and different policies.

INITIAL PRICE: MARK-ON VERSUS AVERAGE MARKUP

It is because of the implications of the preceding paragraphs that marketing experts draw a distinction between *mark-on* and the *average markup*, as the latter term is computed from the year-end income statement. The distinction is based on the fact that many of the items just discussed (markdowns, shortages, damaged merchandise, and employee discounts) are normally not shown on the income statement as such. In most cases it would be impossible to put a dollar amount on these items. Markdowns are recorded at lower sales prices; shortages like shoplifting are not sales at all, but the merchandise lost is still included in the cost of goods sold; damaged merchandise sold at a discount is merely a lessened sales item; and employee discounts are usually recorded as sales at lessened prices. Importantly, however, all of these items must be covered in the initial price set upon the merchandise. Hence the term *mark-on* denotes the total amount added to the cost of merchandise in setting the *initial price*.

In contrast to this, when we refer to average markup shown on an income statement (gross margin divided by sales), we are using the net sales that resulted after all of the above items have had their effect on the sales figure, or have been included in the cost of goods sold when they were shortages instead of sales. The average markup reflected on the income statement may be 38 per cent, but if the items of markdowns, damaged merchandise, shortages, and employee discounts amounted to 4 per cent of net sales, a mark-on of 42 per cent would be necessary in setting the initial price.

The fundamental lesson to be learned by small firm operators is that if you wish to maintain an average markup on net sales of a given percentage, you must use a somewhat higher percentage of sales in setting the initial price.

PRICE CALCULATIONS

If 25 per cent of net sales is required to cover operating expenses, if 3 per cent is required to cover markdowns, shortages, damaged merchandise, and employee discounts, and if 12 per cent is the desired profit, then an average total markup of 40 per cent of sales must be applied to maintain the planned profit. This leaves 60 per cent of sales price for the cost of merchandise.

Looked at another way, the initial price of any merchandise offered for sale can be computed as follows:

Initial price in dollars must equal cost of merchandise, plus operating expenses, plus markdowns, plus shortages, plus damaged goods, plus employee discounts, plus profits.

How is the retail price of a particular item computed when the markup as a percentage of sales is known? Let us take a case which illustrates our figures above. Mark-on is now 40 per cent of sales. If mark-on is 40 per cent of sales price, the cost of the item is 60 per cent of sales price. An item—a dress, say—costing $25 would retail for $41.67. Computations can be made in two different ways:

1

$$\frac{0.4167}{60)\overline{25.000}} \times 100 = \$41.67$$

$$\begin{array}{r} 24\ 0 \\ \hline 1\ 00 \\ 60 \\ \hline 400 \\ 360 \\ \hline 400 \\ 420 \end{array}$$

Explanation of computations:

1   The cost of the dress equals 60 per cent of sales price. We divide the cost ($25) by 60 to find 1 per cent of sales price. Then multiply this 1 per cent by 100 to find 100 per cent of the sales price.

2 $x = \dfrac{25}{0.60} = 41.67$

2 By algebraic formula we would use: $0.60x = 25$ and then solve for x to find the retail price of $41.67.

If the item involved in this calculation were to be sold in various price ranges, it would be placed in the next price range above $41.67. Dresses, for example, might be sold at $35, $45, or $55. The $25 dress would likely be put on the $45 rack.

We should stress here what the retail price would have been if the markup had been computed on cost rather than sales price. We would merely take markup percentage, 40 per cent, of $25 ($10), and add it to cost ($25) to establish a retail price of $35. It is this ease of calculation that had made this method more popularly understood and also contributed to the errors in statement analysis previously mentioned.

QUESTIONS FOR CLASS DISCUSSION

1 What is a table of markup equivalents?
2 What is the difference between "average markup" and "initial price setting"?
3 What does market strategy mean as a price policy?
4 What does price lining mean as a price policy?
5 What is a loss leader? Would you ever recommend its use?
6 Does average markup mean that every item in a store has the same markup?
7 What items must be covered by markup other than normal operating expenses and planned profits?
8 How would you compute the sales price for an item that costs $8 and is to be marked up 20 per cent of sales price?
9 Do you believe employee discounts are justified for most types of business firms?
10 How does a store owner achieve an average planned markup on total sales for the year?
11 If an item sells for $10 and has been marked up one-third of selling price, what did it cost the firm?
12 Do inventory losses usually show up as a specific operating expense on the income statement? If not, how is this expense accounted for?
13 How does target pricing work?

Projects for Home Assignment and/or Class Discussion

1   Prepare a pricing determination for a firm that buys a particular product for $35, desires a 40 per cent average markup, and needs 10 per cent of sales to cover markdowns, employee discounts, and damaged merchandise.

2   As part of pricing policy for your own firm, would you ever condone the use of "loss leaders"? Explain in a brief essay what your policy would be and why you would have it.

REFERENCES FOR FURTHER READING

Sommers, M.S., J. Barnes, W.J. Stanton, and C. Futrell, *Fundamentals of Marketing*, 5th Canadian Edition, McGraw-Hill Ryerson Ltd., Scarborough, Ontario, 1989.

"Control over Direct Costs and Pricing," *Your Business Matters*, The Royal Bank of Canada, 1976.

Minding Your Own Business, Federal Business Development Bank, Montreal, 1982, Vol. 2, Chapter 3.

Chapter

▼▲▼▲▼▲▼▲▼

17

Advertising and Promotion

LEARNING OBJECTIVES

After reading this chapter, you will be able to:

1. **U**nderstand the importance of personal selling, advertising, and promotion to the success of a firm
2. **K**now why the demand for goods and services can be from established customers or can be newly created
3. **R**ecognize the need to identify the target customers who will buy the firm's products or services
4. **K**now the types of direct promotion methods, including personal selling, advertising, publicity, and other techniques
5. **U**nderstand how indirect promotion methods, such as public relations, community goodwill, service, and packaging, increase the firm's potential for success

"Running a business without advertising is like winking at a pretty girl in the dark—you know what you're doing, but she doesn't."[1] The president of one of the largest advertising companies in New York concluded a formal address on the billions of dollars spent on advertising each year in the United States by saying, "We know that half of these billions were wasted. The only trouble is we don't know which half."

These two statements point out the importance of advertising and the size of the advertising bill in the United States and Canada every year, and should caution all business people to make their advertising effective. This warning is even more true for small firms that normally cannot absorb wasteful expenditures as well as larger firms.

THE NATURE OF DEMAND

The total demand for the goods or services offered by any small firm can be divided into (1) established demand and (2) promoted, or newly created, demand.

Established demand is that volume of sales which comes without conscious outside promotion by the firm. It assumes that the firm is established with some degree of attractiveness and relies basically on that fact to bring customers to the firm to buy products or services. Reliance is also placed on the fact that people see the store and think of it, perhaps, when products or services are considered. It is recognized that pedestrian traffic is already in the area and that some of the people will stop en route to other places. Distance from competitors will usually assist in bringing in established demand for most types of merchandise.

Promoted demand, by contrast, is the volume of sales that results from the firm's engaging in all types of activities to draw people to the firm. Promoted-demand customers, if pleased, can become established customers.

It is not true that small firms cannot operate profitably when they rely solely on established demand. However, those firms that supplement this established demand with promoted demand show much better sales volume and profits. Too many small firms restrict their operations by ignoring the possibilities of creating more sales. Case studies often show that the reasons are a *lack of working capital* to pay expenses of promotion, a *belief that their market is inelastic*, or a *lack of knowledge of how to design a sales promotion program*.

All the activities that go into the development of sales can be grouped under the title *sales promotion*. Sales promotion can use either *direct* or *indirect* methods. There are no guarantees that any one method will show a precise dollar return in sales, but the effectiveness of each can usually be measured with some degree of accuracy. Every small firm owner should think about using some of the following types of sales promotion:

---

[1]Copyright, General Features Corporation. Reprinted with permission.

DIRECT PROMOTION METHODS	*INDIRECT PROMOTION METHODS*
1 Advertising	1 Public relations
2 Publicity	2 Customer relations
3 Displays	3 Customer services
4 Special event sales	4 Product styling and packaging
5 Manufacturers' aids	
6 Personal selling	

Each of these promotional methods may be important in the individual case, and surely all of them are valuable ways of trying to expand business sales in the short or long run.

DIRECT SALES PROMOTION

Advertising

It must be recognized that advertising is essential to almost every business. Large-scale advertising has made the benefits of mass production possible by creating a demand for the increased flow of products and services. In turn mass production has created the need for large-scale advertising. Unit costs have been reduced in most cases because the economies of large-scale production have more than offset the cost of advertising.

Advertising can be defined as commercial messages to the public designed to inform potential and established customers and to encourage sales for the advertiser. Advertising can be either *institutional* (designed to sell the firm name) or *direct action* (designed to sell the firm's product or services). An advertisement saying, "Our employees subscribed to the United Way 100 per cent" is an example of institutional advertising. "Raincoats are on sale today at $99.95!" is an example of direct-action advertising. Most small firm advertising is of the direct-action type. Service firms may stress the services available from the firm, but this is still direct action to sell that service.

Types of Advertising Media

Among the media generally used in advertising are:

1 Television
2 Radio
3 Newspapers
4 Magazines
5 Outdoor billboards
6 Specialty advertising (distribution of such items as matchpads, pencils, calendars, blotters, gummed labels, telephone pads, shopping bags)
7 Public transportation

8   Yellow pages

9   Direct mail

10   Other media (catalogues, samples, handout leaflets, etc.)

Small firms have a special problem in choosing the medium or type of advertising that is best for them. Big city *television* is not appropriate for most. Large city *newspapers* are too expensive for a firm that services only a small part of the city (although local newspapers can be used, as we will discuss later). It is worthy of note that some large newspapers have attempted to cope with this problem by having special small firm advertising sections where a dozen or more individual small firm ads can be displayed on a single page. More attractive advertising rates have made such advertising possible for more small firms. Effectiveness of such ads has been demonstrated in many cases. *Magazines* usually cover too much territory for a small local firm. Metropolitan *radio* advertising has adjusted somewhat to the problems of the small firm through multi-sponsored programs. In smaller cities and towns, the local radio station and newspaper may cover the market of the small firm well.

Billboards are most effective when used near the actual site of the small firms. Political campaign use of billboards has demonstrated their effectiveness, although their appeal in elections is usually to a much wider audience than that of the market of a particular small firm. Commercial billboards are quite expensive for individual firms, but they are often custom-made for sites that are available on less expensive terms to the particular firm, such as on another of the owner's buildings or a friend's vacant lot.

Billboard advertising can be effective for small firms as well as large ones.
Courtesy of R.G. Advertising Inc.

Effectiveness of *specialty advertising* has been proved by many small firms. Its appropriateness will vary with the type of business. It can take almost limitless forms. Pencils for children when school begins, calendars distributed in attractive shopping bags to neighbourhood homes, matchpads, telephone pads for firms taking telephone orders, blotters, ball-point pens with company name inscribed, and even gummed labels for various uses have all been effective in particular cases. All should prominently show the firm's name, address, and phone number. Experience will demonstrate the effectiveness of any particular devices used.

Advertising in *public transportation* vehicles has become big business and can be effective for small firms if it is possible to coordinate the particular vehicles used and the firm's market. Local streetcars, buses, subways, and taxis are most popular.

Yellow-page advertising is recommended only when the firm is dealing in shopping goods where buyers compare prices or has a market where customers may be looking for a firm that would first be contacted by telephone.

Despite its abuse over the years, *direct-mail advertising* can be a most effective advertising medium for the great majority of small firms. It has the advantages of being selective in its coverage, inexpensive, flexible, adjustable to any size firm, and subject to measurement of its effectiveness. Because of past abuse, however, it must be done well to avoid being tossed into the nearest wastebasket.

Measuring Advertising Effectiveness

Whenever possible, every advertising program undertaken should be checked for its effectiveness. Some of the ways the small firm can do this are:

1   Advertise one item in one ad only. Have no references to the item on the sales floor. Then count the calls and requests that result.
2   Place identifying marks in an ad which appears in two separate publications. The reader is asked to bring the ad to the firm to obtain a special price or prize. See how many ads come in from each source.
3   Omit a regular advertising project for the intermittent periods and watch for any change in sales.
4   Check sales results when a new advertisement is placed.

While the results of these and similar advertising programs cannot be measured precisely, they can give some indication of effectiveness. Timing, products advertised, weather, and attractions offered, such as valuable coupons, will affect results. If no results are observable, it can be said that the program is not effective as direct-action advertising. Even then it may have notified some people of the existence of the firm, and they may include it on future shopping trips. It will thus have served an institutional purpose.

Are your judgements based on what you know or what you hear?

The Man Who Sold Hot Dogs

There was a man who lived by the side of the road and sold
hot dogs.
He was hard of hearing so he had no radio.
He had trouble with his eyes so he read no newspapers.
But he sold good hot dogs.
He put up signs on the highway telling how good they were.
He stood on the side of the road and cried: ''Buy a hot dog,
Mister?''
And people bought and profits were good.
He increased his meat and bun orders.
He bought a bigger stove to take care of his trade.
He finally got his son home from college to help him out.
But then something happened.
His son said, ''Father, haven't you been listening to the radio?
Haven't you been reading the newspapers?
There's a big depression.
The European situation is terrible.
The domestic situation is worse.''
Whereupon the father thought, ''Well, my son's been to college, he
reads the papers and listens to the radio, and he ought to know.''
So the father cut down on his meat and bun orders, took down his
advertising signs, and no longer bothered to stand out on the
highway to sell his hot dogs.
And his hot dog sales fell almost overnight.
''You're right, son,'' the father said to the boy.
''We certainly are in the middle of a great depression.''

It should be obvious that the most important thing in designing an advertising program for any small firm is knowing your market – knowing where the present and potential customers you seek are located. The more owners know about their customers, the better they can devise ways to get their advertising messages to them. If many live in a condominium, for example, an ad in the local house paper may be most effective. If many live in private homes in a small town and take the local newspaper, newspaper advertising is recommended. These are only obvious examples. Time spent in studying the potential customer market will pay good dividends. Much of the wasted expenditures for advertising can be traced to careless preparation of the advertising, not knowing the market and hence misdirecting the advertising, and using the wrong media.

Once an advertising program has been decided upon, it must be consistent and continuous throughout the year. Special features or special events are appropriate for extra expenditures at certain times, but the basic program must be continuous, with both a long-run and a short-run objective in view at all times.

Publicity

Publicity has often been described as advertising that is not paid for. It includes such things as public news about the owner of the firm that tends to brighten the firm's image or make friends for the business. Notices of support given to community activities, awards won by employees for excellence in their industry, public citations for service rendered, election to office in community organizations, sponsorship of a team in the Pee Wee Hockey League, and notices of new services or techniques available are examples. Such activities give the firm a reputation for being interested in and related to the community interests, for striving to give the latest and best services, for having competent people to serve its customers, or for just being a desirable place to do business. Their effect may often be more indirect than direct promotion, but, in any event, the potential of publicity should be exploited wherever possible.

Displays

Displays are an on-site method of sales promotion. Products that are not normally considered impulse items to most people are often sold through an effective display in the windows or on the sales floor. Displays enable the merchant to add changes, interest, and brightness to the standard layout, and when done well, can do much to increase sales. Even the occasional use of a display as an "obstacle course" item can be effective if not overdone. Remember the L'eggs merchandise-display model in the local supermarket or variety store. Windows can be used for sophisticated displays, such as in men's clothing stores, or for giving information about special sales or events, for example in grocery stores. The use of homemade window signs to advertise prices on Saturday or weekend specials has become a vital activity in many consumer goods firms.

Special Event Sales

Using special events as direct sales promotion has become a well-established feature of most consumer goods businesses. They are also used by industrial goods firms, but less often. The firm's anniversary, Victoria Day, the firm president's birthday, the addition of a new service for customers, the start of the spring and fall seasons, etc. can all be used as occasions to promote sales. Making the most of such events may entail use of other direct promotion methods, such as advertising, but special events justify classification as a separate direct promotion method.

Manufacturer's Aids

Manufacturer's aids are any form of assistance provided by the manufacturer to small wholesalers and retailers for promoting sales. These aids may take the form of national advertising of the products involved, assignment of sales representatives to be in the particular store to demonstrate the use of a product such as cookware, provision of attractive window and floor displays, or monetary contributions to an advertising program. Such products as home appliances, automobiles, television sets, and men's suits and shirts are often accompanied by such assistance from the manufacturer. Firms having franchises and/or distributorships are frequently aided by the parent firm in many of these matters.

Personal Selling

Personal selling means all those activities and characteristics of the individual salesperson that make for successful sales. If it is recognized that all people are not good salespersons, we can appreciate that there are certain things which make good ones. Some of these are being able to discover potential customers, knowing methods of acquainting potential customers with available merchandise, and ability to close a sale. The type of skills required will vary with different types of firms and products.

Attractive store fronts will lure customers. Unattractive fronts will discourage walk-in traffic. *Courtesy of Metropolitan Toronto Convention & Visitors Association.*

Fundamental to all good personal selling is a thorough knowledge of the merchandise by the salesperson. The advantages, various uses, and special qualities of the merchandise must be thoroughly known. Discerning customers look to the salesperson for such knowledge. They know quickly if the salesperson is competent or incompetent in this regard. If a salesperson is only an order taker, this fact is soon obvious to such customers. If equipment or machinery is involved, the salesperson must be able to demonstrate the product efficiently. In retailing, such characteristics as pleasant personality, good appearance, knowledge of prices, and interest in finding a product to fill an expressed need become more important. Confidence in firms is developed through successful personal selling. A positive training program for all sales people should be a must for all small firms, just as it is in large firms. Advertising may produce a first inquiry from potential customers or bring them into a retail establishment. Unless the personal selling that follows is satisfactory, not only the first sale but all potential repeat business is in jeopardy.

The four basic steps in making any sale have often been summarized as follows:

1 Gaining the prospective customer's attention
2 Arousing interest
3 Creating desire for the product—overcoming objections
4 Closing the sale

The detailed sales plan to apply these four steps varies with the type of product and type of business. The drugstore salesperson will need to give less attention to these steps because the customers come in with an interest in a particular product. The person who is selling an electric saw to a prospective customer will need to pay attention to every detail of the sales plan.

INDIRECT SALES PROMOTION

We have observed earlier in this chapter that indirect sales-promotional methods are usually classified as public relations, good customer relations, customer services, product styling, and packaging of products. These may all be applied to the established demand customers we have previously discussed, but they can also be applied to the development of new customers.

Public Relations

A firm's public relations determine its image, or popular reputation, in the general community. The nature of its public relations, good or bad, is reflected in the community's attitude toward the firm. Every business has public relations, either consciously or unconsciously, and a good image cannot normally be purchased; it is the responsibility of every person associated with the firm. Every act of the firm's representatives contributes to the overall image of the firm. Good public relations are a cumulative net result, which is more easily destroyed than built. Good public relations develop goodwill and sales. Every owner should be aware of the importance of good public relations and should be sure that each employee knows their importance and how they are built. Building good relations in the community is a never-ending project. Every proposed business policy should first be analyzed in terms of its effect upon the company image. Every crisis decision must always consider the possible effect upon the firm's image.

Customer Relations

Good customer relations build sales independently and also contribute to the total image of the firm. Satisfied, happy customers are the best form of advertising. Word-of-mouth advertising results from happy customers. Good customer relations are basically the result of past transactions with the firm. Such items as speedy handling of complaints, assistance in emergencies, favours in obtaining items, and abiding by announced policies all assist in developing good customer relations. Courteous, competent, and pleasant treatment of customers is most important.

Customer Services

Customer services can be a part of both public relations and good customer relations. Many customers want special services and seek out firms that supply them. Examples are air-conditioned stores, night hours for shopping, credit accounts, delivery service, and lines of merchandise not generally available. Pricing policy may be adjusted to a particular customer group. Discount coupons may provide an attraction as a customer service. Effective administration of any services offered is essential to making them valuable as sale developers. Firms selling industrial products have found recently that the most valued customer services are on-time deliveries, conformity to specifications of products sold, and efficient accounting procedures.

Product Styling and Packaging

Product styling and product packaging are obvious aids in developing sales volume. Customers who desire to be first with the latest seek out the merchants with the latest styles. When similar products are offered in various styles, they seek choices. Packaging can be an equal attraction. The cosmetic field is an excellent example of products that have been presented in all types of beautiful bottles and packages. Even the choices in packaging bread have recently been of concern to some customers, some preferring the type of package which either has a detachable tie (device to reclose the package after opening) or the inner wrapper supplied by some bakers. Such customer preferences probably reflect a desire for uniqueness rather than utility in the product.

All the indirect sales promotion methods also reflect a conviction that the customer is still the most important part of any successful business. There can be no profit in the absence of sales. Efforts to keep present customers happy and to develop new ones constantly are essential to continued profits and growth.

QUESTIONS FOR CLASS DISCUSSION

1 How would you describe established demand as contrasted with promoted demand?
2 How would you define advertising?
3 Is advertising as important to small firms as to large ones?
4 How is the problem of choosing the advertising media different for small firms than for large ones?
5 What is specialty advertising? Give some examples.
6 Would you recommend advertising on the "Canada A.M." show for a small-town department store? Why?
7 How do you recommend that direct-mail advertising be made effective?
8 What do we mean by "checking the effectiveness of advertising"? What are some of the methods by which this can be done?
9 What is meant by saying that creating an "obstacle course" with a display can increase sales of an item of merchandise?
10 What are the four basic steps in successful selling?
11 Do you agree that good public relations normally cannot be purchased? Why?
12 What is meant by saying that product styling can be an indirect sales promotion device?

Projects for Home Assignment and/or Class Discussion

1 Do you know of a product you or your family prefer because of its packaging and styling? Explain such a case and why you prefer it.
2 List what you think would be the best advertising media for your own hardware store in a suburban area. Prepare a specific ad for the store.
3 Can you name some special events that could be the basis of special sales for a fast-food franchise? How would you advertise them and where?

REFERENCES FOR FURTHER READING

Archer, M., *An Introduction to Canadian Business*, 5th ed., McGraw-Hill Ryerson Ltd., Toronto, 1986, Chapter 11.

Beckman, M.D., W.S. Good, and R.G. Wyckham, *Small Business Management*, John Wiley & Sons Canada Ltd., Toronto, 1982, Chapter 9.

Cunningham, G., *Buy Yourself A Job & Be Your Own Boss*, McGraw-Hill Ryerson Ltd., 1990, Chapter 8.

White, Larry, *How to Make Advertising Work For Your Small Business*, Financial Post/Macmillan Company of Canada Limited, Toronto, 1980.

Wright, John S., Willis Winter, S.K. Zeigler, and N. O'Dea, *Advertising*, 1st Canadian ed., McGraw-Hill Ryerson Ltd., Toronto, 1984.

"Advertising and Sales Promotion," *Your Business Matters*, The Royal Bank of Canada, 1979.

Minding Your Own Business, Federal Business Development Bank, Montreal, 1982, Volume 2, Chapter 5 and Volume 3, Chapter 3.

· ·

MANAGING THE
OPERATION

18

Personnel and Organization for the Small Firm

LEARNING OBJECTIVES

After reading this chapter, you will be able to:

1. **U**nderstand what is meant by the statement ``Good employees are the firm's most valuable asset''
2. **K**now the framework of human resource management programs as they relate to the small firm
3. **K**now what employees want from their employment and how those wants can be met by small business
4. **U**nderstand the basics of a good human resource/personnel policy for the small firm
5. **M**atch individuals to the right jobs through job analysis, job description, and job specifications
6. **U**nderstand how the organization of the firm needs to relate to the human resources within the firm

GOOD EMPLOYEES ARE VALUABLE ASSETS

College students today usually have positive ideas about the personnel policies of business organizations. Their opinions and attitudes have been largely influenced by the eighties, when employers sought employees in what was a seller's market. The demand for workers usually exceeded the supply of able people. Now in the nineties, when unemployment in many areas is high, employers are unwilling to hire people without proper training and ability. Jobs are not so easily obtained in such periods, and applications are scrutinized more closely.

Successful business firms, however, have always recognized the difference between finding and retaining good employees. In big business we have seen great programs of employee on-the-job training, sensitivity training, opportunities to try different positions, merit raises to provide regularly increased income for productive workers, and supervisory and executive programs of various types. All are designed to improve employee productivity, encourage creativity, and generally make workers happy and convinced they have an attractive future with the firm.

At the same time, the past decade and a half have seen an increasing percentage of trained people going into business for themselves in preference to working for large corporations. One large western university reports that regular studies of its graduates show that those who went into business for themselves have the highest average income. This is healthy for small business, but it also means that small business owners must fully understand the problems of obtaining and retaining good employees.

It is a worthwhile experience for students to consider these problems from the employer's viewpoint. They now sit on the other side of the desk. They must devise a personnel program for their contemplated firms, and it must be a good one if the business is to be really successful.

Everyone recognizes that good employees are a firm's most valuable asset. Many customers are "turned off" and do not come back to a business whose employees have been discourteous or incompetent or have given other bad impressions. It is often said that a retailer can lose established customers much more easily than he or she can gain new ones. Customers are the lifeblood of any business. Their continued patronage is essential to its profit objectives. Good employees can do much to assure this objective. Even those not in contact with actual sales contribute much to keeping the entire organization efficient and able to render proper service to customers.

With this in mind, small firm owners can start their personnel programs with a review of those things that are important to employees. These personnel programs are *human resource programs* that seek to communicate company goals and information to employees. The degree of importance may not be in the order presented here, but all of these factors are influential.

THE FRAMEWORK FOR PERSONNEL PROGRAMS

Before taking a look at suggestions about what employees want from their jobs and suggestions for achieving the goal of an efficient, happy, and productive staff of employees for any business, we should recognize the legal framework in which all personnel policies operate. Personnel programs are not left to the sole discretion of business owners in the modern business world. Even well-meaning policies that have proved successful in the past may run into conflict with a barrage of legal regulations that all employers must abide by today.

Chief among the governmental regulations for employers today are minimum wage laws, fair employment regulations, the right of employees to collective bargaining and to form their own unions, requirements for withholding income taxes and other items from employee paycheques for the federal government (Unemployment Insurance, Canada Pension Plan), and public policy relative to being an equal opportunity employer. It is not our purpose here to evaluate such regulations but only to indicate to new firm planners that it is important to check the current status on all such regulations at the time they are starting new firms.

Fringe benefits, health and safety programs, profit-sharing plans, pensions, and vacation policies are all part of a complete personnel program. These benefits can add as much as 25 to 40 per cent to each employee's wages. Surely all successful business owners must recognize today that fair wages which are competitive, fringe benefits which are attractive, desirable working conditions, and a sense of concern for employees are important parts of building a staff of dedicated and productive employees.

WHAT DO EMPLOYEES WANT FROM THEIR JOBS?

1 Fair Wages   Wages must be more than enough to buy the essentials of life. Employees want sufficient money to have adequate insurance, to be able to educate their children, and to provide for their old age. They want real wages to increase from year to year so that they can enjoy an improving status. They want to feel that their wages bear a relation to their contribution to the firm.

2 Continuous Employment   Even when wages are quite satisfactory in all respects, employees still want to know that their employment is assured into the future. They will often take other positions at less pay only because the outlook for permanent employment is better. Yearly earnings are more important than weekly earnings for the majority of employees.

3 Reasonable Hours of Work   Even good employees who truly want to work for a living still want the hours of work to be reasonable. When the eight-hour day was established, it was hailed as a great achievement for all wage earners. Today we are on the threshold of a further reduction in the workday and/or workweek, and small firms must abide by the rules of society. They can often adjust their working hours more easily than the large firms because their employees usually live close to their work and because of the close rapport possible among staff and employers. Some employees are more willing to work split shifts, for example.

4 Pleasant and Safe Working Conditions   Factory workers want a minimum of risk of industrial accidents, occupational diseases, fatigue-creating elements such as noise, disturbances, and vibration. Factory, wholesale, service, and retail employees all want healthy working conditions in a pleasant environment.

5 Sense of Improving Status   Employees desire assurance that they can improve their status over a period of time with the firm. This may take the form of opportunities to use talents other than those that got them their first job, a chance to participate in decision making for the firm, or a chance to demonstrate improved status through a title that their friends will respect.

6 Feeling of Contribution   Despite any contrary impressions that appear in the newspaper during labour strife, most employees really do want to feel that they are making a contribution to the firm. Nothing is more frustrating to good employees than not knowing where their jobs fit into the total operation, not knowing the value of the work they do, and, even more, not having anyone display interest in what they are doing. Here again, the small firm has advantages over the larger firm because of the relative size of the business.

7 Respect for Management   Employees are much happier and better workers when they respect the management of their firm and think that it is competent, fair, and alert to employees' contributions.

Small business has often been accused of being unable to provide all these conditions for employees. Competent owners refuse to accept such an accusation. The numerous small firms whose employees have many years of service with them demonstrate that small business can successfully compete for and keep good employees.

ADVANTAGES OF SMALL FIRM EMPLOYMENT

Among the advantages of employment in a small firm are the following:

1   The small firm can provide employment for people who want to work in the area where they live.

2   Coworkers are often neighbours and enjoy social life and sporting events together, with or without the owner, thereby creating spirit and harmony among the group members.

3   The firm is small enough that employees can be close to the employer at all times. Therefore, complaints and irritations can be solved at once, rather than be sent to a committee.

4   Small firms can readily observe and compliment any exceptional achievements of employees.

5   Employees have greater opportunities to try different jobs in small firms because employers can pay close attention to their talents and desires.

6   Employees can more easily take part in decision making and be made to feel they are part of that process because of their highly regarded and sought-after opinions.

7   Wages can be comparable to the wages paid by large firms while the wage earner maintains the advantages of working for a small firm.

8   Group benefits, such as life insurance and company-supported activities, are equally available in small firms.

9   Profit-sharing plans that aid firm growth and profitability can easily be set up.

10 Employees can easily become shareholders if the legal form of organization is a corporation.

These advantages do not exist automatically. They must be the result of a deliberate personnel policy. Some suggestions for such a policy follow.

PERSONNEL POLICY SUGGESTIONS

The small firm owner can take certain steps to assure a good personnel policy.

1   Create an image that the firm is good to work for. Word of mouth from employees can do much to aid this objective.

2   Don't limit employee applications to people who happen to stop in and ask for a job. Go out and recruit employees. This can be done at schools and universities that maintain job placement bureaus for their students, at established government and private employment agencies, and through referrals from friends and other business firms. Advertising in newspapers or other media can also be very effective.

3   Establish applicants' capabilities before hiring them. Physical examinations are a must, including tests of vision, movement, strength, stamina, and hearing as appropriate to the job. Mental tests are also recommended. Hiring the handicapped is a fine thing, but don't do handicapped persons wrong by expecting them to fill positions they cannot handle.

4   Have all applicants fill out a detailed application form and give references. See the sample form in Figure 18-1. Check references carefully, including credit references and other personal data. Check further than references whenever possible.

SAMPLE APPLICATION FOR EMPLOYMENT

PERSONAL DATA

Position being applied for

Date available to begin work

Last name

Given name(s)

Address

Street   Apt. No.   Home Telephone Number

City   Province   Postal Code   Business Telephone Number

Are you legally eligible to work in Canada?   ☐ Yes   ☐ No

Are you willing to re-locate in Ontario?   ☐ Yes   ☐ No

Preferred location   Category

To determine your qualification for employment, please provide below and on the reverse, information related to your academic and other achievements including voluntary work, as well as employment history. Additional information may be attached on a separate sheet.

EDUCATION

ELEMENTARY OR SECONDARY SCHOOL

Highest grade or level completed

Type of certificate or diploma obtained

BUSINESS, TRADE OR TECHNICAL SCHOOL

Name of course   Length of course

Licence, certificate or diploma awarded?   ☐ Yes   ☐ No

COMMUNITY COLLEGE

Name of Program   Length of Program

Diploma received   ☐ Yes   ☐ No

Other courses, workshops, seminars

UNIVERSITY

Length of course   Degree awarded   ☐ Pass   ☐ Honours   ☐ Yes   ☐ No

Major subject

Licences, Certificates, Degrees

Work related skills

Describe any or your work related skills, experience, or training that relate to the position being applied for.

EMPLOYMENT

Name and Address of present/last employer

Present/Last job title

Period of employment   From   To   Present/Last salary

Name of Supervisor   Telephone

Type of Business

Duties/Responsibilities

Reason for leaving

Name and Address of previous employer

Previous job title

Period of employment   From   To   Final salary

Name of Supervisor   Telephone

Type of Business

Duties/Responsibilities

Reason for leaving

Name and Address of previous employer

Previous job title

Period of employment   From   To   Final salary

Name of Supervisor   Telephone

Type of Business

Duties/Responsibilities

Reason for leaving

For employment references, may we approach:

Your present/last employer?   ☐ Yes   ☐ No

Your former employer(s)?   ☐ Yes   ☐ No

List references if different than above on a separate sheet.

Activities (civic, athletic etc.)

I hereby declare that the foregoing information is true and complete to my knowledge. I understand that a false statement may disqualify me from employment, or cause my dismissal.

Have you attached an additional sheet?   ☐ Yes   ☐ No

Signature   Date

Page 7

FIGURE 18-1 • Application for employment. Sample provided by the Ontario Human Rights Commission. A revised and updated application will be available in 1991.

5   Always have an extended interview with the applicant – in pleasant surroundings – and have his or her application in front of you. The interview should enable you to rate the applicant. The interviewer should direct discussion into various channels to find out as much as possible about the applicant: background, previous employment experience, ambition, sincerity, likes and dislikes, hobbies, sporting interests, living habits, family associations, responsibilities, etc. The applicant's self-evaluation is important also. Discuss past salaries and expected future salaries.

6   Even small firms should have job descriptions[1] available to discuss with applicants. These should be carefully explained, including salaries. The normal sequence of advancement in the firm should be described, including opportunities for such advancement, salary ranges, and average time at each level. If the firm has an organization chart, it should be shown and explained to the applicant.

7   A positive program of orientation of new employees should be established, preferably in writing. When new employees first come to work, a supervisor should be assigned to introduce them to fellow employees, the company layout, the facilities of the firm, and their own positions. Any printed material for employees should be given to them.

8   Have regular meetings with employees to discuss matters of mutual interest. Invite opinions, even contrary ones.

9   If training programs are desirable or necessary, establish them for regular presentation. No exceptions should be made for employees deemed able to benefit. Most small firms will do actual job training on the job.

10   Have a specified trial period for each new employee. Be sure that he or she knows about it. Do not hesitate to terminate a new employee whose work is unsatisfactory during this period. Weak employees hurt the morale of all who carry their share.

11   Provide at least an annual review of each employee's progress and productivity. Such reviews should be discussed with employees so they know how they stand with the firm.

---

[1]Personnel managers have three techniques to assist them in getting people into appropriate jobs:
   Job analysis – A detailed study of jobs, including identification and examination of the elements and characteristics of each job and the requirements of the person assigned to the job.
   Job description – Description of the objectives of the job, the work to be performed, responsibilities involved, skills needed, working conditions, and relationship to other jobs.
   Job specification – Description of the special qualifications required to fill a particular job including experience, education, special skills, and any physical requirements. These are parts of a total job-evaluation program.

12 Keep salaries in line with the competition, or better than elsewhere—if this can be justified. Have a merit system of pay raises within a rank to be put into effect if they are earned. Be sure all new, and older, employees know the salary ranges available to them if they are promoted.

ORGANIZATION WITHIN THE SMALL FIRM

Most small firms do not make a formal chart of their organization, but this may become necessary if the firm grows and additional delegation of authority and responsibility becomes appropriate. A typical organization chart for a drugstore is shown in Figure 18-2. The owner may perform one or more of the functions shown. The size of the firm will determine when more people are assigned to other functions, that is, how many functions are carried out by the owner and how many are delegated.

In any small firm, even one without a formal organization chart, it is important that each employee knows precisely his or her responsibility and authority. If the owner works with the business each day, the owner is the top authority. If he or she is confident of the abilities of the employees, certain authority will be delegated to them to facilitate getting things done and to expedite the many routine decisions that must be made every day. For example, the company may have a policy on customer exchanges of merchandise sold. All competent salespersons should normally be able to handle most steps in this procedure. Approval of credit applications is a

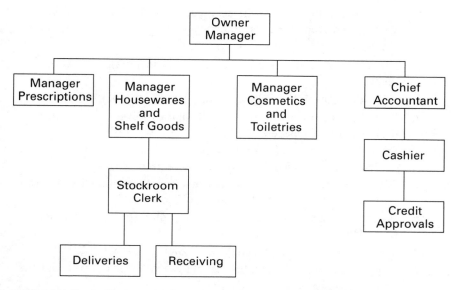

F I G U R E   1 8 - 2 • Organization chart for a drugstore.

different matter. This authority can be specifically delegated, but it carries a responsibility that requires special analytical ability. One person should be assigned final authority in this regard.

All employees, from the stockroom workers to the sales manager, should know what is expected of them and their authority in performing their assigned tasks. It is an old principle of organization that authority must be commensurate with responsibility. This is another way of saying that if you give a person a job to do, give the authority necessary to do it. When policies are established for the firm, all employees should know what the policies are and who is responsible for their administration.

While we have emphasized the small firm in our discussion here, it should be noted that as firms grow they also have to add more division managers, personnel managers, and other staff members to meet their expanding staff needs. All the staff members mentioned here are called "line" employees. Line employees report directly to a superior above them and direct those below them on the organization chart. Growth may bring the need for other staff members, such as legal counsel, who report only to a senior official of the firm. Such persons have no line authority over other employees in the firm.

QUESTIONS FOR CLASS DISCUSSION

1 Would you like the responsibility for keeping a large group of employees happy and productive? Why?

2 Do you believe in a six-month trial period for all new employees? Why?

3 If "good employees are a firm's greatest asset," how would you assure good employees for your business?

4 How can employees do harm to a business?

5 Do you agree that it is easier to lose customers than to develop them?

6 What do you think employees really want from their jobs?

7 Would a 50 per cent increase in all salaries solve the personnel problems of all business firms?

8 Do you agree that most employees really want to feel they are contributing in their jobs? How can this need be achieved?

9 What are some of the advantages that small firms have in assuring that they have happy and productive employees?

10 Would you recommend a profit-sharing plan for your own small firm? How would you devise such a plan?

11 What features would you build into your personnel policy?

12 What is a formal organization chart? Do you think such a chart is appropriate for small firms?

13   What do we mean by "making authority commensurate with responsibility"?

14   What should be the relationship of the warehouse manager and the floor manager in the modest-sized department store? Can this relationship be shown on the typical organization chart?

Projects for Home Assignment and/or Class Discussion

1   Prepare a short report on why "the boss must be the boss" in business and how he or she can retain authority and still have good relations with all employees of the firm.

2   Some companies encourage relatives to become employees of their firm while others positively prohibit having more than one member of a family employed by the firm. What are your thoughts about this?

3   Explain in one paragraph why "personal references" on an application form are normally less significant than reports from former employers.

REFERENCES FOR FURTHER READING

Archer, M., *An Introduction to Canadian Business*, 5th ed., McGraw-Hill Ryerson Ltd., Toronto, 1986, Chapter 15.

Beckman, M.D., W.S. Good, and R.G. Wyckham, *Small Business Management*, John Wiley & Sons Canada Ltd., Toronto, 1982, Chapter 12.

Cunningham, G., *Buy Yourself A Job & Be Your Own Boss*, McGraw-Hill Ryerson Ltd., 1990, Chapter 7.

Tate Jr., C.E., L.C. Megginson, C.R. Scott Jr., and L.R. Trueblood, *Successful Small Business Management*, 3rd ed., Business Publications, Inc., Plano, Texas, 1985, Chapters 9 and 10.

Minding Your Own Business, Federal Business Development Bank, Montreal, 1982, Vol. 1, Chapters 11 and 12.

. . . .

19

Inventory Valuation Methods and Depreciation Methods

LEARNING OBJECTIVES

After reading this chapter, you will be able to:

1. **U**nderstand the importance of purchasing as a part of small business success
2. **K**now the factors to consider when buying for resale and for manufacturing procurement
3. **U**nderstand the value of maintaining good vendor relationships
4. **K**now the considerations for how much inventory to order and the use of the economic order quantity formulas
5. **U**nderstand the advantages of taking all purchase discounts available
6. **U**nderstand the importance of inventory turnover to overall small business success
7. **K**now the methods of valuing inventories and the reasons each can be used

The student who has had a one-year course in accounting, business owners who have become familiar with the accounting for their own businesses, and students who have understood the preceding chapters should now be ready for a more detailed look at the problems associated with valuation methods, which may be applied to inventories, and depreciation rates, which may be applied to fixed assets.

The subjects of valuation and depreciation are particularly appropriate for new firms because the owners have a completely free choice of methods available for both. Final decisions can be postponed until the end of the first year. Operations for the first year can easily affect the choices made. New firm owners can make better decisions if they know the various methods.

Historically, inventories were always valued at the *lower of cost or market*. This method is still popular and it has advantages in many cases. Its chief disadvantage for the small firm is that if the market value is lower than cost, the firm actually takes inventory losses before they have been incurred through sale of the merchandise. This will be explained fully in the following examples and discussion.

METHODS OF VALUING INVENTORIES

The small business firm has a choice of at least five major methods of valuing its inventories. Expediency, tax considerations, the results of operation, and the outlook for the future are some of the considerations that will affect the choice made in the particular case. These five methods are:

1   Lower of cost or market
2   First in, first out (FIFO)
3   Last in, first out (LIFO)
4   Weighted average cost
5   Retail price method

To illustrate the application of each of these methods to a specific inventory, let us consider the small firm that sells a relatively high-priced product. This could be a piano store or a firm selling blockmaking machines. Full data to value its inventory, using the first four methods, follow. A separate example is given showing the retail price method.

Company X sells product A. Its purchases of this product during 1990 were as follows:

January: 10 units at $6,000 each
March: 5 units at $6,500 each
June: 15 units at $7,000 each
September: 10 units at $8,000 each
December: 10 units at $8,500 each

On December 31, the market price from the supplier was $9,000 per unit. Inflation had continued. On December 31, company X had twenty-two units of its product on hand as the year-end inventory. Of these twenty-two units, eight were purchased in December, eight in September, four in June, and two in January.

The company is interested in knowing how these twenty-two units could be valued under each of the five cited methods of valuation.

Detailed computation of the value of the inventory using each of the methods follows.

Lower-of-Cost-or-Market Method

This method necessitates computing two values, cost and market, and then using the lower of these two figures. The market value is easy. Market value on December 31 was $9,000 per unit. Therefore, market value is twenty-two times $9,000 or $198,000. Computing cost value of the twenty-two units in the inventory necessitates finding the invoices for each unit, subtracting the value of those particular units in the inventory, and totalling the result. In our problem, that is done as follows:

8 units purchased in December × $8,500	= $ 68,000
8 units purchased in September × $8,000	= $ 64,000
4 units purchased in June × $7,000	= $ 28,000
2 units purchased in January × $6,000	= $ 12,000
Total cost of the 22-unit inventory	= $172,000

When we compare market value of $198,000 and actual cost value of $172,000, under the lower-of-cost-or-market method the value of the inventory would be $172,000.

First In, First Out (FIFO) Method

This method is the most commonly used method in Canada and it coincides with the normal movement of merchandise in most inventories. At least, almost every small firm owner hopes that inventory will move smoothly through the process of acquisition to sale. Exceptions are, of course, to be recognized in some special types of firms.

FIFO means that the first inventory received is the first sold and, therefore, the remaining inventory is assumed to be the last merchandise purchased. In our problem, the twenty-two units in the inventory would be the ten purchased in December, the ten purchased in September, and two of the units purchased in June. The student will immediately recognize that this statement probably does not conform to the facts of the firm. No doubt some of the units purchased in September and December have been sold. Nevertheless, FIFO is an approved method of evaluation, and its calculation would be as follows:

10 units purchased in December × $8,500	= $ 85,000
10 units purchased in September × $8,000	= $ 80,000
2 units purchased in June × $7,000	= $ 14,000
Total FIFO value of the 22-unit inventory	= $179,000

The student will see that already we have some variation in value. Lower of cost or market gave us a value of $172,000, while FIFO indicates a value of $179,000. The importance of the variation method should begin to unveil itself. But other values are available under the remaining methods. Let us continue.

Last In, First Out (LIFO) Method

As the name of this method indicates, the method assumes that the last units purchased were the first ones sold. Normal retailing activities would not suggest this movement of the inventory in most cases. Yet, in such lines as style merchandise, this may be true more often than suspected. Nevertheless, even though this is an often used method of inventory valuation, Revenue Canada does *not* accept the LIFO method for purposes of income tax returns.

Under LIFO, the twenty-two units in the inventory would be the earliest units purchased – the ten units purchased in January, the five units purchased in March, and seven of the units purchased in June. Calculation of a LIFO value would, therefore, be as follows:

10 units purchased in January × $6,000	= $ 60,000
5 units purchased in March × $6,500	= $ 32,500
7 units purchased in June × $7,000	= $ 49,000
Total LIFO value of the 22-unit inventory	= $141,500

This LIFO value, arrived at under the circumstances of rapidly increasing purchase prices, is substantially less than either of the preceding two value computations. The significance of its potential use will be seen later in this chapter.

Weighted Average Cost Method

This method is more than merely an average cost. It demands that the average cost be weighted to reflect the number of units purchased at different prices. This necessitates that we compute the total cost of units at each price and divide that total by the number of units bought during the year to find the weighted average cost of one unit. This figure is then multiplied by twenty-two to arrive at the inventory value. That calculation is done as follows:

10 units in January at $6,000	= $ 60,000
5 units in March at $6,500	= $ 32,500
15 units in June at $7,000	= $105,000
10 units in September at $8,000	= $ 80,000
10 units in December at $8,500	= $ 85,000
Total cost of 50-unit inventory	= $362,500

First, $362,500 divided by fifty (units purchased) equals $7,250, the weighted average cost on one unit. Then, twenty-two times $7,250 equals $159,500, the weighted average cost of the twenty-two units in the December 31 inventory. Inventory value under this method is, accordingly, $159,500.

Retail Price Method

This method of inventory valuation is particularly appropriate for retail firms that carry hundreds of items in their inventories. Its application involves gathering all costs and expected retail prices on the beginning inventory and the purchases during the year. Freight-inward charges are then added to the cost total and additional markups are added to the original expected retail price total. Markdowns would be deducted from total expected sales price.

The dollar difference between these totals (markup) is then computed in dollars and as a percentage of the sales total. Actual sales are then deducted from this sales value of all merchandise handled during the year to give a retail value of the inventory remaining. By deducting the average markup from this figure, we arrive at the inventory value.

For example, if total invoice costs of beginning inventory, purchases, and freight-inward charges during the year total $60,000, and normal retail prices plus additional markups or less any markdowns total $90,000, the planned markup is $30,000, or 33⅓ per cent of retail. Then, if actual sales at retail are $45,000, the remaining inventory has a retail value of $45,000. By deducting the markup percentage (33⅓ per cent) from $45,000, we arrive at a cost value of the inventory of $30,000.

Adjustments can be made in this method for employee discounts, inventory shortages, etc. in computing the cost percentages. An advantage of this plan for retailers is that employees need only list retail prices when taking inventory counts from the shelves. All cost data and summary work can be quickly completed in the office.

To apply the retail price method strictly to our same problem with company X and the data used in the previous valuation methods, we must set a retail price on the fifty units purchased during the year and record actual sales of the twenty-eight units sold (fifty purchased less twenty-two in the ending inventory), as shown in Table 19-1.

WHICH VALUATION METHOD TO USE

In our various methods, we have seen that the value of the twenty-two units in company X's inventory ranged from $141,500 to $179,000. How is the new small firm owner to make a choice? Several factors may be important in the decision.

First, profits and inventory value vary directly. The higher the inventory, the higher the resulting profit; that is, if closing inventory is overvalued as compared with opening inventory, costs will be understated and profits will

TABLE 19-1

COMPUTATION OF INVENTORY VALUE USING RETAIL PRICE METHOD

	COST	RETAIL
Beginning inventory	0	0
This was a new firm; all units were purchased during the year.		
Purchases during year (50 units)	$362,500	$517,850
The difference between this cost and retail is $155,350, which is the gross margin or markup percentage of 30% of retail. Cost is, therefore, 70% of retail.		
Actual sales for the year (28 units)		$289,350
Inventory value at retail (22 units)		$228,500
70% of retail value is the cost of the inventory		
(30% of markup).		.70
Inventory value under retail price method		$159,950

accordingly be overstated. Taxes may therefore be important in the choice made. The firm owner should also consider the outlook for sales in the immediate oncoming years. Will they be as good as this year? Were there windfall profits or other unexpected profits this year so that profits exceeded expectation? Can such profits continue? Are there some antagonistic shareholders scrutinizing operations to be sure that the firm earned sufficient profit to pay their preference share dividend? Will the firm show a profit regardless of which valuation method is used?

When all these factors are considered, the firm owner will choose the method that will be best for all concerned.

It should be pointed out that in the purposely inflationary market example we used in this chapter, LIFO showed the lowest inventory value and FIFO the highest. In a declining wholesale market, the opposite would be true. The other methods illustrated show a greater tendency to reduce wide variations in resulting values.

The uninitiated are often shocked to learn that a specific inventory of products or merchandise can have different values. Critics often think of this as an inherently evil situation. But who is to say what is the true value of merchandise that is yet unsold or has been on the shelves for a long period? Just as we recognize that there can be no profit in the absence of sale, so it would seem unfair to take an inventory loss in the absence of its sale. Consistency in method used will usually even out the value variations over time. Merchants or manufacturers cannot choose the method that favours their own purposes each year.

It is generally recognized commercial and accounting practice that inventories must be valued in the same manner from year to year and that the method of valuation cannot be changed unless there is good reason for the change and the new method is likely to remain in effect for a considerable time. The *Income Tax Act* provides that the inventory at the commencement of any taxation year is to be valued at the same amount as at the end of the immediately preceding taxation year.

METHODS OF DEPRECIATING FIXED ASSETS

The investment that any business has in its fixed assets must be recouped. Fixed assets wear out, or become obsolete, out of style, or technologically inadequate. As they render their services to the firm, their costs are just as truly business expense as the gasoline for the delivery truck. To provide the firm with capital to replace them, their costs must be charged (allocated) to operations by way of depreciation expense. At the end of each fiscal period, a charge should be made to a *depreciation expense* account (debit) and a credit made to a minus asset account entitled *allowance for depreciation*. Each fixed asset should have such accounts in the records. These depreciation expenses are noncash expenses. No cheques are written for them. But the depreciation expense accounts appear on the income statement as expenses, and the allowance for depreciation accounts are shown on the balance sheet as deductions from the cost value of the appropriate fixed asset accounts. These depreciation charges do not result in the creation of a cash fund to replace the assets, but they do provide a cross section of assets from which demands may be made for necessary capital to replace the assets.

The question for good management is how to charge off the assets as depreciation expense. How much should be charged each year? How long will the asset last before it must be or should be replaced? Small firm owners must make decisions on these matters. When they decide on answers to these questions, they can turn to a method of depreciation.

There are several methods of computing depreciation charges. Each has merit in particular cases. Small firm owners should be familiar with the details of each. The most common are known as:

1   Straight line
2   Use or production
3   Declining balance

It may surprise the new student to know that the depreciation charges on a particular asset can also vary, just as an inventory can have different values. We will illustrate this variation in charges by computing the annual depreciation charge on a specific machinery and equipment fixed asset. The data necessary to illustrate all four methods are as follows:

A small factory has machinery and equipment which cost $150,000. Their estimated life is ten years. It is estimated that their salvage value at the end of ten years will be $20,000. Best estimates indicate that they will turn out 100 000 units of the company's product. During the firm's first year of operation, it produced 15 000 units of its product.

What is the depreciation charge for the first year under each of the three methods listed above?

Straight Line Method

This method provides for an equal charge in each year of the life of the fixed asset. It necessitates knowing the *depreciable value*. Depreciable value is *cost less salvage value*. In our problem, the cost of $150,000 and the estimated salvage value of $20,000 result in a depreciable value of $130,000. Straight line depreciation then spreads this $130,000 out evenly over the ten years of estimated life of the asset. This means an annual depreciation charge of $13,000.

Straight line depreciation is expressed as a formula as follows:

$$\frac{\text{Depreciable value}}{\text{Estimated life}} = \frac{\$130,000}{10 \text{ years}} = \$13,000 \text{ annual charge}$$

Under this method the adjusting entry at the end of each fiscal period would be a debit to depreciation expense, machinery, $13,000, and a credit to allowance for depreciation, machinery, $13,000. Profits will accordingly be reduced this amount for the year, and the asset account value will be modified to this extent by the allowance account, which will be deducted from the cost value on the balance sheet.

Use or Production Method

This method seeks to ascertain what proportion of the total estimated production was achieved in the subject year. This percentage of the total is applied against the same depreciable value used above. In our illustration, the machinery produced 15 000 of the estimated 100 000 units in the first year, or 15 per cent of the total. Accordingly, this method would charge off as depreciation expense in the first year 15 per cent of $130,000, or $19,500.

Expressed as a formula:

$$\frac{\text{Annual production}}{\text{Total estimated production}} = \frac{15\,000}{100\,000} \times \text{depreciable value } (\$130,000)$$
$$= \$19,500$$

Under the use or production method, the depreciation charge will vary from year to year. If only 10 000 units are produced in the second year, for example, the charge would be 10 per cent times depreciable value, or $13,000. If 20 000 units are produced in one year, the depreciation charge would be $26,000.

Declining Balance Method

This method of computing depreciation has the distinction of being the only one that ignores salvage value. It is particularly suited to firms or assets that merit speedier depreciation of the total cost. It uses an accelerated rate and applies to it the cost of the asset. The most commonly used rate is twice the straight line rate which would normally apply. In our problem, this would be 20 per cent. Applying 20 per cent times cost, $150,000, this method produces a first-year depreciation charge of $30,000.

Expressed as a formula:

$$2 \times \text{straight line rate (20\%)} \times \text{cost (\$150,000)} = \$30,000$$
$$= \text{first year charge}$$

It is called the declining balance method because in subsequent years the annual charge is always computed against the new book value of the asset. In our example, the book value of the asset after the first year is $120,000 ($150,000 less $30,000). In the second year, the charge for depreciation would be 20 per cent times $120,000, or $24,000. The book value is then reduced to $96,000, which is the basis for the depreciation charge in the third year. The book value of any asset is its cost less its accumulated depreciation.

WHICH DEPRECIATION METHOD TO USE

The best authorities in the field will usually admit that depreciation methods are only intelligent guesses at best. No asset is going to fall apart on New Year's Eve because that date marks the end of ten years of service. Most business people agree that new assets render more service at less expense when brand new. Even a new delivery truck carries a better image in its first years of service. Yet who is to decide the exact schedule for recouping the investment in any of the firm's fixed assets?

All the methods illustrated are open to a new small firm in its first year of operation, as noted earlier. Government officials insist that the same method be used for taxing purposes unless permission is granted in writing to change it.

Observe that using one method approved by Revenue Canada for income tax purposes and another method for the firm's bank, its creditors, or its shareholders is not illegal or immoral. Full disclosure as to methods used via a footnote on the balance sheet is recommended for both depreciation methods and inventory valuation methods.

The tendency of many small firms to ignore depreciation charges altogether in an attempt to maintain apparent profitability is to be seriously frowned upon. Any "window dressing" of financial statements usually results in the owner's being more misled than the creditors.

The decision as to which method to use will rest on the same factors cited earlier in this chapter relative to choice of an inventory valuation method. A gloomy picture for the next two or three years suggests a faster method of depreciation. Heavy taxes and/or technological obsolescence both suggest faster rates of depreciation. Straight line depreciation is still the most popular among small firms, but it may not always be the best for the particular case. Knowing the preceding details about the major alternatives should help the new firm owner to make the decision best suited to the situation.

Just as uninformed critics of business sometimes mistrust different valuations of the same inventory, they usually respond to knowing that different amounts may be charged as depreciation on a specific asset with a frown and a suspicion that something crooked must be going on. Let us clarify that situation. *In any of the methods illustrated, no firm can ever charge off more depreciation than the cost of the asset.* Whether that cost is charged off faster or more slowly, the total depreciation is limited to the firm's investment. In this modern age, no one has yet found the exact answer that will serve the economics involved. It would indeed be a rarity if a fixed asset were sold or salvaged for exactly the amount of its estimated salvage value. Business people know that fixed assets do depreciate. They use the best methods known to measure when that asset value is used up. They never recover more than they have invested.

Another constraint of note is that of the *Income Tax Act*, which specifies the maximum allowable rates for various kinds (classes) of assets. The rates vary, for example, from 4 per cent per annum for asphalt surface, storage yard (class 1), through 35 per cent per annum for outdoor advertising signs (class 11), to 100 per cent for patterns and moulds (class 12). The taxpayer can claim *less* than the allowable maximum in any given year, but never more.

QUESTIONS FOR CLASS DISCUSSION

1   Using the straight line method for computing depreciation, what would be the first year's depreciation on a delivery truck that cost $9,000, has an estimated life of six years, and a trade-in value of $1,500?

2   What would the depreciation be on the same delivery truck if the firm used the double declining balance method?

3   How would you describe the lower-of-cost-or-market method of evaluating an inventory at the end of the year?

4   What do the letters LIFO stand for in accounting methods? Do you believe there is any logic in this method of valuing an inventory? Does it apply to any business firm you know?

5   What is weighted average? Can you think of any uses for weighted average other than inventory valuation?

6   Do most firms you know move their inventory in the exact order in which it is purchased? Name such firms.

7   If market price is lower than its cost and you are using the lower-of-cost-or-market method for inventories, do you feel the firm should take an inventory loss before sale of the goods?

8   Where would the loss in the preceding question show up in the income statement?

9   Should a physical inventory be taken regularly by all business firms? Why?

Projects for Home Assignment and/or Class Discussion

1   The Jones Grocery Store purchased a new delivery truck for $15,000. It was estimated that the truck would render good service for 120 500 km, have a trade-in value of $8,000 in four years, and have an estimated life of four years. The first year the truck was driven 32 000 km. What would be the first-year depreciation on this truck using each of the three major methods of depreciation?

2   If a piano store purchased five pianos at $6,000 each, eight pianos at $5,000 each, and three pianos at $9,000 each, what is the weighted average cost of all its purchases?

3   Which inventory valuation method would you recommend for your neighbourhood independent grocery store? Why?

4   Do you believe that new showcases render better value to a store in their first year than in their tenth? Why?

REFERENCES FOR FURTHER READING

Archer, M., *An Introduction to Canadian Business*, 5th ed., McGraw-Hill Ryerson Ltd., Toronto, 1986, Chapter 8.

Beckman, M.D., W.S. Good, and R.G. Wyckham, *Small Business Management*, John Wiley & Sons Canada Ltd., Toronto, 1982, Chapter 11.

Meigs, W.B., R.F. Meigs, and W.P. Lam, *Accounting: The Basis for Business Decisions*, 6th Canadian Edition, McGraw-Hill Ryerson Ltd., Toronto, 1991, Chapters 5 and 9.

Tate Jr., C.E., L.C. Megginson, C.R. Scott Jr., and L.R. Trueblood, *Successful Small Business Management*, 3rd ed., Business Publications, Inc., Plano, Texas, 1985, Chapter 14.

"Control Over Inventory Investment," *Your Business Matters*, The Royal Bank of Canada, 1977.

20

Computers and Electronic Data Processing for Small Firms

LEARNING OBJECTIVES

After reading this chapter, you will be able to:

1. Identify the various functions and uses that a small business might have for a computer
2. Understand that the computer program which calculates information must be matched to a specific need for information
3. Understand that the computer must save the firm money in order to be justified
4. Know the types of computers and the advantages and disadvantages of each when owned by a small firm
5. Understand that the process of "going on computer" is time consuming and usually costs more than anticipated
6. Understand the use of the service bureau to provide computer-calculated information for the firm

COMPUTERS AND ELECTRONIC DATA PROCESSING

Business today is highly competitive, and to stay profitable firms must have up-to-date information on which to base decisions. The use of computer information processing or electronic data processing (EDP) provides an answer to this growing need for management information. EDP has proven to be an effective management aid.

The small business owner should keep in mind, however, that a computer is only a tool. Whether the firm owns its own computer or uses a data processing arrangement with an outside company, the tool is not an end in itself. Rather, it is a means to provide information to facilitate better business decisions with the hope of obtaining a better competitive position for the firm, which could mean higher profits.

Fortunately, using a computer has become more simplified during the past few years. The newest small computers are truly "user friendly." Falling prices caused by world-wide competition among the producers of computer equipment (hardware) have helped lower computing costs.

Additionally, computer programs (software) have been developed for just about all business functions. These are standard programs available at reasonable prices. It is important to remember that proper programs are absolutely necessary for the computer to assist in business decision making and operations.

HOW SMALL FIRMS USE ELECTRONIC DATA PROCESSING

Small firms today have found many uses for computers: for such functions as accounts payable, accounts receivable, ledger accounting, payroll, financial statements, financial analysis, and tax planning and preparation.

The operations function in small firms is often improved by using EDP for inventory forecasting and control, job costing, sales forecasting, sales trends, material resources planning, purchasing, production scheduling, computer-aided design, and production control.

Small firm administrative functions that are often computerized include personnel planning, word processing, marketing analysis, general planning, training, communications, staff scheduling, and in some cases, electronic mail.

MATCH PROGRAMS TO NEEDS

The small business owner must always keep in mind that the computer program is what makes the computer useful. The key here is to match available programs to business needs. Quality programs are available for use in every type of small business. They are used by accountants, stockbrokers, small manufacturers, service firms, retailers, wholesalers, engineers, architects, physicians, and other professionals. Contractors talk to architects by computer. Stockbrokers touch a few buttons and have instant, up-to-date information for their clients.

Many small retailers use computerized cash registers and are able to keep perpetual inventories. The computers read the Universal Product Code bar graphs printed on modern packaging to speed checkout. Almost all auto parts outlets keep track of their inventory, print out a customer receipt, and calculate the total amount of the transaction in one simultaneous process using their computer.

CHOOSING A COMPUTER OR ELECTRONIC DATA PROCESSING SERVICE

Most small business owners are no longer frightened by the concept of computers, but many are unaware of the range of capabilities available. As in all business decisions, the selection process should start with a clear statement of the services desired. Before considering the cost of a computer, computer program, or computer service contract, the firm should examine, in great detail, what kinds of information it needs to process. It should first determine what data it uses in its decision-making and management processes. This is a most important step that cannot be stressed enough.

Such an analysis might show the firm it may not need to purchase any equipment at all. It may want to contract with a computerized service bureau, or choose some form of equipment lease agreement.

Only appropriate functions should be computerized. In some cases, after thorough analysis, the firm may wish to delay or be conservative in its use of computers. Some information can be produced adequately by traditional manual systems, and it serves no function to obtain information which has no value.

Computer processing is available today at much lower cost than most people believe, and it should be used if it produces more benefit than it costs. The most popular method is for the small business to own and operate an in-house computer with standard programs purchased from software companies. The cost of owning an adequate computer with adequate programs is no longer prohibitive for most small firms.

Until recently, a majority of small firms using electronic data services have emphasized the production of payrolls and inventory control as their chief objectives. But so much more data and analysis can be made available if desired. Many firms have a complete basic accounting system produced in this manner. In fact, it is possible for all of the following functions to be conveniently programmed for easy reporting to management: the accounting functions (from inventory and payroll control to financial statement production); the finance functions (cash flow analysis, auditing, and government reporting); the marketing functions (advertising, market analysis, and development and market research); personnel functions (training, placement, insurance, wage schedules, and recruitment programs); the production functions (procurement, production control, quality control, and schedule maintenance); and even distribution functions (routing, shipping, and business logistics). No single small firm would need all of these possibilities. The needs vary with the type of firm—retailers don't have production functions, manufacturers emphasize production control, and so on.

When the individual management has determined what it needs from any electronic data processing system, the firm's management can look at the following alternatives to find the best system for providing information for those needs.

DOES YOUR FIRM NEED ELECTRONIC DATA PROCESSING???

	How many of these do you have each month?	Give yourself these points	Your points
Number of cheques written	_____	10 points for each 100	_____
Number of employees (including salesmen)	_____	1 point per employee	_____
Number of customers' accounts receivable	_____	10 points for each 100	_____
Number of invoices you prepare	_____	10 points for each 100	_____
Number of purchases or purchase orders	_____	10 points for each 100	_____
Number of different items you carry in inventory	_____	10 points for each 1,000	_____
Do you have very large items in inventory, such as trucks?	_____	10 points if answer is yes	_____
Do you need help in keeping track of your inventory?	_____	10 points if answer is yes	_____

Total points for your business _____

If you fill in the blanks honestly and your total comes to 100 or more, you would probably benefit from using a service bureau. Even if your total is less than 100, you might be able to benefit. But no simple test such as this can make the decision for you. Look into it carefully. Remember that EDP should reduce costs or increase income enough to repay every dollar you put into it. Other points that will help you decide will be discussed later.

FIGURE   20-1 • Does your firm need electronic data processing?

Mr. John D. Caley, Senior Consultant to the international accounting firm of Laventhol, Krekstein, Horwath and Horwath, designed the chart shown in Figure 20-1 to help small firms decide if they can truly benefit from using some form of electronic data processing. Notice that this is only a suggested aid. Specific circumstances of the firm will alter the final decisions. Firms with less than 100 points on this chart may still need EDP. Others with more than 100 points may not. Notice the warning that "EDP should reduce costs or increase income enough to repay every dollar you put into it."

FIRM-OWNED AND -OPERATED COMPUTERS

The firm-owned and -operated computer is very popular today. This ownership may be in the form of a small microcomputer or a medium-sized minicomputer, and occasionally some small businesses use a larger mainframe computer. All three can do essentially the same functions, although, in general terms, the larger the machine, the faster it can calculate, the more variables it can use, and the more items it can hold in its memory. However, all of these machines are quite versatile and may be used individually or may be linked together if more speed or capacity is needed.

The three basic types of computers are:

1 Microcomputer   A microcomputer, called a personal computer (PC) or micro, is a small desk-top machine which can do many, many tasks and which can be operated by persons with no special computer knowledge. These machines generally handle only one task at a time, although some of the newer models can process information as fast as the large mainframes of the 1970s. These are called supermicros, and they can be linked together or to a mainframe or minicomputer to form a computer network. The truly portable laptop models give the owners a great deal of flexibility in utilizing the computer while away from the business on travel or working at home on evenings or weekends.

2 Minicomputer   A minicomputer is a medium-sized machine into which information can be entered directly, such as inventory changes, as they occur. Minicomputers have large storage capacities and computing ability and can be operated by persons with no special computer knowledge. These units can support several terminals and are good for networking with micros.

3 Mainframe   A mainframe is the traditional large, room-sized computer with vast computing and storage capacity. Mainframes require trained specialists to input data, but they have enormous capacity. Generally these computers provide electronic data processing capabilities beyond the needs of a small business.

The choice for more and more small businesses is the microcomputer. They have plenty of power for many small firms. The supermicros currently on the market, such as the models produced by Compaq, IBM, AT&T, and Unisys, have the power of a 1975 mainframe. They can perform the needed business functions at incredible speed and accuracy.

Micros make it possible economically for even very small businesses to own their own computer. While the prices for supermicros will range from about $10,000 to $12,000, very usable machines can be purchased for from $1,000 to $1,500 for cloned reproductions of the IBM PC. The micro is easy to operate and hundreds of programs will run on it.

The minicomputer is popular because it can do a big job and be linked with micros in a networking system. It provides expanded capacity over micros and can cost from $20,000 to $200,000. It has speed, storage, and flexibility.

As stated above, the large mainframe computer is not what most small businesses need. It provides incredible computing capacity and speed, and as a result, is expensive. It requires specialists to input or change programs.

Advantages of a Firm-Owned Computer

Having a computer in-house provides the small business with many potential advantages:

1 Easy access to information processing
2 Availability of substantially more decision-making data than with manual systems
3 Ability to link several machines together and other expansion possibilities
4 Control and security of the system

Having the computer at hand allows greater flexibility and ready access to information. Special uses are possible, too. Single-use plans and budgets can be computerized in-house. Most modern microcomputers and minicomputers can be expanded to provide additional file storage and processing capacity.

Computer programs (software) are now readily available for just about all business functions at reasonable prices. It is important to remember that proper programs are absolutely necessary for the computer to assist in the business.

The ability of minicomputers is awesome. Small firms can now program an entire accounting system into a small computer that does not need special atmospheric conditions or floor strength to operate efficiently. Minicomputers are available to small firms today that have all the features of their predecessors. These include the basic components of (1) an input unit, (2) a control unit, (3) a memory unit, (4) the arithmetic and logic unit, and (5) the output unit.

It was only in the latter years of the seventies that technological developments made these modern machines available. Their wide acceptance, combined with the economies of size, has brought their cost within the reach of many small firms which never contemplated such a development. Their wide acceptance is reflected in their rapidly expanding sales. In 1988, over 800 000 PCs were sold in Canada. New manufacturers are appearing all the time and selling their merchandise nationwide. There are still wide variations in design and recommended uses. Growth will be explosive over the next few years.

While the market today has been described by some experts in the field as "fragmented" (meaning that other products such as desk-top calculators and copiers and various designs of microcomputers are also in the field), it is clear that the general use of computers is bound to become an important part of more and more small firm operations.

Before buying a microcomputer, the small business firm owner must check out the supplier and talk to former customers to gain insight into the vendor's track record. The ground rules (and costs) for installation and training as well as after-sale service must be firmly established. In fact, the selection of a vendor is probably just as critical as the equipment itself. The advice of an independent consultant/expert could be invaluable.

What Does a Micro- or Minicomputer Cost?

The variety of equipment on the market makes it difficult to define a small business computer (SBC) precisely. It is generally defined as a micro- or minicomputer system with a purchase price of between $50,000 and $100,000. A typical general-purpose minicomputer system such as the IBM AS400 with appropriate software may be purchased for $50,000 to $100,000. Digital Equipment Corporation's MicroVAX would cost $40,000 to $50,000 for similar hardware described above.

A small business computer is a valuable tool. *Courtesy of IBM Corporation.*

The so-called personal computers costing $3,000 to $5,000 are getting more and more powerful and have wide-ranging business applications. There is a rapid development of a new generation of personal computer software that will support sophisticated applications that were previously beyond the capabilities of most personal computers. An excellent example of such software programs is Lotus 1-2-3 or Symphony. Often referred to as an "electronic spreadsheet," it can be used for all kinds of budgeting and cost-estimate calculations. Its cost is less than $300.

Disadvantages of Operating a Computer

For all its advantages, an in-house computer operation has its disadvantages as well:

1 The cost of hardware and software
2 The time required to learn to operate the system
3 Confusion during conversion from the original manual system to the computer system
4 The requirement of someone to operate the system
5 The possibility of having too much information available

Buying a computer, its companion programs, and the needed side equipment like printers and tables costs money. This represents a significant investment for a small firm. For example, literally hundreds of programs exist for various business functions; these can cost from $25 to $50 to more than $500 to $700. Some companies will lease computer equipment to firms. The monthly cost can start as low as $300 per month, with higher costs for greater capacity.

Learning to put programs into the computer and operate the system takes time. It is not baffling, but it does take time that the small firm owner may be reluctant to give. Another block of time must be spent during the conversion period when the firm transfers its information from the manual systems to the computer. The small firm owner should be cautioned to recognize that this conversion is often a bigger job than anticipated. After the computer is installed, someone must be assigned to run the system and to keep it operational. This is an expense, whether that person is a current employee who has been trained or whether a new person is hired.

Another concern is that when computers are in full use they can provide reams and reams of paper full of information. While this information pertains to the business, it is often more than is needed. Unusable information is a costly waste.

Going on computer the first time is no bed of roses for most firms. It usually means keeping the old manual systems going while the computer is being set up, sometimes for six months to a year. Running two systems at the same time can be quite time consuming and sometimes frustrating to both employees and management, but some form of backup system is needed to safeguard against information loss. Many firms have regretted not being prepared for the change-over from manual systems to a computer system and have found change-over expenses far exceeded estimates.

The small firm undertaking this type of electronic data processing must have trained programmers and computer operators or may employ independent consultants/contractors on an "as-needed" basis. A normal requirement for the firm that first installs a complete computer system usually involves changes in the forms and procedures of the accounting system. Computers may replace some jobs in the firm, but they will create other jobs for their operation. It is hoped that existing employees can be trained in the new system or that they may find other employment within the firm. Minicomputers have the advantage of fitting into existing office space without requiring special rooms, they are relatively simple to use, they are more reliable than their predecessors because of their simpler design, they require little or no scheduled maintenance, and their costs are coming down as manufacturers share the economies of scale.

SERVICE BUREAUS

Service bureaus are designed to relieve the individual firm of the cost of buying computer equipment. The bureau sells its service to many firms: the service is to process the data of the firm into reports. Most service bureaus have a computer of their own on which the work of the clients is processed, although some lease time on computers owned by still a third party. Most have trained programmers and computer operators on their staff. All cities with a substantial business community have such bureaus.

Small firms using this alternative arrange with the bureau to have the desired data available at specified periods. This involves an arrangement whereby the firm delivers *transaction data* (such as receipts, cheque payments, sales slips, and journal entries not covered otherwise) to the bureau on a specific schedule. The bureau staff then enter information into their system's data storage devices. Their computer processes that *input* and prints the reports desired by the client firm. This procedure is comparable to the "Mail-Me-Monday" service that was popular when all accounting was done manually. Merchants at that time could send the same transaction papers to an accounting service firm for recording.

Many service bureaus provide facilities for electronic file transfer of information. The user completes "screens" of data input and then electronically transmits files of data to the service bureau for processing. This is common for payroll with Comcheq, ADP, and most of the chartered banks, to name a few providing such a service.

The specified reports, of course, vary with the individual firm, but a fairly comprehensive system for fulfilling most basic accounting needs is now quite popular. This can include deriving reports from all transactions involving a cash receipts journal, cash register, payroll register, sales journal, and general journal plus ledgers for receivables, payables, and property accounts. Where financial statements are a part of the system, the reports produced most often include balance sheets, income statements, inventory status, and payroll reports for government agencies. Accounts receivable reports and even budget reports and operating ratios may easily be added.

It should be noted that the earliest use by small firms of service bureaus included chiefly the preparation of payroll cheques and/or inventory control data. Because even this limited service successfully provided a real cost saving to small firms, the wider use of service bureaus for additional services today has been encouraged.

What Do Service Bureaus Cost?

Small firms expecting to use this type of electronic data processing can expect two charges:

1   One charge for designing system
2   A monthly processing charge

The service bureau will design and program a specific, custom-made system for the individual small firm, or they can also offer a standard system that is adaptable to the needs of most small firms.

A specifically designed system will cost from $1,000 to $2,000 for most small firms that require the usual reports to which we have referred. This is a one-time charge. If an available standard system is adopted, the design charge is eliminated or greatly reduced. Some service bureaus provide such systems at no charge but then have a slightly higher monthly processing charge to compensate. It is recommended that a firm have an adequate system made available at the very beginning, since changes in the system involve additional design charges.

Monthly processing charges vary with the volume of transactions, of course. The trend is toward charging per transaction rather than billing for processing time. The normal monthly charges range from $200 to $500 for small firms. Use of Figure 20-1 will assist firms in determining their volume of transactions and make possible an estimate of monthly processing charges involved.

Summary Thoughts on Service Bureaus

Service bureaus were the first companies to make available the wide use of electronic data processing for the average small firm. They remain a large and significant service to thousands of small firms in our country and abroad. Their costs remain the most economical for small firms that have limited their data needs to basic accounting data. They easily record all types of accounting transactions and can easily produce basic accounting statements. If desired, service bureaus can introduce analysis of particular items into the basic program.

Service bureaus first proved their cost effectiveness in producing payrolls and inventory records, but the economies they can now provide for producing general accounting systems for the typical small firm are well established. They involve no investment in equipment by the firm, they can eliminate routine clerical and accounting jobs, and they guarantee consistent, accurate reporting. They offer their customer clients the option of doing their own data entry if they want—this may be economical when the volume of transactions becomes large. They ideally fit the plans of small firm owners who wish to avoid any direct involvement or investment in computer hardware or software. They have proved their cost-benefit merits in most cases when their services have been sought after the customer has made a careful scrutiny of costs and the firm's needs.

TIME SHARING

Since the late sixties, small business firms have had the services of time sharing generally available to them. It is called time sharing because the individual firm shares the time of a computer that is owned by someone else. This type of service has been vastly reduced in use in recent years for small businesses, replaced by personal computers and LANs (Local Area Networks). They still exist for specialized, complex applications that would cost far too much money to design and operate individually.

Time sharing requires that the small firm using this service have a terminal device installed in its place of business. See the photo on page 295 for an example of a terminal. The terminal is connected to a computer in another location via telephone lines. The basic computer may be many miles from the individual customer using the time-sharing service.

The customer firm must have a trained operator to enter the basic information into its terminal. The terminal transmits the information to the computer over the telephone line, which can be either a part-time "dial-up" or a full-time "dedicated" service provided by the telephone company. When the "host" computer is available, it can return final results back to the customer firm's terminal in a matter of seconds. The average time for lengthy reports is usually less than two hours. This is known as *turn-around time*. With time sharing, there is no wait for messenger delivery or mail delivery of reports.

Time sharing reached its maximum utilization in the seventies, before technological developments made possible the very popular microcomputers or personal computers (PCs) of today. There has been a clear trend throughout the eighties where small mini- and microcomputers are replacing time sharing. However, it is clear that thousands of small firms today still use time sharing in preference to either service bureaus or owning their own computers.

What Does Time Sharing Cost?

Total costs of a time-sharing system involve the cost of a terminal and the price of the actual amount of computer time used. Terminals similar to that shown in the photo on page 295 may be rented in most cities at a charge of $50 to $100 per month, including a maintenance contract. Computer time charges are fairly well standardized in most cities. Lengthy reports are more expensive than one-page reports because of the time involved in recording and processing the data. It is not unusual, however, to find a cost as low as $5 to $8 per standard sheet, including specified calculations.

Summary Thoughts on Time Sharing

A big advantage of time sharing is the speed with which reports can be produced. The author's experience indicates that this is not a major concern of the typical small retailer, wholesaler, or service firm. Two-day service from a service bureau seems quite satisfactory in most cases. It is true that the cost of time sharing is moderate when the vast computer power it is capable of supplying is recognized. The individual small firm must consider what its basic data needs are rather than get carried away by the complete facilities offered by connecting with enormous computer capacity. Time sharing can be most efficient for special jobs, when the firm has a need for such special reports. Firms operating on a closely regulated budget system, for example, can have ready access to any variances from the budget. Any computer service eliminates much clerical time involved in making rough drafts, making involved calculations, and typing and reproducing reports.

Unless the customer firm is able to use a predesigned system, it will have to design its own. This involves the need for a programmer on the staff of the firm. Our experience has been that most small firms can use a "canned" system well. A programmer will need to know a basic computer language, but this is no longer a difficult task.

Time sharing has no limit as to the type of data it can produce for the individual firm. Cheque writing, sales analyses, cost analyses, inventory controls, purchase order production, and receivables and payables control and analyses all can benefit from the advantages of time sharing. We can only repeat that the special system adopted by any firm should be based on an authoritative analysis of its data needs. Trade associations, bankers, accountants, service bureaus, time-sharing firms, and computer firms are all available to help the individual small firm owner in making the best decisions. Small firm owners are well advised to confirm the costs of the alternatives that are presented. Historically, the service bureau arrangement has been more economical in providing for the basic accounting needs for the typical retailer, manufacturer, wholesaler, or service firm. Today, however, firms make a wider use of EDP possibilities using time sharing, and even more with their own computer.

SUMMARY

As small firms are finding the economies of electronic data processing more and more necessary to maintain competitive positions, they have three alternatives to consider: (1) service bureaus, (2) time sharing, or (3) purchasing a minicomputer. There are no precise rules for answering which of these alternatives the individual firm should pursue. Many small firms have admitted to buying machines or services that they could not justify on a cost-benefit basis. No firm should use EDP unless it means increased benefits and unless it makes fiscal sense. Yet the need for reducing costs and getting better information for decision making is more and more pressing. The best procedure to follow is a close study first of the needs of the firm and then of the relative costs and savings provided by the three EDP alternatives we have studied in this chapter.

QUESTIONS FOR CLASS DISCUSSION

1   What does the term *electronic data processing* mean to you?
2   As a small firm owner, what alternatives would you have available if you decided to turn to electronic data processing?
3   How should a small firm proprietor decide among the alternatives available in electronic data processing?
4   How do service bureaus render their service to the individual firm?
5   How are service bureau charges determined?
6   Can a service bureau maintain a complete accounting system for a small-firm client?
7   How does using a time-sharing plan for electronic data processing vary from using a service bureau?
8   How do minicomputers differ from their predecessors?
9   From your study of this chapter, how would you summarize the relative costs of the three options available for obtaining electronic data processing?

Project for Home Assignment and/or Class Discussion

Discuss with your instructor the possibility of having a minicomputer available for a class period. Classmates will appreciate a chance to have its operations explained during the class period.

REFERENCES FOR FURTHER READING

Archer, M., *An Introduction to Canadian Business*, 5th ed., McGraw-Hill Ryerson Ltd., Toronto, 1986, Chapter 19.

Blumenthal, Susan, *Understanding and Buying a Small Business Computer*, Copp Clark Pitman, Toronto, 1982.

Bullock, Jerome, "Small Business Computers." Part 1 "What Do You Need?" Part 2 "Selecting Hardware and Software." *C.A. Magazine*, Vol. 113, Nov. 1980, pp. 74–80, Vol. 114, Jan./Feb. 1981, pp. 66–70.

Cunningham, G., *Buy Yourself A Job & Be Your Own Boss*, McGraw-Hill Ryerson Ltd., 1990, Chapter 12.

Meigs, W.B., R.F. Meigs, and W.P. Lam, *Accounting: The Basis for Business Decisions*, 6th Canadian Edition, McGraw-Hill Ryerson Ltd., 1991, Chapter 6.

. . . .

21

Exporting and Importing: A Challenging Opportunity for Small Business

LEARNING OBJECTIVES

After reading this chapter, you will be able to:

1. **U**nderstand the scope of international marketing and markets as they affect both small and large businesses
2. **U**nderstand the Canada–United States Free Trade Agreement and its implications to small businesses
3. **K**now the special requirements for entering the export trade
4. **U**nderstand the different types of financial assistance that are available to exporters
5. **K**now the kinds of help that are available to assist in developing foreign markets
6. **K**now techniques for selling export products and services and the methods for receiving payments for them

Exporting domestic products abroad and selling foreign products in Canada has always held a special fascination for some small firm owners. The lure is apparently based upon a number of things: the satisfaction derived from comparing the cultures and products of various countries; the uniqueness of the products involved; the general satisfaction that comes with travel; and the handling of international transactions. Being the sole distributor of special products in a certain market also has sound business attractions.

Along with this fascination for foreign business, however, there is a popular misconception that only very large firms are able to engage in the exporting and importing of the vast number of goods that are sold regularly in foreign markets. It is not generally recognized that the great majority of firms that export domestic products to foreign countries or import foreign goods for sale in Canada are very small firms from the standpoint of capital invested, number of employees, or total sales within a year. A lack of understanding of these facts has deterred many small firm owners from seriously investigating the possibilities of exporting their products or services, or importing other merchandise for domestic sale. Others have been discouraged by the unfamiliar procedures involved in dealing in foreign currencies; obtaining foreign markets; bills of lading; permits; consular invoices and regulations; dealing through letters of credit issued by banks; investigating buyer or seller reliability and financial soundness; and concern for some foreign governments' stability.

Competent business people look upon these features of the export and import business only as a challenge. They properly prepare themselves for the conduct of foreign business in order to gain the potential profits. Familiarity with all the features cited is essential to successful conduct of such a business. Authoritative information on these procedures is easily available. Some of the sources will be cited in this chapter and others will be listed as references at the end.

It should be emphasized that the federal government as well as the provincial governments are heavily committed to the development of exporting Canadian products abroad. They have invested much time, energy, and money in preparing publications and other aids for those who are in the exporting business or who are planning to enter this field. Most of these publications are available free by writing to the Small Business Secretariat, Ottawa, or the Export Development Corporation, Ottawa, or by visiting a local office of these departments. Most major banks' international departments also have publications and guides to aid small businesses in understanding export trade. Developing exports is indeed in the national interest. There is, now, a Minister of State for International Trade, a federal Cabinet post.

Because of the demand of Canadians for goods of all types, foreign imports of consumer goods have vastly exceeded the volume of Canadian consumer goods sold abroad. Much of this can be traced to the fact that it is easier to import foreign goods than it is to establish markets and sell domestic goods abroad. And that is why the Canadian business community has been challenged to expand its exports.

The emphasis in this chapter will be on developing export business because export operations are admittedly more demanding. The chief concern of importers is finding desired products, determining their landed cost, and setting prices to cover overhead and profits. Full knowledge of customs duties and tariffs on specific products is, of course, a part of determining the landed costs in this country.

THE CANADA–UNITED STATES FREE TRADE AGREEMENT (FTA) – INTERNATIONAL OPPORTUNITIES FOR SMALL BUSINESS

The Free Trade Agreement represents a historic development in North American commercial relations and offers exciting new opportunities to small business while at the same time threatening noncompetitive, inefficient operations. It is a far-reaching partnership that will change many ways businesses operate in North America to create the largest free trade area in the world. Until the FTA, Canada–United States trade had been governed almost entirely by the multilateral rules of the General Agreement on Tariffs and Trade (GATT). Only the automotive and defense industries have been regulated by specific bilateral (between two countries) accords, enabling these sectors to engage in long-term planning. Over ten years the FTA will eliminate all bilateral tariffs; increase procurement opportunities on both sides of the border; relax or eliminate dozens of rules, procedures, and standards that create nontariff barriers to trade; and set up a dispute settlement mechanism to resolve trade conflicts.

Advantages of the FTA include: the general feeling of entrepreneurial optimism that accompanies a major change in the economic climate; the opportunity for business expansion represented by the American market; lower Canadian labour costs for the next few years; less stringent U.S. approval and labelling standards for products.

On the downside, many firms that are content to service the domestic market may find themselves competing with cheaper American products. Also, small companies may be hurt if their branch plant customers are closed down or repatriated.

The small business community is not traditionally perceived as a major source of exports or international trade. Nationally, companies with fewer than 100 employees or less than $2 million in sales account for about 8 per cent of direct exports, according to Statistics Canada. However, when sales of components and services to exporters are included, small businesses account for about 29 per cent of indirect exports – roughly the same as the total small business contribution to the national economy.

When Canadian firms export, they almost always do so to the U.S. This is partly because of convenience. Serving the U.S. market usually means little product modification. Additionally, the product instructions and guarantees can be in English. All that is really needed is a marketing and service network, and sometimes this can be handled from the Canadian base. Its proximity makes it very accessible, and it can easily be reached by rail, truck and air. Also, it is a politically secure market.

Servicing Europe or the Orient is more difficult as it involves diverse cultures, distinct languages, and varying technical standards. As well, traditional standards of design and functionality may be higher than in the Canadian market, limiting the ready acceptance of Canadian products. Finally, it is more difficult to service these markets from a Canadian base and an indigenous marketing organization or agent is usually required. We shall discuss those in more detail later in this chapter.

Effect of the FTA on Small Business

Many of the provisions of the FTA will particularly benefit small businesses seeking to export to the United States:

- *Elimination of Tariff Barriers*   Tariff barriers particularly hinder smaller firms, which may have lower profit margins. The additional cost of a tariff often eliminates any possibility of a profit and prices small firms' goods out of the American market. Smaller firms are less able to avoid tariff restrictions by options such as locating manufacturing facilities in the United States. In addition, reduction or elimination of customs and duty requirements will assist small firms that cannot afford the added expense of hiring personnel to handle the substantial paperwork burden.

- *Procurement Opportunities*   New procurement opportunities that will be created under the FTA are particularly beneficial to small businesses. The FTA will lower the threshold of United States government contracts available to Canadian bidders from those above approximately $171,000 to those above $25,000. The result is that approximately $500 million U.S. worth of potential Canadian government purchasing will be opened up to American companies and $3 billion U.S. in American government purchasing will be opened to Canadian companies.

- *Coordinating Standards*   Another provision of the FTA of particular interest to smaller firms is the agreement to recognize laboratory accreditation systems and to work together to coordinate government standards. Small businesses are much less able to afford dual testing requirements than larger firms. As a consequence, such nontariff barriers can virtually preclude small firms from entering new markets in the United States.

- *Freer Trade in Services*   The FTA is the first major trade agreement to establish rules for trade and investment in service industries. Small service firms, which have led the dramatic employment growth in the service sector since the mid-1970s, will particularly benefit. Over 150 service industry sectors are covered by the agreement, including construction, computer services, tourism, telecommunications, accounting, architecture, business services, and insurance. The two countries now have a relatively open market with regard to services; the FTA goes further to ensure that future laws and regulations do not adversely affect service providers of either country. The FTA also guarantees the right of establishment and the right to sell across the border.

- *Dispute Resolution*   Finally, the FTA establishes dispute resolution and consultation procedures. A Canada–United States Trade Commission made up of Cabinet-level representatives from both countries will monitor implementation of the agreement. If consultation does not resolve a trade conflict, the Commission may refer the matter to a binational arbitration panel, which must deliver a binding decision. This process should operate much more quickly and less expensively than judicial review procedures in either country, to the benefit of small firms that cannot afford to wait out delays or pay extensive legal expenses.

Photo: Tom Bochsler Mainway Studio. Courtesy of Zenon Environmental Inc.

Directly related to the FTA, External Affairs and International Trade Canada, in cooperation with provincial trade departments, have created the *New Exporters to Border States* (NEBS) program, which introduces groups of nonexporting companies to the possibility of doing business in the U.S. Small groups of business people are taken to the nearest Canadian trade office in the U.S. for an intensive two-day program that demystifies U.S. customs clearance procedures, immigration requirements, and financial and legal issues related to doing business in the United States. They also meet with American manufacturers' agents and distributors to learn more about American business practices.

The *New Exporters to the U.S. South* (NEXUS) program takes "graduates" of NEBS, together with those companies whose experience is limited to doing business just across the border, to the southeastern or southwestern states, usually to a trade post or selected trade fair. There, they receive a briefing from post trade officers, who organize meetings with manufacturers' agents, distributors, and buyers.

Later on in this chapter we will discuss in detail the major incentives and assistance programs provided by the government to encourage small businesses to enter export markets.

SPECIAL REQUIREMENTS FOR ENTERING EXPORT TRADE

No special federal licence or permit is required to conduct an import/export business. Permits are required, however, for the import or export of certain commodities under the authority of the *Export and Import Permits Act*. Import permits are required for a number of commodities itemized in the Import Control List, including certain dairy products, poultry products, sugar and coffee, various textile and clothing items, endangered species and their by-products.

Export permits are required for a wide range of goods, in particular those deemed to be of strategic nature, such as electronics, firearms, munitions, atomic energy related materials, etc. These are enumerated in the Export Control List. In addition, there are a number of countries specified in the Area Control List, and any exportation to these countries requires a permit.

The *Export and Import Permits Act Handbook*, which reproduces the Act, Control Lists, Regulations, etc., and its amendment service, is available from the Publishing Centre, Supply and Services Canada, Ottawa. Other government departments issue regulations governing the importation and/or sale of various goods including certain drugs, food, seeds, plants, animals, motor vehicles, and potentially hazardous products. Accordingly, prospective importers should consult regional Customs offices or other appropriate federal officials before arranging purchases.

Export selling often has paperwork requirements from foreign government regulations as well as from rules of our own government. Special emphasis, for example, is placed upon the shipping documents that accompany every shipment abroad. Packing lists and domestic bills of lading are essential. A shipper's export declaration is needed. This statement facilitates movement of the shipment through Canadian Customs and also provides statistical information that is used to provide summary information on total export trade. Detailed invoices are essential, just as they are in domestic transactions. Some foreign countries have special requirements for such documents as consular invoices, certificates of origin, inspection certificates, certificates of manufacturer, dock receipts, warehouse receipts, and insurance certificates. The list looks more awesome than it really is. The consuls of the various countries will clarify the requirements in a particular situation and assist in their preparation and handling.

While there is certainly a great deal of paperwork associated with exporting to both the United States and overseas markets, more and more attention is being given to standardizing and simplifying export documentation.

IS FINANCIAL ASSISTANCE AVAILABLE FOR EXPORTING FIRMS?

Yes, there are many types of financial assistance available, especially to established firms with a record of successful business performance. As in all business firms, there is no substitute for having your own working capital. All credit is dependent upon the proper infusion of an adequate amount of investor capital in any firm. Your own line of credit at your bank is always a bulwark of strength to support international operations. Banks with international banking departments can be of great value since they maintain relations with their own branches or with other correspondent banks throughout the world.

Generally, the extent of the financial support that a bank will provide depends on the product or service itself, the company's security, etc. However, a better line of credit from a regular financial agency or banker can be obtained if the company is able to insure export sales with the Export Development Corporation (EDC).

A would-be exporter can insure foreign accounts receivable against commercial and political risk in export markets. This is one of the main functions of the EDC, which offers a wide range of insurance, guarantee, and loan services to facilitate and expand Canada's export trade.

The exporter is often referred to EDC by his bank, by the CMA, or the CEA. EDC is affiliated through the Berne Union in Switzerland with similar organizations worldwide that aim at stabilizing credit terms. As such, EDC has access to international information related to economic change in world business. The corporation, whose head office is in Ottawa, has offices in Toronto, Montreal, Vancouver, and Halifax.

Export Insurance

Canadian firms of any size can insure export sales against nonpayment by a foreign buyer through EDC's export credit insurance. Normally, EDC assumes 90 per cent of the commercial and political risks involving insolvency or default by the buyer; blockage of funds; war or rebellion; cancellation of import licences in a foreign country; and cancellation of export permits in Canada.

Almost any kind of transaction involving the export of goods, services, or technology may be insured through EDC. Insurance is available to cover sales of general commodities and services normally made on short term of up to 180 days and capital goods and services made on medium-term credit of up to five years. It is also available to cover performance bonds, cross-liabilities in consortia, and foreign investments of various types.

Export Guarantees

It is EDC's policy to achieve maximum private-sector involvement in Canadian export financing. To this end, EDC provides guarantees—although not normally for short-term transactions—to banks and financial institutions without recourse to them in order to facilitate the exporter's banking arrangements. Obviously the deal must be exceedingly beneficial to Canada and all the capital goods and services must be insured by EDC.

When export insurance is involved, EDC will agree to pay any proceeds payable under an exporter's policy to a bank or other financial organization providing financing in respect of the sale. The corporation also issues guarantees to banks making export loans or issuing performance and bid securities.

Export Loans

EDC makes long-term loans at both fixed and floating rates to foreign buyers of Canadian capital goods and services. Funds are paid directly to Canadian suppliers on behalf of the borrower.

These loans in themselves do not cover all payment risks to the exporter. A condition of financing is that the exporter take out EDC insurance services.

The corporation will consider all projects that, on their own merits and within the framework of internationally accepted practices, normally justify financing for a period of five years or more and provide significant benefit to Canada. In its loan program, EDC works with the chartered banks and other financial institutions in a number of ways consistent with the requirements of international competitiveness. This includes providing part of the financing required, including down payment, construction period, and local cost financing that is not normally provided by EDC itself. This involvement may take the form of parallel loans, co-lending, or participation in EDC loans.

Under this program, EDC is extending lines of credit to a number of countries as a means of opening the door to Canadian exporters to bid on foreign projects. These lines of credit serve mainly to encourage foreign countries to look seriously at Canadian manufacturers and consultants as a potential supply of capital goods and services to the recipient country.

In all export transactions, it is important to contact EDC and the chartered bank at the earliest point to ensure maximum benefit from the programs available.

IS ANY HELP AVAILABLE IN DEVELOPING FOREIGN MARKETS?

Emphatically, yes. There are no limits to creative individual ways of finding customers, or to the use of intermediary representatives to sell Canadian products in export trade. Many firms develop their foreign markets completely on their own. However, if you desire assistance, it is as close as your nearest Industry, Science and Technology Canada office. The people there will gladly reply to mail inquiries if personal visits are difficult. This department has developed various programs to assist Canadian firms in locating representatives or markets.

Regional Offices of Industry, Science and Technology Canada

The Regional Offices across Canada assist exporters and potential exporters with design and implementation of market plans; they help in locating and evaluating new markets and in expanding existing ones; they bring to bear departmental financial assistance for market development and explain opportunities in trade fairs, missions, and in-store promotions. Counselling is available on pricing, documentation, tariffs, labelling, and modes of transportation, as well as on financing and insurance abroad. The offices have detailed knowledge of current regulations on export and import controls and can help to identify licensing and joint ventures abroad.

Canadian Commercial Corporation (CCC)

This government-owned agency specializes in facilitating export sales by Canadian suppliers to foreign governments and agencies, such as the U.S. Defense Department and the United Nations. The CCC can assist the small business owner by simplifying the process, reducing paperwork and onerous terms, and adding credibility in the eyes of the foreign buyer. More than 50 per cent of CCC's $740 million business fell within the corporation's small business category, that is, those with sales of less than $5 million or fewer than 100 employees.

Trade Commissioner Service

The External Affairs and International Trade Canada Commissioner Service maintains a worldwide network of offices to assist companies seeking export markets. It deploys approximately 400 officers among ninety-one posts in sixty-seven countries. First appointments of Trade Commissioners (then Commercial Agents) commenced in 1892.

The objectives of the Trade Commissioner Service are as follows:

1 Act as the focal point in foreign markets for the Government of Canada's efforts to promote the export of Canadian goods and services.

2 Represent and defend Canadian trade interests before the local government and analyze and report on local legislation and commercial practices that impact on Canadian trade relations and trade policy.

3 Advise and assist Canadian companies seeking out and securing foreign joint venture and licensing opportunities of benefit to Canada.

In the course of their daily activities, Trade Commissioners carry out a variety of functions. They prepare periodic reports on trade, business, and financial conditions. They make assessments of new market opportunities in overseas markets by identifying market requirements and alerting potential Canadian suppliers. Trade Commissioners are a source of tariff and trade regulations information specific to the country where they are posted. They report on competition in the marketplace and on a variety of other data necessary to Canadian exporters, including guidance on how to quote in the market, banking information, and economic and business conditions.

Trade Commissioners can assist Canadian exporters by preparing the steps for their establishment as a new exporter in the marketplace. They can identify firms suitable as agents and can place Canadian suppliers in direct contact with these firms. Trade Commissioners are able to provide credit and other information on potential business partners in other countries and will encourage new exporters to visit the marketplace when conditions look particularly favourable to access for the commodity or service in question. Trade Commissioners also are a source of continuing assistance to Canadian firms already established in various marketplaces. They maintain close contact with new agents; intercede on behalf of exporters with local authorities; and help cut red tape and smooth out difficulties in order to keep Canadian trade moving. External Affairs and International Trade Canada also sponsor trade shows, selling trips and exhibits that introduce Canadian products and producers to foreign markets. External Affairs and International Trade Canada use a computer data base, called WIN, which contains information on some 21 000 Canadian companies wishing to export. The *Info Export* group, which can be reached through a toll-free number (1-800-267-8376), provides answers and assistance to export questions and problems.

Program for Export Market Development (PEMD)

The Program for Export Market Development was established in 1971 to encourage and assist established Canadian suppliers of goods and services to enter new export markets or to undertake additional export development activities. By sharing the incurred costs, PEMD reduces the risks to the suppliers.

The incentives offered under PEMD are in the form of financial contributions where there is a proven need to share the risk of developing and/or maintaining overseas markets; the high cost of bidding on capital projects of unusual size or complexity; and the risk of unusual international competition or creating an export consortium to meet sales opportunities abroad. These contributions are repayable to the Crown if export sales are achieved. Repayment is not required if sales or contracts are not obtained.

PEMD offers financial assistance to Canadian businesses that wish to participate in or undertake various types of international trade promotion and export activities. The Program covers projects initiated by industry as well as projects initiated by government that business participates in by invitation. PEMD is designed to assist companies regardless of size.

Financial assistance is available to eligible participants and applicants for the following export marketing activities:

Government-Initiated

- **Trade Missions** outside of Canada, and for foreign business and officials coming to Canada or to trade shows where Canadian business participation is substantial.
- **Trade Fairs** abroad in specific industrial sectors or for specific types of products. Participants in government-initiated trade fairs pay a participation fee.

Industry-Initiated

- Participation in recognized **trade fairs** outside Canada.
- **Visits** outside Canada to identify markets, and visits of foreign buyers to Canada or to another approved location.
- **Project bidding**, or proposal preparation, at the pre-contractual stage, for specific projects outside Canada involving international competition and formal bidding procedures. Covers the supply of Canadian goods and services for major capital projects including consulting services, engineering, construction, and equipment.

- The establishment of **export consortia** for companies that would be better able to exploit export opportunities by pooling their resources and sharing costs and risks with other companies.
- The establishment of **permanent sales offices abroad** (excluding the U.S.) in order to undertake sustained marketing efforts outside Canada.
- **Special activities** for nonprofit, nonsales, food, agriculture, and fish organizations, marketing boards and agencies (for the benefit of their members). Activities include participation in trade fairs, visits, technical trials, product demonstrations, seminars and training, and commodity promotion.

The assistance provided for PEMD industry-initiated activities is repayable if export sales result.

Applications must be made prior to undertaking the activity.

Business Opportunities Sourcing System (BOSS)

In order to promote Canadian-made products within Canada and around the world, the BOSS system was established as a comprehensive national sourcing directory. It is providing an authoritative data base on Canadian companies, their products, and the markets they serve. BOSS takes individual information from Canada's manufacturing and international trading companies and incorporates it into a system that quickly and efficiently identifies Canadian suppliers for international and domestic markets. In 1986 it had on file more than 20 000 manufacturers, trading houses, and service companies.

It works like this. Information, exactly as provided by the company, is transferred into microfiche and distributed to each of Canada's international trade offices, Industry, Science and Technology Canada, Business Information Centres, and provincial departments of industry across Canada.

Statistics Canada's Canadian International Trade Classification is the base for the information identification system, providing 16 000 product codes and 32 000 product descriptions.

The main advantages of using BOSS are:

- The system reduces paper burden as other government departments and associations use the data rather than make individual demands upon business.
- Companies in BOSS are automatically included in other reference sources and directories.
- Multinational companies access relevant data to fulfill offset commitments with Canada and to aid in day-to-day sourcing requirements.
- Special data distributions are planned to domestic purchasers not always aware of Canadian sources. For example, some 1400 hospital procurement departments will receive special data on medical

devices manufactured in Canada. This program will eventually help replace the import of medical devices.

- It is used to locate appropriate representation for trade missions and trade fairs, both in Canada and abroad.
- There is no registration fee.

Under the Business Services programs, additional assistance for exporters is provided through specialized government trade missions. These are actually groups of business people who have been recruited from a specific industry to promote the sale of the products of their industry or at least to establish local representatives in specific countries. The government provides marketing information and pays the expense of missions' operations. Members pay their own expenses and conduct business for the firms they represent.

Other sources of assistance for market development are trade shows or other types of commercial exhibitions in which the Government of Canada may be participating. These usually offer wide exposure for products and services of participating firms. The government also aids exporters who travel abroad by giving them information about local markets. Our embassies and consulates publish newsletters and other sources of information for the use of prospective exporters.

Governments have realized that the pool of science and technology (S & T) is international and that no country can unilaterally develop all the S & T it needs. The Canadian government is supporting firms and research organizations to obtain the most advanced S & T wherever possible and to bring it back to Canada for development.

This strategy of scouting the world for new S & T to gain a competitive edge complements the traditional national policies of indigenous research and development and leads to the establishment of international S & T programs and agreements.

Canada has Science and Technology Counsellors posted to missions in the U.S.A., Japan, U.K., France, Belgium, Netherlands, West Germany, and the European Community to assist Canadian firms and research organizations to establish relationships abroad.

Canada has eleven full-time Technology Development Officers (TDOs) and more than thirty part-time Trade Officers in thirty-five missions abroad to assist small- and medium-sized Canadian firms to acquire foreign technology. The TDOs and Trade Officers respond to specific requests and act as intermediaries. Each year, the TDOs respond to about 3000 requests for information. They provide support to the Technology Inflow Program.

International scientific and technological cooperation is facilitated through umbrella agreements between Canada, France, Belgium, West Germany, and Japan, which set the framework for collaboration. There are also less formal arrangements with the U.K. and Norway, as well as more narrow sectoral S & T arrangements between government agencies, both federal and provincial, and their counterparts abroad. There are over 250 such arrangements managed by about twenty science-based government departments and agencies.

Financial support is also offered to Canadian companies through the Technology Inflow Program (TIP), which covers a portion of the travel costs for firms visiting potential sources of technology development or exchange. There are seven TDOs stationed in western Europe and Trade Officers in all other offices to assist with identifying technologies requested by companies and arranging such visits. The National Research Council (NRC) is the official delivery agency of the TIP program throughout Canada. Firms planning to apply for this program or seeking assistance should first contact the NRC's Industrial Research Assistance Program representative in their region. These Industrial Technology Advisors (ITAs) are listed under "Technology Assistsance" in the yellow pages of regional telephone books.

All provinces have facilities in place to provide financial support to resident exporters. This assistance can vary from cost-sharing arrangements on product promotion activities and new market development to export credits in some cases. Many of these facilities are normally not provided when assistance is also available from the federal government. Interested exporters should also note that for the most part the maximum support that can be extended on individual projects is subject to specified limits. Companies requesting provincial assistance must demonstrate financial and management strengths and an ability to succeed in export markets. In most cases, companies must apply several weeks in advance of the proposed event or project for which funds are requested.

In the private sector of the economy there are also many efforts made to promote foreign sales. Industry-organized, government-approved trade missions are frequently sponsored by private groups who wish to promote their own sales or develop reliable representation abroad. Trade associations, chambers of commerce, industry groups, or single large firms often sponsor or finance promotions of foreign sales. Small firm operators will find that their local bank can be valuable in gathering data through their international departments or through correspondent banks. Airlines, ocean freight carriers, and port authorities also have significant data to assist potential exporting plans. Many of them publish booklets of data for potential customers. Business and travel magazines from abroad, often privately sponsored, are another source of market information.

It is important to point out here that finding the names of potential agents or distributors to represent a Canadian company is one thing. As in all domestic business, it then becomes important to investigate the reliability of such representatives before entering into detailed and obligatory contractual relationships. This can best be done with assistance from commercial credit reporting firms or from your local bank and its affiliated banking institutions.

ARE THERE DIFFERENCES IN PRICING GOODS FOR EXPORT?

In the sense that all prices must be set to return a profit, there are no differences. But there may be philosophical or psychological policies that will accrue to the benefit of both buyers and sellers if adopted. Canadian goods are generally expensive in foreign currencies, and sales can be greater if the product can be sold at lower than domestic prices. Some of the recommendations that have been made by international trade experts in this regard include:

1   Omit domestic marketing costs such as advertising and sales expense from the price of that portion of the output that is sold abroad. This is not usually done but has much to commend itself to Canadian exporters.

2   Determine marginal costs of the increased production that goes into foreign trade. Then use this figure, rather than full average costs, to compare with competitive prices to determine profits.

3   Modify your product so that it can meet consumer demand levels in a specific market. This may mean packaging it in smaller packages or making a simplified product that serves the basic use.

4   Be sure that the customer understands the full landed cost of your goods in his or her city. If freight charges are not clear, be sure the customer knows they are to be added to the prices you have quoted.

Many well-intentioned foreign relationships are severed early because of a lack of understanding of some of the business terms used in correspondence. It is essential that shipping terms be clear to both the buyer and the seller. The great majority of present exporters merely send their shipments under a "c.i.f." designation. This means price plus cost, insurance, and freight. The final cost under these circumstances may be quite different than the invoice price quoted. It is absolutely essential that any terms used are clear to both buyer and seller. There are other terms used in the terms of sale that are often not understood thoroughly by domestic business people, to say nothing of foreign citizens. Some of these are "c. & f." (cost and freight) to the named overseas port; "f.a.s." (free alongside ship) at named Canadian port; "f.o.b." (free on board) to which is added the point of origin, the port of exportation, or the vessel employed. Time spent in clarifying these terms of sale will preserve good friendships established in export trade.

HOW ARE SPECIFIC MARKETS CHOSEN?

Despite all the data presented in the preceding section, it is recognized that most small firm exporters are not interested in attempting coverage of the more than 100 foreign countries as export markets. They would prefer to know which foreign markets have evidenced demand for the particular types of products or services that they offer for sale. Unless they already have information about how to choose the particular markets to be pursued, they can find assistance from both government and private sources. Some of these sources are the following.

Statistics Canada issues the monthly *Summary of Canadian International Trade* No. 65-001. This publication provides a summarized presentation of two-year quarterly totals of exports and imports, seasonally adjusted, by seven geographic areas and selected commodity groupings; current and previous month and three-year cumulative totals by country and commodity categories; exports by province of lading and imports by province of clearance; charts, indexes of prices and volumes. A monthly information bulletin releasing preliminary merchandise trade statistics is also available from the External Trade Division.

There are several, more detailed monthly, quarterly, or yearly publications of Statistics Canada related to external trade and one should consult libraries for them.

Market Share Reports is a publication of the U.S.A. Department of Commerce. It summarizes international trade in manufactured products and includes more than 75 per cent of the total exported output of the factories in the free world. Imports of more than ninety countries including over 1100 commodities are included. The libraries of the U.S. Consulate usually have current copies of this report.

From the private sector of the economy additional information can be obtained from trade associations, foreign freight forwarders, international bankers, local chambers of commerce, and from other firms in the exporting business.

Foreign markets are extensive. They are dynamic. They are often changing and challenging. Those who would actively pursue them should take advantage of all information available to keep current on developments in the markets they choose to share.

GETTING PAID FOR YOUR EXPORTS UNDER VARIOUS FINANCING PLANS

One of the reasons some firms have neglected foreign market possibilities is that they are concerned about getting paid for their merchandise once it has been shipped. Exchange rates are considered an added risk that must be undertaken. Again, only a bit of study is required to remove these concerns and assure payments from any of a variety of plans. The problems of collection of amounts due is not a peculiarity of the export trade. As experienced business people will testify, that problem is important for domestic firms as well. It is an axiom of business that careless extension of credit is bound to result in some losses from uncollectable accounts.

There are at least six different methods used in securing payment for export sales. A brief word of explanation for each is appropriate here.

1 Letters of Credit   This is the traditional method for handling foreign shipments. The letter of credit is issued by a bank at the buyer's request in favour of the seller. It promises to pay the seller the agreed amount when documents covering the sale are received. Such letters of credit are usually irrevocable so that once the credit has been accepted by the seller it cannot be altered without his or her permission. The bank pays the seller in full upon proper delivery of the merchandise and presentation of the documents to the bank. Bank charges and government regulations abroad have made this method unpopular with buyers.

2 Sight Drafts   Whenever the seller wishes to retain control of the goods, or title thereto, shipment is made on a negotiable bill of lading. This bill must be properly endorsed by the bearer and given to the carrier before the cargo can be released. A sight draft is sent to the buyer's banks, along with the other documents. The bank notifies the buyer that the documents have been received and that as soon as the amount of the sight draft is paid, he or she may have the bill of lading and obtain receipt of the merchandise.

3 Time Drafts   These drafts operate in the same manner as sight drafts except that they are drawn for thirty, sixty, or ninety days in the future. When the buyer signs the draft he or she can receive the merchandise, but payment is not made until the due date of the time draft. The signed draft becomes a note payable.

4 Consignment Sales   Such sales operate the same for export as for domestic sales. The merchandise is delivered to the buyer, but title is retained by the seller. When the buyer sells the merchandise, then payment is made to the seller. The added risks of buyer responsibility and economic and political stability of the foreign government are assumed. Political risk insurance is available.

5 Open Accounts Receivable   When selling to buyers of unquestioned integrity, some exporters sell to foreign accounts just as they do to preferred customers in this country. The normal risks of collection are assumed. The exporters' capital is tied up in such receivables until payment is received. This method is the least complicated.

6 Cash in Advance   This happy state of affairs is seldom available to exporters. Buyers usually object to this method because their capital is unavailable until the merchandise is received and resold. Small sales are still made this way in many cases.

It can be noted that factoring firms exist that specialize in collecting foreign accounts receivable. This method is not recommended in most cases, not only because of the fees involved but because of the importance of maintaining customer goodwill.

CHANNELS OF DISTRIBUTION FOR EXPORTED PRODUCTS

In the vocabulary of modern marketing the term *channels of distribution* refers to the paths taken by merchandise and/or its title as it moves from the manufacturer to the ultimate consumer. In exporting circles, *direct selling* means that the Canadian manufacturer deals with foreign firms and is usually responsible for shipping the products overseas. *Indirect selling* means that the manufacturer deals with another Canadian firm that acts as a sales intermediary, and this firm will normally assume the responsibility for moving the products to their foreign destination.

Direct Selling

There are various methods of direct selling. The Canadian firm may operate with a foreign representative (or agent), a distributor, or a foreign retailer, it may sell directly to ultimate consumers or to state-controlled trading companies.

Sales Representatives In export selling, sales representatives are comparable to manufacturers' representatives in this country. They have product literature or samples to present the products to potential buyers. They usually work on commission, assume no risk or responsibility, take no title, and are under contract with the manufacturer for a specified but renewable period of time. They need not be exclusive representatives. Orders received are sent to the manufacturer for delivery.

Foreign Distributors These are merchants who purchase their products from the Canadian manufacturer at the best prices they can get and resell them at a profit. Title to merchandise is assumed at once. This method is particularly suited to products that need servicing if the distributor will stock necessary parts and provide the service for a fee. This is also a highly popular method for selling household and consumer products.

Foreign Retailers Direct selling in this case is largely limited to consumer goods. There is much reliance upon travelling salespersons, but catalogues and brochures can be useful as well.

Selling Directly to Ultimate Consumers This has been a small part of the total export business in this country. Difficulty is often encountered when a foreign buyer places an order based upon an advertisement in a magazine that reaches foreign cities. The buyer often does not know foreign trade regulations that may impair delivery.

State-Controlled Trading Companies These exist in various countries in the world. The chief activities of these companies in recent years have been in the purchase of raw materials, agricultural machinery, and manufacturing and technical equipment. Countries that use such firms are primarily concerned with improving their self-sufficiency. Only a few have purchased consumer and household goods.

Indirect Selling

These other Canadian firms, or intermediaries, to whom manufacturers sell their products in indirect selling can be commission agents, country-controlled buying agents, export management companies, export merchants, or export agents. Exporting manufacturers have to choose the type of operation that seems best suited to their needs. These firms can be distinguished as follows:

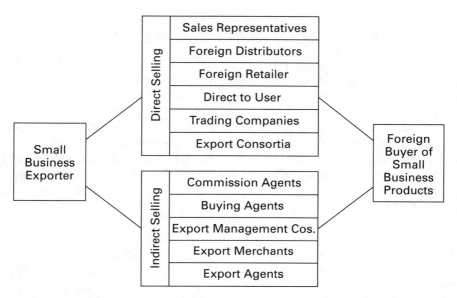

FIGURE 21-1 • The small business exporter can distribute products through direct selling or indirect selling methods, depending upon the types of products to be sold, the customer's requirements, and the type of regulations in use in the country where the products are to be sent.

Commission Agents   These firms are also known as buying agents. They are hired by foreign firms as "finders" of Canadian products that are desired by the foreign firms. It is their function to find the requested merchandise at the lowest possible prices. Their remuneration is a commission paid by the foreign firm.

Country-Controlled Buying Agents   These firms are agencies or quasi-governmental firms representing foreign governments. They are given power to find desired products of all types for those countries.

Export Management Companies (EMCs)   These firms are of special value to small manufacturers endeavouring to promote foreign sales. The EMCs act as the export department for several manufacturers of noncompetitive products. Through their foreign contacts they solicit and transact business sales in the name of the manufacturer they represent. They do not buy or sell for their own account, they never take title to specific merchandise, and they do not finance any of the transactions. They may be paid on a straight commission basis, on a salary basis, or have a retainer fee plus commissions. They can be of exceptional value to a small firm that hasn't the time, personnel, or money to operate its own export department.

Export Merchants   These merchants purchase products directly from the manufacturer, take title, and have the packaging done to their own specifications. The merchandise is then sold overseas throughout their own contacts and in their own name. They assume all risks.

Export Agents These agents operate like manufacturers' representatives in Canada. Title to merchandise and risks are retained by the seller.

The firm desiring to do export business must first make a decision as to whether it prefers and can manage direct selling or indirect selling. A second decision involves the choice of alternatives we have reviewed in each category. Small firm owners should recognize that in some of the marketing methods outlined they do not have direct control over the marketing and promotion of their product abroad. They should clarify their method and the timing of payment under each method to be sure that the financing is compatible with their financial resources. These decisions merit close study by those desiring export business. Circumstances will vary for each firm. Figure 21-1 charts the various means of selling to foreign markets.

THE TRADING HOUSE

A trading house can be a valuable connection, particularly if the company is small and can't afford to visit a foreign trading territory on a regular basis. It is becoming more and more important, depending on the product, to visit the market personally.

A reliable, efficient trading house whose people know all about the company's products can be invaluable. Involved with a large range of products, they can often arrange to have one person trained to service a variety of products, thus reducing the across-the-board costs for clients who would otherwise have to send individual service people abroad.

Many trading houses have offices worldwide or associates in major markets. The name "trading" implies two-way commerce, and trading houses can be mainly export, mainly import, or a combination of both.

There are about 400 trading companies of varying size in Canada. Some represent a certain number of manufacturers and take their catalogues to market their products. Others – literally sourcing houses – sell the idea of using a Canadian trading house and will encourage potential exporters to seek exposure to overseas markets, perhaps for new products.

Canadian trading houses tend to specialize in specific markets, primarily (but not exclusively) in the Third World and in certain product areas, but they may trade in everything from large machinery to consumer goods.

Some trading houses also provide factoring and confirming services. Others are in the warehousing business, lease/rent warehouses, and hire outside brokers. Some also specialize in carrying out export market surveys and studies.

EXPORT CONSORTIA

A number of companies, often as a spin-off of their industry trade association, are in the process of forming or have formed export committees that address themselves primarily to the export function of their members. Technically, they become their own consortia and can cooperatively work toward a common objective, along the lines of a trading house.

SUMMARY

Export business is good business. Its challenges can be met with good management. Abundant assistance is available from government agencies and private organizations for those who wish to enter the field. The assistance ranges from finding customers to giving financial assistance in completing transactions. It is national policy to encourage our private business firms to consider more export business. The potentials of export marketing represent a very real opportunity to expand sales and profits for many firms.

Small firms may engage in importing and exporting at the same time. Importing has been well developed in Canada, in fact, so well developed that national policy is concentrating upon expanding exports and replacing imports instead.

REFERENCES FOR FURTHER STUDY

Importing into the United States
Published by:
The Treasury Department
U.S. Customs Service

Available from:
The Superintendent of Documents
U.S. Government Printing Office
Washington D.C. 20402-9325

Revised periodically, this ninety-page book is directed to companies planning to export to the United States. It covers such areas as customs organization; clearance and duty; entry of goods; duty assessment; invoices; marking; refunds and allowances; special laws and foreign trade zones. Current price is $4.50 U.S. funds. For fast service, order by stock number 048-002-00109-5.

Export News Service
Published by:
Canadian Export Association
Suite 250, 99 Bank Street
Ottawa, Ontario
K1P 6B9

The association provides several newsletter services designed to keep Canadian exporters up to date on export techniques, markets, and services plus developments in international business.

EDC Information Circulars
Published by:
Export Development Corporation
National Bank Building
150 York Street
Suite 810, P.O. Box 810
Toronto, Ontario
M5H 3S5

These circulars provide detailed information on EDC services and are available, without cost, from Export Development Corporation, 151 O'Connor Street, Box 655, Ottawa, Ontario K1P 5T9.

Gateway to Canada
Published by:
Canadian Imperial Bank of Commerce
Corporate Information & Development
Commerce Court West
Toronto, Ontario
M5L 1A2

This ninety-eight-page booklet is a guide to doing business in Canada. Chapters deal with customs/tariffs, international agreements, and financial services offered by the bank.

Exporting-Importing
Published by:
The Royal Bank of Canada
Independent Business Section
20 King Street West
Toronto, Ontario
M5H 1C4

An eighteen-page booklet, part of a series called *Your Business Matters* (No. 4), this guide for independent business people contains information on exporting including ways to build export sales, export financing tips, and sources of export information.

Directory of Industrial Development Contacts
Published by:
Ontario Ministry of Industry, Trade & Technology
Plant Location & Municipal Liaison
5th Floor, Hearst Block
Queen's Park
Toronto, Ontario
M7A 2E1

A ninety-three-page listing of key contact personnel in the Division of Industry & Tourism, Small Business Operations Division, the Ontario Development Corporation, Ontario International Corporation, the Federal Business Development Bank, the four chartered banks, CN and CP, the

Ontario Northland Transportation Commission, industrial development personnel, contacts in the various provincial utility companies and municipalities in Ontario.

A Guide to Documentary Credit & Collections
Published by:
Toronto Dominion Bank
Public Affairs Department
P.O. Box 1
Toronto-Dominion Centre
Toronto, Ontario
M5K 1A2

A 136-page book by D.W. Bisset, with seven chapters, plus index, covering contracts between buyers/sellers, arbitration of disputes; currency of payment, trade terms, documentation of foreign shipments; documentary credits and special aspects and uses of documentary credits. Mr. Bisset was divisional administration officer in the bank's international field. *This is a free publication.*

QUESTIONS FOR CLASS DISCUSSION

1   What factors have drawn small firms into the import-export business?

2   Can American companies compete for Canadian federal government purchasing contracts under the FTA? What effect will it have on small Canadian businesses?

3   Can a Canadian manufacturer sell its products in the U.S.A. without paying duties? What about a service company such as software consulting?

4   What are the advantages of the FTA to a small business?

5   Are there specific government assistance programs available to promote exports under the FTA?

6   How does the Canadian dollar's exchange rate affect imports?

7   How does it affect exports?

8   What is the chief way in which the Export Development Corporation assists exports?

9   Can a small firm receive any help in developing new foreign markets that it desires to develop?

10   Does the private sector develop foreign markets on its own?

11   How can foreign prices for Canadian markets differ from domestic prices?

12   What do the terms "c. & f."; "f.a.s."; "f.o.b."; and "c.i.f." mean as they are used in export trade?

13   Which of the various methods for getting paid for exports would you prefer? What are the other methods?

14   How do foreign distributors operate in the buying and selling of export products?

15   Is direct selling to foreign consumers a large part of Canadian export business?

16   How can commission agents assist the development of export trade for Canadian products?

Project for Home Assignment and/or Class Discussion

With your instructor's assistance you can probably arrange for a guest speaker to visit your class from Industry, Science and Technology Canada or the Export Development Corporation, or a local business owner who sells abroad or imports products for sale. He or she will be glad to explain the details of engaging in exporting or importing products.

REFERENCES FOR FURTHER READING

Archer, M., *An Introduction to Canadian Business*, 5th ed., McGraw-Hill Ryerson Ltd., Toronto, 1986, Chapter 18.

· ·

Small Business and The Law

LEARNING OBJECTIVES

After reading this chapter, you will be able to:

1. **U**nderstand that there are many, many legal responsibilities for the small firm owner
2. **R**ecognize that some regulation of private citizens and businesses is necessary
3. **K**now the various areas of management that may contain some legal implications
4. **K**now some specific laws and regulations which apply to small firms and the significance of each
5. **U**nderstand the four basic laws which govern the labour–management relations within a business

No small business management text could include a detailed coverage of all the laws and regulations that apply to small firm operations. In fact, the avalanche of laws and regulations themselves requires many volumes of government documents just to state them. Dealing with regulations and laws is one thing that small and large firms share equally. The universal complaint of small business groups is that their very existence is endangered by the endless numbers of required reports and regulations to which they are subjected. These regulations are issued by the federal, provincial, and local governments. The most recent expansion has come from the endless bureaucracies at all levels of government. Compliance has involved endless costs, time, and legal entanglements.

Despite the frustration involved with all these regulations, it is important for small firm owners and planners to be familiar with the laws that apply to them, whether they come from national, provincial, or local government bodies.

Our approach here is to point out the various areas of business management that can lead to legal entanglements if not properly handled and then to review many of the major laws and regulations that apply to large and small firms. In this way it is hoped that small firm owners or planners will recognize when it is necessary to get professional advice and assistance from their attorneys or accountants.

SOME REGULATION OF THE BUSINESS WORLD IS NECESSARY

Most people agree that some regulation of the business world is desirable. As the government exercises its policing powers to protect the health, safety, and welfare of its citizens, such laws as regulation of food ingredients, sanitary requirements, and protection against fraudulent or unscrupulous operators are deemed essential. Controlling legal forms of business organizations through corporate laws is generally accepted everywhere. The federal government's power to control exports and imports in the national interest is generally accepted. No one argues with laws to protect business firms and citizens from harm and the destruction or theft of their property. Compliance with new social legislation of recent years has been accepted by the business world with some reservations since it is recognized as being in the best interests of the nation. Tax laws are accepted as essential – the business world asks only for a better cost-benefit ratio for the vast amounts of taxes collected from it. Stability of government, the national defence, adequate law enforcement, and tax funds are essential. The business world does, however, object to government waste and meaningless reports and regulations.

THE AREAS OF MANAGEMENT WITH LEGAL IMPLICATIONS

The inexperienced small firm operator may well ask why or when legal knowledge or assistance is necessary. What phases of small firm management involve technical legal knowledge? A list of the many areas in which legal requirements must be met will be helpful to the small firm owner. Some of them are:

Real estate transactions

Payroll procedures and withholding taxes

Obligations under all types of contracts

Preparation of legal documents for use with lending institutions or landlords

Obligations under contracts with suppliers or customers

Tax laws and their latest changes

Insurance claims

Need for audited statements of the firm

Tort or negligence actions for damages to property

Minimum wage laws and other personnel regulations

Sales contracts

Agency relationships

Branch and subsidiary relationships

Unemployment compensation laws and workers' compensation laws

Collective bargaining agreements

Product liability laws

Purchasing contracts and other types of contracts

Consignment, installation, and open account sales

Local laws governing licences, competency, zoning, and land uses

Negotiable instrument transactions

Leases of real or personal property

Bankruptcy and insolvency proceedings

Occupational Health and Safety Act

Trademarks, copyrights, and patents

Libel laws and their ramifications

Human rights legislation

Before looking at some of the specific laws that apply to all business firms, we should note again that the above list includes only some of the areas with legal implications that the small firm owner should be familiar with. The complete list is almost endless.

SOME SPECIFIC LAWS AND REGULATIONS APPLICABLE TO SMALL FIRMS

The *Constitution Act, 1982*, Canada's new constitution that came into force in April 1982, will affect many areas of employment, human rights legislation, and pensions. The Act does not replace existing federal and provincial human rights legislation, but it is intended after three years to override any inconsistent provisions in federal and provincial laws.

The *Canadian Human Rights Act* came into force March 1, 1978. In the words of the Act "every individual should have an equal opportunity with other individuals to make for himself or herself the life that he or she wishes to have, consistent with his or her duties and obligations as a member of society, without being hindered in or prevented from doing so by discriminatory practices based on race, national or ethnic origin, colour, religion, age, sex or marital status, or conviction for an offence for which a pardon has been granted or by discriminatory employment practices based on physical handicap."

The Act applies to all federal government departments and agencies, Crown corporations, and businesses and industries under federal jurisdiction, such as banks, airline and railway companies. It applies to their employment policies as well as their dealings with the public.

In areas not under federal jurisdiction, protection is given by provincial human rights laws. Each of the ten Canadian provinces has its own antidiscrimination laws that are broadly similar to the federal law.

The Act also protects the privacy of personal information stored in government files. It ensures that any person may find out if there is personal information in these files, check its accuracy and the use to which it is being put, and request that inaccurate information be corrected.

Standards for employment are established in all provinces and are wide ranging, including hours of work, minimum wage, public holidays, overtime pay, vacation pay, equal pay for equal work, benefit plans, termination of employment, severance pay, etc.

The Canada Pension Plan was enacted in 1965 and operates in all provinces of Canada except Quebec. The Quebec Pension Plan contributions are identical to those of the federal plan, while the benefits, although not identical, are similar. The Canada Pension Plan provides earnings-related pensions to all contributors over age sixty-five. There is an option to take early retirement after age sixty; however, the pension is reduced by one-half per cent for each month under age sixty-five. All employers are required to match their employees' contributions to the plan. Self-employed individuals must contribute 3.6 per cent of their pensionable earnings subject to the same maximum pensionable earnings as employees ($28,900 in 1990) and a maximum contribution.

All provinces have *Workers' Compensation Acts* to provide compensation to workers in most industries who suffer occupational diseases or personal injuries in the course of their employment. The compensation is paid from an Accident Fund administered by a Workers' Compensation Board. Employers (but not employees) are required to contribute to the fund. In return, they are relieved of individual liability.

The *Unemployment Insurance Act* established an unemployment insurance fund to which employers and employees must contribute according to a published schedule of rates. Employees contribute to the fund through payroll deductions made by their employer. The employer has the task of accounting for the employees' contributions and remitting them regularly along with his own. In 1990 the typical rates were $2.25 for the employee and $3.15 for the employer per $100 insurable earnings ($33,280 maximum for 1990). Unemployment insurance benefits are payable out of the fund to workers who have contributed in the past and are currently unemployed.

LICENCES AND LOCAL LAWS GOVERNING BUSINESS FIRMS

Many (but not all) types of businesses require a municipal licence. The fees can vary from a few dollars to a thousand dollars or more, but in most cases the fees are nominal.

In addition, the business and industry must conform on zoning regulations. Most municipalities have a planning board that designates areas within the municipality that are reserved for residential, commercial, light industry, heavy industry, noxious industry, green belt or parkland. Construction, reconstruction alterations, or additions to a building require that the drawings first be approved by the building commissioner of the borough or municipality.

In addition to the approval of technical and structural details, the building commissioner must be satisfied that the proposed construction will meet with all the health and safety factors which must be provided for the workers and the general public using the building. This approval should be obtained before making application for a municipal building permit. Most municipalities also require that a building permit be obtained before alterations or new construction takes place. For details of fees and application requirements, contact the buildings and development office of the city or borough in which the premises are located.

It is extremely important, therefore, that the business should check zoning regulations before signing a lease, and the owner should obtain the necessary building permit before making alterations or starting new construction.

For the regular business licences, check with the municipal licensing board or commission.

Typically the following types of businesses and trades require licences:

Category I
(stationary businesses)

Places of amusement

Billiard and bowling parlours

Butcher shops

Convenience and variety stores

Laundromats

Movie theatres and public halls

Parking lots

Salvage yards

Grocery, fruit, or fish markets

Bake shops

Barber and hairdressing shops

Drug stores

Pet shops

Public garages and gas stations

Secondhand shops

Sign painters

Pawnbrokers and old-gold dealers

Any premises where food is prepared for consumption on or off the premises is required to be licensed.

Category II
(mobile businesses)

Taxicab owners/drivers

Catering truck owners/drivers

Driving school owners/instructors

Cartage vehicle owners/drivers

Tow truck owners/drivers

Car/truck rental operators

Category III
(trades and other)

Plumbing/heating/electrical contractors

Renovators

Auctioneers

LAWS GOVERNING TRADEMARKS, COPYRIGHTS, AND PATENTS

Many small firms operate with the advantages of trademarks, copyrights, industrial designs, and/or patents on their products. Proper protection and registering of each is very important.

A *trademark* is a word, name, symbol, logo, shape or mode of packaging used to distinguish one firm's products from other companies. Examples are Kodak, Coca-Cola, and McGregor. Trademarks and brand names may be registered with the government to protect their exclusive use. Trademarks are valid for fifteen years and are renewable for further fifteen-year periods. Legal life of a trademark depends on continued use. Trademarks are administered by the Registrar of Trademarks, Consumer and Corporate Affairs Canada.

Copyrights can be secured to protect an owner's exclusive use and distribution of creative work, such as literature, music, art, films, and drama. They are automatically effective upon completion of such works. Copyrights provide protection for a term through the life of the author, plus fifty years after his or her death. Anonymous works are protected for fifty years from publication. Copyrights are administered by the Copyright and Industrial Design Branch, Consumer and Corporate Affairs Canada.

An *industrial design* is any original shape, pattern, or ornamentation applied to an article of manufacture, such as the shape of the table, the pattern of the fabric, or the decoration on the handle of a spoon. The article must be made by an industrial process. The protection offered is for an initial period of five years and a renewal may be obtained for a further five years. Many designs, being works of art, are automatically protected under the *Copyright Act*. However, once the original artistic work is used or intended to be used as a model or pattern to produce more than fifty single articles or sets of articles, the artistic work then becomes an industrial design, which can only be protected under the *Industrial Design Act*.

Patents are designed to stimulate the development and use of new discoveries. Such discoveries protect the owner by issuance of patent giving him or her exclusive use of the invention for seventeen years. The patent may not be renewed after that period. Applications are to be made to the Patent Office, Consumer and Corporate Affairs Canada.

CONSUMER LEGISLATION

In Chapter 16 we have briefly mentioned the federal *Competition Act*. The provincial governments are also extensively involved in consumer law. In addition to legislation, departments of consumerism have been set up at the federal level and in most of the provinces. As a means of illustration we are listing here just a few federal laws: the *Consumer Packaging and Labelling Act* regulates packaging, labelling, sale, importation, and advertising; the *Food and Drugs Act* is concerned with the quality and marking of food and drugs; the *Meat and Canned Foods Act* regulates the branding and marking of meat and meat products; the *Weights and Measures Act* maintains standards of weights and measures and prohibits the sale of articles otherwise than in accordance with such standards. Each province has its own Acts to protect consumers; for example, the *Business Practices Act* of Ontario, the *Trade Practices Act* of British Columbia, and the *Unfair Trade Practices Act* of Alberta, to cite a few.

SALES AND CREDIT LEGISLATION

Wide-ranging federal and provincial statutes regulate sales and credit. Some examples of relevant provincial legislation are the *Sale of Goods Act*, the *Bills of Sale Act*, the *Chattel Mortgage Act*, the *Collection Agencies Act*, the *Mechanics' Lien Act*, and the *Assignment of Book Debt Act*.

The federal *Bankruptcy Act* provides protection of creditors, and the *Bills of Exchange Act* regulates drafts, promissory notes, and cheques.

ENVIRONMENTAL LAW

The public concern for the protection of the environment in the seventies and eighties has led to several legislations at both the federal and provincial levels. Accordingly, businesses must be aware in general terms of the applicable laws and include an environmental impact assessment in their planning.

The *Clean Air Act* regulates air pollution and sets up procedures for specifying emissions limits. The *Motor Vehicle Safety Act* provides for detailed safety standards. Other typical federal environmental laws include the *Canada Shipping Act*, the *Canada Water Act*, the *Fisheries Act*. In addition, every province has many more specific Acts (e.g., the *Pesticides Act,* the *Lakes and Rivers Improvements Act, Livestock Health Regulation Act, Pulp and Paper Industry Emission Regulations*) to protect the environment. There are over 400 in total! Deposits or discharges in any form of any contaminants into the natural environment are prohibited. Breaking these laws will result in heavy fines. Every small business planner and owner must pay appropriate attention to such legislation.

Tax Laws and Withholding Requirements on Employers The statement of federal tax laws is a full-volume production. It reflects the eternal search for new sources of tax funds by the federal government. It covers all types of taxes from income taxes to property taxes and from corporation taxes to the Goods and Services Tax. We also have *ad valorem* taxes, business taxes, capital taxes, capital gains taxes, and many others. It is indeed a keen and capable small business owner who is able to become an authority on all the taxes that may be applicable to the firm. Unique to business firms is the requirement that they must withhold taxes from the paycheques of all employees and send them regularly during the year to the federal government to be applied to the individual employee's federal income tax for the current year. This procedure alone requires extensive bookkeeping expense and equipment. Yet, again, the business community recognizes the government's need for revenue to maintain essential and desirable governmental functions. The objections are based only on the waste in government bureaucracies and on the very poor cost-benefit ratio that most government expenditures represent. The disproportionate contributions of all persons to government revenues is also a major concern of many citizens in our society.

The Endless Reports Demanded by Innumerable Government Bureaus   By far the most serious objections of business people are against the seemingly endless requests made for special reports by so many different government units. Even a list of such reports and the bureaus that request them defies our space allotment here. One small firm reported that it had received a total of 122 requests for special reports on the firm's operations during a single year. Fines and jail terms are threatened to those who do not or cannot comply. In most cases, much time and expense is needed in order to comply. These requests for regulatory reports deal with energy, ecology, personnel composition, financial details, compliance with special laws, special reports for different branches of the federal government, and almost any other phase of business imaginable. While the federal government is the chief offender here, some provinces also have carried this practice to the point of rousing serious objections from the business community.

SUMMARY

This brief survey of the matter of small business and the law could easily discourage new firm planners. We hope it will not. But it should be clear that compliance with the many laws and regulations in effect demands professional assistance, at least in the stage of setting up compliance procedures. Owners cannot afford the time to meet all regulatory needs. Fortunately, professional assistance is easily available from the firm's accountants. Every small firm should also have a capable attorney available on a retainer basis, or, at least, definitely available when needed.

REFERENCES FOR FURTHER READING

Archer, M., *An Introduction to Canadian Business*, 5th ed., McGraw-Hill Ryerson Ltd., Toronto, 1986, Chapter 17.

Beckman, M.D., W.S. Good, and R.G. Wyckham, *Small Business Management*, John Wiley & Sons Canada Ltd., Toronto, 1982, Chapter 8.

Smyth, J.E., and D.A. Soberman, *The Law and Business Administration in Canada*, 5th ed., Prentice Hall of Canada Ltd., Scarborough, Ontario, 1987.

Willes, John A., *Contemporary Canadian Business Law*, 3rd ed., McGraw-Hill Ryerson Ltd., Toronto, 1990.

· ·

6

ACCOUNTING, TAXES, DAY-TO-DAY MANAGEMENT

23

Essential Accounting Records and Simplified Accounting System

LEARNING OBJECTIVES

After reading this chapter, you will be able to:

1. **U**nderstand why accounting information is essential to the decision-making process in small businesses
2. **K**now the types of accounting and financial information needed for the small firm
3. **I**dentify the techniques used to gather appropriate accounting data and the sources of that data
4. **U**nderstand the time commitment required to keep, record, and maintain good accounting records
5. **M**ake the proper entries in a simplified journal-ledger accounting system

Telling owners or planners of small firms that they must keep good accounting records seems to cause a reaction of bewilderment, and they have visions of countless hours spent on ledgers, journals, and posting. A good double-entry bookkeeping system is too often thought of as something requiring at least one full-time employee who makes decisions under divine guidance. Nothing is further from the truth.

At the same time, in too many small firms the owners do not understand accounting and fail to keep proper records. It is amazing that many proprietors do not know whether their business operated at a profit or a loss until many weeks after the close of their fiscal year because they are waiting for an outside accountant to come in and summarize their operations for the year. Audit reports are valuable, but timely knowledge on operating results is even more important to successful business management.

The objective of small firm owners should be to find ways to get essential accounting information economically, quickly, and with a minimum of desk effort. Unless the owners are completely unable to record figures, they can easily obtain the basic information using the methods outlined in this chapter. We studied basic accounting statements in Chapter 10. Now we must devise ways to obtain the underlying information for those statements. Mini- and microcomputers and other electronic data services for securing this data were covered in Chapter 20. This chapter explains the accounting involved in a manually operated double-entry accounting system.

By now it should be obvious to the student that if the firm would keep records of at least its daily cash and credit sales, its cash receipts and payments, its invoices for purchases of merchandise, and all expenses paid or owed, the basic information for making an income statement could be obtained. Likewise, if purchases, sales, and exchanges of fixed assets are recorded at least in memorandum form, a balance sheet could be produced. Accountants employed to prepare these statements often have little else to work with.

It is nevertheless surprising how many firms do not keep even this basic information readily available in their files. Substantial guesswork is often necessary to produce the barest details for annual statements. Even when this basic information is available, however, the owner does not have the benefit of an analysis of operations from month to month or week to week. It is this type of owner who doesn't know the firm's profit position until long after the fiscal period has ended. Such neglect of good accounting information is a prime measure of management incompetence.

Day-to-day decisions in any business must depend upon the financial condition of the firm. Adverse income/expense relationships cannot be corrected, or even detected, without good accounting information. The sooner financial problems or undesirable trends are detected, the more quickly corrective action can be taken.

The simplified recordkeeping and the basic accounting system outlined in this chapter are designed particularly for retailers and wholesalers, but they can easily be adjusted for manufacturing. The discussion is divided into three parts:

1 Minimum information needs
2 How to gather the required information
3 Operation of a combined journal-ledger and a summary work sheet

MINIMUM INFORMATION NEEDED FROM ACCOUNTING RECORDS

1 Sales The owner should know not only the total sales by day, week, month, quarter, and year but should also be able to easily break these sales down into departments, products, or types of merchandise as may be appropriate to the particular business. A grocery store usually divides its sales into meats, produce, dairy, and staple groceries. A separate division may be needed for a delicatessen if one is part of the store. Drugstores may divide sales into prescriptions, housewares, shelf medicines, tobacco, and magazines, and even have a separate category for gift cards.

These divisions of sales are necessary for the owner to be able to decide on the profitability of each department or line and make decisions about it.

2 Operating Expenses Information is needed for total expenses, departmental expenses, product expenses, and any other appropriate divisions. Retailers' expenses may be classified into selling expenses and general expenses. Owners of factories will want to divide total expenses into manufacturing, selling, and administrative expenses.

3 Accounts Receivable Records of total sales for cash and total sales on account must be available. A current record of balances owed by credit customers is fundamental. Sales to be charged to credit card companies must be easily accessible so that statements may be submitted to those companies for payment.

4 Status of Accounts Payable Every debt incurred must be recorded and the total debts outstanding at any time must be easily accessible. The records must provide a way to pay invoices within discount periods. Other due dates must be known and observed.

5 Inventory The accounting records must provide ways to give the owner regular information on the total inventory and its major divisions. We will discuss inventory control in Chapter 25.

6 Payroll Record Payrolls involve much more than issuance of weekly, bimonthly, or monthly cheques to employees. The requirements of withholding taxes, payments toward Unemployment Insurance, Canada Pension Plan, Health Insurance Plans, and other payroll deductions must be noted in detail for each payday.

7 Taxes Municipal, provincial, and federal taxes are an unavoidable part of managing any business. Details will vary from one location to another, except for federal income taxes. Requirements must be determined, and then provision for getting the proper information can be arranged.

HOW TO GATHER INFORMATION

1 Cash Register   Use a modern cash register. This essential piece of business equipment can be invaluable in assuring accuracy in recording transactions. But it can do much more. Modern cash registers can provide classification of sales and expenses paid in cash into almost any groups desired. Sales can be divided into departments, products, or lines of merchandise. The register will then provide daily subtotals for each classification as well as total sales for the day. It will also provide subtotals for cash sales and credit sales. The representatives of companies selling these machines will show the individual firm how best to use their potentials.

2 Accounts Receivable and Accounts Payable   Set up records for accounts receivable and accounts payable. If sales are made on credit and the company is carrying its own receivables, a record for each customer is essential. Such a record sheet need not be elaborate. Many small firms use a 5 in. by 8 in. (12.5 cm by 20.5 cm) card for each customer on which each credit sale and each payment on account is recorded. A simple book of lined paper with a separate sheet for each customer will also suffice. Copies of sales slips are necessary to post each sale. This book is known as an *accounts receivable ledger*.

When sales are made on credit cards, it is only necessary to keep all such sales slips together by credit company to form a basis for sending statements to the company for collection.

A record of accounts payable operates similarly to the accounts receivable record. In both cases, it is important to be able to tell immediately the current amount owed by a customer or the amount owed to a creditor. The record of amounts due to others is known as an *accounts payable ledger*.

3 Payroll Sheet   Devise an adequate payroll sheet. Before each payday a complete payroll sheet must be completed. This sheet must have columns for employee identification, pay rate, overtime worked, taxes withheld, UI and CPP contributions, and other authorized deductions such as United Way, Canada Savings Bond, etc. Once the form has been devised, it can be completed easily for each succeeding payday. Standard payroll sheets are available in stationery stores (Figure 23-1). Employers must also contribute to the Unemployment Insurance (UI) Fund and to the Canada Pension Plan (CPP). The employer's premium rate is 1.4 times the employee's premium for UI, and every employer is required to make a contribution to CPP of an amount equal to the contributions deducted from the employees.

4 Inventory Control   Establish an inventory control procedure. The procedure will vary with the type of firm. Many retailers keep inventory records by accumulating price tags from merchandise sold. Accumulated tags show when reordering is appropriate. Other firms set minimum inventories and regularly check shelves and warehouse to see that stocks are above that minimum. Alert cashiers can report when sales of particular items suggest an inventory check. Analysis of sales records shows which items are getting more

PAYROLL JOURNAL

DEPT. OR PLACE _____

NAME	EMPL. NO.	PERIOD ENDING	TIME WORKED		RATE	EARNINGS			TOTAL EARNINGS	U.I.C. INS. EARNINGS
			REGULAR	O TIME		REGULAR	OVER-TIME			
R. SIMONS	07	Oct. 26	40	—	5.50	220.00	—		220.00	220.00
J. REJTO	12	Oct. 26	40	8	5.65	226.00	67.84		293.84	293.84
B. GAUDELIUS	13	Oct. 26	40	4	6.90	276.00	41.40		317.40	317.40
D. NAYDA	14	Oct. 26	40	—	7.15	286.00	—		286.00	286.00
C. BRADY	29	Oct. 26	36	—	5.40	194.40	—		194.40	194.40
F. CARVAILLE	30	Oct. 26	40	—	5.70	228.00	—		228.00	228.00
B. SIMPSON	31	Oct. 26	40	10	6.75	270.00	101.30		371.30	371.30

FIGURE 23-1 • A sample payroll sheet. A separate record of cumulative totals for each employee must be kept throughout the year for tax purposes, etc.

or less popular and whether inventory size needs checking. Physical inventories should be taken regularly, never less often than once a year. A perpetual inventory may be appropriate for some kinds of firms—which means checking each item sold as a deduction and each item received in stock as an addition in the inventory. Owners should devise their own plans for keeping themselves informed on adequacy of inventories.

5 Office Supplies Provide the firm with a businesslike set of supplies. Any firm's image, its public relations, and its accuracy in recordkeeping are all served by using attractive and businesslike supplies. These include sales books, statements to be sent to customers, invoice forms, receipt forms, letterheads and envelopes, and wrapping and packaging supplies.

6 Business Papers Carefully preserve all underlying business papers. All purchase invoices, receiving reports, copies of sales slips, invoices sent to business firm customers, all cancelled cheques, all receipts for cash paid out, and all cash register tapes must be meticulously retained. They are not only essential to maintaining good records but may be important if legal involvement is ever incurred on any of these items.

7 Accounting Records Install a basic set of accounting books in a combination journal-ledger system. Such a system is illustrated in the

PAYROLL PERIOD ENDING_____ SHEET NO.   OF   SHEETS

HEALTH INSCE	CANADA PENSION PLAN	INCOME TAX	HOSP. INSCE	UNEMP. INSCE	CAN. SVGS. BONDS				MISCELL. CODE	AMOUNT	TOTAL DEDNS	NET PAY	CHEQUE NUMBER	
6.87	3.96	30.64			5.17	—			CF	2.00	48.64	171.36	820	1
6.87	5.28	52.51			6.89	4.34			CF	2.50	78.39	215.45	821	2
13.73	5.72	30.63			7.45	—			CF	2.75	60.28	257.12	822	3
13.73	5.15	30.63			6.73	2.17			CF	2.50	60.91	225.09	823	4
														5
														6
6.87	3.50	25.38			4.56	2.17			CF	1.75	44.23	150.17	834	7
13.73	4.11	15.25			5.36	—			CF	2.00	40.45	187.55	836	8
13.73	6.69	47.00			8.72	6.51			CF	2.75	85.40	285.90	837	9
														10
														11

FIGURE 23-1 • (continued)

remainder of this chapter. This is the heart of the accounting records. This basic record, plus a worksheet to summarize operations at the end of the month or fiscal period, will enable the owner to make formal balance sheets and income statements regularly. Any student who has had a high school course in bookkeeping should easily handle both. Others can teach themselves by reviewing Chapter 10 and studying this chapter.

TIME REQUIRED TO MAINTAIN GOOD RECORDS

If the foregoing system still sounds as if it requires much time and expert knowledge to maintain, the following statements may help to dispel such thoughts. A men's clothing store which installed a similar system reports that less than thirty minutes a day of uninterrupted time was all that was needed to maintain daily recordings. A small department store with annual sales in excess of $700,000, with an average of eighteen credit card sales per day and twenty purchase invoices per month, reported that less than one hour per day was sufficient. The owner handled this work himself as the system was established. He then trained one of his sales people to do the work, and she did

H. JONES COMPANY
Journal-Ledger
October 19– –

Date	Description or Explanation	Cash and Bank		Accounts Receivable		Sales
		Debit	Credit	Debit	Credit	Credit
1986 oct. 1	Jones opened Business with $2,000 Cash; $1,500 Store Fixtures and $2,000 Merchandise – Total $5,500	2 000 —				
2	Paid Oct. Rent – Cheque #1		200 —			
3	Cash Sales	300 —				300 —
4	Credit Sales			350 —		350 —
5	Merchandise purchased from Fincher Co. on account					
6	Store Supplies – Rex Co. – Chq #2		200 —			
8	Cash and Credit Sales	600 —		200 —		800 —
9	Purchased Insurance on Inventory from Acky Ins. Co. – Chq #3		75 —			
10	Collections on Acct. (Hernandez)	100 —			100 —	
11	Jones withdraw cash		100 —			
12	Paid Fincher Invoice 206 – Chq #4		600 —			
13	Merchandise received from ABC Co.					
15	Sales Return (from Cook)			25 —	DR. 25 —	
16	Payroll – Chqs 5-8		480 —			
23	Paid ABC Co. Invoice of 10/13 – Bus disc.		980 —			
	Omitted Transactions					
31	Sent gov't. checks for withholding taxes – U.I. – C.P.P. Chqs 10, 11, 12		440 —			
31	Purchased showcases – XYZ Co. – Chq. 13		100 —			
		9 300 —	6 500 —	4 100 —	3 000 —	11 600 —

FIGURE 23-2 • A segment of one page of a journal-ledger.

it during her slack periods on the sales floor or before the store opened each morning. Monthly summaries involving completing a worksheet, preparing formal statements, and preparing and mailing customer statements do require additional time. Many small firms engage a student as a part-time employee to handle the accounting details. Owners should not be occupied in these details when their valuable time can be spent on other things.

THE JOURNAL-LEDGER ACCOUNTING SYSTEM

Figure 23-2 is an example of a segment of one page of a journal-ledger. It illustrates most of the possible types of entries that a small firm will have during the course of a month. The entries and their explanation are on the pages following. The column headings can be arranged to fit any desires of the owner. For example, we have combined operating expenses with a column of brief explanation to facilitate finding subtotals for each type of expense.

Date	Description or Explanation	Due to Government Agencies Debit	Due to Government Agencies Credit	Fixed Assets Debit	H.Jones Withdrawals Debit	H.Jones Capital Credit
1986 Oct. 1	Jones opened business with $2,000 Cash; $1,500 Store Fixtures and $2,000 Merchandise- Total $5,500			1 500 -		5 500 -
2	Paid Oct. Rent. Cheque #1					
3	Cash Sales					
4	Credit Sales					
5	Merchandise purchased from Fincher Co. on account					
6	Store Supplies -Rex Co.- Chq#2					
8	Cash and Credit Sales					
9	Purchased Insurance on Inventory from Acky Ins. Co.-Chq#3					
10	Collections on Acct.(Herman dez)					
11	Jones withdrew cash				100 -	
12	Paid Fincher Invoice 206-Chq#4					
13	Merchandise received from ABC Co.					
15	Sales Return (from Cook)					
16	Payroll -Chqs 5-8	220 -				
23	Paid ABC Co. Invoice @1%-Bus. disc.					
	Omitted Transactions					
31	Sent govt checks for withholding taxes -U.I., C.P.P. Chqs 10,11,12	440 -				
31	Purchased showcases-XYZ Co.chq#13			400 -		
		440 -	440 -	1 900 -	400 -	5 500 -

FIGURE 23-2· (continued)

Explanation of Journal-Ledger Entries

October 1   H. Jones opened a retail store, investing $2,000 in cash, store fixtures valued at $1,500, and an inventory of merchandise valued at $2,000. All assets were paid for in full, so no liabilities existed on opening day.

Debit cash (for increases) $2,000, debit Fixed Assets (for increases) $1,500, debit Merchandise Inventory $2,000, and credit H. Jones, Capital (for increases) $5,500. The assets invested are explained in the description column so that any transaction can be traced later.

October 2   Paid rent on the store building for October, $200, by cheque. Debit Operating Expenses (for increases) $200, credit Cash (for decreases) $200. The description column notes that the expense was for October rent so that all the items in the Operating Expenses column can be subtotalled at the end of the month.

October 3   Cash sales for the day, $300.
             Debit Cash (for increases) $300, credit Sales (for increases) $300.

October 4   Sales on account for the day, $350, as follows: Nicla Dattolico, $100; Alan Cook, $150; Marie Smith, $100. Debit Accounts Receivable (for increases) $350, credit Sales, $350. It is then necessary to go to the accounts receivable ledger and post debits to Ms. Dattolico's, Mr. Cook's, and Mrs. Smith's individual accounts. This ledger is a supplemental record and does not require equal debits and credits.

October 5   Purchased merchandise for the inventory, $600, on account, from the Fincher Wholesale Company.
             Debit Merchandise Inventory $600, credit Accounts Payable $600.
             It is then necessary to record the liability owed in the accounts payable ledger by opening a sheet for Fincher Wholesale Company and crediting it for $600. This record is also a supplemental record and does not require equal debits and credits.

October 6   Purchased supplies for the store, $200. Gave cheque in full payment.
             Debit Supplies $200, credit Cash $220. The description column will indicate what was bought and from whom to enable the owner to analyze details at the end of the month.

October 8   Sales for the day, $800, of which $600 was for cash and $200 on account.
             Debit Cash $600, debit Accounts Receivable $200, credit Sales $880.
             Then debit the individual customers in the accounts receivable ledger for their purchases from the copies of the sales slips.

October 9   Purchased insurance policy covering the inventory and fixtures in the store. Premium, $75, paid by cheque. Debit Operating Expenses $75, credit Cash $75.
             If insurance coverage extends beyond the period when the books are normally closed, the premiums may be charged to a Prepaid Expense account, which is an asset. Then, at the end of each period, the amount used up may be taken from the account and placed in the Expense account.

October 10   Received cheque for $100 from Nicla Dattolico to pay for her credit purchase on October 4.
             Debit Cash $100, credit Accounts Receivable $100.
             Then go to the accounts receivable ledger and credit Ms. Dattolico's account for $100.

October 11   Mr. Jones withdrew $100 from the business for personal expenses.

Debit Mr. Jones, Withdrawals $100, credit Cash $100.

October 12 Sent cheque for $600 to Fincher Wholesale Company to pay for invoice covering merchandise purchased on October 5.

Debit Accounts Payable $600, credit Cash $600.

Then go to accounts payable ledger and debit (for decreases) the account for Fincher $600.

October 13 Purchased and received merchandise from ABC Company. The terms of sale are 2/10, n/30. Invoices for $1,000.

Debit Merchandise Purchases $1,000, credit Accounts Payable $1,000.

October 15 Alan Cook returned merchandise, $25, which was part of his credit purchase on October 4. Merchandise was defective. We gave him full credit on his account.

Debit Sales Returns $25, credit Accounts Receivable $25. Then credit Mr. Cook's account in the accounts receivable ledger for $25.

If such transactions are infrequent, it is not necessary to open a special column for sales returns. Such entries can be placed in the Sales Credit column and circled to indicate that they are debits. The circled items can be totalled at the end of the month to find sales returns for the income statement.

October 16 Issued paycheques to employees covering the bimonthly payroll. Gross pay was $700, but withdrawals were made as follows: Withholding taxes, $175; UI, CPP, and Health Insurance, $30; United Way, $15. Take-home cheques, therefore, totalled $480.

Debit operating Expenses $700, credit Cash $480, credit Due to Government Agencies $220.

All this information will come from the payroll sheet (see Figure 23-1). The amounts due various governmental agencies will be kept current from the payroll sheets and sent on due dates to those agencies.

October 23 Sent cheque to ABC Company for $980, covering invoice for $1,000, dated October 13, less 2 per cent discount for payment within 10 days.

Debit Accounts Payable $1,000, credit Cash $980, credit Purchase Discounts $20.

October 31 Sent cheques to government agencies for withholding taxes collected for the government out of employees' pay cheques, $350, UI, CPP, and Health Insurance payments of $60, United Way payments, $30.

Debit Due to Government Agencies $440, credit Cash $440.

The amounts due will be taken from the payroll sheets since the last payment to the agencies.

October 31 Purchased new showcases for the store, $400. Paid $100 cash and signed contract for $300 to be paid in three months.

Debit Fixed Assets $400, credit Cash $100, credit Accounts Payable $300.

Again the description column will identify what was bought and from whom so that analysis of the Fixed Assets column can be made whenever desired.

GOODS AND SERVICES TAX AND ITS IMPLICATIONS TO SMALL BUSINESS

With the introduction of the Goods and Services Tax (GST), small business owners will have to keep more accurate records of purchases and sales than ever before. With the new GST, the government eliminated the federal sales tax (FST) and replaced it with this new tax on consumption of most goods and services. While from a consumer's perspective the GST will appear similar in nature to provincial retail sales taxes, in fact it differs in many respects. The major differences are its multistage nature and the input tax credit mechanism.

Unlike the various provincial taxes, which are levied only at the retail or consumer level, the GST is applied at each stage of commercial activity— importing, manufacturing, wholesaling, retailing, and consumption. Since the GST is a tax on domestic consumption, it applies to imports. Exports, however, are not subject to tax, and any GST previously paid will be recovered through input tax credits.

A business collects the GST at a rate of 7 per cent on domestic sales and pays the GST on goods and services bought for business purposes. The tax paid is recovered using something called an "input tax credit."

This is how it works: when you file your GST return, you will only remit the difference between the tax you have charged on sales and the tax you have paid on purchases.

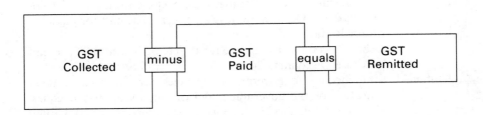

Sometimes the GST paid on purchases may exceed the amount collected on sales over a given period, for example, if your business is seasonal or when you invest in new equipment. In such situations, the government will refund the difference within twenty-one days of receiving your return or pay interest on any refund not made within that period.

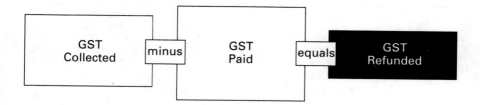

This, in essence, is how the GST operates for taxed goods and services. However, some goods and services are not taxed: there are "zero-rated" goods and services and "tax-exempt" goods and services.

Zero-rated Goods and Services

Zero-rated goods and services are those to which a "zero" rate of tax applies. Examples include:

- any product or service that is exported
- most agricultural and fish products
- certain major purchases by farmers and fishermen
- basic groceries
- prescribed medical devices
- prescription drugs

If a business sells zero-rated goods and services, it does not collect GST from customers on these sales but will be able to recover all GST paid on business purchases related to these sales by claiming a refundable input tax credit on the GST return. Small retailers who sell a combination of taxed and zero-rated goods and services will be able to use a streamlined system to account for the GST.

Tax-exempt Goods and Services

Tax-exempt goods and services are those on which no tax will be collected from customers. These include:

- most educational services
- most financial services (including insurance)
- health and dental care services
- long-term residential rents
- daycare services

Business owners will **not** be able to claim any input tax credits for the GST paid on business purchases related to tax-exempt sales.

The table at the top of the next page illustrates the multistage structure of the GST with tax paid and input tax credits claimed at each level of production and distribution and the eventual imposition of tax on the end consumer. The

PERSON	COMMERCIAL ACTIVITY	TAX CHARGED ON SALE	CREDIT FOR TAX PAID ON PURCHASE	NET TAX PAID
Sawmill	Cutting of trees, manufacture of lumber, sale of lumber for $100	$ 7	$–	$ 7
Woodworker	Purchase of lumber, manufacture of table, sale of table for $300	$21	$ 7	$14
Wholesaler	Purchase of table, distribution to local markets, sale to retailer for $400	$28	$21	$ 7
Retailer	Purchase of table, delivery to retail outlet, support services, sale of table for $600	$42	$28	$14
Total tax paid by consumer				$42

Source: Deloitte & Touche

example follows the manufacture of a table from the raw materials stage through to the sale to the consumer. To simplify the example, the sawmill is assumed to have no taxable purchases.

At the second level of commercial activity, the woodworker adds $200 of value in converting the lumber into a table. Although the woodworker charges $21 tax on the sale of the table, he remits only $14; the sawmill has already collected and remitted $7 on the value it added in producing the lumber. That $7 is the input tax credit taken by the woodworker. At each successive level, tax is charged and input tax credits claimed on purchases from the preceding level, ultimately moving the tax to the final consumer. The total of the net tax paid at all stages of commercial activity is the same amount that would have been through a single-stage tax on the retail sale to the consumer. However, the government has not opted for a single stage retail tax because such a tax is more susceptible to avoidance and evasion and is therefore a less reliable source of revenue.

Compliance Burden Eased for Small Businesses

All businesses with annual sales above $30,000 must register to operate the GST. The cost of collecting and remitting the GST is adding considerable expense to small business owners. Value-added tax systems in other countries show that small businesses bear a disproportionate share of the compliance burden. A study conducted in the U.K. found that the compliance costs of the smallest businesses as a percentage of sales averaged over forty times higher than those of the largest businesses.

In Canada, qualifying small businesses are able to use an alternative method called the "Quick Method" to calculate the GST to be remitted. This optional calculation is directed at most small businesses, it allows them to use a prescribed per cent to calculate the net GST to be submitted.

TABLE A
PRESCRIBED RATES FOR QUICK METHOD

TYPE OF BUSINESS	MAXIMUM ANNUAL SALES	PRESCRIBED RATE
Manufacturer	$200,000	5%
Services*	200,000	5%
Retailers	200,000	3%
Wholesalers	200,000	3%
Grocery & Convenience Stores		
−25% to 50% groceries	500,000	1.75%
−More than 50% groceries	500,000	1%

* Excludes legal, accounting or financial consulting businesses.

TABLE B
EXAMPLE OF QUICK METHOD CALCULATION

ASSUMPTIONS:

1. Shoe store annual sales $180,000 (1)
2. Cash register purchase. 5,350 (1)

QUICK METHOD CALCULATION:

Annual sales $180,000
Prescribed rate . . . .   × 3%
= 5,400
Input tax credit on capital purchase. . . . .   (350) (2)
Net GST. $5,050

(1) Includes GST   (2) 7/107ths × $5,350

Source: Peat Marwick Thorne

This approach does not mean that eligible small businesses charge the Quick Method rate on their taxable sales. They will still collect 7 per cent on taxable sales and pay the 7 per cent tax on their purchases. The benefit is that qualifying small businesses will calculate their remittance to the government based on a simple formula. They are not required to track all GST collected and then deduct the amount of GST paid that is eligible for an input tax credit. In addition, they can claim an input tax credit on capital purchases.

Assistance to Small Business

Compliance has been made as simple as possible to minimize administrative costs for small businesses. In addition, several types of assistance to businesses are included in the GST package.

Small Supplier's Threshold

Businesses and individuals with annual sales (from taxable and zero-rated transactions) of $30,000 or less will not be required to register and collect GST. Those who choose not to register will not collect tax on sales, nor will they claim input tax credits on their purchases.

This arrangement may suit some small businesses that are small suppliers who sell directly to consumers. However, if selling mainly to business, it may be an advantage to register as this will allow both the business and its customers to claim input tax credit. If a business does elect to register, it will be bound by that choice for the balance of the fiscal year and for the following fiscal year.

Assistance to Upgrade Cash Registers

Although operating the GST will not require it, some business owners may want to purchase equipment that simultaneously shows the GST and the provincial sales tax. For those who choose to upgrade, the government is providing assistance in two ways—by exempting electronic point-of-sale and related inventory control equipment from the current federal sales tax as of December 19, 1989, and by allowing retailers who wish to buy such equipment to fully write off the cost in one year. Together, these measures will reduce the after-tax cost of acquiring this equipment by about 20 per cent. The special 100 per cent write-off is in effect between August 8, 1989, and December 31, 1992.

The assistance applies to specified types of equipment, including electronic bar-code scanning equipment, cash registers or similar machines, equipment and computer software to adapt existing cash registers to the new system, and other related equipment.

Transitional Credit

Many small businesses will be eligible to receive a one-time transitional payment from the government to help offset the costs involved in changing over from the federal sales tax to the GST. This payment will be available to registered businesses with revenue (from taxable and zero-rated sales) of $2 million or less in a fiscal year. If a business' total annual sales (from taxable and zero-rated goods and services) are between $60,000 and $2 million, it will receive 0.5 per cent of total sales, up to a maximum of $1,000. If revenue is between $30,000 and $60,000, the business will receive $300.

QUESTIONS FOR CLASS DISCUSSION

1   After studying this chapter, does bookkeeping still seem a great mystery to you?

2   Can you think of situations where small firm owners could make wrong decisions because they lacked good accounting information?

3   Why should the owner of a drugstore want to have sales broken down by departments?

4   Have you ever closely observed a modern cash register? What things can it do for firm owners to help them have good accounting information available?

5   What is an accounts receivable ledger? How does it work?

6   What is an accounts payable ledger? How does it work?

7   What type of inventory control system would you recommend for a business firm you would like to own and operate?

8   Are withholding taxes taken from employee salaries an expense to the business or a part of its total salary expense? Explain.

9   Why are attractive supplies important to any business firm?

10   Why can underlying business papers, such as invoices, become important in case of legal involvement?

11   Could you post eighteen credit sales and one purchase invoice to a system such as outlined in this chapter in one hour?

12   If you had not taken a course in bookkeeping, do you think you could learn to operate a journal-ledger system as outlined here? How much study would it take?

REFERENCES FOR FURTHER READING

Cunningham, G., *Buy Yourself A Job & Be Your Own Boss*, McGraw-Hill Ryerson Ltd., Toronto, 1990, Chapter 6.

Kao, R.W.Y., *Small Business Management: A Strategic Emphasis*, 2nd ed., Holt, Rinehart and Winston of Canada, Ltd., Toronto, 1984, Chapter 4.

Meigs, W.B., R.F. Meigs, and W.P. Lam, *Accounting: The Basis for Business Decisions*, 6th Canadian Edition, McGraw-Hill Ryerson Ltd., Toronto, 1991, Chapter 2.

Tate Jr., C.E., L.C. Megginson, C.R. Scotto Jr., and L.R. Trueblood, *Successful Small Business Management*, 3rd ed., Business Publications, Inc., Plano, Texas, 1985, Chapter 20.

. . . .

24

Worksheet, Formal Statements, and Cash Flow Statements

LEARNING OBJECTIVES

After reading this chapter, you will be able to:

1. **U**nderstand how the multicolumned accounting worksheet provides a complete summary of operations

2. **P**repare a worksheet of the financial transactions of the operation, including the trial balances necessary to make operational adjustments

3. **P**repare the income statement and balance sheet using the journal-ledger and worksheet

4. **P**repare a cash flow chart listing estimated or planned cash receipts and expenses

5. **C**omplete the cash flow chart month by month by posting actual income and expenses to be compared to those projected

Experienced bookkeepers can prepare a balance sheet and an income statement directly from the totals of the columns in the journal-ledger. They will make the necessary adjustments in the process. A worksheet as a permanent record is recommended.

The worksheet has been described as the best friend a bookkeeper ever had. On this one multicolumn sheet there is a complete summary of operations for the period, from a trial balance through the adjustments to the formal statements.

All accounts in the journal-ledger are listed in the left column. In the first set of dollar columns, the totals of each account are inserted. These are the totals at the bottom of the journal-ledger. If an account has a column for both debits and credits, the difference between these amounts is inserted. This is the account balance.

In the second set of columns, adjustments are made to bring the accounts up to date. This usually involves recording the new merchandise inventory, the supplies used, and any depreciation expenses that are to be charged. Other adjustments may be necessary. Actual debits and credits are made to the specific accounts involved.

When the adjustments have been completed, the first and second sets of columns are combined to make an adjusted trial balance. All additions and subtractions are made as we read across the page to the third set of columns.

Completing the worksheet from the adjusted trial balance involves transferring the income statement accounts to the income statement column and the balance sheet accounts to the balance sheet column.

On the completed worksheet shown in Figure 24-1, adjustments were necessary for the following items:

1   New merchandise inventory $3,000
2   Depreciation expense on store fixtures $25
3   New inventory of store supplies $400

Each step in completing the worksheet and the method of preparing statements from it are explained in the following pages.

COMPLETING THE WORKSHEET

Trial Balance Columns

All accounts in the journal-ledger are listed horizontally in that record. Their names are listed vertically on the worksheet. Opposite each account name, insert the totals from the bottom line of the journal-ledger in the trial balance columns. Four of our accounts (cash, accounts receivable, accounts payable, and due to government agencies) have both a debit and a credit column. In these cases, insert the difference between the debits and credits (the account

H. JONES COMPANY
Worksheet
October 19—

Account	Trial Balance Debit	Trial Balance Credit	Adjustments Debit	Adjustments Credit	Adjusted Trial Balance Debit	Adjusted Trial Balance Credit	Income Statement Debit	Income Statement Credit	Balance Sheet Debit	Balance Sheet Credit
Cash	2 800				2 800				2 800	
Accounts Receivable	1 100				1 100				1 100	
Sales		11 600				11 600		11 600		
Merchandise Purchases	10 620			(1) 7 620	3 000				3 000	
Purchase Discounts		20				20		20		
Accounts Payable		2 225				2 225				2 225
Supplies on Hand	550			(3) 150	400				400	
Operating Expenses ($1,975)										
Rent	200				200		200			
Employee Salaries	1 400				1 400		1 400			
Advertising	200				200		200			
Delivery Charge	50				50		50			
Insurance	75				75		75			
Miscellaneous Exp.	50				50		50			
Due to Gov't Agencies	0	0			0	0				
Fixed Assets ($1,900)										
Store Fixtures	1 500				1 500				1 500	
Show Cases	400				400				400	
H. Jones, Withdrawals	400		(4) 400		0					
H. Jones, Capital		5 500		(4) 400		5 100				5 100
Cost of Goods Sold			(1) 7 620		7 620		7 620			
Deprec. Exp.- Store Fix.			(2) 25		25		25			
Accum. Deprec.-Store Fix.				(2) 25		25				25
Supplies Used			(3) 150		150		150			
	19 345	19 345	8 195	8 195	18 970	18 970	9 770		9 200	7 350
Net profit for month (before income taxes)							1 850			1 850
							11 620	11 620	9 200	9 200

FIGURE 24-1• A completed worksheet.

balance) in the trial balance column. Be sure to list the balance on the appropriate side of the trial balance. When all accounts are inserted, add the debits and credits to be sure that the books are in balance.

Where a summary account title has been used, such as Operating Expenses, the trial balance can break the total down into any classification desired. By inspecting the individual items in our Operating Expense column, we have broken the total of $1,975 into Rent, $200; Employee Salaries, $1,400; Advertising, $200; Delivery Charges, $50; Insurance, $75; and Miscellaneous Expense, $50. The Fixed Assets total of $1,900 has been similarly divided into Store Fixtures, $1,500 and Showcases, $400. If this detail is not desired, only the totals can be used.

Adjusting Entries

Adjusting entries are necessary to update trial balance figures. For example, the Merchandise Inventory account shows a balance of $10,600. But we have an inventory, taken as of October 31, which tells us that the merchandise actually on hand is $3,000. The difference in these two figures must be the cost of the merchandise sold. Therefore, we make an adjusting entry in the second set of columns to take $7,600 out of the merchandise account and put in a new account, Cost of Goods Sold. This new account and any others needed for the other adjustments are opened at the bottom of the worksheet, below the Trial Balance totals. It is a debit to Cost of Goods Sold because such expense accounts are increased by debits, and a credit to Merchandise Inventory because assets are decreased with credits. The Merchandise Inventory account now shows a debit balance of $3,000, which is the value of the current inventory. This amount will be carried over to the Adjusted Trial Balance. This adjustment is marked (1) in the Adjustments column.

The second adjusting entry is to record $25 of depreciation expense on the store fixtures. We open a new account, Depreciation Expense—Store Fixtures, and debit it for $25. The credit is to an account entitled Accumulated Depreciation—Store Fixtures for $25. This is technically known as a minus asset account and is deducted from the Store Fixtures account on the balance sheet. It is carried across the worksheet as a balance sheet account with a credit balance. This entry is marked (2) in the Adjustments column.

Adjustment (3) is necessary to bring the asset account Supplies on Hand up to date. On the trial balance it shows a balance of $550. But we have taken an inventory and know that only $400 of these supplies are still on hand. The difference of $150 represents the supplies used up during the month. Therefore, we credit Supplies on Hand $150 and debit a new expense account, Supplies Used, for $150. This entry reduces the balance of the Supplies on Hand account to $400, which is the value of supplies still in inventory.

Adjustment (4) is to close the owner's withdrawal account into his capital account. Withdrawals are not operating expenses but capital reductions. We therefore credit H. Jones, Withdrawals $400, and debit H. Jones, Capital $400.

This removes any balance from the Withdrawals account so that no figures need to be carried across the sheet. The debits and credits in the adjustments column are added.

Adjusted Trial Balance

This set of columns is only a total of the first two set of columns. Unless a debit or credit has been added in the Adjustments column, the same trial balance figure will be carried across the Adjusted Trial Balance, as illustrated in the case of Cash, Accounts Receivable, and Sales. Merchandise Inventory has a debit in the trial balance for $10,620 but a credit in the Adjustments column for $7,620. The debit balance of $3,000 is accordingly carried over to the Adjusted Trial Balance column. Supplies on Hand has a $550 debit in the trial balance but a $150 credit in the Adjustments column. The difference of $400 is carried over to the Adjusted Trial Balance. Every account, including the new ones opened at the bottom of the Adjustments column, must be carried to the Adjusted Trial Balance.

TABLE 24-1

H. JONES COMPANY
INCOME STATEMENT
OCTOBER 1-31, 199–

Gross sales			$12,000
Less sales returns			400
Net sales income			$11,600
Cost of goods sold:			
Inventory, October 1		$ 2,000	
Purchases during month	$8,620		
Less purchase discounts	20	8,600	
Goods available for sale		$10,600	
Less inventory, October 31		3,000	
Cost of goods sold during month			7,600
Gross margin			$ 4,000
Operating expenses:			
Rent		$ 200	
Employee salaries		1,400	
Supplies used		150	
Advertising		200	
Delivery charges		50	
Depreciation expense		25	
Insurance expense		75	
Miscellaneous expenses		50	
Total operating expenses			2,150
Net profit from operations before income taxes			$ 1,850

TABLE 24-2

H. JONES COMPANY
BALANCE SHEET
OCTOBER 31, 199–

ASSETS			*LIABILITIES*	
Current assets:			Current liabilities:	
Cash		$2,800	Accounts payable	$1,925
Accounts receivable		1,100	Contract payable	300
Merchandise inventory		3,000	Total current liabilities	$2,225
Prepaid expenses		400	Fixed liabilities:	
Total current assets		$7,300	None	0
			Total liabilities	$2,225
Fixed assets:				
Store fixtures	$1,500			
Less accumulated			*NET WORTH*	
depreciation	25	1,475		
Showcases		400	H. Jones, Capital	$6,950
Total fixed assets		$1,875		
			Total Liabilities Plus	
Total Assets		$9,175	Net Worth	$9,175

INCOME STATEMENT AND BALANCE SHEET COLUMNS

Once the Adjusted Trial Balance is complete, the remainder of the worksheet involves only transferring each account on across the sheet to its appropriate column. All income and expense accounts go into the Income Statement column, and asset, liability, and Net Worth (capital) accounts go to the appropriate side of the Balance Sheet columns. When each account has been transferred, the columns should again be added.

Now notice that the difference between the debits and credits in the Income Statement column ($11,620 less $9,770) is the same as in the Balance Sheet columns ($9,200 less $7,350). This difference ($1,850) is the net profit from operations for the month. Another entry is made below these totals to transfer this profit from the Income Statement to the Balance Sheet, where it will appear as part of the owner's new Capital account balance.

We can now prepare formal statements. Items needed are on the worksheet. Samples taken from the worksheet are shown in Tables 24-1 and 24-2.

To prepare the journal-ledger for the next month's operations, insert the balance sheet account balances under the date of November 1.

TABLE 24-3

CASH FLOW STATEMENTS

(The estimated figures [typed] are projected for a full year; the actual figures have been inserted for 3 months only.)

CASH FLOW STATEMENT – MILLER'S AUTO SUPPLY – 19__

	JANUARY Estimated	JANUARY Actual	FEBRUARY Estimated	FEBRUARY Actual	MARCH Estimated	MARCH Actual	APRIL Estimated	APRIL Actual	DECEMBER Estimated	DECEMBER Actual	YEARLY TOTALS Estimated	YEARLY TOTALS Actual
1. Cash on Hand, 1st of Month	$5,000	$5,000	$3,400	$4,025	$2,400	$2,625	$1,975	$1,900	$3,700		$3,700	
2. Cash Receipts During Month												
a. Cash Sales	3,000	3,800	3,500	4,000	4,000	4,200	4,000		8,000		$72,600	
b. Payments on Accounts Receivable	1,800	2,000	2,000	2,000	2,400	2,200	2,400		4,000		32,000	
c. Bank Loans	0	0	0	0	0	0	0		0		6,000	
d. Other Sources (list)	0	0	0	0	0	0	0		0		0	
3. Total Cash Receipts	$4,800	$5,800	$5,500	$6,000	$6,400	$4,400	$6,400		$12,000		$110,600	
4. Cash Available During Month	$9,800	$10,800	$8,900	$10,025	$8,800	$9,025	$8,375		$15,700		$49,000	
5. Cash Outlays for Month												
a. For Merchandise	$1,200	$1,500	$1,200	$2,000	$1,500	$1,800	$1,500		$4,500		31,000	
b. For Wages & Salaries	3,600	3,600	3,600	3,600	3,600	3,600	3,600		4,600		43,200	
c. Payroll Expenses	100	100	100	100	100	100	100		150		1,800	
d. Rent	400	400	400	400	400	400	400		400		4,800	
e. Utilities	100	125	100	150	100	150	100		200		1,600	
f. Insurance	50	50	50	50	50	50	50		50		600	
g. Interest	0	0	0	0	0	0	0		0		100	
h. Repairs & Mtce.	0	50	100	100	100	50	100		100		1,000	
i. Advertising	100	200	100	200	100	200	100		200		2,000	
j. Supplies	75	75	75	150	100	150	100		200		2,100	
k. Delivery Expenses	150	150	150	125	150	25	150		250		2,200	
l. Taxes	25	25	25	25	25	25	25		25		300	
m. Misc. Expenses	100	50	200	200	100	200	100		200		1,800	
n. Other Expenses (list)	0	50	0	0	0	0	0		0		0	
Total Mdse. & Opr. Exp.	$5,900	$6,475	$6,000	$7,100	$6,325	$6,825	$6,325		$10,875		$98,600	
Loan Repayments	0	300	0	0	0	0	0		0			
Withdrawals	500	300	500	300	500	300	500		500		6,000	
Equipment Purchases	0	0	0	0	0	0	0		0			
6. Total Cash Paid Out	$6,400	$6,715	$6,500	$7,400	$6,825	$7,125	$6,825		$11,375		$104,600	
7. Cash Balance End of Month	$3,400	$4,025	$2,400	$2,625	$1,975	$1,900	$1,550		$4,325		$6,000	

OMITTED MONTHS

CASH FLOW STATEMENTS

Because any firm's cash position is important to its economic health, firm managers should use all tools available to keep abreast of cash flow and current cash position. One of the best of these tools is the cash flow chart. It is designed to estimate future cash receipts, outlays, and balances and then compare actual results with the estimate at the end of each month of operations. Careful preparation and use of the chart provides a schedule of cash flow and a ready device for ascertaining if the schedule is being met.

If cash shortages are anticipated, arrangements can be made to meet these shortages. Periods needing expanded credit from the bank, for example, can be anticipated and planned for. If surplus funds are anticipated, arrangements can be made for profitably investing such funds. An estimated cash balance and an actual cash balance at the end of each month is provided.

The cash flow chart provides two columns for each month. One is the planned or estimated cash receipts, outlays, and balances. The second column provides for inserting at the end of each month the actual receipts, outlays, and balances. Disparities between the estimated and actual amounts merit close attention. Adverse trends can be detected early and management decisions can be influenced by studying the results.

The estimated columns should preferably be completed for a year in advance. Great care should be exercised in completing the estimates in each area. Many discrepancies between estimates and actual results are caused by failure to recognize lags in collecting accounts receivable and by failure to recognize all cash outlays.

It should be emphasized that we are dealing here only with actual cash flow. Credit sales are not cash receipts. Payments received against accounts receivable are. Bank loans represent cash received. Repayment of such loans are anticipated as a cash outlay. Starting from cash on hand at the beginning of the month, we add all cash received to find cash available during the month. From this amount all cash paid out is deducted to arrive at cash position at end of the month.

Improving cash position by ignoring liabilities and purchase discounts is not to be recommended. When all liabilities are paid as due and cash flow shows a healthy cash position, the firm has a healthy all-around condition.

QUESTIONS FOR CLASS DISCUSSION

1   How would you describe the worksheet?
2   Do you think the worksheet can be called "the bookkeeper's best friend"?
3   Where do the figures for the trial balance columns come from?
4   Why are adjusting entries necessary? Give some examples of necessary adjusting entries.

5 Once the adjusted trial balance columns are complete, how does the worksheet proceed?

6 Can you explain why the difference between the debits and credits in the income statement columns and the balance sheet columns is the same?

7 How did Mr. Jones's capital account go from $5,500 to $6,950?

8 On what amount will Mr. Jones pay income taxes for October?

9 Is the entire $1,850 of profits for October still in the business?

10 Can you find every item on the formal income statement and balance sheet in the columns of the worksheet?

REFERENCES FOR FURTHER READING

Cunningham, G., *Buy Yourself A Job & Be Your Own Boss*, McGraw-Hill Ryerson Ltd., Toronto, 1990, Chapters 9 and 10.

Meigs, W.B., R.F. Meigs, and W.P. Lam, *Accounting: The Basis for Business Decisions*, 6th Canadian Edition, McGraw-Hill Ryerson Ltd., Toronto, 1991, Chapter 4.

Tate Jr., C.E., L.C. Megginson, C.R. Scott Jr., and L.R. Trueblood, *Successful Small Business Management*, 3rd ed., Business Publications, Inc., Plano, Texas, 1982, Chapter 22.

25

Purchasing and Inventory Control

LEARNING OBJECTIVES

After reading this chapter, you will be able to:

1. **U**nderstand the importance of purchasing as a part of small business success
2. **K**now the factors to consider when buying for resale and for manufacturing procurement
3. **U**nderstand the value of maintaining good vendor relationships
4. **K**now the considerations for how much inventory to order and the use of the economic order quantity formulas
5. **U**nderstand the advantages of taking all purchase discounts available
6. **U**nderstand the importance of inventory turnover to overall small business success

The term *merchandising* is used very broadly in business. It usually covers all facets of the business that have to do with merchandise: acquiring it, handling and displaying it, seeking out potential customers for it, selling it, and rendering services to customers who have bought it. These activities can be divided into at least the following subjects:

1   Purchase of inventories
2   Inventory control
3   Sales promotion and advertising
4   Publicity
5   Displays of merchandise
6   Selling activities
7   Pricing policies
8   Customer services

Each of these subjects is a large one and many books have been written on the theory and practice of each. For the student or new firm planner, we can attempt here only to summarize some of the key considerations in each area. Such a summary can also be used to check the actual performance of an existing firm. This chapter will cover purchasing and inventory control.

THE IMPORTANCE OF PURCHASING

Retailers and wholesalers who buy items for resale must buy at the right price in order to be successful. Manufacturers must purchase their inputs correctly, too. It is obvious that this process of buying inputs is critical to business success. This topic is called *buying* for most retailing and wholesaling firms and *procurement* or *purchasing* for most manufacturing firms. It is one of the more important functions small business managers undertake.

The following information helps illustrate the importance of this function. When the purchasing is done properly, hundreds of dollars can be saved. This saving should make the product lower priced and more competitive. Since manufacturers can spend as much as 65 to 80 per cent for purchases, wholesalers as much as 65 to 75 per cent, and many retailers as much as 50 to 75 per cent for their purchases, it becomes a lot of money.

The people involved in retail and wholesale are called *buyers*, and most manufacturing procurement is done by *purchasing agents*. Most companies who provide the products purchased are called *vendors*.

BUYING FOR RESALE

Most retailers and wholesalers buy with an eye on the target customers. They try to identify items which they can buy at a low price and which they can sell at a profit. This requires a lot of buying decisions. For example, many retail stores carry in excess of 20 000 items.

There are essentially three basic ways to buy for resale:

1 Automatic rebuy of standard items as inventory goes down without review of items
2 Seeking and buying new products based on customer wants
3 Partial rebuy with some review of items

MANUFACTURING PROCUREMENT

Manufacturers need raw materials, semimanufactured (components) products, equipment, and supplies. Each need is unique and will be slightly different for every firm and will depend upon a materials planning schedule developed for the production process. A bill of materials should be developed and the factors listed below considered.

1 Determine the proper quantity needed.
2 Set and follow quality standards.
3 Get the items where they are needed on time.
4 Purchase at the right value.

Purchasing at the right value involves many factors. Price is often most important, but quality, delivery, service, and reliability are also a part of the value equation.

THE IMPORTANCE OF GOOD VENDOR RELATIONSHIPS

Vendors are important to the success of the small business. They supply many things as well as the product. They are responsible for delivery, reliability, and service. They set the prices charged and determine the quality.

A good vendor relationship is essential. Nothing is more difficult than having customers and no merchandise to sell to them. As an example, a local restaurant recently changed bread suppliers to get a lower price. Unfortunately, the new supplier could not meet agreed-to delivery schedules. As a result, the restaurant went back to the original vendor. The price was higher, but the delivery was reliable.

PURCHASING MERCHANDISE

The key questions that the small firm owner must ask himself or herself are: Am I buying through the established channels of distribution for this type of business? Is there another source which would give me the same dependability and service? Am I getting the best prices available for comparable quality? In what quantities should I be buying merchandise?

Most small retailers have wholesale houses available in their own locality that are eager and willing to serve them. Most consumer goods are normally distributed from manufacturer to wholesaler to retailer. In addition, there are salespeople from out-of-town suppliers who will call on the merchant to present their products. Job-lot dealers may operate in the area and have special quantities of merchandise for sale. A basic decision the new owner must make is whether to buy only from established wholesalers who serve the area or to buy wherever needed types of merchandise are available. If the firm has a distributorship for a particular line of merchandise, the source of supply is assured as part of the distributorship arrangement. Most small firm retailers carry similar merchandise in different price lines. Each price line may be served by a different wholesaler or distributor. Experience will soon tell the owners which are the most popular lines with their customers, and they will buy accordingly.

The inventory investment is usually the largest investment in the new small firm. Because of this, the owner must constantly be concerned with making this investment as profitable as possible.

DIFFERENT TYPES OF WHOLESALERS

New retailers are often confused as to the various types of wholesale establishments that are available to serve their procurement needs. New wholesalers are often not sure of how their planned firms fit into the generally accepted organization of the wholesale function. The following comments should clarify the situation for both groups.

Wholesalers are generally classified as:

Full-service wholesalers (also called merchant wholesalers)

Limited-function wholesalers

Agent middlemen (also called intermediaries)

Full-service Wholesalers   These are the most numerous in most lines of consumer goods. They usually buy their inventories directly from the manufacturers and thus take title to the merchandise. They store the merchandise in their own warehouses, deliver and/or assemble the products involved, and maintain a location where customers may inspect the products and place orders. They do not work on commission but rely upon their ability to sell their products at a profit to make their own operations successful. They are called full-service wholesalers because of the extra services they extend to their customers—such as granting credit on sales, providing delivery service, and supplying current market information.

Limited-function Wholesalers   These wholesalers render fewer marketing functions for their customers. *Jobbers*, who specialize in off-lot sales only, are often placed in this category. Wholesalers who merely sell merchandise that is delivered by the manufacturer to the customer are another example. They are often called *drop shippers*. Wholesalers who do not grant credit to their customers but make cash sales only are similarly classified.

Agent Middlemen or Intermediaries   These are wholesalers who actually provide a procurement function for their customers. Most do not take title to the merchandise they buy or sell for their customers, they merely arrange for such sales through their customers and contacts. They usually work on commission only. Any extra services extended to their customers are the exception, not the rule. Examples of this group are *brokers*, who arrange sales for their clients without ever taking title or possession of the merchandise products involved; *selling agents*, who often contract to take the entire output of a small factory and sell it wherever the market may be; and *manufacturers' agents*, who usually represent their manufacturer in only a certain specified territory and make sales of their product for delivery by the manufacturer.

Commission Merchants   These wholesalers are also usually classified as agent intermediaries, but they operate somewhat differently. They do not take title but usually assume physical possession of the merchandise they are employed to sell. They often provide temporary storage until they have completed their sales. They usually provide delivery of the merchandise sold. Sometimes they grant credit to firms to which they sell, but this is not uniform practice. They are paid for their services by a commission on the selling prices they develop. Special arrangements with the principal they represent may add other compensation.

HOW MUCH TO ORDER AND WHEN

How much of each item should be purchased on each order? The most important consideration here is to avoid stockouts while keeping the investment under control and the working capital active and available. Most retailers determine a minimum size in the inventory of any item as the reordering point. This minimum stock must take into consideration the time necessary to get a new order placed and delivered. Some allowance for contingencies in this regard is usually advisable. For example, if canned milk is sold at the rate of a case per week and it takes one week to get a new order placed and delivered, such an order could be placed when the stock is down to one case. Prudence suggests ordering a bit sooner.

But how many cases should be ordered? If local wholesalers are easily available with speedy delivery or pick-up service, if there is no price advantage in ordering more, and if storage space is limited, grocers cannot be accused of hand-to-mouth buying if they keep a reserve of one case and just have one case delivered each week. Such a situation does not usually exist. Even the problem of bookkeeping and totaling several invoices during the month would probably suggest that the grocers buy one month's supply each time. More likely, they have opportunities for purchase discounts for prompt payments of invoices and lower prices for larger quantity purchases. These factors would cause them to increase their ordering quantities. Larger orders would be encouraged by their wholesalers. Keeping track of every item in a large inventory is a big job, and some system should be established for keeping information available. Some small firms use tags taken from each item to post against inventory on hand. Others determine monthly usage and order just that amount each month until a physical inventory is taken.

THE ECONOMIC ORDERING QUANTITY (EOQ): THE SQUARE ROOT FORMULA FOR INDUSTRIAL BUYING

Industrial buyers have several basic square root formulas that apply more effectively to their type of buying. The use of modern computers make the calculations easy. One formula computes the economic ordering quantity (EOQ) in dollars. We will illustrate this formula first here.

For each item being purchased, the formula considers the dollar amount of the product used in the previous year; the cost of issuing a purchase order; and the cost of storing, insuring, protecting, and maintaining inventory on hand. When these factors are known, the formula is as follows:

$$\text{Economic ordering quantity} = \sqrt{\frac{2AB}{i}}$$

where A = the annual usage in dollars
B = the cost of issuing a purchase order, in dollars
i = the cost of carrying inventory, expressed as a percentage of the inventory value

We can illustrate the use of this formula with an actual example: if a factory used $75,000 of a product last year, the cost of issuing a purchase order was $6, and it cost 12 per cent of the inventory value to store, insure, protect, and maintain the inventory (0.12 per cent), we can insert these figures into the formula as follows:

$$\begin{aligned} \text{Economic ordering quantity (EOQ)} &= \sqrt{\frac{2(\$75,000)6}{0.12}} \\ &= \sqrt{\frac{\$900,000}{0.12}} \\ &= \sqrt{\$7,500,000} \end{aligned}$$

The square root of $7,500,000 is $2,738.

The most economic ordering quantity is, therefore, $2,738 each time an order is placed. If each unit costs $50, the number of units ordered would be 55 ($2,738 ÷ 50).

This formula uses a square root, but the time spent calculating it is worthwhile. It takes the guesswork out of the buying process. (Tables of square roots are available.) Different product groupings with similar usage patterns can be placed together so that calculations are minimized. The ordering quantity is recorded on each inventory sheet for future use. The formula does have some limitations, such as schedule changes, price changes, commercial practices, packaging limits, and perishable nature of products, that will prevent strict adoption in some cases. These can all be handled as adjustments, however, in the initial calculations if they can be estimated in advance.

The foregoing example of computing the EOQ shows the order in total dollars. During periods of rampant inflation which started in the late 1970s, continued into the 1980s, and is, still, a constant threat in the 1990s, it is often deemed best to compute the EOQ in terms of number of units because the prices are so subject to regular increases. Thus, we have another formula available that computes the EOQ in terms of units and uses the current price at the time a new order is being placed. Under this plan the formula becomes:

$$\text{EOQ} = \sqrt{\frac{2 \times U \times O}{P \times i}}$$

In this formula U = sales for past period (in units)
P = price per unit (now)
O = processing cost per order
i = inventory carrying charge as a percentage of inventory value

When this formula is used with the current price inserted, it will give the number of units to be ordered in the ideal ordering quantity. Notice that it again involves the computation of a square root. This formula is often referred to as "the standard formula" for computing EOQ.

Beginning inventories for a new factory must be based upon close scrutiny of available industry statistics and planned production schedules. As experience is gained in operations, the techniques of the square root formulas can be applied.

As factories grow larger, management will usually find it desirable to utilize even more refined economic purchase order formulas that can be operated on computers. Many of these formulas have as many as fifteen variables to be considered in arriving at precise ordering quantities.

In small factories the responsibility for initiating new purchase orders for materials and supplies must be the responsibility of the person in charge of inventories. A minimum inventory is established that allows for the normal lead time in getting stocks replenished (the time necessary to get purchase orders issued and new materials received). When that minimum is reached, immediate action is necessary. Notice that the minimum inventory reached can be given in different ways. One is to have the minimum stock in separate bins or shelves. Another is to post to a current inventory record all materials issued to production. This record adds all incoming shipments, deducts material issued, and thus has a perpetual inventory of balances on hand. The size of that minimum inventory may be adjusted because of new business developments such as transportation strikes, supplier problems, etc. It may also be affected to attractive prices available or changes in the production demands due to new products or extra usage of particular items in the total inventory.

Regardless of which system is used to keep control of inventory, the most important thing is to work the system. Practising the old idea of always having more than enough on hand to avoid stockouts or machinery shutdowns without regard to the adequacy of the inventory or the investment involved is prime evidence of inefficient management. Special circumstances may create exceptions. Too much inventory is wasteful. It ties up working capital, increases storage costs, and increases the risks of obsolescence and deterioration of the products.

INVENTORY CONTROL CONSIDERATIONS FOR RETAILERS

What is the ideal amount of inventory? For retailers, it is that inventory which does not lose profitable sales and can still justify the investment in each part of its total. For manufacturing firms, it is that inventory that maintains production schedules with a minimum investment in inventory.

Let us quickly admit that the ideal inventory is easier to describe than to determine in particular cases. Some examples will serve to illustrate the rule. If a drugstore has repeated requests for an aerosol spray product but does not have this item on its shelves, it is losing profitable sales by not stocking that item. If the owner's reason for not carrying the item is that it is only bought seasonally, the reasoning is faulty; such a policy is driving potential customers to competitors. If it is seasonal, the owner should arrange the stock so that little or no investment is tied up on the item during the off-season.

Carrying too many brands or sizes in a particular item can easily produce a situation where the total investment is not justified. Stocking many brands of toasters in one drugstore would be an example. People who want to buy a toaster in a drugstore are not usually concerned with the particular brand. Brand-conscious customers in this case would likely go to the brand distributor. Other consumer items that can easily fall into this category for various types of retailers are dishware, shirts, hammers, men's suits, and dresses. A choice may be desirable but excessive brands are not usually necessary. The type of store and type of customer must, of course, always be considered, but the underlying principle of inventory control remains important. Knowing the customers you have or are seeking is the best information to have in this regard.

Some items that are not generally popular may still have to be carried in minimum quantities for other reasons. For example, few drugstores still carry bar shaving soap. In one case, the druggist admitted that his shelves always had one dozen bars in stock because of two customers who regularly made substantial purchases in the store and who demanded this product from time to time. Giving up the small investment in bar shaving soap would have driven those customers together with their profitable purchases to another store. A slow-moving item was justified here, even though its sales probably could not justify even the small investment.

Retail Inventory Control Techniques

The problems of inventory control are really more difficult for most retailers than for factories. The factory has a specific production schedule, and the inventory of raw materials is adjusted to that positively planned usage. Retailers, however, may have the demands on their inventories change with the whims of their customers, with style changes, which are often unpredictable, or with the changing character of their market. They may drop or add new products or new lines of products at any time. Yet for most retailers the importance of efficiently managing this largest investment remains. Even if the ideal inventory has been approached, it is often subject to change on short notice. And the problems of different retailers vary in many ways. Some of the techniques that can be used to assist inventory control are:

1   Keep a constant surveillance of sales results and inventories. There is no substitute for this. All other techniques only assist actual experience.

2   Set minimum reordering point and maximum inventory on all basic stock items. Such basic stock is not susceptible to most frivolous demand changes.

3   Obtain data from modern cash registers to identify key items for sales. These will reflect increased or decreased sales of such items.

4   Have a detachable portion of sales slips that will record sales of particular items. A two-part price tab, half of which can be detached at time of sale, will accomplish the same purpose. Summaries of this data will provide sales information to govern purchases.

5   Rely on suppliers who regularly visit the store to maintain proper inventories without wasteful expenditure. (The bread truck driver knows how many loaves of each kind of bread to leave each morning.)

6   Use wholesaler or manufacturer recommendations for certain brands.

7   Use advanced computerized cash registers to assist inventory control.

PURCHASE DISCOUNTS

Good management demands that all purchase discounts should be taken. The excuse that cash is not available is not valid. A purchase discount is a reduction in the price on any invoice offered in return for prompt payment of the invoice. The most common discount offered by suppliers is 2/10, n/30. This means that if the invoice is paid within ten days, 2 per cent of the gross amount can be deducted, but in any event the entire amount is due in thirty days. An invoice for $1,000 of merchandise can thus be settled in full for $980 if paid within ten days, instead of $1,000, which would be due on the thirtieth day. Net savings is $20. A saving of 2 per cent for paying bills twenty days sooner is saving at the rate of 36 per cent per year. (It is earned in twenty days and there are eighteen periods of twenty days each in the year.)

This formula calculates the true percentage rate:

$$\frac{\text{Discount}}{\text{percentage}} = \frac{\text{Number of days in year}}{\text{Net days} - \text{Number of days for discount}} \times \text{Discount \%}$$

$$= \frac{360}{30 - 10} \times 0.02$$

$$= \frac{360}{20} \times 0.02 = 18 \times 0.02 = 36\%$$

Note that the number of days are 360 per year. The common business practice uses that number rather than 365.

The often-observed tendency to avoid paying such bills within the discount period represents neglect of good financial management. The typical drugstore must sell many units of shaving cream, cigarettes, or magazines to clear $20 in profit. One of the differences between efficient and inefficient firms lies in the attention given to this matter.

A study some years ago of over 1000 small firms showed that most were lax in taking advantage of purchase discounts. It also showed that 2 per cent of purchases were more than the majority of these firms paid in federal income taxes.

If adequate cash is not available, the competent proprietor with a good credit standing can borrow the necessary amount from a bank for the twenty days involved in the case above. At 12 per cent interest, the $980 would cost $6.54 in interest. Even deducting this interest from the $20 saved, the proprietor is still $13.46 ahead by paying the invoice within the discount period. Such clear gains cannot be ignored.

While advocating taking advantage of all purchase discounts for prompt payment and all quantity discounts where the quantities involved are justified by the company's inventory policy, we should also caution against ordering too large quantities in order to receive quantity discounts. One year's supply should be the maximum order placed regardless of attractive prices on larger quantities. In many cases, an order of even this size cannot be justified.

THE PROBLEM OF SLOW-MOVING MERCHANDISE

One of the hardest lessons for new retailers to learn or to accept is the desirability of selling slow-moving merchandise at less than normal markup or, in some cases, at less than cost. Every firm faces this problem to some degree. Stores selling style merchandise are particularly vulnerable to the risk of being stuck with an inventory of slow-moving products that will lose value as the style fades. Bathing suits and fashion shoes are examples of products that should be marked down as seasons or styles pass. Merchants sell Christmas cards at half-price the day after Christmas to combat this problem. They don't want working capital tied up in the cards for a whole year. Other products are subject to deterioration, fading, or other defects when kept in stock too long. Wise merchants who find such items in their inventory act to sell them as best they can as soon as they can. Special sales, markdowns, and advertising are some of the devices employed.

The Federal Business Development Bank and the Royal Bank have prepared several aids for small firm owners. They include long lists of ideas on how to move such products and generally reduce the problem. All proprietors should take advantage of these services. The typical report includes the following suggestions for liquidating slow-moving inventory:

1   Make traffic obstacles of large displays of the items.
2   Offer special discounts for quantity purchases.
3   Put specially coloured lights on displays.
4   Offer 1-cent sales.
5   Place slow-moving goods next to best sellers.
6   Have grab-bag sales.
7   Use specially coloured price tags.
8   Offer "Special of the Day" items.

MERCHANDISE INVENTORY TURNOVER

Some attention was paid to inventory turnover in Chapter 6, where we needed to know the average turnover for our type of firm. We can now return to that concept with more experience.

We have found that the ideal merchandise inventory is the one that does not lose productive sales and can still justify each part of its investment. We have investigated many of the ramifications of achieving that happy state. We know that the turnover is computed by dividing cost of goods sold by the average inventory. It is also clear now that too much inventory can lessen the turnover and result in inefficiency in total operations.

A time-honoured measure of efficiency in management has been this turnover figure. When comparing two firms, the one with the higher inventory turnover is usually assumed to be the more profitable. We are regularly reminded in these instances that a profit is made every time the inventory is turned. It is assumed, therefore, that the higher the turnover, the higher the profits. This is not always true. This measure does not take into account profitable sales lost because no merchandise was available. To illustrate with an extreme case: consider the hardware store with an inventory consisting of one hammer. No other merchandise is on the shelves. The owner sells a hammer each day. After the sale, the owner goes to the nearby supply house and buys another hammer. At the end of the month, there is a merchandise inventory turnover of thirty times per month, or 360 times per year. But has it been efficient? Many profitable sales may have been lost through lack of inventory. A proper inventory with a turnover of five times per year would have produced much better results.

Experience has demonstrated that too much inventory is usually less harmful than inadequate inventory and stockouts. The ideal inventory as described earlier may never be exactly achieved. Nevertheless, it has great value as a principle and should always be pursued.

QUESTIONS FOR CLASS DISCUSSION

1 What is meant by saying that "the ideal inventory should be able to justify the investment in each part of its whole"?
2 Have you ever been the victim of a stockout? What was your reaction?
3 What are the advantages, if any, of buying regularly from the same wholesaler?
4 How can it be dangerous to buy very large quantities of a particular item in order to receive an extra discount?
5 How do distributorships assure a steady supply of merchandise?
6 Do you agree that the merchant's inventory is usually the largest investment of small firms?
7 What is the ideal inventory for a retailer?
8 What is the ideal inventory of raw materials for a factory?
9 What is hand-to-mouth buying?
10 If a factory uses $20,000 of one raw material this year, should it order this amount on January 1 next year? Explain.
11 What are the possible advantages of placing large orders if doing so is consistent with inventory needs?
12 How can carrying too many competing items adversely affect the inventory investment and consequent profits?
13 Why can an efficient merchant not afford to neglect purchase discounts?

14 A saving of 2 per cent in twenty days represents an annual rate of 36 per cent. Explain how this is true.

15 Can the merchandise turnover ever be too high? Explain.

Projects for Home Assignment and/or Class Discussion

1 Make up your own problem on economic ordering of quantities for a factory and solve it with each of the formulas in the chapter. Do you get the same answer with each?

2 In your own firm, which type of wholesalers would you prefer to do business with? Are there advantages in dealing with different ones? Explain.

REFERENCES FOR FURTHER READING

Archer, M., *An Introduction to Canadian Business*, 5th ed., McGraw-Hill Ryerson Ltd., Toronto, 1986, Chapter 8.

Beckman, M.D., W.S. Good, and R.G. Wyckham, *Small Business Management*, John Wiley & Sons Canada Ltd., Toronto, 1982, Chapter 11.

Cunningham, G., *Buy Yourself A Job & Be Your Own Boss*, McGraw-Hill Ryerson Ltd., Toronto, 1990, Chapters 9 and 10.

Tate Jr., C.E., L.C. Megginson, C.R. Scott Jr., and L.R. Trueblood, *Successful Small Business Management*, 3rd ed., Business Publications, Inc., Plano, Texas, 1982, Chapter 14.

Minding Your Own Business, Federal Business Development Bank, Montreal, 1982, Vol. 1, Chapter 7 and Vol. 2, Chapter 4.

. . . .

26

Fixed and Variable Expense Analysis: The Break-Even Chart

LEARNING OBJECTIVES

After reading this chapter, you will be able to:

1. **K**now the process for break-even analysis to find the break-even point of operations
2. **D**etermine if expenses are fixed, variable, or a combination of both, called *semivariable*
3. **K**now the steps necessary to construct a break-even chart for an individual firm based upon that firm's expenses and income
4. **U**nderstand what can be learned from examination of a break-even chart
5. **U**nderstand the methods used to determine operating capacity
6. **K**now the formulas commonly used to calculate the break-even point

A business that has only variable expenses, all varying directly and proportionately with sales, cannot possibly operate at a loss. Such a business would be very unusual. Yet the idea is more than merely an academic or theoretical concept.

The foregoing statements are offered here in the hope they will stimulate the student's interest in a study of the nature and consequences of fixed and variable expense relationships in any business firm.

Basic to such a study should be recognition of the fundamental law of business that the greater the risk, the greater must be the potential profits. It follows that when the risk of loss is removed or even lessened, the potential profits must be less. Some sacrifices must be made in exchange for the protection against loss. In the case of the firm that has only variable expenses which vary directly and proportionately with sales, the sacrifice is that the profit margin on the first dollar of sales is the same as the profit margin on the last dollar of sales. Such a firm, which has total expenses of 85 per cent of sales, will have a profit of 15 cents on the first dollar of sales and a 15-cent profit on the one hundred-thousandth dollar of sales. Many small firm owners of long experience would likely welcome such an arrangement in exchange for this protection against loss if, indeed, it were possible to attain such an expense position. Although such a position is extremely rare, in fact impossible in almost all cases, the facts involved can be useful in making decisions for any business.

WHAT ARE FIXED EXPENSES?

Fixed expenses are defined as those that do not change with the sales volume. No matter what the sales are, the expense stays the same. A good example is the set monthly rent paid for the store or factory premises. The rent may be $400 per month. This is known as a flat rental. Such a rental has no relation to the volume of sales made by the business during the month. It must be paid every month whether sales are good or bad. This is a true fixed expense. Other fixed expenses in a typical small firm are depreciation expenses on fixed assets, skeleton-staff salaries, property taxes, amortization of organization expense, and most insurance premiums. In all these cases, too, the expense goes on at the same amount without reference to sales made.

WHAT ARE VARIABLE EXPENSES?

Variable expenses are defined as those that change with the sales volume of business. One type varies directly and proportionately with sales, the best example being commission expense. If all salespersons, for example, receive commissions only and no sales are made, there is no commission expense. As sales grow larger and larger, the commissions grow accordingly. If all salespersons receive commissions of 10 per cent of sales, the commission expense account grows directly and proportionately to total sales. Such expenses are the exception.

Most variable expenses do *not* vary directly and proportionately with sales. In fact, there are all degrees of variability. As a result, most variable expenses are really *semivariable*. Let us examine some of the typical variable expenses to determine how closely they vary with sales.

1 Cost of Goods Sold   Normally, the expense of cost of goods sold will bear a close relationship to sales made. But it may vary somewhat if there are increases in the price paid for merchandise that cannot be offset by increases in sales prices, or if special bargain purchases are made that increase profit margins. The situations seldom make a large percentage change in the relationship between cost of goods sold and sales. Strong competitive pricing situations may force owners to adjust their prices unwillingly in order to maintain average margins. Cost of goods sold can, therefore, be considered in most cases as bearing a direct and almost proportionate relationship to sales.

2 Utilities Expenses   Utilities expenses cover the cost of such items as telephone, electricity, water, and gas. If these expenses are billed on a flat per-month charge, they are truly fixed expenses. If they are charged on a usage basis and the use varies from period to period during the fiscal year, a distinctly variable factor is involved. Telephone and telegram expenses usually have a tendency to rise with increased sales volume. Heating in the winter by electricity or gas, or cooling in summer may bring variability into these utility charges. Many firms have a policy of charging the basic telephone bill as a fixed expense and the extra charges for long-distance calls and telegrams as variable expenses. Where the variations are small from month to month in total utilities expenses, most firms consider the total as a fixed expense.

3 Advertising and Promotion Expense   If a specified amount is set aside for these items in the yearly budget and if it is spent on a regular program or at specified periods, the total can be considered a fixed expense. If the policy of the firm is to increase or decrease its expenditures for advertising and promotion on a basis of monthly decisions, for example, it becomes a variable expense. Many firms have a policy of planning a specific advertising budget but remain open to extra advertising for the special occasions. In these cases, the planned budget could be considered a fixed expense and the extra expenditures would be considered variable when analyzing the total operation for a specific period.

4 Salaries for Sales Staff   A common mistake is failure to analyze the expense of salaries for sales staff and to assume that it is a completely variable expense. So doing neglects the concept of skeleton staff: the minimum number of salespersons who must be on hand to keep the doors open for business. Salaries for these people are a fixed expense. The variable portion of sales salaries is all salaries which will be expanded or contracted with changes in the sales volume. Competent managements study the need for adding sales people

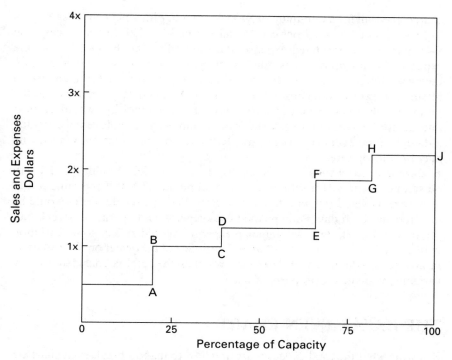

F I G U R E   2 6 - 1 • Relationship of sales and semivariable expenses.

as sales grow. Often they find the need for part-time people in certain seasons or on certain days of the week, or even during certain hours of the day. Sales salaries still do not vary directly and proportionately with sales volume. As sales increase, new salespersons are added to the payroll so that four people are doing the work in a leisurely way that three persons were doing last week under considerable pressure. Thus sales and sales salaries do move in the same direction but not proportionately at any given time. Figure 26-1 illustrates the relationship of sales and most semivariable expenses. Points A, C, E, and G might represent the addition of a new salesperson, a new bookkeeper, or a second delivery person. At these points there is a vertical increase in the dollar total of the variable expenses. Between points B and C, D and E, F and G, and H and J, the variable expenses stay the same. As sales increase, each semi-variable expense tends to increase also.

5 Rent Expense and Percentage Lease Rentals   Landlords have long demonstrated that they are more competent in knowing the value of store or factory space than most small firm owners. In most big cities, especially, the percentage lease rental arrangement is replacing the flat rental previously mentioned. A percentage lease provides a minimum flat fee plus an additional charge made on sales above certain amounts. For example, the total rental charge may call for a minimum of $400 per month plus 1 per cent of sales over $100,000 annually and 2 per cent of sales over $200,000. In such a case, the $400 flat charge is a fixed expense and the additional charge is a variable expense. Small firm planners must be prepared to evaluate the type of lease they are offered. Under the flat rental plan, the proprietor has a chance to retain more profits when business is very good. Under the percentage lease, the proprietor shares the profit of extra sales with the landlord. It would be most unusual for the landlord to give the firm a completely variable rental contract, although some instances are known. Requests for such rental arrangements may be appropriate.

6 Delivery Expenses   Are they fixed or variable? Would the delivery person be discharged if sales were down 50 per cent? Not if the same routes were to be covered but with fewer deliveries. Perhaps the deliveries would be less frequent each day. Perhaps the bookkeeper would operate the truck half the time. Gas, oil, and maintenance expenses should reflect some variation with a wide variation in sales volume. The policy of the owner on these matters in any given situation will determine whether the total is considered fixed, variable, or divided into parts of each.

THE BREAK-EVEN CHART

Knowing what the total expenses are and how to make a break-even chart are essential to good management. A correct break-even chart is valuable as a supplement to budget making, pricing policies, decisions on sales policies, and expense control and expansion plans, among other things. The completely competent businessperson should know what sales volume is necessary to break even (the point where there is no profit and no loss). The break-even chart can indicate the profits to be achieved at different levels of expanded sales. It can tell the results of changes in price policies and the benefits of expense reductions which might be available.

A break-even chart shows the relationship of fixed, variable, and total expenses to sales at all volumes of sales. It measures all expenses and income from sales on the vertical axis and the units sold or percentage of capacity on the horizontal axis. Profits at any level of capacity or at any volume of sales are measured by the vertical distance between the total expense line and the sales income line.

An accurately drawn break-even chart tells firm owners what sales volumes are necessary to reach the break-even point and the percentage of their capacity this sales volume represents. It tells them the profits to be derived from any planned expansion of sales. These relationships are measured against a presently existing set of facilities and expense analysis. Any change of store space, for example, would call for the creation of a new chart for the expanded facilities and expenses.

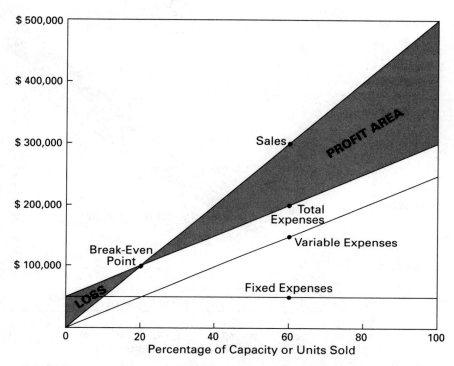

FIGURE 26-2 • Break-even chart for the Jones Department Store.

An example of a complete break-even chart is shown in Figure 26-2. It has been prepared for the Jones Department Store, which had sales for the year of $300,000, fixed expenses of $50,000, variable expenses of $150,000, and total expenses of $200,000. The firm operated at 60 per cent of capacity during the year. Students should study this chart to see how each line is plotted and identify where the sales line intersects the total expense line and profit generation begins. Be sure you can tell how to measure the profit for the year on this chart at any given point.

Making Your Own Break-Even Chart

Most students and most owners of small firms will recognize the preceding example of a break-even chart and appreciate its usefulness. The actual construction of such a chart for a specific firm is not so widely understood. All small firm owners should know how to construct a break-even chart and how to use it to analyze their operations.

The following is a step-by-step explanation of how to construct a break-even chart for any business when the percentage of capacity is known. Each step is illustrated on the break-even chart shown in Figure 26-3.

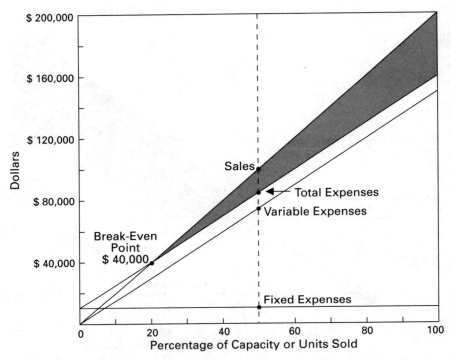

FIGURE 26-3 • Break-even chart for 1991 for the ABC Company when the percentage of capacity is known.

Step 1 Analyze each operating expense on the income statement (or planned income statement) to determine whether it is fixed, variable, or divided between these two according to the policies of the owner. List the fixed expenses in one column and the variable expenses in another column. Total the columns and add the cost of goods sold to the variable expense column. For this illustration we will use the ABC Company, which had sales of $100,000 for the year, costs of goods sold at $50,000, and operating expenses of $35,000, broken down into fixed and variable expenses as follows:

FIXED EXPENSES		*VARIABLE EXPENSES*	
Flat rental paid	$ 6,400	Sales salaries	$15,000
Taxes	1,200	Office salaries	8,000
		Percentage lease, extra payment	500
Depreciation	400	Telephone & telegrams	500
Delivery expense	1,400	Advertising & promotion	1,000
Utilities expense	600		
		Subtotal	$25,000
		Cost of goods sold	50,000
Total fixed expense	$10,000	Total variable expense	$75,000

Step 2   On a blank sheet of paper (or graph paper), draw the vertical and horizontal axes for your chart. The chart should be about 5 in. (12 to 13 cm) square. Label the vertical axis "Dollars (sales and expenses)" and the horizontal axis "Percentage of Capacity" or "Units Sold." Divide each axis into equal parts and mark each division with a dot. Place dollar amounts on each dot on the vertical axis, beginning with zero at the lower left corner and increasing in equal amounts to the top of the vertical axis. The dollar amount at the top of the vertical axis should represent sales at 100 per cent of capacity if known. This amount is broken up into ten equal amounts. In our example, we will assume that *operations for the year were at 50 per cent of capacity and use $200,000 as the top figure on the vertical axis*, with cumulative divisions of $20,000 each as the scale starts from the bottom.

Step 3   Draw a solid line from the lower left corner of the chart to the upper right corner. This will become the sales income line.

Step 4   Find the point of 50 per cent capacity on the horizontal axis. Draw a vertical dotted line from the bottom of the chart to the top of this at 50 per cent capacity point.

Step 5   On the vertical dotted line, mark the points representing $10,000, $75,000, $85,000, and $100,000, all measured against the left axis. These points mark the total of fixed, variable, and total expenses and the sales volume at 50 per cent of capacity.

Step 6   On the left axis, mark the point for $10,000. This is the total fixed expenses and total expenses at zero sales, or zero percentage of capacity.

Step 7   Every complete break-even chart should have four lines. We drew the sales line in Step 3, which bisects the square chart. Now draw the other three lines. Fixed expenses, by definition, are the same regardless of sales volume. Therefore, connect the $10,000 mark on the left axis and the $10,000 mark on the vertical dotted line, and extend the straight line on across the chart. Variable expenses, by definition, are zero at zero sales and $75,000 at 50 per cent of capacity. Therefore, connect the point zero on the left axis with the $75,000 mark on the vertical dotted line, and extend the straight line on across the chart. Total expenses are the combination of both fixed and variable expenses. That total is $10,000 at zero sales and $85,000 at 50 per cent of capacity. Therefore, connect the $10,000 point on the left axis and the $85,000 mark on the vertical dotted line, and extend the straight line on across the chart.

We now have a break-even chart for the ABC Company. It tells us many things about the operations. Among these things are the following:

1   The break-even point for the firm is a sales volume of $40,000. This is the point in sales volume where neither profit nor loss will result. On the chart it is found at the point where the sales line and the total expense line cross. Any sales less than $40,000 would put operations in the loss area of the chart. As sales expand into the profit area, profits become larger and larger.

2   Only 20 per cent of possible capacity is necessary to reach the break-even point. This is found by comparing the break-even point with the horizontal scale. It follows that $40,000 of sales represents 20 per cent of the capacity.

3   Profit on the $100,000 of sales for the year was $15,000 – measured by the vertical distance between the total expense line and the sales line, read against the vertical dollar axis.

4   As sales volume expands, the profits on each succeeding dollar of income is greater than on the preceding dollar. A sales increase from 50 to 60 per cent of capacity will not yield as much profit as an increase from 70 to 80 per cent of capacity. The reason is that after we pass the break-even point, all fixed expenses are covered and only the variable expenses must be borne by subsequent sales.

5   We can measure the profit results of a 10 per cent increase in prices, for example, by superimposing another sales line from the lower left corner across the chart connecting through the vertical dotted line at the point of $110,000 ($100,000 plus 10 per cent). We can also observe the results of a 10 per cent reduction in total expenses by superimposing a line from $9,000 ($10,000 less 10 per cent) through the point $76,500 ($85,000 less 10 per cent) on the vertical dotted line. This type of analysis may be necessary if the firm is faced with the necessity of increasing income or reducing expenses. In any event, it provides good information for decision making and study of the operation.

6   If sales could be expanded to 100 per cent of capacity, profits would rise to $40,000 – again the vertical distance between sales and total expenses on the right axes. As a practical matter, we can observe that if this point is even approached, most small firms have already made plans to expand their facilities.

Finding the Break-Even Point by Formula

If the only objective is to ascertain the dollar volume necessary to break even when sales, fixed expenses, and variable expenses are known, the following formula will give a ready answer:

$$\text{B.E.P.} = \frac{\text{Fixed expenses}}{1 - \text{Variable expenses over sales}}$$

Applying this formula to our problem above will show the same 40 000 break-even point in dollars:

$$\frac{\$10,000}{1 - \$75,000/\$100,000} = \frac{\$10,000}{1 - 0.75} = \$40,000$$

Finding the break-even quantity by formula:

If you would like to calculate the volume of output to break even (that is, total revenue is exactly equal to total costs) at a given selling price, use the following formula:

$$\text{B.E.Q.} = \frac{\text{Fixed expenses}}{\text{Price per unit sold} - \text{Variable expenses per unit}}$$

In our example, if the variable expenses are $1.00 per unit and the selling price is $1.33, then:

$$\text{B.E.Q.} = \frac{\$10,000}{\$1.33 - \$1.00} = \frac{\$10,000}{\$.33} = 30\ 000 \text{ units}$$

THE PROBLEM OF MEASURING CAPACITY

The problem of determining at what percentage of capacity the firm operated has prevented many small firms owners from making maximum use of a break-even chart. This problem can be easily removed.

A factory operation that has machines which can produce 100 units of its product a day can easily determine 100 per cent of its capacity. It merely multiplies working days times 100 units to find what production will be if full production is maintained during the month or year. By then comparing actual production with this capacity, the percentage is determined. For example, if the plant operates 250 days per year and 100 units is capacity per day, maximum production at 100 per cent capacity would be 25 000 units. If actual production is 15 000 units, the percentage of capacity for operation during the year is 60 per cent (15 000 divided by 25 000).

For retail and wholesale operations, the measurement of utilized capacity is not easily determined. Some retailers use a flat amount of sales per salesperson (for example $300 per day) to represent 100 per cent of capacity. This method must include the number of salespersons who can conveniently operate in the available sales space. Others attempt to combine average sales, time required per sale, sales people's time on the sales floor, and number of sales people who can conveniently operate in the sales space to arrive at a figure that would represent 100 per cent capacity sales for a given period. Store hours must be considered in any such calculation.

HOW TO MAKE A BREAK-EVEN CHART WHEN PERCENTAGE OF CAPACITY IS NOT KNOWN

It is not necessary to resort to these types of calculations to have the benefit of a break-even chart. The chart shown in Figure 26-4 has been constructed with-

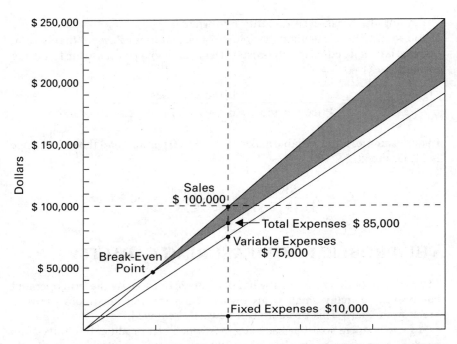

F I G U R E   2 6 - 4 • Break-even chart for 1991 for the ABC Company when the percentage of capacity is unknown.

out reference to the percentage of capacity at which the firm operated. Its construction is explained in detail following the chart.

Figure 26-4 shows the break-even chart when the percentage of capacity or number of units is not known. The same ABC Company data is used.

Step 1   Find any convenient point on the vertical scale to insert the $100,000 sales volume. A point about midway up the scale is normally used unless it is felt that close-to-maximum capacity has been achieved. In that case, choose a higher point on the vertical scale.

Step 2   Bisect the angle on the grid at the lower left corner. Extend this line far enough across the grid so that it allows for the maximum length of the horizontal and vertical lines. This is the sales line on any break-even chart.

Step 3   Scale the vertical axis in even units from the point where you inserted the $100,000 amount for sales.

Step 4   Draw a horizontal dotted line from the $100,000 sales point completely across the grid. Where the horizontal dotted line crosses the sales line, draw a vertical dotted line from bottom to top of the grid.

Step 5   On the vertical dotted line, plot the points for fixed, variable, and total expense against the vertical axis scale.

Step 6 Draw the lines for fixed, variable, and total expenses from the left axis to the plotting points on the vertical dotted line. Remember sales and variable expenses connect at the point zero on the vertical axis, and fixed expenses and total expenses connect at the point of fixed expenses ($10,000) on the vertical axis.

When we compare this chart with Figure 26-3, it will be seen that the scale is different, but all readings are identical. The break-even point calls for the same volume of sales, and profits are the same at all sales volumes. The only thing unknown is the percentage of capacity represented at each measuring point. The profit effects of an increase in sales can still be measured in the same manner.

QUESTIONS FOR CLASS DISCUSSION

1 Do you believe that cost of goods sold is a variable expense of any business? Why?

2 Why is it better to compute a firm's percentage of capacity on the basis of actual business days, rather than using 365 days for the year?

3 Is it possible for any business to be immune to loss? How?

4 What sacrifices must a business make to reduce risk?

5 What types of expenses increase directly and proportionately with sales?

6 What expenses increase directly but not proportionately with sales?

7 If the rent is $400 per month plus 1 per cent of sales over $50,000, how would you classify the total rent expense?

8 What do we mean by the "skeleton staff expenses"?

9 What are the three most important things you believe a break-even chart tells you?

10 Does an annual break-even chart reflect seasonal variations in sales volume?

11 Why is the cost of goods sold added to the variable operating expenses when making a break-even chart?

12 Is it true that the greater the fixed expenses, the farther to the right is the break-even point? Why?

13 What other uses can an owner make of an accurate break-even chart?

14 Do you consider delivery expenses a fixed or a variable expense? Explain.

Projects for Home Assignment and/or Class Discussion

1   Write a short essay explaining the importance of an adequate inventory, the extra costs of having too much inventory on hand, and the dangers of having too little inventory on hand.

2   What would your policy be on markdowns in your firm? Explain the reasons for each part of your policy.

3   a Write a short paper on the value of a break-even chart for any small firm.

     b How often do you think it would be wise to make a break-even chart? Monthly? Quarterly? Or annually?

REFERENCES FOR FURTHER READING

Archer, M., *An Introduction to Canadian Business*, 5th ed., McGraw-Hill Ryerson Ltd., Toronto, 1986, Chapter 12,

Cunningham, G., *Buy Yourself A Job & Be Your Own Boss*, McGraw-Hill Ryerson Ltd., Toronto, 1990, Chapters 9 and 10.

Meigs, W.B., R.F. Meigs, and W.P. Lam, *Accounting: The Basis for Business Decisions*, 6th Canadian Edition, McGraw-Hill Ryerson Ltd., Toronto, 1991, Chapter 25.

Tate Jr., C.E., L.C. Megginson, C.R. Scott Jr., and L.R. Trueblood, *Successful Small Business Management*, 3rd ed., Business Publications, Inc., Plano, Texas, 1982, Chapter 21.

27

Selling on Credit: Administering a Credit Program

LEARNING OBJECTIVES

After reading this chapter, you will be able to:

1. **U**nderstand that the use of credit by a business will increase sales
2. **K**now the different types of consumer credit and how consumer credit is different from trade credit
3. **U**nderstand the costs involved in granting credit
4. **K**now the steps involved to administer a credit program—including methods for handling delinquent accounts
5. **C**alculate accounts receivable turnover and age accounts receivable
6. **K**now the scope of laws concerning consumer credit practices and how the small business should deal with them

CREDIT SELLING WILL INCREASE SALES

There are very few axioms in the world of business, but one of them is "if you sell on credit you will increase sales, even to the same customers to whom you previously sold for cash only." This alluring proposition has great appeal to small business firms. Sales are the foundation of profits, and anything that will help to increase sales commands the attention of competent business owners.

But there is more to credit selling than meets the eye. Every retail business must first decide whether it will offer credit arrangements to its customers. If credit is to be available, a decision must be made about the kind of credit to be extended. Will the firm sell to its customers on open account and carry these accounts receivable on its own books until they are paid? Or will it sell to credit card holders who have been approved for credit by one or more of the many credit card companies now so active throughout Canada? In this chapter we will review the details of both of these types of consumer credit.

TRADE CREDIT VERSUS CONSUMER CREDIT

Trade credit is credit extended from one business firm to another. *Consumer credit* is credit given by retailers to their customers, who are the final users of the products or services sold. Sales by manufacturers and wholesalers are almost always made on a credit basis. Retail sales on credit are now about half of the total retail sales in the country. Only the growing popularity of chain grocery stores and others that sell for cash only has kept retail sales on credit from growing larger.

Trade credit almost always carries a sales discount for prompt payment. We have seen in Chapter 25 that "terms of sales 2/10, n/30," for example, means that 2 per cent of the total amount may be deducted if the invoice is paid within ten days, but the entire amount is due in thirty days. Such discounts are extremely rare in consumer credit. The trend is quite the opposite. Most retail sales on credit charge customers for the privilege of postponing their payment to a later date. Large firms have adopted this practice more than small firms. Various types of consumer credit accounts will be discussed later in this chapter.

THE BUSINESS WORLD MUST OPERATE ON CREDIT

Our business world could not operate without credit. There is not enough currency and coin in the country to finance the business transactions carried on every day. Total bank deposits exceed the actual money in the country several times over. The key is credit extended throughout the economy.

Without credit from banks, credit from other business firms, and the sale of securities, large and small manufacturers could not operate. Without credit from manufacturers, banks, and other sources, wholesalers could not operate. Retailers depend on credit from banks and wholesalers. Without credit terms available, the average family could not buy a home, an automobile, major appliances, or finance expensive vacations. The importance of the credit standing of the business firm and of individuals is obvious. Unless a reputation for prompt payment of obligations is developed, credit sources will not be available. A good credit standing is essential to business success. Business owners must look for the same good credit standing of firms or individuals to whom they grant credit.

OPEN ACCOUNT CREDIT

Open account credit means that the merchant allows customers to say "charge it" when they make purchases. Data from the sales slips for each purchase is recorded on the firm's books. The total charges for each customer are added and shown on a statement, which is sent to the customer, usually on the first of the following month. Unpaid balances appear on the firm's balance sheet as accounts receivable. Open account credit operates quite differently from credit card credit, which we will investigate later in this chapter.

Great care in granting open account credit is most important. We have seen in Chapter 12 that even when such credit is carefully granted, the firm will soon have a total investment in accounts receivable of forty-five to sixty days' credit sales when they are selling on a thirty-day credit basis. Careless credit granting will greatly increase this amount. Accounts receivable tie up the working capital of the firm. We have stressed in Chapter 12 the importance of the firm having sufficient cash in the business to be able to invest in such accounts receivable.

The Cost of Open Account Credit

Whenever a business firm, large or small, makes open account credit available to its customers, it automatically assumes additional costs. These should be seriously considered before a business owner embarks upon a general credit policy. Too many new small firms fail to recognize some of these costs. They include:

Bookkeeping costs to record customer purchases and payments received

Printing of sales slips, statement forms, letterheads, envelopes, and credit memos

Postage costs for mailing statements

Interest on working capital invested in accounts receivable

Collection costs for delinquent customers

The inevitable bad debts which are never collected

Full recognition of these costs has caused more and more small firms to turn to credit card sales rather than carrying customer accounts on their own books.

The seriousness of the credit problem is emphasized by the aggregate losses on bad debts incurred every year by Canadian business firms. The most conservative estimates run into the millions. The most efficient firms are satisfied to keep their bad-debt losses below 2 per cent of their credit sales. Studies show that small firms which exercise inadequate control over their credit extensions have often had losses on bad debts that exceed 5 per cent of their credit sales. Profitability can be seriously affected in such cases. Such data point up the need to be careful in extending credit.

The longer a credit sale is carried on the books, the greater is the likelihood of its not being collected in full. This fact shows the necessity of close follow-up on accounts that become past due. Small firms too often have been lax in enforcing good collection procedures.

With the benefit of the foregoing facts about the world of credit, new firm planners can make choices for their firms. If they decide to sell on open account, either exclusively or in connection with credit card sales, they must turn their attention to the question of which customers should be granted credit and on what basis.

ADMINISTERING A CREDIT PROGRAM

It has been seen that credit sales may increase total sales and profits. This is only true, however, if the increased sales do not cost more in administration expenses and bad-debt losses than the profits on the credit sales. Every firm should therefore have a procedure for granting credit. Any customer who asks for credit desires the use of the firm's capital. In exchange, the customer should be willing to comply with reasonable rules for granting of that credit. No exceptions should be made.

The credit manager always wants to be sure that the account will be paid. The manager must find out the applicant's record for payment, capacity to pay, and how much credit the applicant can properly handle. Everyone is worth some credit; the question is how much. No business does its customers favours by granting them more credit than they can handle. Such a credit policy only invites ill will from the customers in the long run and might even force them to consider bankruptcy. Giving credit is a serious responsibility.

Well-managed companies take the following steps in granting credit:

1   Have the applicant for consumer credit fill out a credit application form, which calls for such basic information as name, address, age, present and past employment, length of employment, salary, home ownership details, past credit extended, payments now being made on other accounts, bank accounts, family status including

PLEASE PRINT IN BLOCK LETTERS

| LAST NAME | FIRST NAME | INITIALS | TELEPHONE NO. | | SOCIAL INSURANCE NO. | NO. OF CARDS REQUIRED 1 2 |

| NO. AND STREET NAME (SPECIFY ST., AVE., RD., ETC.) | APT. NO. | SINGLE   SEPARATED / MARRIED   DIVORCED / WIDOW(ER) | DATE OF BIRTH MONTH DAY YEAR | SPOUSE (FIRST NAME) |

| CITY | PROVINCE | POSTAL CODE | AT PRESENT ADDRESS OWN   RENT $_____ WITH PARENTS   PER MONTH | NO. OF DEPENDENTS (EXCLUDING SPOUSE) | DRIVER'S LICENSE NO. |

| PREVIOUS ADDRESS (IF AT PRESENT ADDRESS LESS THAN 2 YEARS) | | HOW LONG? |

| EMPLOYER—NAME AND ADDRESS | TELEPHONE | OCCUPATION | HOW LONG? | GROSS MONTHLY INCOME $ |

| PREVIOUS EMPLOYER (IF WITH ABOVE LESS THAN 2 YEARS) | TELEPHONE | OCCUPATION | HOW LONG? | GROSS MONTHLY INCOME $ |

| SPOUSE NOW EMPLOYED BY—NAME AND ADDRESS | TELEPHONE | OCCUPATION | HOW LONG? | GROSS MONTHLY INCOME $ |

| NAME AND ADDRESS OF NEAREST RELATIVE NOT LIVING WITH ME | | RELATIONSHIP |

REFERENCES

| BANK | BRANCH | LOAN $ / SAVINGS ACCT. NO. | PCA NO. / C/A NO. |

| HOME: FINANCED BY | | ESTIMATED VALUE $ | AMOUNT OWING $ | MONTHLY PAYMENT $ |

| AUTO: YEAR AND MAKE | FINANCED BY | $ | $ | $ |

OTHER LOANS, CREDIT CARDS, DEPT. STORES, FINANCE CO'S, ETC.

NAME	ADDRESS		AMOUNT OWING $	MONTHLY PAYMENT $
NAME	ADDRESS		$	$
NAME	ADDRESS		AMOUNT OWING $	MONTHLY PAYMENT $
NAME	ADDRESS		$	$

I, the undersigned, hereby certify the above information to be true and, if this application is accepted, request _____ card(s) be issued to me, and renewals or replacements thereof from time to time. In connection with such issuance, renewal or replacement, the undersigned authorizes and consents to the receipt and exchange of credit information and agrees to abide by the terms of the issuing _____ Cardholder's Agreement. Use of such card shall evidence receipt of such Cardholder's Agreement.

DATE _____   APPLICANT'S SIGNATURE X _____

FIGURE 27-1 • Typical application for credit used by large firms. Small firms should be equally careful in extending credit.

dependants, and other asset information. An example of a credit application form is shown in Figure 27-1. Applicants for trade credit should submit their companies' official financial statements.

2 Check the applicant's credit record with local credit bureaus and other credit agencies. Find out what limits were placed on the applicant's credit by other firms. Remember, you are always looking for evidence of the applicant's possession of the "four Cs of credit." These are character, capital, capacity, and conditions. Trade-credit applicants are checked by credit bureaus and/or by Dun & Bradstreet, a general trade-credit agency. (See Figures 27-2 and 27-3.)

3 On the basis of knowledge gathered from an independent investigation plus confirmation of information on the application, determine the limit of credit you feel can safely be granted. If the investigation proves that an applicant is a high risk, the decision must be to deny any credit at all. Assuming that investigation proves an applicant worthy of credit, compare the desired merchandise purchase with the limit you have set. This will determine whether the applicant should be granted credit on an installment-loan basis, a revolving-account basis, a budget-account basis, or an open charge account. (These accounts are explained below.)

NAME AND ADDRESS OF BUREAU MAKING REPORT

TORONTO REGIONAL CENTER
60 BLOOR STREET WEST
TORONTO, ONTARIO
M4W 3C1

ACB OF C = 96100

REPORT TYPE

SUMMARY	SINGLE REF	TRADE
SHORT	FULL	PREV RES
DATE RECEIVED 11/09/90	DATE MAILED 11/09/90	ACB REPORT
DATE TRADE CLEARED RE:D/RPTD	DATE EMPL VERIFIED	INCOME VERIFIED YES NO

CONFIDENTIAL Factbilt® REPORT FOR | IN FILE SINCE 08/23/79

This information is furnished in response to an inquiry for the purpose of evaluating credit risks. It has been obtained from sources deemed reliable, the accuracy of which this organization does not guarantee. The inquirer has agreed to indemnify the reporting bureau for any damage arising from misuse of this information, and this report is furnished in reliance upon that indemnity. It must be held in strict confidence, and must not be revealed to the subject reported on.

REPORT ON (SURNAME) MR., MRS., MISS: KENT,CLARK,RALPH,JR,	SOCIAL INSURANCE NUMBER: 111-111-514		SPOUSE'S NAME: LOIS
ADDRESS / CITY / PROVINCE: 1234A,MAIN,ST,EAST,,THUNDER BAY,ON,	POSTAL CODE: L4B1X3	RESIDENCE SINCE: 04/88V	SPOUSE'S SOC. INS NO: 111-111-514

COMPLETE TO HERE FOR TRADE REPORT AND SKIP TO CREDIT HISTORY

PRESENT EMPLOYER AND KIND OF BUSINESS	POSITION HELD	MONTHLY INC	SINCE
SAVE OUR LIVES HOSPITAL	MEDICAL DOCTOR	$2500	01/86

COMPLETE TO HERE FOR SHORT REPORT AND SUMMARY REPORT AND SKIP TO CREDIT HISTORY

DATE OF BIRTH	NUMBER OF DEPENDENTS INCLUDING SPOUSE			
01/25/55	2	[X] OWNS	[ ] BOARDS	[ ] RENTS

FORMER ADDRESS / CITY / PROVINCE	FROM	TO
999,GREEN AVE APT21,,MONTREAL,PQ		

FORMER EMPLOYER AND KIND OF BUSINESS	DATE VERIFIED	POSITION HELD	MONTHLY INC	FROM	TO
MCGILL UNIVERSITY		STUDENT	$	12/79	12/85
SPOUSE'S EMPLOYER AND KIND OF BUSINESS: NESBITT THOMSON	04/89	CHARTERED ACCT	$2258	07/87	04/89

CREDIT HISTORY (Complete this section for all reports)

```
* BUS/ID         RPTD     OPND     H/C     TRMS   BAL   P/D    RT 30/60/90   MR   DLA

ROYAL BANK VISA
  *650ON28       03/89

EATONS (416) 343-3375
  *650DC32       04/89    09/79    2000    150    750   315    R2 01 02 00   12   03/89
   PREV HI RATES: R3 02/89.
   AMOUNT IN H/C COLUMN IS CREDIT LIMIT

ROYAL BANK
03/89    626BB400        09/83    5MED
PERSONAL CHEQUING,OVERDRAFT,
4 NSFS IN 1988

PUBLIC RECORDS AND/OR SUMMARY OF OTHER INFORMATION
02/89  JUDGMENT DC THUNDER BAY,,$750, DEF-SUBJECT,CASE NO-9999999,ONTARIO HYDRC
VERIFIED 04/89
SUBJECT STATES MERCHANDISE FAULTY - VOLUNTARILY RETURNED

04/89  SECURED LOAN CENTRAL REGION THUNDER BAY, CREDIT BANK OF NOVA SCOTIA
55 PARK AVE THUNDER BAY $4000  MATURES 09/90

12/88  PAID COLLECTION,COLL THUNDER BAY,$500,,,03/89,BRN-123456789 SEARS,
BALANCE-0  SUBJECT DISPUTES THIS ACCOUNT

*INQS-
04/11/89  626BB400    ROYAL BANK
04/11/89  626LP23     COLOR YOUR WORLD
03/24/89              CB MIAMI FL
   BB    A12/86  01/70  500      0     R1       09/86
12/86 SAVAC    BB 03/70  2LOW

 NARRATIVE             RPTD  04/89       PURGE  04/90
 SUBJECT WAS UNEMPLOYED FOR 2 MONTHS, CREDIT GRANTORS WERE NOTIFIED AND ALL
 PAYMENTS WERE MADE, PLUS INTEREST, WHEN HE RETURNED TO WORK &
```

AFFILIATED WITH

FORM C100T ASSOCIATED CREDIT BUREAUS OF CANADA

FIGURE 27-2• Credit Report. This type of report may be obtained from local credit bureaus when a business owner is checking on the eligibility of credit applicants.

Courtesy Credit Bureau of Greater Toronto.

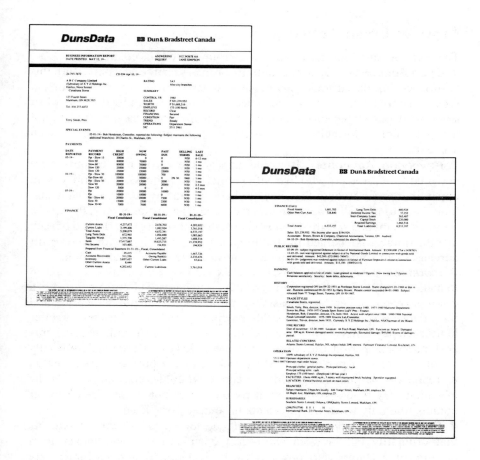

F I G U R E   2 7 - 3 •   A typical business report by Dun & Bradstreet Canada Limited/Limitée.

4   Discuss your decision with all applicants. Explain the reasons for the decision if asked. Support your decision by explaining that applicants' payments must be in line with their available income and that you are protecting them from getting too far in debt.

5   Follow up on new credit accounts regularly. This can be done even before an aging of accounts receivable (to be explained later in this chapter) is made. When payments are delinquent and notices and other steps taken have been ignored, it may be necessary to exercise right of repossession if it is available. If all has worked out well, it would be desirable to inform the customer that better credit terms can be arranged in the future.

Types of Credit Accounts

There are at least four basic types of consumer credit accounts.

1 Open Accounts   Open accounts are ordinary charge accounts. With this type of account the customer charges all purchases throughout the month and is expected to pay the total charges when a statement is sent by the firm. Most firms send out statements monthly, but full payment each month is not insisted upon. Normally no interest charges are made against such accounts.

2 Revolving Accounts   It would appear the revolving accounts were designed for customers who live with eternal indebtedness. The firm sets an upper limit to the amount that may be charged, and any purchases below that limit are automatically approved for credit sale. The customer must then pay a certain amount or a specified percentage of the total charges at the end of each month. Interest is charged on the unpaid balance each month, and credit purchases can continue to be made against the account up to its limit.

3 Installment Accounts   Installment accounts were specifically designed to make possible the sale on credit of larger purchases. The customer makes a down payment, preferably at least 20 per cent of the total purchase price, and the balance is spread over a monthly payment plan. Good business practice limits such payments to not more than three years. Many installment accounts are for a shorter period. Carrying charges are added to the amount due, usually about 1½ per cent per month. Most such sales are protected by a chattel mortgage on the item being sold or a conditional sales contract, so that the merchant may repossess the item if payments are not made. The customer obtains title only when the payments have been completed.

4 Budget Accounts   Budget accounts are designed to handle payments that ordinarily fall between short-term open accounts and longer term installment accounts. No down payment is required and customers are normally given three months to remit the total price in equal payments. Customers are expected to make payments without reminders in the form of statements from the seller. Service charges are made only when the original plan of payment is not maintained.

Each of these four types of accounts necessitates special forms and clear identification to the buyer. Payment plans for each must be explained and understood.

ACCOUNTS RECEIVABLE TURNOVER

The accounts receivable turnover is the relationship of the credit sales made during the year and the average amount of accounts receivable carried on the books. It is computed by dividing the total credit sales for the year by the average accounts receivable.

$$\frac{\text{Credit sales for the year}}{\text{Average accounts receivable}} = \text{Accounts receivable turnover}$$

When seasonal variations in credit sales are normal during the year, it is especially important to average the accounts receivable to obtain a more accurate measure of their turnover. Firms selling to one another on a basis of trade notes receivable should include the balance of any such notes receivable in their receivables in computing the turnover.

Every good management keeps a close check on the turnover figure and makes decisions based on the trend of this turnover. This figure also serves as a check on the paying habits of the firm's credit customers and on the credit-extension policies of the credit department. Increasing turnover indicates that customers are paying their accounts more quickly. If the turnover is decreasing, customers are paying more slowly, and/or the credit department is granting unjustified credit.

An example will illustrate computation of the accounts receivable turnover and its significance in evaluating performance.

The AAA Company is a small department store that sells to many customers on a thirty-day credit basis. In 1990 its credit sales were $300,000. The average accounts receivable on the first of each month was $50,000. Its accounts receivable turnover, therefore, was six times per year. In other words, it took one-sixth of a year (sixty days) to collect the average amount of receivables carried on the books. But the firm was selling on thirty-day credit. If all customers paid their account balances on the first of the month, the turnover would have been twelve times per year. Management considerations in such a situation involve answers to questions such as the following:

1   Can the company carry these receivables without impairing its cash position?

2   Has credit been granted unwisely to customers who average sixty days to pay thirty-day accounts?

3   Is the account-paying schedule normal for this type of business?

4   Has the loss on bad debts been increased because customers take sixty days on the average to pay current charges?

5   If bad-debt losses are not out of line, would it be desirable to arrange financing to enable the firm to carry its accounts receivable for this longer period?

6   Can anything be done to encourage more prompt payment of credit accounts by customers?

7   Would an interest charge on past due accounts stimulate more prompt payment?

Circumstances will vary from firm to firm as answers to these questions are sought. The important thing is to know the facts in regard to the accounts receivable turnover and to make policies accordingly. New restrictions may have to be placed on credit granting. Or perhaps credit will be granted only through credit cards. On the brighter side, a turnover of twelve times per year for the AAA Company may suggest that profits could be expanded by further granting of credit. Such a turnover rate indicates that customers are paying their bills on schedule and that losses on bad accounts are at a minimum.

AGING OF ACCOUNTS RECEIVABLE

To combat the problem of delinquent accounts, an *aging of accounts receivable* should be regularly made by the small firm owner. An example of such a statement is presented in Table 27-1. The first two columns show the customer's name and current balance. In the other columns, that balance is broken down into what portion of it was charged in the last thirty days, what portion has been on the books thirty to sixty days, what portion sixty to ninety days, and what portion over ninety days. As we observe our axiom that the longer an account is on the books the more likely is its failure to be paid in full, we can see that prompt action should be taken via an established collection procedure whenever a balance gets past due. The exact point and exact steps will be decided by firm policy. Alternatives are presented later.

TABLE 27-1

ABC COMPANY
AGING OF ACCOUNTS RECEIVABLE
OCTOBER 1, 199–

CUSTOMER NAME	CURRENT BALANCE	NUMBER OF DAYS ON BOOKS				
		0–30	*31–60*	*61–90*	*91–120*	*OVER 120*
M. Jones	$375	$ 75	$300			
H. Harris	160	60	50	$ 50		
G. Salzman	50	50				
P. Miller	500	300	100	100		
G. Geipel	50	–	–	–	$ 50	
B. Thompson	75		75			
H. Strauss	35	10	–	25		
J. Hegner	125	100	–	–	–	$ 25
T. Nathan	400	100	100	100	100	
A. Cohen	425	25	200	200		
G. Young	75					75
J. Osborg	200				100	100
Totals	$37,000	$22,000	$8,000	$5,000	$1,000	$1,000

In this case, $37,000 represents the balance of the accounts receivable account for the firm. The total of all other columns is also $37,000. This statement shows the proprietor that $22,000 is current month charges, $8,000 is less than sixty days old, $5,000 is less than ninety days old, but $1,000 is more than ninety days old, and $1,000 is over 120 days old. When the proprietor estimates the bad-debts expense for the year, serious consideration should be given to charging off the last $2,000. Its collection is definitely in doubt when it has been on the books so long. Accounts once charged off as a loss can always be reported as income if their unlikely collection should occur.

NUMBER OF DAYS' SALES IN RECEIVABLES

An even more precise measure of customer paying habits is the number of days' sales represented in the accounts receivable on a given date. This figure is found by dividing the total accounts receivable at the end of the year by the average daily credit sales. The latter figure is found by dividing the credit sales for the year by 365. If the firm has $50,000 of accounts receivable on December 31 and the average daily credit sales are $1,000, the receivables represent fifty days of credit sales. This calculation can also be made in terms of business days rather than calendar days by dividing the credit sales for the year by the number of business days the firm is open for operation rather than by 365, as stated above.

We should note that the example of the AAA Company's selling on thirty days' credit and having fifty days of credit sales on its books is not a far-fetched one. You will recall that in the planning of an opening day balance sheet (Chapter 12), it was recommended that we be prepared to finance 1½ to 2 times the credit sales in the maximum credit period. Most new firms that carry their own receivables will reach such a position within the first or second year of operation.

HANDLING DELINQUENT ACCOUNTS

Credit customers who do not pay on schedule cause the firm several problems. Their credit is cut off so that they are lost as future customers even if their finances improve, the old balances restrict liquidity of the working capital, and the net result is usually an uncollectible account which becomes bad-debts expense. Partial collection by attorneys or collection firms incurs much expense. No merchant likes to make credit sales in good faith and then have the sales cause these problems. The best course of action when accounts become overdue is to minimize the eventual losses by taking the following steps:

1   Send a second statement sixty days from purchase. This could include a note to the effect that "Perhaps our first statement was not received or was mislaid. We know you would not want your credit status impaired. Please advise us if there is any complaint about our products or service."

2   Telephone the customer or send a telegram in seventy days, asking the reasons for nonpayment.

3   Send a third statement in seventy-five days. Include a note to the effect that "Your credit status is at stake. We are forced to turn over accounts seventy-five days old to our collection agency or attorney."

4   Send a registered letter in eighty days, including a certified copy of the statement, saying that the account is being referred to the collection agency.

5   Turn the account over to the agency or the firm's attorney for legal action in ninety days.

Small firm owners usually have an advantage over large firm owners in this situation since they know their customers better. If this is so, they can usually accomplish more through personal contact with the customer than by resorting to the steps just described. If they find that a genuine customer complaint exists, they may open the door to make a fair adjustment and keeping the customer. But the possible delinquent situation should always be anticipated by picking the right credit customers in the first contact.

PERSONAL AND COMPANY CHEQUE CASHING AS ANOTHER FORM OF CREDIT

Credit extension is normally thought of as allowing customers to charge their purchases to the firm at the time of purchase, with the balances due to be paid at least once a month. Cashing cheques for customers and companies, however, is another form of credit extension. Many merchants will confess to having cashed cheques for customers that came back from the bank marked "NSF" (not sufficient funds) or "no account here." One major airline admitted it had accepted more than $2 million in bad cheques in one year. It now encourages the use of credit cards whenever possible. These facts point up the necessity of a policy on cheque cashing. The natural result has been an increasing reluctance to accept such cheques.

Devices are now available to aid in this problem. "Debit cards" have been introduced. These are plastic cards, held by customers, that may be inserted into an electronic box by the merchant to confirm that cheque writers have funds in their accounts to cover their cheques. Cheque-guarantee companies, which will guarantee personal cheques to the merchant, now exist. Many banks have machines available twenty-four hours a day to enable their card holders to get cash from the machines by inserting their cards. These machines not only make it easier for customers to get cash, they also reduce the use of personal cheques. Merchants must be cautious in cashing cheques for people they do not know. We will see more and more evidence in this chapter that the small firm should restrict its credit sales to credit cards and not attempt to carry many open account receivables on its own books. Neither should it accept personal cheques without substantiation of the customer's identification and/or assurance that the cheque is good.

CREDIT CARD CREDIT

The huge increase in the use of credit cards in Canada in the past ten years has truly been one of the major merchandising and financial developments. In 1990 it was estimated that there were more than 35 million individual credit cards outstanding. In effect, many families have as many as ten cards. Outstanding dollar balances exceed $9 billion, or over $1,500 for every family in the country. Credit cards are used for more than half a billion transactions each year. The interest charges alone are more than $1 billion.

Credit cards are being used today for ever-increasing types of purchases. They originally were designed to assist travelers with the problem of cashing personal cheques when they were away from home. They were used most often for purchasing airline tickets and paying hotel bills, auto rentals, and gasoline purchases. *Today, retail purchases of consumer products and services represent their widest use.* In California, credit cards can be used to pay property taxes, buy auto tags, and even to pay state income taxes. Other newer uses could include payments to doctors and dentists, political parties, churches, etc. Many credit cards are issued free of charge for approved applicants. Each card specifies the maximum credit the holder may charge.

Usually there is a charge of an annual fee to holders of some credit cards; for example, American Express and Diners Club. These charges were as high as $55 per year in 1990. The Royal Bank offers its VISA customers a choice of paying either a flat yearly fee of $12 or a charge of $0.15 every time they use their card.

The cards named above are all issued by general credit card companies. Many can be used around the world. But we should also observe that many individual service and product companies still issue their own credit cards. These are called *single-firm credit cards.* Oil companies, department stores, hotels, and chain restaurants are the most prominent examples. The objective is to stimulate sales of the firm's own products or services while avoiding the costs of the general credit card companies. Some oil companies even honour the credit cards of other oil companies. Oil companies charge no fee to service stations, garages, or other firms using their cards. Most of these individual company cards carry no service charge to customers who pay their monthly balances promptly. When such cards are issued by smaller firms, the effect is usually comparable to open account selling. They may still have good advertising and sales development value.

How Credit Cards Operate for the Customer

When a cardholder wishes to make a purchase against a credit card, he or she must first ascertain whether the firm honours that card. Most small firms which accept credit cards have signs displayed in their front window or door indicating the types of cards accepted. To make a purchase, the customer merely hands the merchant the credit card. The merchant, who may phone the credit card company or a credit bureau to confirm the customer's credit limit,

Small firms offering credit card sales find it profitable to tell customers the specific cards they honour by listing them either on the front door or at the cash register. *Photo courtesy of Dan Kewley.*

processes a multiple-copy bill called a *charge notice*. The customer signs the notice and keeps one copy. The merchant files the other copies and returns the credit card to the customer.

At the end of the month, the credit card company sends the cardholder a statement of the total charges and the minimum payment required on the total. A due date for the payment, in full or in part, is indicated on the statement. There is usually a grace period, typically twenty-one to thirty days, before interest is applied. If the cardholder decides to make the minimum payment only, he or she is charged interest on the unpaid balance. (In 1990 the annual rate of interest charged on such outstanding balances was about 22 per cent.)

Credit card companies prefer customers who do not pay in full each month – but who do pay in full, with interest, some time in the future.

How Credit Cards Operate for the Merchant

When sales are made on credit cards, the business is assured of full collection of those sales, less the credit card company charge, each month. The owner merely tallies the total credit card sales slips and takes them to the credit card company. The settlement date is usually the fifth of each month. With some credit cards, sales slips may be deposited in a commercial bank in the same manner as currency or cheques. Credit card charges to large and small business firms vary from 1 to 6 per cent. The rates are lower now than when credit cards were first introduced.

The charge to the specific firm varies with two basic factors: (1) The total volume of credit card sales, and (2) the average dollar sale. Thus, an airline that discounts $2 million per week with a credit card company and has an average sale of $100 may receive a charge of 1 per cent. The average charge for small volume of credit sales and a much lower average sale is 5 to 6 per cent. For an additional 1 per cent discount, merchants may cash in their slips sooner. Most small firm owners do not know that the rate they are charged is negotiable. Competition between credit card companies is keen, and small firm owners should always take advantage of this fact in requesting a lower rate from their credit card companies.

Are Credit Card Companies' Charges Too High?

Credit card companies are not philanthropic organizations. We would not wish them to be. They render positive services to business firms, small and large, and are organized to make a profit. They have large administrative costs. One credit card company executive reports that the average cost of each computerized entry is 28 cents.

The companies suffer losses from misuse of stolen cards and when accounts for which they have advanced funds to the individual merchants are not paid. Credit card companies "buy" accounts without recourse to the merchant. This means that unpaid accounts are losses to the credit card company. They cannot collect losses from the merchants to whom they advanced the money.

The companies' only source of income are the discounts charged to merchants when accounts are bought and the interest charged to cardholders who do not pay in full each month. In addition, the major general credit card companies face stiff competition. Their reported profits have not been out of line with the services rendered, and many companies report that any profits were long in coming.

Should Small Firms Encourage Credit Card Credit?

The predominant answer to this question that we have gathered from successful small business owners is *yes*. There may be communities where customers still demand open account credit. In such circumstances the individual small firm must satisfy the customers and meet the competition. However, the general trend throughout the country is obviously toward wider and wider consumer use of credit cards. Manufacturers and wholesalers who supply small firms must abide by the prevailing trade credit terms. As we have noted, little if any business between firms is done on a credit card basis.

The small retailing firm that is adequately financed to carry its own open accounts receivable must measure its costs of open account credit against the cost of credit card credit. Experienced firms can do this most effectively. If the total costs of bookkeeping, printing, postage, interest, collection costs, and bad debts are less than the discount paid to the credit card company, it pays to have open accounts available. If the individual firm is inadequately financed to carry its own receivables, if the owner does not want the bother of the bookkeeping and other aspects of administering a credit program, and if no community demand exists for open account credit, a program of credit card credit seems preferable. The cost differences between the two plans of credit are often slight. Many small firms still offer both open account and credit card credit, but the trend is definitely toward more credit card selling.

LAWS GOVERNING CONSUMER CREDIT PRACTICES

The great current interest in consumerism in our country has been accompanied by new legislations designed to protect consumers. Chief among these are:

- provincial Consumer Protection Acts
- provincial Credit Reporting Acts
- amendments to the federal *Bills of Exchange Act*

It is most important for all business firms that extend credit on their own books to become familiar with these Acts and related regulations. Space prohibits even a condensed summary here; we can only note the main provisions.

All disclosure Acts in Canada now require disclosure of both the dollar costs and the effective annual rate of interest to enable credit consumers to discover the terms of their borrowing before actually purchasing a good on credit. If the full cost of credit is not disclosed, the borrower is only required to pay the amount disclosed. Nondisclosure is also a criminal offence, punishable in Ontario, for example, by imprisonment for up to one year, a $2,000 fine, or both.

In recent years, legislation has been passed in several provinces to control the activities of credit reporting agencies: a *Personal Investigations Act* was passed in Manitoba in 1971; a *Credit Reporting Agencies Act* was passed by Saskatchewan in 1972; the *Ontario Consumer Reporting Act* was passed in 1973; and similar Acts were passed by Nova Scotia and British Columbia in 1973. The main purpose of these Acts is to ensure the consumer's right to expect responsible conduct from businesses engaged in gathering, storing, assembling, or using credit and personal information; the right to know what is being reported and to whom it is reported; and the right to correct false information. Figure 27-4 shows the Code of Operating Standards prepared by the Credit Bureau of Greater Toronto.

ASSOCIATED CREDIT BUREAUS OF CANADA
CODE OF OPERATING STANDARDS

The Associated Credit Bureaus of Canada are dedicated to protecting the individual's right to information security. Our **Code of Operating Standards** clearly states the business principles under which we operate to protect consumers' right to personal privacy.

The purpose of the Credit Bureau is to gather and maintain the credit histories of consumers. The availability to credit granters of such information is essential in ensuring that consumers receive quick service when applying for credit.

1. **TO COMPILE FINANCIAL INFORMATION:**
   We pledge to record information related only to an individual's financial history, compiled only from the consumers' credit applications, credit account histories and information already in public records. We do not record data on race, religion, health, political affiliation and personal habits.

2. **TO GIVE INFORMATION ONLY TO AUTHORIZED INQUIRERS:**
   We ensure that credit information will be provided only to Bureau members, after proper identification, and meeting certain criteria, the most important of which is a clear need to know. The consumer has the right to inquire about his/her own credit history.

3. **TO GIVE INDIVIDUALS THE RIGHT TO REVIEW THEIR OWN FILES:**
   We recognize the consumer's right to review his/her own file. After proper identification has been verified, the file may be reviewed, and if amended, appropriate Bureau members are notified.

4. **TO KEEP ACCURATE INFORMATION ON FILE:**
   We are committed to recording accurately the information provided by individuals on their credit applications.

5. **TO OPERATE EFFICIENTLY AND QUICKLY:**
   We utilize high-speed, sophisticated technology whenever possible to transmit responses to credit granters so they can make timely credit decisions, ensuring fast, accurate and convenient service to consumers.

6. **TO MAINTAIN TIMELY INFORMATION:**
   We are committed to deleting outdated information from a consumer's file, in accordance with the relevant Provincial Act.

7. **TO UPHOLD THE LAWS OF THE LAND:**
   We not only operate within the letter of provincial regulations (which vary by province), but with due regard to the spirit and intent of laws designed to ensure consumers' right to protection of their information privacy.

Members of the Associated Credit Bureaus of Canada are committed to this Code of Operating Standards in their continuing efforts to provide convenient, accurate and excellent service on behalf of all consumers.

F I G U R E   2 7 - 4 •   Code of Operating Standards.

Credit Bureaus of Greater Toronto.

In order to give greater protection to the consumer, the federal *Bills of Exchange Act* was amended in 1970 to require that a promissory note signed in connection with a sales agreement, such as a conditional sales contract, must be marked "consumer purchase." This has the legal effect that the creditor cannot sue the consumer on the basis of the promissory note if the seller has not met his or her obligations under the sales contract, for example, has sold defective goods.

Another federal legislation to be noted is the *Small Loans Act*, enacted in 1939, which provides for uniform, all-inclusive credit charge ceilings for all loans of $1,500 or less.

All of this legislation has contributed to the increasing use of credit cards by customers and the increasing encouragement of credit card sales by small business firms. Only large firms and credit card companies can normally stand the expense of staff experts to administer credit programs and to make sure the firm complies with the abundant rules and regulations. Key details and forms may be obtained through trade associations or bankers or other friends of small firms.

Credit card sales now give the customer more protection than ever. As one credit card company executive reports, "The consumer who doesn't use credit cards today is short-changing himself." It seems a fair prediction for the decade of the 1990s that more and more credit programs will be under the jurisdiction of credit card companies, which have the expertise to make their programs comply with the abundant legislation that now governs credit granting. The same expertise may also help to protect people from using excessive and unwarranted credit.

It May Still Be Worthwhile for Customers to Pay Cash

Another feature of the current wave of consumer legislation makes it legal under the *Competition Act* to give a discount of up to 5 per cent to retail customers who pay cash. This law was deemed necessary to avoid charges of price discrimination.

SUMMARY

The business world operates on credit. From the providers of raw materials to manufacturers, distributors, transportation companies, or retailers, business operations necessitate credit. Consumer credit to buyers of all products is a vital part of the entire credit system in this country.

Trade credit is that offered by one business firm to another. Consumer credit is that offered by retailers to buyers of consumer goods. Without credit, most families would be unable to purchase their homes, their cars, their major appliances, and many other items.

Granting of credit must always be based upon the applicant's ability to repay debts incurred within a specified schedule. For the small firm, this necessitates careful granting of credit in the first place and careful administration of a credit program once it is established. The costs of a credit program are significant. They include bookkeeping costs, postage, supplies, interest on investment in receivables, costs of collection, and eventually bad debts expense for those accounts that are never collected. Some loss on bad debts should be anticipated whenever a general program of credit is undertaken.

Small firms usually have a choice of carrying their own receivables on open accounts or restricting their credit sales to credit cards. More and more small firms are finding it desirable to accept credit cards, even though the average charge is still about 5 per cent of all credit card sales discounted with the credit card companies. It is a genuine service to small firms to be able to collect their credit sales in full by the fifth of the following month, less the credit card company charge, and avoid the expenses and losses of their own program. New credit legislation suggests that businesses of the future will have more credit based on credit cards and administered by experts in the field.

QUESTIONS FOR CLASS DISCUSSION

1   Do you agree that if a customer desires credit from your store he or she should be able to get an established credit card? How should this fact govern credit policies for small retailers?

2   What is meant by the phrase *the number of days credit sales in receivables*?

3   Would you sell on credit and carry the accounts on your own books if you owned a dress shop? Why?

4   What are the advantages to small firm owners of selling on customers' credit cards? The disadvantages?

5   What is an "aging of accounts receivable?" How often would you recommend that one be made for small firms?

6   What is the difference between trade credit and consumer credit?

7   How would you explain the statement, "The world operates on credit?"

8   Do you believe the statement that "a firm will sell more merchandise, even to its present customers, if credit accounts are made available?" How do you explain this?

9   How does a revolving account work?

10   Is an installment account different from a revolving account? How?

11   When would you recommend use of a budget account?

12   How is the credit reputation of an applicant checked?

13   Do you agree that you do not do a person a favour by granting credit that he or she cannot likely afford? Explain.

14   What kind of a policy would you establish to handle delinquent accounts?

Projects for Home Assignment and/or Class Discussion

1   Explain how you would handle the matter of granting credit to customers in your retail business. Would you carry your own accounts, insist on credit cards, have no credit at all, or a combination of all methods?

2   Do you agree that the expenses of operating an accounts receivable ledger could exceed the 5 per cent charge of a credit card company? If so, explain how this could happen.

REFERENCES FOR FURTHER READING

Cunningham, G., *Buy Yourself A Job & Be Your Own Boss*, McGraw-Hill Ryerson Ltd., 1990, Chapter 10.

Paulsen, T.R., *Collection Techniques for the Small Business*, 2nd ed., International Self-Counsel Press, North Vancouver, B.C., 1983

"Credit Management and Collection," *Your Business Matters*, The Royal Bank of Canada, 1978.

"Financial Analysis for Credit Managers," Canadian Institute of Credit & Financial Management, Toronto, 1987.

"Insurance Guide for Credit Managers," Canadian Institute of Credit & Financial Management, Toronto, 1989.

Minding Your Own Business, Federal Business Development Bank. Montreal, 1982, Vol. 1. Chapter 10

"Significant Aspects of Credit Management," Canadian Institute of Credit & Financial Management, Toronto, 1987.

"Types of Security Available to Credit Managers," Canadian Institute of Credit & Financial Management, Toronto, 1987.

28

Risks and How to Deal with Them

LEARNING OBJECTIVES

After reading this chapter, you will be able to:

1. **R**ecognize the types of risks faced by the small firm
2. **K**now what to do about business risks and what devices to use to cope with them
3. **U**nderstand the different types of insurance which can be used to protect against business risks
4. **K**now the elements that are involved in property and casualty insurance, including the concept of co-insurance
5. **U**nderstand the different types of health and welfare insurance available for the employees of the business
6. **K**now the different types of life insurance available and how each type can be used by small businesses

Every business firm operates daily with risks. The small firm is no exception. A risk can be defined as the chance of damage, injury, or loss. The total dollar costs incurred from risks may be much greater for large firms, but they are relatively more important for small firms. The small firm is characteristically less able to absorb losses from risks. These facts make it very important that every small firm understand the risks to which it is subject. Once these are known, a policy can be established on how best to handle the risks so as to keep losses to a minimum.

Risk is a vital part of everyday life. Each of us takes chances in driving to work, crossing the street, owning a house, traveling on public transportation, buying food, attending the movies, and eating in restaurants. Accidents happen in the best-regulated routines, and they may result in injury, damage, or loss to the person affected. Individuals, like businesses, take steps to protect themselves from many of these risks. People install burglar alarms and window guards in their homes as protection against risk of loss from robbery. Generally, they tend to guard themselves and their families by shifting the chance of loss to an insurance company. They purchase life insurance policies to protect their families in case of death; they buy title insurance on their homes to be sure that they are protected against any defects in the title that may be discovered later. Most automobile owners buy insurance to protect them in case of collision damage, bodily damage, and property damage to others. Almost any type of risk can be insured against, but the question is, how much can one pay in insurance premiums? If every possible risk in an individual's life were insured against, the cost of insurance would be prohibitive for most people.

The small business owner has all the previously mentioned risks and many more. For small firm owners, competence demands that they give serious attention to what risks they assume when they start operations. They face the same losses, damages, and injuries that are faced by individuals, and the losses, damages, or injuries to the business may be even more serious to the success of the business. Most common risks are generally recognized, but a serious investigation may reveal some that are not usually noted.

During the 1980s insurance premiums for businesses skyrocketed. For small businesses the cost of carrying appropriate protection often became prohibitive. During the 1986 White House Conference on Small Business, the delegates voted overwhelmingly that this is the most critical problem facing the small business community and demanded action and relief. Unfortunately, even at high cost, the owner must protect the business against the common risks.

RISKS FACED BY THE SMALL FIRM

1 Damage to Property The property of most small firms is represented by its inventory and its building if it is owned by the firm. The building and the inventory are constantly subject to the risks of damage and loss from fire, theft, floods, hurricanes, and riots. Cars and trucks owned by the firm are also open to loss through theft or damage.

Property damage to business firms in Canada is estimated to be as high as $450 million yearly, placing it at the top of the list of possible risks for most firms.

2 Liability to Employees   All employers are responsible for the health and safety of employees while they are performing their duties for the firm. Legislation giving employers such responsibility has been one of the greatest developments in social responsibility in recent years. The employer's liability is no longer left to individual court action but is assured by the requirement that workers' compensation insurance be carried by employers to provide this protection to employees.

3 Liability to the Public   This type of risk is often illustrated by the proverbial slip on a banana peel by the customer in the store. Store owners are liable for injuries received by persons on their premises. This liability applies to apartment houses, factories, and wholesale establishments, as well as to popular retail establishments. This risk includes not only physical injuries, but also damage to the property of others. It further covers liability for the defects in merchandise that the firm has sold. Readers may recall cases in which cosmetic firms have been sued for alleged harmful results from using cosmetic products of a particular firm; canned food companies were sued because people were made ill by spoiled contents; restaurants were sued for illness from eating on the premises; airlines and railroads and bus companies were sued for injuries incurred when traveling; or theatres were sued for injuries sustained in a theatre fire or accident. All these risks are examples of possible liability to the public.

4 Death of Key Employees   Valuable employees are a firm's best asset. Real losses could be sustained if they should die suddenly. Fortunately, this is a possible loss that can be insured today.

5 Excessive Loss from Bad Debts   We have noted in other chapters the importance of extending credit carefully and on the basis of a well-established procedure. Losses due to inability to collect accounts receivable can be severe. Protection against such losses can be expensive, as we shall see later in this chapter.

6 Faulty Title to Real Estate   Students may not recognize the importance of being sure that real estate purchased does, indeed, have a clear title that cannot be challenged at law. Typically, in Canada, the purchaser will rely on a solicitor's "certificate of good title." However, there are a few insurance companies providing real estate title insurance policies.

7 Shoplifting   This serious management problem seems to be growing in our society. It cannot be dismissed, because no firm seems free from the attendant losses. Legal action is expensive and difficult to administer. We will consider management ideas on the problem later in this chapter.

8 Loss Through Dishonest Employees   No business people like to admit that they have dishonest employees. Countless cases of employee theft are reported every year. This is another risk that must be recognized and coped with.

9 Financial Hardship   Financial hardship has probably caused more small firms to go out of business than any other single risk. It is especially sad to see a firm with otherwise excellent prospects suffer because illiquidity has been allowed to dominate its financial condition.

10 Marketing Risks   Marketing risks cover such things as having an inventory of merchandise suddenly fall in value because the market price has dropped. The risk of having a location lose its value is a marketing risk. In the sale of style merchandise, situations occur where the style has fallen out of favour and the remaining merchandise on the owner's shelves has lost most of its value. The small miller may have bought a large supply of wheat, for which he or she paid the market price two months ago. The finished product, flour, will bring a price that reflects the price of wheat when the flour is sold. All merchants face some of these types of marketing situations and should be cognizant of their existence. When all prices are rising, as in a period of inflation, the risk will not be present. In a period of declining prices, the risk becomes greater.

These risks are only ten of the more prominent types faced by many small firm owners. Individual cases may produce other risks which should be recognized.

WHAT TO DO ABOUT RISKS

When the existing risks are known, business owners may turn their attention to the matter of what to do about them. They will realize that some risks are easier to control than others. In all cases, good management will do some of the following:

1   Eliminate risks
2   Minimize risks
3   Shift risks
4   Absorb risks

The action taken will vary with the desired policy, services, and circumstances of the individual firm, and the business owner has several choices.

DEVICES AVAILABLE TO COPE WITH RISKS

1 Remove the Cause   If losses are being incurred from injuries to workers handling dangerous equipment, install safety guards on the machinery. Replace equipment that has proved it is defective. Faulty wiring should not be tolerated. Employ an outside delivery service if necessary to remove the risk associated with operating your own delivery equipment.

2 Create Self-Insurance   Under a self-insurance plan, a specified amount is set aside in a reserve fund each year to be available to cover any losses incurred. Rather than the owner paying premiums to an insurance company, the cash is held in this reserve fund. Unfortunately, this plan has been used with bad results by many one-store small firms. This self-insurance plan can be recommended only when the business has several geographically separated units. School systems and small chains of hamburger shops or grocery stores are ideal candidates for self-insurance. A small loss on one will usually be covered by the reserve fund. A significant loss for a one-store firm usually results in a net loss for the firm because the reserve fund has not yet become large enough to cover losses. Unless the reserve fund is well built up, the risk remains and protection is inadequate.

3 Purchase Outside Insurance An insurance policy shifts the risk to the insurance company. Insurance can be purchased from established insurance firms to cover many of the risks listed here. These are considered normal business risks. In addition, Lloyd's of London will insure any nonbusiness risks—for a price.

As we review the ten risks listed earlier and consider the case of a typical small firm retailer, it would appear that there is no alternative to buying insurance to protect the inventory and building against various possible losses such as fire, theft, floods, or hurricanes. Owners are required by law to carry workers' compensation insurance to cover their employees. They surely should carry public liability insurance to cover risk of liability to people on their premises. If key personnel are sufficiently valuable to the business, owners may buy life insurance on their lives, with the proceeds payable to the company.

For loss from excessive bad debts, only the loss in excess of what is normal for the particular line of business can be insured. Credit insurance is not available to cover what are considered normal losses. The cost of such insurance is very high, and it is not recommended for small businesses. Proper administration of a credit program, as outlined in Chapter 27, is preferable.

Fidelity bonds may be purchased to protect any firm from losses incurred by employee thefts. Only established losses are reimbursed, and to establish such losses is often difficult. In business practice these bonds have been used much more to cover cash losses than merchandise losses. Too many firms buy such protection only for those employees who operate cash registers or handle money in other operations. It is common knowledge today that the losses incurred by business firms from merchandise stolen by employees far exceed losses in the form of cash. This situation suggests that fidelity bonds should be used more widely to cover losses of both cash and merchandise.

Surety bonds, which will protect the firm against losses incurred as a result of the failure of others to perform on schedule, may be purchased. Failure of a contractor to complete an important addition to the store in time for the Christmas trade under the terms of a contract would be an example. In such a case, the insurance company would pay the firm for the established loss incurred.

Title insurance is available on all real estate purchases for a small sum, and it should always be requested.

Insurance is either not economically available or not usually recommended to cover the other risks on our list.

4 *Practise Hedging*   Any small firm that buys quantities of products quoted on well-established commodity exchanges should know about hedging and should practise it to protect normal profits. Hedging is often misunderstood as a device to make additional profits, but it is only to protect normal profits.

A few of the commodities regularly traded on the commodity exchanges are sugar, wheat, corn, citrus fruits, soybeans, soybean oil, cocoa, wool, oats, rye, silver, and copper. Whenever merchants buy large quantities of a product listed on the exchanges for use in manufacturing and sell it later as a part of their final product, they can protect themselves against losses in the price of the commodity by *hedging*. On the day they purchase the material, they also sell a futures contract on the exchange. The difference between the price paid for products delivered today (spot price) and the price in the futures market is roughly the cost of insuring and storing the same commodity for the period of time from today to the date of the future contract. When the merchants sell their manufactured products, they will neutralize any loss in the price of the raw material commodity by buying a future contract. The profit or loss on the commodity (spot) sales will be offset by the profit or loss on the purchase and sale of the futures contracts.

5 *Good Management*   Good planning and good management are probably the best protection against most of the other risks we have considered. Price fluctuations of any normal retail inventory may be upward or downward. Good management will keep itself informed of price trends. Study of population trends and business activity will warn merchants early if their location is losing its value. Good accounting records and study of operations against a budget will warn of any developing adverse trends. To handle the risks of shoplifting and dishonest employees, good management will provide devices for detecting shoplifters, such as internal security guards and signal systems. These are often expensive but necessary. Personnel policies will provide means of checking employees whose honesty is questioned. Inspection of employees at checkout time is being used by manufacturing firms. It is recommended for wholesalers and retailers when losses in this area are deemed a high risk. As we have seen, fidelity bonds may be purchased to protect the firm from losses by dishonest employees.

The risk of financial hardship can best be coped with by proper financial planning and financial management. This popular risk has caused the downfall of many firms that otherwise had a most profitable future. Good planning along the lines we have reviewed in this text, watching the key financial ratios in the financial statements, the cash adequacy rule, the investment in receivables, and having a cash flow statement are devices to protect against this risk. Having a good performance record for honesty and fair dealing will help the businessperson secure financial help when it is needed.

Chapter 29 is devoted to managing the daily operations of the firm. It will demonstrate how danger signals may appear that may affect the financial standing of the firm. Thus warned, the owner can quickly apply corrective action.

CO-INSURANCE FOR BUSINESS FIRMS

Small firm owners should know how co-insurance works. It is a subject often misunderstood. For example, a building owner who has a $40,000 building insured against fire loss of $20,000 would not collect in full for an $8,000 fire loss.

Insurance companies are not in business for charity, nor should they be. As business organizations, their function is to pool the risks of many and pay those who incur losses. There premiums must provide them with adequate income to cover these losses, their operating expenses, and a profit. They know from experience that fire damage to business buildings, for example, rarely results in complete loss of the building. To protect themselves and the client against having to pay insurance on the total cost of the building only partially destroyed, for example, they offer a co-insurance clause in their policies. Co-insurance means that owners of a building can literally share the potential loss with the insurance company if they are willing also to share the premium cost.

The risk of fire damage is so great that all small merchants should insure their firms against damages to property. *Courtesy of the City of Toronto Fire Department.*

Business buildings, like residential buildings, may be protected against losses in varying degrees under such co-insurance clauses. This means that potential losses may be shared by the owner and the company while major protection is still given to the owner.

For example, a building owner may wish to insure the building at 50 per cent of its market value. The savings in annual insurance premium costs may be considered as an offset to any potential losses incurred. This does not mean, however, that any losses incurred up to 50 per cent of the building value will be paid in full by the insurance company. Policyholders become subject to the co-insurance clause in their policies.

The most common percentage of market value of buildings used in co-insurance is 80 per cent. If the building is insured at 50 per cent of its value and 80 per cent is the co-insurance percentage, the owner will recover fifty-eightieths of losses incurred. If there is an $8,000 loss, $5,000 will be recovered. Co-insurance truly means a shared risk.

Let us review a more detailed illustration of how co-insurance works.

ABC Manufacturing Company has a small factory building valued at $40,000. It is insured under a co-insurance policy at 80 per cent of market value, or $32,000. This amount is the face value of the owner's policy ($32,000). The insurance company will be liable for the full amount of any losses up to $32,000. A complete loss on the building, or $40,000, would result in the owner's bearing an $8,000 loss and the insurance company's paying him or her $32,000.

The formula for computing insurance company liability in such cases is as follows:

$$\text{Insurance company liability} = \frac{\text{Face value of policy}}{80\% \text{ of property value}} \times \text{Amount of loss incurred}$$

As we apply this formula, we can see that if the ABC Company had insured its building for only $16,000 (less than 80 per cent of market value) and then incurred a $16,000 loss, it could collect only $8,000 ($^{16}/_{32}$, or ½, times $16,000). This is true even though the face value of the policy was $16,000.

If a building is insured for more than 80 per cent of its market value, the insurance company pays any losses in full up to that of the face value of the policy. Insurance never pays more than the face value of the policy.

OTHER FACTS ABOUT CASUALTY INSURANCE FOR SMALL BUSINESSES

The small firm owner should be aware of the following facts:

1   A regular (standard) fire insurance policy pays the policyholder only for losses that are directly due to fire. Other indirect losses,

known as consequential losses, may be even more important to the small firm's welfare. Some of these consequential losses are:

a Loss of use of the building

b Continuing expenses after a fire, such as salaries, rents paid, and interest obligations.

c Loss of rental income on buildings owned and rented out.

d Extra expenses of obtaining temporary quarters.

Most fire insurance policies have available a consequential loss clause to cover such losses. An extra premium is charged for such a clause, of course.

2   Fire losses caused by windstorms, tornadoes, or hurricanes are not covered by a standard fire policy. A windstorm policy is essential to have protection in such cases.

3   Flood insurance is designed to protect buildings and inventories against such risks as overflowing rivers and tidal waves. Water damage insurance, as distinct from flood insurance, covers such risks as roof leaks, bursting water tanks, and leaking pipes.

4   Marine insurance covers merchandise while it is in transit. There are two types:

a Ocean marine insurance, covering transportation of merchandise and products on water.

b Inland marine insurance, which covers both land and water transportation.

5   Automobile collision insurance is considered a must by prudent business people. Business cars and trucks, as well as personal cars, should be insured. This insurance can be purchased under both a full-coverage policy, which pays all losses from collision damage in full, or a deductible policy, which carries a lower premium but provides that the owner be responsible for the first $50 or $100 in damage from each accident.

6   Comprehensive policies are available to cover fire and theft losses on automobiles. They can protect the owner against many risks of damage or loss, including flood, windstorm, riot, glass breakage, robbery in the car, theft of the car, fire damage, or even hail damage. Collision damage is not included in these policies. Rates on policy premiums vary from region to region in accordance with the loss record for the particular area.

7   The *relative incidence of loss* means the likelihood of the risk's causing a loss to the firm. The relative chance of an automobile collision, for example, is greater for most people than the risk of losing a limb. Thus, collisions are said to have a higher incidence of risk. It follows that the higher the incidence of loss, the more important it is to have insurance protection.

8 An *insurable interest* means that the person buying insurance is subject to a loss if the property or person insured should be damaged or die. An insurable interest is a prerequisite to the purchase of any insurance policy. Key-person insurance, the right of a company to insure the life of particularly valuable employees, is a relatively recent large development in the business field. A business firm, large or small, has an insurable interest in the lives of its key employees when the business would suffer should those persons be removed by death. Under certain conditions, group insurance policies on the lives of employees may be charged as expenses to the firm.

BASIC FACTS ABOUT LIFE INSURANCE FOR BUSINESS AND FOR BUILDING PERSONAL ESTATES

We have seen the importance of having adequate protection against casualty risks in business management. Whenever the incidence of such risks as fire, theft, and other damage is high, most business owners shift the risks to insurance companies. But the matter of life insurance is of growing interest and value to small firms as well. Small firms, like large ones, can carry key-man (or woman) life insurance on the lives of valuable employees to protect them against the loss of such employees. The fact that a company can carry a group life insurance policy on all of its employees up to $50,000 each and charge the premiums as a business expense can be a major part of a personnel policy and help retain good employees.

Because life insurance can be used to serve business purposes or in the building of personal estates, it is important for all informed citizens to know the basic facts about different kinds of life insurance policies. But first we should be sure that we understand the basic terms used in connection with such policies. Some of these follow:

Terminology of Life Insurance

Face amount of the policy	The amount paid by the insurance company in the event of the death of the insured, for example, $1,000.
Premium	The amount paid annually to maintain the face of the policy in force, for example, $20 per year.
Beneficiary	The person designated to receive the face amount of the policy in the event of the death of the insured.
Insured	The person whose life is covered in the policy.

Cash value of policy (Cash surrender value)	The amount the insurance company will pay if the policy is cancelled.
Loan value of policy	The amount the insurance company will loan to the insured if he or she wishes to borrow against its cash value.
Paid-up policy	A policy on which no further premiums are required, or a new policy for less than the face value, given to an insured person who desires to cancel the original policy, to take a policy for less than the original face, and to pay no more premiums.

Types of Life Insurance Policies

There are four basic types of life insurance policies. Some special policies may include features of more than one of these types. If we understand the basic types, we can evaluate special policies which may be under consideration at any time. These four basic types, their characteristics, and their uses, plus a word of explanation of each, are as follows:

1 Term Life Insurance Policies   This is the least expensive type of life insurance (see Table 28-1). It can be written for short periods, such as one year, or for longer periods of years. It is seldom written for more than twenty years. It provides full payment of the face of the policy to the designated beneficiary if the insured dies during the life of the policy. Term insurance is unique in that no payment of face value is ever made if death occurs after the stated expiration date of the policy. This very feature, plus the inexpensive premiums, have made the policy extremely valuable in the business world. The premium rates fluctuate between smokers and nonsmokers.

Such term policies are increasingly used to provide collateral security for firm or personal obligations. Bank loans or mortgage debts on plant and equipment can have a provision that the borrower take out a term policy in his or her life payable to the creditor, which will assure full payment of the obligation in the event of death. It is often called *credit life insurance* when used in this manner. Only a small addition to regular payments on such obligations is needed in most cases to pay for the insurance. Creditors thus are not forced to interfere with the business firm's operations to collect the debt.

Financial advisors recommend to all young married couples with a mortgaged home or condomimum that they take out a term life policy on the life of the breadwinner of the family to assure that the mortgage will be paid in full in the event of the insured's death. The home is thus fully paid for and the remaining spouse is no longer faced with this debt. Many mortgage companies and other financial institutions are encouraging, if not requiring, such insurance protection for both the borrower and the lender. Family protection and estate building usually suggest that the amount of any life insurance carried should be proportionate to the current debts and present versus future earning powers of the family.

Term life insurance is unique in other ways. Historically it has no cash value, no loan value, and no paid-up policy is available. These features are also part of the price paid for the inexpensive premiums required.

TABLE 28-1

APPROXIMATE ANNUAL PREMIUM COSTS OF
LIFE INSURANCE AT AGE 22*

TYPE OF INSURANCE	*ANNUAL PREMIUM PER $1,000 FACE VALUE*
Term	$ 1.5–2
Straight life	12–13

* These rates assume no dividends are paid on the policies.

2 Straight Life Insurance Policies   This is the type of life insurance on which the great insurance industry was built. Premiums are based on actuarial figures of life expectancy, as in all insurance. When a policy is once taken out on the life of an individual, that person normally pays the annual premium until death. The face amount of the policy is then paid to the designated beneficiary. In recent years, many insurance companies have introduced provisions that no further premiums are to be paid after some ripe old age, such as ninety or ninety-nine, is reached, if the policy has been in effect a minimum number of years. The policies are considered paid up for the full face value at that time. Face value plus any accumulated dividends or interest are paid to the beneficiary at the death of the insured.

Most straight life policies may be cancelled after a minimum existence and the insured given a paid-up policy for a lesser face value than the original policy. The insured may also borrow against active policies up to the amount of the cash value or cancel the policy if desired and receive the cash value. Straight life insurance is more expensive than term insurance but less expensive than other types.

LOAN VALUE OF LIFE INSURANCE POLICIES AS A SOURCE OF TEMPORARY WORKING CAPITAL

When any life insurance policies, except term, have been in force a few years, they build up a loan value, as we have noted. This loan value may be used to assist business owners in times of cash shortages or special needs. The interest rate charged on such loans against life policies is not as high as that charged by most financial institutions. Such loan values can be counted on to be available without risking a refusal on a loan application elsewhere. If death occurs, the full face value of life insurance policies remains in effect during the period of such loans, although the amount of the loans and accrued interest would be subtracted from the proceeds paid to beneficiaries.

From this brief review of the fundamentals of casualty and life insurance it should be clear to students and the experienced small firm owner that *every business needs a good insurance agent*. Competent business owners today *buy* insurance to fit their needs and do not have to be *sold* insurance protection. They analyze the relative incidence of each risk to which they are subject and plan their casualty insurance accordingly. They then decide how they can use life insurance for business purposes or personal estate building and choose appropriate policies. A thoroughly competent and conscientious insurance agent who specializes in the problems of small firms can be an invaluable asset to any small firm owner.

QUESTIONS FOR CLASS DISCUSSION

1   What is meant by saying that we all live with risks every day of our lives? What are some of these risks?

2   What risks are incurred by ownership of a building?

3   If you rent a building for your store, should you still insure the inventory of merchandise? Why?

4   What is workers' compensation insurance? How does it work?

5   What kinds of risks does the owner of a department store incur as far as the general public is concerned?

6   How do risks of a restaurant vary from those of a department store?

7   What is title insurance? Do you think it is important?

8   How would you cope with the risk that your location may lose its value?

9   What is the best way to protect a business against the risk of financial hardship?

10   What do we mean by "shifting the risk" as a means of coping with possible loss?

11   When is self-insurance a practical idea?

12   Have you considered a term life insurance policy on your life with your parents as beneficiaries? Why?

13   Should you protect against all risks by buying insurance?

14   If your answer to Question 13 is no, give an example of risks you would not insure against. How would you handle them?

Projects for Home Assignment and/or Class Discussion

1 If you were the owner of a business that was subject to all of the risks listed in this chapter, which ones would you try to eliminate, which ones would you be willing to absorb, and which ones would you transfer to an insurance company? Prepare a written report explaining your answers for each.

2 Write a short report explaining to some business friends how much fire insurance they should carry to be protected on all fire losses up to 80 per cent of the value of their $150,000 building.

3 Explain the difference between cash value, loan value, and a paid-up policy as these terms relate to life insurance.

REFERENCES FOR FURTHER READING

Tate Jr., C.E., L.C. Megginson, C.R. Scott Jr., and L.R. Trueblood, *Successful Small Business Management*, 3rd ed., Business Publications, Inc., Plano, Texas, 1982, Chapter 23.

29

Day-to-Day Management of the Ongoing Business Firm

LEARNING OBJECTIVES

After reading this chapter, you will be able to:

1. **U**nderstand the scope of day-to-day management of the small business and the need for continual decisions by the manager
2. **K**now the importance of experience in the process of judgement and decision making
3. **U**nderstand the wide responsibilities of the small business owner as contrasted to most executives of large firms
4. **K**now that time demands upon the small business manager or entrepreneur often conflict with achieving management control
5. **K**now the essential data for effective ongoing control in terms of those items that need to be reviewed in short-term intervals and those items that can be reviewed less frequently

Day-to-day management of any successful business demands that the owners have available data of all types that become the basis for making current decisions. The gathering of those data can be a time-consuming and expensive process, yet its importance cannot be exaggerated. Fortunately, today's developments in small computers and other electronic data processing techniques have made that data-gathering process available to and economical for many small firms that never suspected they could afford such "luxuries." In fact, true cost reductions are available in most cases of successful firms with a growth record.

There are a number of ways to gather information necessary to run a business. Chapter 20 dealt with the various electronic data processing services that are available to speed the gathering of those data. This chapter deals with the various types of information that entrepreneurs need in daily management.

It is appropriate in this final chapter that we take a look at the small firm owner's activities as daily decisions are made governing the total operations of the business. The dynamics of the business world call for decisions almost every day. Problems arise, priorities change, policies are questioned, market developments arise, and countless other things call for the exercise of judgement in arriving at sound management decisions. The "management of change" is often a daily process.

Experience is a great developer of wisdom. Experienced owners carry many facts in their heads, facts that help them make decisions on new developments as well as facts governing daily operations. Owners with less experience should seek to learn key facts relative to the firm and the industry or to the total business scene in which operations exist. Better judgement will result.

If each step in a good planning procedure has been thoroughly completed, much time and effort has been expended. After the firm has begun operations, the owner cannot rely on automatic fulfilling of the firm's objectives. Management must keep itself aware of key items that affect or may affect the firm's best welfare. The basic management function of control demands regular analysis of operational results and facts for all phases of the total activities of the firm, as well as analysis of outside factors that may have an influence on operations.

The individual small firm owner must normally assume a wider responsibility in giving the firm this management control than does the head of a particular division of a very large firm. In fact, this difference in total responsibility has caused many learned business authorities to say that more ability is needed to manage a substantial small firm than to be a specialized vice president of a very large firm. For example, the vice president for finance of a large automobile manufacturing firm is charged only with keeping advised on matters of finance. These would include cash flow, current cash position, advice on security markets, capital structures of the firm, financial ratios, dividend capability and policy, anticipated cash demands, and so on. The vice president for marketing is charged with decisions and recommendations only in the area of marketing and distribution activities of the firm. The vice president for manufacturing handles problems of production and production schedules. Each of these senior executives carries heavy responsibilities, but each is concerned with only one general area of the total firm activities.

These duties and many more must all be the responsibility of the small firm owner. Every phase of the business is the owner's responsibility. He or she must be concerned with matters of daily sales, personnel, inventory control, supply sources, credit policies, new products, policy changes, market studies, public relations, advertising, location and site reviews, balance sheet data, income statement relationships, economic trends, all of the financial details, and many other issues. The owner's duties call for the management of change as well as the effective control of established procedures.

It is a long-established truism in management that early detection of adverse developments provides speedier correction thereof and thus a minimum loss of efficiency. With so many areas to control, it is obvious that the demands upon the small firm owner are most significant and time-consuming. Yet effective managerial control is most essential.

TIME DEMANDS VERSUS ACHIEVING MANAGEMENT CONTROL

The time demands upon the owner in conducting normal operations may be so great that time for gathering data and analyzing key controls may necessarily become overtime hours. We have all seen many small firms where the presence of the owner is a key part of having the firm open for business. Fine restaurants often build their image around a well-known proprietor. Customers come to see the owner, to be greeted by the owner, and perhaps to have a visit with the owner at their table. If the owner is not available, the customers lose a good deal of the image they have of the firm and lose part of their desire to patronize the restaurant.

If this owner is also one who wants to be at the produce market at five in the morning to pick out the freshest vegetables and fruits for the kitchen, even more time is consumed in normal operations. All these demands mean that analysis time to study controls of the firm is further limited. Analysis must be performed when the business is not open to customers, probably very late in the evening.

Small firm owners have another problem in that most small firms cannot afford to hire personnel purely to study operational results. As firms grow larger, more delegation of authority becomes essential. If department heads have been appointed or a full-time bookkeeper employed, these people can be most helpful in getting information to the owner to assist in control analyses. The drugstore organization chart studied in Chapter 28 shows that the owner-manager could call upon three department managers and an accountant to supply much data on current operations. Many small drugstores do not have this degree of organization because the volume of business is too small to allow it. In such cases, the entire responsibility for accumulating data for analysis falls upon the owner.

ESSENTIAL DATA FOR EFFECTIVE ONGOING CONTROL

Interviews with many successful small firm owners reveal that they usually divide their management information into two categories:

- Data that they analyze daily, weekly, or monthly
- Long-range data that they check less often or whenever the occasion presents itself

In the first category they include:

1 Sales data and trends
2 Production records
3 Cash position and cash-flow outlook
4 Inventory data and need for adjustments
5 Analysis of the accounts receivable ledger
6 Policy violations and need for change
7 Price policy questions that may have arisen
8 Effectiveness of shoplifting and theft-prevention procedures
9 Suggested new products or new lines
10 Weekly results compared with weekly break-even chart
11 Public-relations effectiveness

In the second category they include:

1 Adequacy of accounting data
2 Personnel policies
3 Outlook for expanding or contracting operations. (These aspects of planning and forecasting are a continuing concern at all times.)
4 Effective measures in adjusting to seasonal variations
5 Review of lease arrangements
6 Review of location and site values
7 Possible changes in legal form of organization
8 Additional asset needs that might improve efficiency
9 Adequacy of risk coverage
10 Efficiency in purchasing and possible new sources of supply
11 Study of broader economic data and local developments that might affect expectations for the firm

The priorities given to the various items on any owner's list will vary with the other demands upon his or her time and the circumstances surrounding the particular firm. For example, a small private water company would have less need for checking income records so often. A restaurant would need this data almost daily. A small department store would need regular data, at least weekly, on a new department just opened. Owners would be more concerned with inventory movement and inventory control in style goods departments.

Use of Data

It is one thing to gather the management data to which we have referred in the preceding paragraphs; it is quite another to use that data in making day-to-day decisions for the firm. It took considerable time for the authors to recover from the shock of hearing a small firm proprietor say, "Why collect all of those facts? They are history and you can't change them now." Many college students and experienced operators realize that business history is studied to make improvements in efficiency for the future. We can take a brief look here at each of the items on our data lists to indicate when a management decision might be appropriate.

Data Analyzed Daily, Weekly, or Monthly

Sales Data and Trends   If sales are increasing steadily and are in accordance with budgeted income statement plans, they can be looked upon with pleasure. If they are increasing faster than had been expected, the fact may call for a look at the adequacy of inventory to support the increased sales volume. If sales are dropping below expectations, the owner should find out why, in what departments, in what lines, or if the decline is general. Decisions to be made would deal with how to reverse the trend. Would more advertising help? Has advertising been effective? Have we measured that effectiveness? Is the market changing so that total purchasing power in our market will remain lower? When did this trend start? Are there any other reasons for it?

Production Records   If the factory was expected to produce 5000 units of the product in September and only 4000 were finished, management should ask why. When the reasons are found, decisions must be made to correct the problems. This may involve new machines, inefficient employees, faulty maintenance, absenteeism, labour turnover, poor training methods, or other things. Management must find the reasons and make decisions to prevent repetition. Perhaps it was only a matter of poor timing of employee vacations.

Cash Position and Cash-Flow Outlook   Management's concern here is with providing assurance that obligations of the firm can be paid on time—within the discount period if discounts are offered. We have seen the trouble that can result when the cash position is inadequate. Very few small firms have complete cash-flow statements (Chapter 24), but experienced small firm owners have a pretty good idea of what cash receipts to expect in the immediate future. If the cash position is really hurting, the reasons for it must be found. Perhaps it is slow collection of receivables. Is a campaign to collect delinquent accounts appropriate? It may be that enlarged inventories were purchased to take advantage of special buys. If so, should we arrange an additional line of credit to carry the firm until that invenotry is sold and funds replenished?

Inventory Data and Need for Adjustments   Where departmentalization of a firm is established, inventories must be checked by departments and/or particular lines of merchandise. If sales are up, is the inventory adequate to support sales in each department and in each line? If sales are down, is the decline general or confined to specific departments? It is dangerous to order general inventory reductions if the sales variations are limited to certain departments. When sales are off for a particular department, the inventory of that department may have to be reduced. When requests for items not carried in the inventory have been received a few times, a decision to add such items to the inventory may be appropriate.

Analysis of Accounts Receivable Ledger   Even if the firm does not have a cash position problem, it should still make a regular analysis of its total accounts receivable. This will reveal which customers are getting behind in their payments and suggest caution in further credit to some customers. An aging of accounts receivable (Chapter 27) is a regularly used current management device. Decisions that may result from its analysis may include a new campaign to collect delinquent accounts, cutting off credit for certain customers, a policy of expanding credit more widely if the account receivable turnover is more than twelve times a year on thirty-day credit, terminating open accounts, and resorting only to cash and credit card sales. Without the facts, necessary corrective action cannot be taken.

Policy Violations and Need for Change   If it is found that there is public objection to some of the policies of the firm, a management decision to change certain policies may be called for. For example, a grocer has a policy of selling all soft drinks only in nonreturnable bottles. Public resentment is great, and some customers actually change their patronage to other stores for this single reason. Decision: Bring back returnable bottles to the shelves and change the policy decision against their use. Advertise the new policy change. (In Ontario it is the law now to stock returnable bottles if nonreturnables are sold in the store.)

Price Policy Questions That May Have Arisen   It may be found that customers are being driven away because the firm is selling one or two specific items a few cents higher than a competitor down the street. Should those prices be lowered? Is that type of customer valued? Is the item purchased in isolation or as part of larger orders? A decision is important. Another possible decision could be on the desirability of cleaning out that slow-moving inventory of certain items via obstacle-course displays, at special prices, or even as loss leaders.

Effectiveness of Shoplifting and Theft-Prevention Procedures   This problem never ends, and the alert merchant is always looking for evidence of the effectiveness of present procedures to combat both shoplifting by outsiders and employee thefts. Whenever an incident of this nature is discovered, a new look at established procedures is appropriate to see if greater effectiveness can be achieved.

Suggested New Products or New Lines   Most merchants keep a record of calls for merchandise they do not carry. Not all such calls merit adding the item involved. But if such requests are repeated, a decision is appropriate on the advisability of adding those goods to the inventory. If the firm sells dresses in two price lines or in two brands and receives numbers of requests for another price line or another brand which is available, this may suggest that the inventory should be expanded to include them. This could again be a recognition that an original policy was not suited to the particular market and that the facts suggest it be changed.

Coincidence of Weekly Results with the Break-Even Chart   If an accurate break-even chart has been divided into weekly, monthly, and quarterly periods as well as the annual measure of income-expense relationships, the manager-owner will always have in mind a sales total which will reveal whether sales for any period have placed the operation in the profit area. Many small firm owners have such a figure in mind even without formal break-even charts. This is why they can tell you, "This was a good week," or a good month, or even a good day.

Public Relations Effectiveness   Measures of good or bad public relations may appear at any time during any business day, or even at a social gathering. Compliments may be received over participation in a community project, a special service rendered, support of a good cause, or innumerable other things. Likewise, complaints may be received. A manager notes both compliments and complaints to measure total effectiveness and govern future decisions on public-relations activities.

We have taken this brief look at some of the key data managers must have at their fingertips to help in the many decisions they are regularly called upon to make. These were the items in the first category as we described priorities here. Not all owners will agree with this division of priorities, but none will disagree with the importance of each item on the list. Any owner having all this key information readily available will make better decisions for the welfare of the firm.

Data to be Checked Occasionally

Adequacy of Accounting Data   If an owner is often faced with a decision requiring accounting data that are not readily available, the decision to add financial analysis to the present accounting records will usually be forthcoming. A decision to request a bank loan that demands supporting data on cash flow would be an example. Total accounting value is more than routinely recording operations and preparing the basic statements at the end of a fiscal period. Daily decisions on matters such as ability to make an attractive purchase may be dependent on basic accounting facts. Expansion plans cannot be properly judged without detailed accounting data. Daily decisions are enhanced with analytical accounting information. There is no uniformity of accounting adequacy for all firms. Each owner must decide the extent to which he or she needs details to govern daily operations.

Personnel Policies   Excessive absenteeism and labour turnover are usually signs that something is wrong with the personnel policies of the firm. If unskilled labour requiring little training is being utilized, labour turnover is not as serious as absenteeism, as long as replacements are always available. The public image of the firm, however, is adversely affected by either excessive absenteeism or labour turnover. When these are facts of the firm, a serious look at policies in effect is called for. Excessive absenteeism needs investigation concerning its reasons, its legitimacy, and its incidence for particular employees. Small firms are usually less able than larger firms to absorb absenteeism because of greater dependence upon fewer employees. Ability for one employee to fill in for an absent employee is usually severely limited in the small firm. For example, if two salespersons are handling the retail counter, one person would find it extremely difficult to serve all the customers. It is true that good organization should always anticipate replacements in any position, but opportunities to do so successfully are fewer in a small firm. After reviewing the facts, it may be decided that certain persons must be terminated, salaries may justify review to cope with the problem, personal conflicts between employees may be uncovered, or other corrective measures may be necessary. The important thing is that the manager know the facts and speedily apply corrective action.

Outlook for Expansion or Contraction of Operations   Not all small firm owners want to expand, even if the possibilities of profitably doing so exist. Many are staisfied just to keep the business at its present level. The optimists and true entrepreneurs (venture managers) are always looking for profitable ways to expand the firm to become an ever-enlarging part of the total scene in their industry. Basic planning and forecasting are continuous activities. Contracting operations is sometimes dictated by the facts of recent firm history. Market changes and market opportunities represent the kinds of facts needed to make the proper decisions in this area. That is why the efficient manager wants to keep informed on total markets, competition, available locations, detailed costs, and financing possibilities to support any necessary decisions. These are truly long-range considerations, yet they can be of utmost importance to the eventual welfare of the firm.

Adjusting to Seasonal Variations   It is most important to have a clear picture of just how important seasonal variations have been in the firm's recent history. Management decisions must then be made concerning the in-evitability of these variations and whether they can be evened out through special sales, production policies, or other devices. Changes in buying policies, employee vacation schedules, part-time employment, and even inventory control may be dictated. Nothing can be done authoritatively without detailed facts upon which to base those decisions.

Review of Lease Arrangements   Most retailers and many manufacturers lease their business facilities. As a result, the continuation of the business at a particular location is dependent upon renewal of the rental lease. It is very sad to see a successful small firm forced to move only because of its inability to renew its lease at prices the firm can stand. Options for renewal may be written into an existing lease. Percentage leases (a flat rental charge plus a percentage of sales over a stated amount) provide additional rental income for landlords if business sales exceed normally expected totals. Effective management always has one eye on this matter, looks for options, and tries to ensure continued favourable locations for the firm's operations.

Review of Location and Site Values   Just as the lease terms are important, so is a review of the value of an existing location and site. Those firms that rent their facilities have the advantage of not being forced to remain in an unfavourable location if the location is losing its true value. When the current lease expires, the owners may not want to renew it because they have found a more favourable location at the right price.

Possible Change in Legal Form of the Firm   With all the new legislation by the federal government designed to assist small firms, it is important that the owner know of those opportunities. We covered the details in Chapter 8.

Additional Asset Needs   Experience in operations may often suggest that a new piece of equipment, a new showcase, a different type of cash register, or other assets would materially improve the efficiency of the firm. Daily observation of procedures will clarify such needs and indicate which acquisitions are necessary.

Adequacy of Risk Coverage   The eternal problem of risks and how best to cope with them must be continually under review. New types of insurance protection appear often. The manager may see that the incidence of loss from certain types of risk has increased and now demands insurance coverage, whereas in the past the firm had relied upon good management to absorb that risk. The limits of public liability insurance that the firm carries may be found to be inadequate, and a decision to increase such coverage may be in order. New features are often written into some insurance policies, such as those which cover inventory losses. Costs and protection may be affected. Fidelity and surety bonds may become appropriate, even though they had previously been deemed completely unnecessary. Minimum losses in some areas of risk may suggest that they be coped with only by good management in the future. The facts of current operations will supply details to justify any appropriate decisions.

Efficiency in Purchasing and Need for New Sources   Study of results may reveal lapsed discounts, availability of new sources at better prices and improved quality, better transportation arrangements, or better terms of sale. These matters must also be carefully noted by managers as they make decisions for the ongoing firm.

Economic Data and Local Developments   All the information available about general business trends nationally, regionally, and locally should be a concern of management. Trade associations, chambers of commerce, daily newspapers, and business periodicals are all sources of such information. A manager's ability to make decisions on the basis of such data may have a great effect on the firm's welfare. Changing styles, lessened purchasing power in the area, new plant developments and new payrolls, trends in population growth, and changes in buying habits are some of the items falling in this category. It behooves efficient managers to keep themselves apprised of as much information as possible on these matters.

SUMMARY

We have approached the subject of managing the ongoing firm from the standpoint of the key data which must be readily available to the manager and how the manager should use that information. It is hoped that this approach has given the student an appreciation of the many duties that fall upon managers' shoulders and how they prepare themselves to make the proper decisions. With all the planning and operating details we have covered in this text, we feel sure that new small firm owners who have studied with us will be better qualified as successful managers. Good luck.

REFERENCES FOR FURTHER READING

Archer, M., *An Introduction to Canadian Business*, 4th ed., McGraw-Hill Ryerson Ltd., Toronto, 1982, Chapter 13.

Kao, R.W.Y., *Small Business Management: A Strategic Emphasis*, 2nd ed., Holt Rinehart and Winston of Canada Ltd., Toronto, 1984, Chapter 2.

CASE STUDIES

Customer Relations

Mrs. Royer's husband operated a small independent bakery in their home town of 50 000 people. Mrs. Royer often worked with him during the rush hours. The bakery had been very successful in competing with the larger bakeries. His breads, cakes, and pastries were popular with everyone who tried them, and the bakery had consistently made a good profit for many years.

As small firm owners, the Royers encouraged all their friends to patronize small firms. They made their own purchases at small firms whenever possible. They truly believed that a prosperous small business community was in the best interests of the people.

One of their friends was the proprietor of a small independent paint store located two blocks from the bakery. They had made intermittent purchases of paints, brushes, wallpaper, and allied products there for many years. Service was usually very good. But one day Mrs. Royer stopped by to purchase an additional litre of red cement paint. They had used four litres to paint a back porch landing but needed just a bit more to finish one corner.

The first time she stopped at the store she found it was closed at 2:00 p.m., contrary to the business hours posted in the front window. The second time she came by she was stopped at the door with an explanation that a robbery had just occurred in the store and the police were inside investigating. The third time she returned she asked for a litre can of the same paint. She was advised by a new clerk that they carried this particular paint only in 4-L sizes and, therefore, she couldn't buy just one litre. When she said, "I'm surprised that you don't have litre cans," the clerk replied with a smirk, "So, you're surprised," and turned away to prepare another order for delivery.

Mrs. Royer felt deeply offended. She then went to another paint store that was a serious competitor of the one she had patronized for so long. As a stranger in the store, she was greeted warmly. She explained her desire to get one litre of this particular brand of red cement paint. The clerk there said, "We don't carry this paint in litres, but we will get one at the wholesale house this afternoon and deliver it to your house later today."

Quite happy to be assured that her needs were now taken care of, Mrs. Royer returned to the bakery. But she was most upset at the treatment received from the first store, which she had patronized for so long. She recited all the details to her husband. Together they decided that the customer relations of their friend's store needed some attention.

What would be your reaction to this situation and what action would you take? Would you advise the owner of the incident? Would you return to the store as a customer? What does the term "customer relations" mean to you? What violations of good customer relations do you observe in this case?

Are Independent Grocers Doomed?

Dick Hafner was a proud man who established his own independent grocery store thirty years ago. In its early years it faced tough competition from many similar independent grocers who seemed to be located every few blocks from his location. Each provided all the usual services of the neighbourhood grocer in those days—delivery service, sales on open account, and personal counter service by competent clerks. Customers could call in their orders and have their groceries, fruit, meats, and produce delivered on either the 10:00 a.m. or the 4:00 p.m. delivery. When he started his business, most payrolls were paid on the first of the month. The customers often brought their paycheques to the store for cashing and payment of their monthly credit charges from the store. It was traditional for the owner to "send home a bag of candy for the children" free of charge when the accounts were paid each month, as a gesture of patronage appreciation.

Almost from the beginning Hafner made a good profit with his store. He was always among the first in the wholesale produce markets early in the morning. He picked the best products and proudly displayed them for the pleasure and purchase of his customers. Fresh bread and other bakery products were delivered to the store each morning. He carried various lines of canned goods, always including the nationally advertised brands and a lesser known brand that was lower-priced. He hired his own butchers and insisted upon good quality meats. They always had a free bone for a customer's dog.

He had a separate tobacco counter, a candy counter where young children could pick out their choices of penny items, and a long counter where customers could designate their purchases to the clerk either to take along or to be delivered.

During the past twenty years, Mr. Hafner has seen one after another of his independent grocer competitors go out of business. In most cases the buildings they had used were not purchased by other grocers but were turned into bicycle repair shops, garages, sewing goods shops, barber shops, or just torn down and the property converted to other uses.

The predominating factor in all of these closings was the complaint that the independent grocer could no longer compete with the ever-expanding chain grocery stores. Mr. Hafner watched these developments with a great deal of concern. He noticed that he was losing some of his customers to the new chain store competition. He also noticed, however, that he was picking up from his former competitors about as many customers who still wanted the special services that he rendered and the chain stores did not. The chain stores sold for cash only (or allowed the use of their own credit card), did not provide a delivery service, and all customers were obliged to go around the store with a cart to pick up their purchases and then go through a cashier's line to check out their total and make payment.

Some of these developments were very new at that time, and some skepticism existed among remaining independent grocers that the idea would ever catch on with the public.

After five years of the growing chain store competitions, Mr. Hafner found that his sales had held steady or increased each year. But now he faced retirement and hoped that his son would take over.

Among Mr. Hafner's employees was his only son, Jerry. Jerry had worked throughout his school years and had continued with his father into his middle twenties. Jerry wanted to have his own store, but a different kind of store from his father's, and still different from the large chain stores. He had in mind a convenience store that did not extend credit, did not have delivery service, and did not always carry the most expensive kinds of merchandise. He would sell prepackaged meat and produce. His father was against the idea. However, he wanted to encourage Jerry to go out on his own and do his own thing. He had always hoped that the present store would be maintained under its present operation, with Jerry as its owner.

1   What would your advice be to Jerry?
2   Could Jerry be successful operating the store as his father had for so many years?
3   Do you think that the independent full-service grocer has a future?

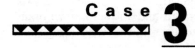

C a s e **3**

Inadequate Investor Capital

ALL THAT GLITTERS IS NOT GOLD

Maxie Stein was a personable young man who graduated from a good business school with a major in management. He always felt that the principles of conservative financing he learned about in his business courses were just too restrictive.

Maxie was particularly critical of such ratios in an opening day balance sheet as a 50 per cent proprietorship ratio; he didn't believe in paying a credit card company 5 per cent of his credit sales, even if doing so guaranteed him full payment of the balances by the fifth of the following month; and he had been

TABLE C3-1

STEIN'S DEPARTMENT STORE
OPENING DAY BALANCE SHEET
JANUARY 1, 19–0

Current assets:		
Cash	$ 5,000	
Merchandise inventory	10,000	
Prepaid supplies	1,000	
Total current assets		$16,000
Fixed assets:		
Store equipment	$ 8,000	
Office furniture and fixtures	2,000	
Delivery truck	3,500	
Total fixed assets		13,500
Total assets		$29,500

Current liabilities:		
Accounts payable (for inventory)		$ 8,000
Fixed liabilities:		
Notes payable	16,500	
Total liabilities		$24,500
Net worth:		
M. Stein, proprietorship		5,000
Total liabilities and net worth		$29,500

told that it is foolish to invest too much of your own money in your business because it is difficult for owners to withdraw money from the business.

After working for another firm for five years to gain business experience, Maxie opened his own small department store. He didn't think it wise to pay incorporation fees, so he decided to operate as a proprietorship. Following his convictions about business, he prepared the opening day balance sheet shown in Table C3-1.

Maxie was smart enough to employ an accounting firm to keep his records and give him annual financial statements, but he instructed the accountant not to charge off any depreciation on the fixed assets because "after all, we don't write cheques to anyone for that kind of expense."

From the day he opened the business, sales exceeded his planned sales volume. Maxie was careful about taking money from the business for himself and restricted himself to $200 per week to cover his own expenses.

The accountant prepared the annual income statement and balance sheet each year. In his optimism that he had proved his points about financing, Maxie looked only at the net profits from operations figure at the bottom of the income statement. During the first four years of operation the income statement showed that he had averaged net profits from operations somewhat in excess of $16,000 per year.

Maxie became conscious of an inability to take advantage of good inventory purchase deals in the third and fourth years. He borrowed $5,000 from the local bank to improve his cash position. He made regular payments on the long-term note with which he had started the business, but he was later forced to borrow $5,000 from his father to meet current obligations.

When he received his annual statements at the end of the fourth year, Maxie was furious. His balance sheet for that year is shown in Table C3-2.

Maxie made an appointment with his accountant the next morning. He questioned the accountant's ability and accused him of being responsible for the fact that Maxie's vendors now sold him C.O.D. only and were pressing him for payments on his outstanding balances to them, for the fact that the bank was pressing him for payments on the bank loan, and for the fact that he was not able to keep his inventory up to date or large enough to support his declining sales volume.

Some of Maxie's specific questions included the following:

1   How is it possible that the firm could have earned more than $64,000 in four years and still be in such poor financial condition?

2   Where are those profits now? I only took out $200 per week.

3   Can I get a refund on the income taxes I paid due to my financial situation now? After all, I paid my income taxes with company cheques.

4   Are those income statements correct for the first four years of operation? How can they be?

If you were the accountant, how would you explain the situation to Maxie? Can you explain where most of the profits have gone?

T A B L E C 3 - 2

STEIN'S DEPARTMENT STORE
BALANCE SHEET
JANUARY 1, 19–4

Current assets:		
Cash	$ 200	
Accounts receivable	23,500	
Merchandise inventory	6,000	
Supplies on hand	200	
Total current assets		$29,900
Fixed assets:		
Store equipment	$ 8,000	
Office furniture and fixtures	2,000	
Delivery truck	3,500	
Total fixed assets		13,500
Total assets		$43,400

Current liabilities:		
Accounts payable	$17,000	
Note payable, bank	5,000	
Fixed liabilities:		
Note payable (original loan)	10,000	
Note payable (father)	5,000	
Total liabilities		$37,000
Net worth:		
M. Stein, proprietorship		6,400
Total liabilities and net worth		$43,400

Case **4**

Administrative Problems—

Personnel Management

A GOOD MARKET DOES NOT ASSURE SUCCESS

Three young men were looking for a business in which to invest their savings and at the same time give themselves good jobs. All had good business experience and some college training. One was a personable sales type, one a factory supervisor type, and the third a good accountant and office manager. They greatly desired to own a business and preferred to make a product rather than own a retailing outlet.

While investigating possibilities in the Niagara Peninsula, they had a meeting with several growers of grapes and other fruits and vegetables. The growers liked the three young men and indicated the great need in their area for a factory that would manufacture crates in which to ship produce. They offered assistance in making a market survey of the reasonable demand for crates and even showed them a small warehouse that could be used for setting up such a plant. The building was available on a long-term lease at a price that seemed reasonable.

The three men liked the idea, investigated the total costs, and found they could finance the business with their joint savings and a small amount of help from their families. They then went to work to get the business going.

The market survey, the growers practically assured them, showed that a total of 1 200 000 crates annually was a minimum they could sell. Only two types of crates were involved. Of the total, 75 per cent would be one type, 25 per cent the second type. But the seasonal variation in the demand for the crates was immediately noticed by the factory man. The total demand was broken down into months as follows:

January	40 000 crates
February	50 000
March	50 000
April	60 000
May	70 000
June	90 000
July	200 000
August	200 000
September	250 000

October	80 000
November	60 000
December	50 000
Total	1 200 000 crates

Obviously the demand called for five times as many crates in September as in the slack months of the winter. The proportion between the two types of crates stayed the same throughout the year.

When they purchased the necessary machines, work tables, and tools, they found that their building could only handle enough of this production equipment to produce an average of 4600 boxes per day, or a total of 1 150 000 in the 250-day work year. To cope with this shortage from the 1 200 000 sales expected, the owners decided that they would request all factory employees to work on Saturdays and Sundays for seven weekends in April and May to provide the extra crates needed to meet anticipated sales. This would produce the extra 50 000 crates with an average of only 3571 crates per day.

Fortunately the factory opened in February during the lighter demand season. The owners hired eight supervisors and twenty-four bench workers from local employment agencies. Some workers needed training, which the owners were able to provide as on-the-job training. Workers with the most experience were made supervisors when first employed.

Things went very well, profits were good, and the employees increased their efficiency to the point that the planned average daily production was approached. Each owner applied his special talent in selling, factory operations, and general management.

They easily filled orders and built up an inventory of crates on hand. This inventory began to be a problem almost immediately because of the lack of warehouse space.

When the seven overtime weekends were announced, the owners had no idea the supervisors would not co-operate 100 per cent. The bench workers were to receive time and a half, but the supervisors were expected to work without extra pay because they were management employees. This meant that for those fourteen days the bench workers earned just about as much as the supervisors. Supervisors received monthly salaries, the workers hourly rates.

The first weekend only four supervisors showed up for work, and production fell off significantly. The owners talked to each supervisor the next week and advised them that strict action would be taken if they failed to show up the next weekend. The next weekend five supervisors showed up, but two who had been there before didn't report. Inventory was also very high by this time in anticipation of the heavy July, August, and September demand. Crates were stored in every available spot. Even the loading docks and empty truck bodies were filled with crates. Rafter space was used. No other warehouse space was available in the town.

The three owners decided on Saturday afternoon to have a meeting to solve the two problems of employee dissatisfaction and storage space.

How would you advise them to solve these problems?

Case 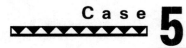 5

Operating Expense Analysis

HOW FAR DO YOU GO WITH STATISTICS?

Ms. Lucille Schwartz and Ms. Olga Olsen started a beauty supply business eight years ago. Ms. Olsen handled public relations and concentrated on the sales end of the business. Ms. Schwartz was the business person who watched after the profits and losses and internal management of the firm. From the beginning they were very successful. They incorporated the firm and charged generous salaries for themselves to corporate expense. They equally divided the outstanding stock. Their commercial bank held a line of credit open for them, but they rarely used it. They paid their bills promptly and took advantage of all sales discounts offered by their suppliers.

Their income statement for the eighth year of operation was in line with the previous years and was as follows:

SCHWARTZ AND OLSEN
CONDENSED INCOME STATEMENT
YEAR ENDED DECEMBER 31, 199–

Net sales	$936,000
Cost of goods sold	702,000
Gross margin	$234,000
Operating expenses	171,600
Net profits from operations	$ 62,400

Ms. Olsen was delighted when the accountant delivered the report for the year. Ms. Schwartz, however, felt that profits should be higher, even though she recognized that both owners had been paid good salaries, which were included in the expenses.

She asked the accountant to prepare a break-even chart for the firm. It showed that their break-even sales volume was far below their present sales volume. But Ms. Schwartz didn't like making deductions from those lines of the chart, so she set about to study the operational figures with good, plain seventh-grade arithmetic.

She took each figure on the annual income statement and divided it by fifty-two to find the weekly results. She then divided those weekly figures by six to find the average daily results. She produced the following table to show Ms. Olsen.

	YEARLY	WEEKLY	DAILY AVERAGE
Sales	$936,000	$18,000	$3,000
Cost of goods sold	702,000	13,500	2,250
Gross margin	$234,000	$ 4,500	$ 750
Operating expenses	171,600	3,300	550
Net profit from operations	$ 62,400	$ 1,200	$ 200

She showed this table to Ms. Olsen, whose reaction was, "Isn't that nice. We're making an average of $200 per day over and above our salaries. What an excellent return on our modest investment."

Ms. Schwartz wasn't satisfied yet. She decided to compare average daily sales with average daily margin and average daily expenses. She spent hours on the past records to find the daily average sales for each day of the week. She then computed the 25 per cent markup on average daily sales and compared these figures with the average daily expenses. She then produced the following table:

	AVERAGE DAILY SALES	AVERAGE DAILY GROSS MARGIN @ 25%	AVERAGE DAILY EXPENSES
Monday	$ 1,800	$ 450	$ 550
Tuesday	1,200	300	550
Wednesday	1,800	450	550
Thursday	3,600	900	550
Friday	4,200	1,050	550
Saturday	5,400	1,350	550
Weekly totals	$18,000	$4,500	$3,300

Ms. Schwartz was very pleased now. She suddenly realized why she and Ms. Olsen had been able to play golf, enjoy the theatre, and spend more time with their families on Monday, Tuesday, and Wednesday. She triumphantly showed her figures to Ms. Olsen. She insisted that she had proved that the business was losing money on Monday, Tuesday, and Wednesday and that the only way to avoid this loss was to close the business on those days.

Ms. Olsen was shocked. The idea of staying closed three days a week just didn't sound right to her. She asks you to evaluate the situation.

Case 6

Layout for Factories

SAMMY'S JAM AND JELLIES INC.

When Sammy Westhoff started making jams and jellies in the kitchen of his home to sell to the public, he never expected that his products would be in such great demand. His success forced him to find larger and larger facilities to produce his excellent products. After eight years he was determined to find a factory building which would make his production more efficient. The problems he currently faced included much cross hauling of raw materials, inadequate storage space, poor loading and unloading areas, and inability to use conveyor belts or horizontal escalators in the manufacturing process. He knew that his labour cost was higher than that of his competitors because of the inefficiency of his factory operations.

He found an available building that he believed would be ideal for his operations. The building was 50 m by 80 m and had a railroad sidetrack on the north side. It was set back 30 m from the south side of a busy industrial street. On the east it reached to within 2 m of a side street. On the west the property had open ground space of 60 m by 80 m. The north, west, and south sides of the building had a 3 m loading platform covered with a roof that reached 1 m beyond the platform. Ceilings in the building were 12 m high, and sliding partitions reached across the entire floor space from east to west at 15 m intervals. Some doors were in those partitions, and others could be added.

His manufacturing operations consisted of cooking the fruit, cooling, adding sugar and other ingredients, filling the jars, packing the cases, storing the finished cases, and getting shipments out to buyers. The labelling of jars was done by machine on the production line and the printing on the cases was done before purchase. Most of the fruit, sugar, and other materials were received in carload or truckload lots. Trucks could enter the loading platform area on the three sides of the building with loading docks. The jams and jellies were cooked in 500-L steel drums, which had to be moved from the gas stoves in the process of adding other ingredients to the fruit. Each operation required a maximum of 15 m of operation area in width and varied in length down the line from 5 to 10 m.

Sammy was satisfied that he could easily meet his production schedule of 600 cases of jam per day and still have space to expand if his demand continued to grow.

He provides you with the above sketch of the building and surrounding area and requests that you make a layout of his new factory.

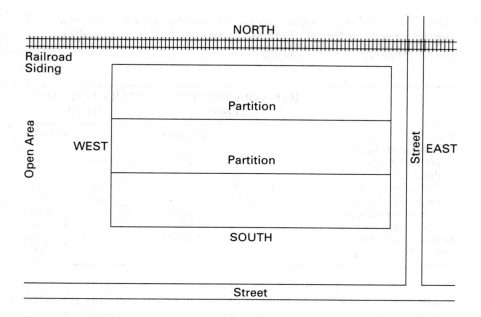

C a s e **7**

Inventory Management

SIMILAR FIRMS MAY HAVE GREAT DISSIMILARITIES

Barbara Bowens and Mary Hopkins each operated small business firms of the same type. Each had hired the same firm to make a market survey before they opened their respective businesses. The market surveys revealed that each was located in an area that should produce about the same sales volume at the same prices to similar customers. Because the women were fellow members of the Chamber of Commerce, they had occasion to meet quite frequently. They enjoyed comparing notes on their operations. They were not in direct competition, since their stores were in different parts of town, but they felt that their discussion of operations could be mutually beneficial.

Their discussions led them to the matter of their inventories. They were amazed to find a large discrepancy in the inventories each maintained in her store. They decided to compare income statements for the past year and see if they could account for the variations. Condensed income statements were as shown below.

	BARBARA BOWENS' STORE		MARY HOPKINS' STORE	
Sales		$200,000		$190,000
Cost of goods sold:				
Inventory, Jan. 1	$ 75,000		$ 15,000	
Purchases	150,000		150,000	
Goods available	$225,000		$165,000	
Inventory, Dec. 31	75,000		15,000	
Cost of goods sold		150,000		150,000
Gross margin		$ 50,000		$ 40,000
Operating expenses		20,000		25,000
Net profits from operations		$ 30,000		$ 15,000

The women knew how to compute average markups, inventory turnovers, and operating expenses as a percentage of sales. They compared all three. When they concentrated on the problem of why they had such different inventories, they turned to their trade association for comparative statistics. They found that the average inventory turnover for their type of firm was five times a year.

When they saw how far they each varied from this average inventory turnover, they decided to see if they could do something about the variations.

Barbara admitted that she had always figured it was better to have plenty of merchandise on hand than to lose a sale due to "stockouts." Mary admitted her dislike for having too much working capital tied up in inventory. She was located close to a wholesale house, which made it easier to send one of her employees there or to drive there herself to get merchandise quickly. She paid for the gas for employee automobiles on such trips. She admitted that she had frequent "stockouts" and that, despite assurance to customers that the item would be available in a short time, those customers often did not come back.

Mary and Barbara decided to resolve their discussions around the following questions, and they asked you to comment on each.

1   What was the average markup, inventory turnover, and profits as a percentage of sales for each store?
2   What are the disadvantages of having too much inventory on hand?
3   What are the disadvantages of having too little inventory on hand?
4   What is the ideal inventory?

5   In what ways can the profitability of the firm be affected by its inventory policy?

6   What recommendations would you make to each woman?

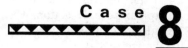

Case 8

The Over-Aggressive Sales Rep

The Specialty Shoe Store was a prosperous retail business in a large western city. It sold both men's and women's shoes. Jack Jones, the owner, prided himself on the capabilities of the six salespersons, many of whom had been with him for several years. The three women and three men salespersons averaged thirty-four years of age, were not unionized, and often gave extra time to their work without extra pay when busy periods occurred. Jones instituted a profit-sharing plan, which was based on the earnings for the year and distributed at Christmas.

In June he was forced to replace one of the salesmen, who moved to another city to open his own store. Jones hired Byron Smith, who had just graduated from the local community college. Smith was cleancut, twenty-three, had some previous selling experience, and appeared very personable. He was interviewed by the other five sales people, as well as by Jones, before he was employed. All gave their approvals.

Within two weeks Jones started receiving complaints from the other sales people about Smith's over-aggressive tactics on the sales floor, especially when Jones was not around. Young Smith rudely interrupted the others when they were making sales or considering choices of shoes with customers. He offered his positive opinions to the point that the customers resented them. He sometimes took customers away from the other staff members. His favourite comment to the others was "Stick with me! Some day I will own this store." He interrupted the person assigned to balance the cash register at closing time. He insisted he could improve the established procedures because "After all, I've been to college."

At first the other sales people tried to make kind suggestions to Smith, but they failed to change his method of operation. When Jones first became aware of the situation, he talked to Smith. He pointed out that Smith's sales record was good but the customer complaints and the complaints of his fellow sales people had to stop. Smith said he would try to change his behaviour. Jones felt particularly concerned about this situation because Smith's father was a personal friend and a fellow golfer at the local country club. As a result, he put off any final disciplinary action as long as possible.

In December Jones received a memorandum signed by the five senior staff members. It indicated that unless this aggravating situation were corrected immediately, they would not attend the Christmas party and would look for other jobs because they all planned to resign as of January 1. They also said that they would like an opportunity to have a full staff meeting to air their grievances. Jones knew he could no longer postpone positive action. He decided, in view of the total situation and his friendship with Smith's father, that he should have the requested meeting with the entire staff.

If you were Mr. Jones, how would you conduct the meeting and what decisions would you make?

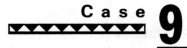

Case 9

The Heartaches of Credit

Management

Mrs. Alice Billings is the credit manager for the ABC Department Store in Halifax. Her duties include making the final decisions on applications for credit after her staff has concluded the regular investigation of formal applications. The ABC Department Store encourages open credit accounts for qualified applicants. It has maintained a good record of efficiency in administering its credit program. Losses on bad debts have been minimal. Few accounts get more than ninety days past due because of the store's effective program for handling delinquent accounts.

One morning Mrs. Billings found an application from Mr. Ned Albers on her desk. She knew Mr. Albers as a fellow church member, a regular contributor to charity, and a very kind and considerate person. He had four children in the public schools. His wife made most of the children's clothing and was also active in the church. They were known as people of modest means and limited income. None of these facts were known to the staff member who investigated the information and references on the application for credit.

The staff member had attached a long, handwritten note for Mrs. Billings to the application. It said that the application should never be approved, that the information given was inaccurate, the income was overstated, and the prior references reported that their credit experience was most unsatisfactory.

It was company policy that the credit manager must have a personal meeting with all credit applicants to advise them of the firm's decision to approve or reject credit and the limits placed on credit extended. Before setting up the appointment, Mrs. Billings learned from a mutual friend that the Albers' application was made in the hope of buying a badly needed kitchen stove.

If you were Mrs. Billings, how would you handle the required meeting with Mr. Albers?

C a s e

▶▲▶▲▶▲▶▲▶▲▶▲▶

10

If There Is a Will, There May

Be a Way—to Get Started

Bill Jacobs was attending university in Regina. His best friend was Jack Evers, who operated a small sporting goods store in Bill's home town. Both young men had always hoped and planned to move to Winnipeg and establish a larger sporting goods store as partners. They planned their move for next June when Bill would graduate with a degree in business administration. When Bill came home for his last spring vacation, he found Jack very downhearted. When he inquired, he found that Jack had figured out the investment they would need to open their Winnipeg store. Jack saw no way they could arrange for sufficient capital. Together they went over the asset needs and came up with the statement of assets to be used which follows:

STATEMENTS OF ASSETS TO BE USED

Cash	$　3,000
Funds to invest in accounts receivable	3,000
Merchandise inventory	20,000
Prepaid insurance and supplies	1,000
Land and building	65,000
Store equipment	10,000
Office furniture and fixtures	2,000
Delivery truck	3,000
Total assets required	$107,000

Jack figured that he could net $15,000 from the sale of his present store. Bill had $10,000 available to invest. Bill had studied small business management in college. He knew that with certain constraints or decisions on providing needed assets they could open the business with their $25,000.

1　Set up your own constraints (decisions) and make an opening day balance sheet for the new Winnipeg firm.

2　What are your four basic ratios on the balance sheet? Can they be improved? How?

Case 11

The Unknown Per Cent of Capacity

When Harry Wong graduated from the university, he was employed as assistant office manager by the Supreme Auto Parts Company. Harry was a keen young man and was anxious to show in practice the many things he had learned in his college study. His first assignment was to establish a combined journal-ledger bookkeeping system for the young but fast-growing business. The owner was so pleased with the resulting saving in bookkeeping time and efficiency of the system that Harry received his first raise after only two months with the firm. His next assignment was to establish a better system of inventory control. Again he did a good job; he installed a perpetual inventory system for the parts department that included signed receipts for every part issued, every part returned, and every part received from vendors. The system gave management better control of the inventory and seemed to eliminate the unknown losses in inventory which had occurred in the past.

Over coffee one morning Harry asked the owner, Ms. Worlish, if she had ever considered the use of a break-even chart to analyze the results of operations. He pointed out the many uses that could be made of such a chart by showing the relationship of expenses and income at all levels of income of the business. Ms. Worlish replied that she would love to have such data available. She said the reason it had not been done in the past was that no one could establish a percentage of capacity at which the firm operated.

Harry saw a chance to further prove his value to the firm. He promised to make a break-even chart for the firm for the past year. Sales were $300,000; total expenses were $250,000, of which $50,000 was fixed. The per cent of capacity was not known.

1   Can you prepare the break-even chart in a 12.5 cm grid?
2   How does your chart vary from one in which the per cent of capacity is known?

Case
▼▼▼▼▼▼▼▼ **12**

Overall Personnel Policy

Mr. Baker, Mr. Carter, Ms. Johnson, and Ms. Garcia are the equal owners, the board directors, and the officers of the Bild Manufacturing Company. The company manufactures dishware and pottery products of various types, including a very popular line of dinnerware. The firm has been in business for seventeen years and was started by the present owners and their relatives. It has seventy-five employees, including fifty factory workers, twelve sales people who travel the sales territory, and thirteen office employees. Profits are modest but steady.

One day the owners were called to a special emergency meeting to evaluate possible changes in their personnel policies. The day before, the Provincial Labour Relations Board had conducted an election in the plant to decide upon a collective bargaining agent for the employees. The vote was close, but a 55 per cent majority voted for no unionization and no formal collective bargaining.

The directors were shocked and saddened that the vote was so close. They had always prided themselves on the loyalty of their employees. They felt they always rewarded their employees well and that surely they were happy and satisfied people who valued their jobs.

In the meeting with the employees this morning the directors requested information on the complaints that had motivated the election and its close results. They were pleased to learn that the chief complaint was not wages, although they did pay slightly less than their bigger competitors. The complaints revolved around fringe benefits. They can be summarized as follows:

1. Present vacation policy is one week after one year, two weeks after five years, and three weeks after ten years' employment. The employees want two weeks after one year, three weeks after five years, and one month's vacation after ten years' employment.

2. Employees want a guaranteed annual salary. They are willing to do other jobs, such as maintenance painting, if the factory does not have enough orders to maintain year-round full employment — which has rarely happened in the past.

3. Employees resented it when the management placed much routine accounting and inventory control on a terminal computer service. This eliminated two bookkeepers, who were later given other jobs. Net saving was $12,000 yearly.

4. Employees feel that the sales people make too much money compared with factory workers. Sales people work on a straight commission basis.

5   Employees complain that the company does not follow through on its policy of dismissing new employees whose work is not satisfactory after a three-month trial period. They want a voice in the retention or dismissal decision. They feel that keeping weak employees is hurting plant efficiency.

6   Because a group life insurance policy for employees is a tax-deductible expense for the company, employees want their group policy increased to $25,000 for each employee. This is a legal maximum under the Income Tax Act without it being deemed a taxable benefit in the hands of the employees.

7   It is felt that some supervisors are not enforcing company work rules uniformly for all people under them.

Some of the employees who are known to have agitated for the union frankly indicated that their agitation will cease if acceptable answers can be found to these complaints. They indicated that the rank-and-file employees do not like a plan of union dues writeoff from their salaries, and that they believe in the right-to-work laws, which remove the necessity of being a union member in order to work in their province.

In tomorrow's meeting the directors must recover from their disappointment and shock and take positive action on each of the employee complaints.

If you were a member of the board of directors, what would your recommendations be on each complaint? Can you defend your recommendations? How?

Case 13

Inventory Valuation

The piano department of Rizzo's Music Store showed the following purchases in 1991 after being completely sold out in the Christmas trade of 1990.

January–5 pianos at $2,000 each
February–8 pianos at $2,100 each
March–6 pianos at $2,000 each
April–5 pianos at $2,200 each
May–5 pianos at $2,200 each
June–5 pianos at $2,300 each
July–5 pianos at $2,300 each
August–6 pianos at $2,400 each
September–8 pianos at $2,400 each

October—10 pianos at $2,500 each

November—10 pianos at $2,500 each

December—15 pianos at $2,500 each

On December 31, 1991 the department had an inventory of twelve pianos on hand. The selling price then was $2,500. Of the twelve pianos on hand, two were purchased in January, three in May, five in November, and two in December.

How would the remaining twelve pianos be valued under LIFO, FIFO, weighted average cost, and lower of cost or market methods?

C a s e

▼▲▲▲▲▲▲▲▲▼ **14**

An Existing Firm Versus a

New One

Everett and Jeanie were childhood sweethearts who married after they graduated from high school. Jobs were scarce in their home town, so they opened a small restaurant of their own "on a shoestring." They were such a good team that they prospered from the beginning. As their finances improved, despite raising four children, their thoughts turned to their lifetime desire to move to the West Coast. When a chain restaurant offered them $75,000 for their restaurant, they decided the time had come to move west. They settled in New Westminster, British Columbia, and immediately set about finding the location for a new restaurant.

They found an attractive suburban location and proceeded to plan the financing necessary to get under way. The building they planned to rent was new, and no equipment of any kind was available from the landlord. With careful planning they determined that they could equip the place and start business with a minimum investment of $40,000. The market survey suggested a profit of $20,000 per year.

Jeanie came home from shopping a short time later and reported to Everett that she had found a For Sale sign on "that cute little restaurant" they had visited some time before. She visited the owner and found that the business could be purchased for $35,000. The owner even showed her his bank deposits and income tax returns to prove that he had averaged between $18,000 and $21,000 net profit each year for the past ten years. His desire to sell was explained as a wish to retire.

The ensuing discussion between Everett and Jeanie was the bitterest of their entire married life. Everett was screaming the disadvantages of buying an established business and praising the advantages of starting a new firm in the fine location they had found. Jeanie favoured buying the restaurant that had been established for years and was a proven moneymaker. She cautioned Everett about the additional risks undertaken in starting a new firm.

1   Can you help them resolve the dispute?
2   What specific factors should enter into their discussion?

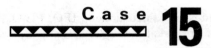

C a s e **15**

To Buy or Not to Buy

Igor Siminkowski has decided that he has worked for someone else long enough. For the past four years, he has been taking business classes at the local community college and attending seminars offered by the Small Business Administration. He and his wife, Jean, have been saving several hundred dollars each month, and they now have $31,500 in savings.

The Siminkowskis have been investigating buying one of the small, neighbourhood grocery stores that are for sale in Edmonton. These convenience stores are each independently owned and operated, and most have been in business for several years. The Siminkowskis have found two operations they like. Here are the facts:

	STORE A	STORE B
Sales (average for 5 years)	$177,000	$192,000
Cost of goods sold	132,750	140,160
Operating expenses (including owner's salary)	40,000	50,760
Net profit	4,250	3,000

1   Calculate the value of each store using the capitalized-earnings method of determining value. Assume a 15 per cent CAP rate. Since these types of stores are considered to be high risk, refigure the value using a 25 per cent CAP rate.
2   The depreciated value of the store fixtures has a value of only $6,500 for Store A and $9,000 for Store B. Inventory on hand in Store A is worth $14,000 and in Store B is worth $16,000. What would the replacement cost be for each store?
3   The selling price for either store is $25,000. Would you recommend the purchase of either store? Why or why not?

Case **16**
▼▲▼▲▼▲▼▲▼

Ficklin's Recycling

Marlow Ficklin had been office manager for the large regional distribution centre of Nationwide Products, Inc. for eleven years. He liked what he did, and because the firm had been successful, Marlow had done well in terms of expanded responsibility and income. His salary was quite good and the fringe benefits he received were excellent. Last year his profit-sharing bonus had been $6,300.

Although Marlow liked what he was doing, he was disturbed by all the waste he saw at the distribution centre. Each day several tons of cardboard and paper were discarded. Additionally, dozens of loading pallets were thrown out because they were cracked or had a broken section. The waste computer and typing paper was discarded, along with other items.

One day as a huge garbage truck pulled away with several hundred kilograms of scrap cardboard boxes, Marlow could take it no longer. He marched into Vice President Belle Bevins' office with a proposition. Could he have the waste paper and cardboard? He would dispose of it in a responsible way and save the company the hauling charges.

Belle immediately said she thought it would be okay with the company. He would have to agree to remove the scrap on a regular basis without involving Nationwide in any way and to do the work on his own time.

With that Ficklin's Recycling was born. Soon the business began to produce income. Marlow stayed after work a few evenings a week and put in a couple of Saturdays a month. With the help of his two college-aged daughters he was able to keep up with the disposal of the cardboard and paper, as well as to repair and recycle the broken pallets. In fact, the net income the first year of operation was enough to pay the tuition for the girls at a local college.

Then Marlow reached a crossroads; he was offered the same type of opportunity by another large firm in the community. If he accepted the additional business, it meant he would have to change his operational methods. It would mean hiring more help and, perhaps, he might even have to quit his job to "go into business for himself."

1   Could a real-life small business start the way Ficklin's Recycling did? Do you know of examples of businesses with this type of beginning? Explain.

2   What might the future have in store for Marlow Ficklin if he decides to "go into business for himself"?

3   What would you advise Marlow to consider before he makes a decision to go into the business full time?

4   Can some of the business principles which make Nationwide Products successful apply to Ficklin's Recycling? What principles would apply?

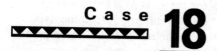

Case 17

The Tornado Rock Crusher

For many years Gadke Machine Works specialized in machine tooling specific parts to be used as components by manufacturers in the Sault Ste. Marie area. Gadke did not consider manufacturing products under their own name until a customer from Manitoba requested a mid-sized rock crusher to be built. The product was a success, and it was delivered at a good profit.

Top management decided it was time to go into the rock crusher business. With the help of consulting engineers, a design was perfected and a prototype called the Tornado was built. It was a handsome model (as rock crushers go) and could be priced competitively.

Now decisions had to be made about how to market the new Tornado. The company also needed to decide how to position the product.

1   What kind of target market does the Tornado have? How should the product be promoted?

2   Should the product be sold directly to the user, or should distributors be used? Why?

3   What kind of selling effort should be used? What about installation and service?

4   What should be done to position the product correctly?

Case 18

Valvco Manufacturing Company

Willis Mumfert, general manager of Valvco Manufacturing Company, has designed a new type of self-cleaning gate valve that he is sure will be a winner. Valves currently used to close the tubes at hydroelectric facilities are hard to close because sand and grit can build up in the seating trench at the bottom making it sometimes difficult to screw them down tightly. Tests show the new self-cleaning valve will eliminate that problem. This feature will be a breakthrough.

Willis has been assured that the new valve meets governmental safety requirements, and preliminary test marketing research shows a high probability for product acceptance. Willis knows, however, that the market is limited to outfitting the few new hydroelectric dams to be constructed plus possibly some replacements in existing facilities.

Yet, Willis is so confident about the new product that he feels he should analyze changing the system of distribution Valvco uses. He has a couple of choices to make in this regard.

First, the valve could be marketed directly to the final customers using the present sales force. This channel would involve Valvco's manufacturing the valves and selling directly to the contractors building the dams. The second choice would be for Valvco's sales to be handled through a strong system of merchant wholesale distributors.

Willis decided to compare the two choices. He began by estimating the cost to produce the new valve at $11.70 each. His market research indicated a total potential of 15 000 in sales, of which he felt Valvco would sell two-thirds, or 10 000 units. He felt this amount would be the same for either of the choices.

The wholesalers would be allowed to purchase the valves for $18.00 each and then resell them to the final users at a suggested price of $23.00. This channel would require $10,000 in cooperative advertising and the shipping costs would be $1.50 per unit.

If Willis used an in-house sales force, he would have to add an additional salesperson at a cost of $35,000 for commissions and expenses, plus spend $30,000 on additional advertising. The direct selling price would be $21.50. Shipping cost would be $0.50 per unit.

1   Calculate the expected sales income from the two choices Willis is considering. Subtract related expenses from each choice. Which method would be best? By how many dollars?

2   Why is the price of the valve reduced to $18.00 for the merchant wholesalers? Why are advertising costs lower for them? Why are shipping costs higher?

3   Why does the selling price to the final customer change when the products are sold direct? Explain in detail.

1

Management Consultant's Checklist

The following pages give the student or small firm owner a basis upon which to evaluate an existing firm's effectiveness.

The chart on page 467 shows some of the causes of business failure. The checklists show:

1   What an outside consultant looks for in evaluating an existing firm.

2   What owners should check in evaluating their own business.

The subjects covered are:

1   The firm's market

2   Asset adequacy

3   Adequacy and use of accounting records

4   Financial condition

5   Location analysis

6   Layout analysis

7   Proper legal form of organization

8   Sales development program

9   Pricing policies

10   Merchandising of lines of goods

11   Seasonal variations and their implications

12   Purchasing and inventory control

13   Expense analysis and break-even chart

14   Credit policies in effect for sales and purchases

15 Risks and protection provided
16 Personnel policies

1 FOR EVALUATING MARKETS

- Is the firm's major problem a lack of sales?
- What has been the trend of sales in recent years?
- What factors can be determined to be responsible for the trend of sales?
- Was a proper market survey made when the firm started?
- If so, what were the predicted results in sales volume?
- If not, should such a survey be made now?
- Have the basic sources of market survey data been studied?
- Does population growth, new competition, or competitor change in methods justify new ways of serving this market?
- Has the character of the population in the trading area changed, aside from general growth or decline? Has this affected sales?
- Has the ratio of population to number of firms in this trading area changed since the firm was established? If so, what has been done by management to keep current with these changes?
- Does the future look good, fifty-fifty, or bad for this firm in this market?

2 FOR EVALUATING ASSET ADEQUACY

- Does the firm lack any assets that would improve its capacity for service, its image, or its profitability?
- Are its store fixtures, office fixtures, and/or machines modern? Would newer ones improve image, service, or profitability?
- Are present fixed assets consistent with the floor plan, available additional space, and customer comfort?
- Does the firm have the necessary capital to finance its own receivables? Should this be done?
- Are cash balances and working capital adequate for the volume of business being done?
- Do growth requirements of the immediate future suggest the need of any other current or fixed assets? If so, are plans satisfactory for their acquisition?
- Could the firm expand sales and profits with more assets in its present operation? How?

3 FOR EVALUATING ADEQUACY OF ACCOUNTING RECORDS

- Does the proprietor have monthly statements easily available?
- Does a complete accounting system exist?
- Does the present system involve excessive posting?
- Would a combined journal-ledger system reduce the work of the system?
- Can the owner tell quickly the amounts owed by credit customers? (Is there an accounts receivable ledger of some kind?)
- Can the owner quickly ascertain the balance due to creditors? (Is there an accounts payable ledger of some kind?)
- Can sales easily be broken down into departments, chief lines of merchandise, or special items?
- Does the system in effect provide a means of telling the profitability of individual departments or lines of merchandise?
- Are the monthly adjustments properly included in the charges for depreciation, amortization, and new inventories?
- What type of information not now easily available does an owner need?
- Does the firm take advantage of purchase discounts? Do the records provide adequate notice of discount periods?
- Do procedures include a regular aging of accounts receivable?

4 FOR EVALUATING FINANCIAL CONDITION

- What is the relationship of assets and liabilities?
- What is the relationship of current assets and current liabilities?
- Are the current assets truly current?
- Are the liabilities properly classified?
- What is the working capital? Is it adequate?
- What is the current ratio? What is the quick ratio? What is the proprietorship ratio?
- Is the firm trading on too thin an equity?
- Does it have trouble paying its current bills? Why?
- Have the accounts receivable been aged recently? What is the firm's policy on charging off uncollectible accounts?
- How much of current profits is going to pay for fixed assets?
- Are any creditors withholding credit because of the company's debt-paying habits or its other financial problems?

- Does the firm need additional investment capital? Are any sources available?
- Is the inventory turnover a cause of financial stress? Has it been reviewed for slow-moving merchandise lately? Are there other problems?
- Is the gross margin consistent with that of comparable firms? If not, why not?
- Are operating expenses in line? If not, why not?
- Do company policies indicate that the financial condition will be improved? How?
- Are any other financial weaknesses apparent?

5 FOR EVALUATING LOCATION

For Retailers

- Is the firm located in a high-rent or a low-rent area? Should it be? Is the rent paid by the firm competitive?
- If in a low-rent area and competing with firms in high-rent areas, how does it compensate in attracting customers?
- Is the location good from the standpoint of meeting competition?
- Is the total traffic in the area adequate?
- Do neighbouring stores draw potential customers?
- Is there a parking problem for customers? Would it be worthwhile to pay for customer parking?
- Is the location good for development of sales via promotion?
- Is this site appropriate to the principles of location for convenience, shopping, and specialty stores?
- Is there a better site available in the area?
- Is the going-home side of the street or the sunny side of the street important to this firm? Does it have that advantage?
- Do the community and general area suggest adequate payrolls, population trends, living habits, and attitudes to encourage firm development here?
- Are any other disadvantages of this location observed?

For Wholesalers

- Is the location economically accessible to its market?
- Are shipping costs in receiving inventory the lowest available? Would additional rail, truck, or air facilities improve efficiency and reduce costs?

- Do competitors have advantages in costs of delivery to customers due to better location?
- Do customers visit the plant in person or call in orders by phone? If they visit, is the accessibility and customer convenience satisfactory?
- Does this location make possible the best layout of merchandise to expedite order filling and minimize labour costs?

For Factories

- Should this type of factory be close to its markets or to its raw materials? Is it?
- Do the facilities at this location make possible the best use of the appropriate production layout?
- Is the location appropriate to hiring the types of labour required? Is adequate labour of the desired type available?
- Are utility costs consistent with those available at other potential locations?
- Are adequate shipping facilities available at competitive costs? Would additional competition by shippers be helpful?
- Are government attitudes and community facilities encouraging?
- Do alternative locations offer reduced costs or better profits? Why?

For Service Firms

- Is customer visitation an important part of the business? If so, are facilities for customer comfort adequate?
- Is the location consistent with the type of clientele sought and its habits in buying this service?
- Does the firm need a high-rent location? Is it in one?
- If efficient working conditions for employees are important, do they exist?
- Is the firm paying an expensive rental for space when most of its business comes via telephone? Is this necessary?
- Is drop-in business important? Does it exist in adequate quantity? Can it be developed by advertising?

6 FOR EVALUATING LAYOUT

For Retailers

- Is the present layout encouraging to sales because it reflects buying habits of customers?

- Could the present layout better reflect a good "selling machine"? How?
- Is merchandise attractively displayed?
- Is merchandise displayed to facilitate easy comparisons and easy examination?
- Is customer comfort properly provided to meet the particular shopping habits of the firm's customers?
- Are associated lines of merchandise displayed adjacently?
- Does the layout reflect maximum use of light, ventilation, and heat?
- Is maximum view of store space by customers, employees, and managers desirable? If so, is this view now possible?
- Are selling and nonselling activities properly separated?
- Are convenience, shopping, and specialty goods properly located in the floor plan?
- Does the image of the store reflect colours, fixtures, and displays that are compatible with the type of customers sought?

For Wholesalers

- Does the layout make order filling easy?
- Are most popular lines of merchandise located adjacently?
- Is maximum use made of rolling equipment in filling orders?
- Do customers visit the firm often? If so, is the image the one desired?
- Are receiving doors convenient to inventory stacks? Are more doors needed?
- Is the line of travel from merchandise collection for orders to location of loading deliveries direct? Could it be shortened to reduce costs of order filling?
- Are aisles wide enough for efficient operation?
- Can the height of merchandise stacks be reduced in the present space?

For Factories

- Does the firm now use a process or a product layout?
- Is maximum use made of the advantages of the present layout?
- Can the unproductive movement of raw materials, goods in process, or finished products be reduced?
- Are testing and quality-control stations located in the best spots on the production line? Should there be more quality-control locations?
- Are materials to be placed in production located close to the point where they are introduced into production?

- Are material-receiving areas located as close to storerooms as possible?
- Are luncheon areas, restrooms, drinking fountains, and other employee areas located for maximum efficiency?

7 FOR EVALUATING LEGAL FORMS OF ORGANIZATION

- Under what legal form of organization is the firm now operating?
- What are the major risks to which the firm is subjected?
- Does the legal form of organization give the firm proper protection against these risks?
- Does the firm need public liability insurance? Is the amount adequate?
- Is unlimited liability a serious potential problem for the owner(s)?
- Has the present form limited financial needs in any way?
- Has the owner considered changing the legal form?
- What is the relative incidence of the major risks of the firm?
- Are there tax advantages available by changing the legal form of organization?
- Is the owner fully aware of the management advantages of the alternative legal forms available for the firm?
- Is the firm utilizing all the advantages of its present legal form of organization?

8 FOR EVALUATING SALES DEVELOPMENT

- Has the firm properly distinguished between established demand and promoted or created demand for its goods?
- Has the owner considered all the direct and indirect sales promotion methods?
- Are the applicable sales promotion methods being used in effective quantities?
- Is the present advertising program being checked for its effectiveness?
- Is the present sales volume consistent with the potential for the firm in this trading area? If not, how could it be increased?
- Do customers generally reflect a feeling of satisfaction in doing business with the firm?
- What is the firm's image in the community it serves?

- How could the firm's image be improved if deficiencies are found?
- Is personal selling by employees consistent with the best practices?
- Do any suggestions seem apparent for improving sales promotion?

9 FOR EVALUATING PRICING POLICIES

- Do prices now produce an average gross margin consistent with the sales volume for this type of firm? If not, why?
- Is the firm's pricing policy influenced by fair trade laws, nationally advertised prices, or competitor prices?
- Is market strategy employed in setting prices?
- Is the owner reluctant to adopt less-than-average markup prices when good judgement dictates their use?
- Do prices reflect attempts to sell slow-moving merchandise?
- Are proper methods used in moving slow merchandise?
- Is style merchandise a factor in markups and markdowns?
- Does original markup policy reflect normal markdowns, employee discounts, damaged merchandise, and shortages?
- Does the firm use adequate markups to produce desired results?
- Are markups based on cost or retail prices?
- Have loss leaders ever been used? Were they necessary or productive?
- Does the firm's overall pricing policy reflect a dynamic management?
- Do above-average markup sales cover the sales of less-than-average markup items?

10 FOR EVALUATING MERCHANDISING

- Does the owner recognize the differences between convenience, shopping, and specialty goods?
- Is the merchandise inventory arranged to reflect these categories?
- If sales effort is primarily in one category, does the merchandising policy properly reflect this fact?
- Is the merchandising policy generally in line with the majority of customers in the trading area?
- Are selling policies and services (credit plans, delivery services, etc.) in line with the products?
- If selling industrial goods, does the firm recognize the differences in merchandising its goods and consumer goods?

- Is the location consistent with the type of merchandise sold and the price policies in effect?
- Is employee capability consistent with the needs of the type of merchandise being sold?

11 FOR EVALUATING SEASONAL VARIATIONS

- Does the firm have distinct variations in sales in different months and/or seasons of the year?
- Is the management using accepted methods of adjusting operating expenses to these variations?
- Is purchasing policy consistent with the noted variations?
- Would the addition of different lines of merchandise or different products help to even out the seasonal variation in sales?
- If seasonal variations are drastic, would it be better to close the business entirely for some periods in the year?
- If a manufacturing firm, would it be more profitable to use the slack periods to build up inventory and to cut down factory overtime in the busy seasons?

12 FOR EVALUATING PURCHASING AND INVENTORY CONTROL

- Are the proper sources of supply now being used?
- Is the firm taking advantage of all purchase discounts?
- How are minimum inventories and ordering points determined?
- Has the firm suffered from stockouts of finished merchandise or raw materials?
- What is the record of quality, service, and price of its present suppliers? How about dependability and assistance in periods of sellers' markets?
- How does the firm set its minimum ordering quantities?
- Has buying policy led to buying quantities that are too large to be justified by carrying costs?
- What is the cost of carrying inventories in stock until needed?
- Does the firm owner know what the best average inventory is and use it to guide purchasing policy?
- Could more effective purchasing contribute profits to the present results of operation? How?

13 FOR EVALUATING EXPENSES AND A BREAK-EVEN CHART

- Have fixed and variable expenses been thoroughly determined?
- Are there advantages to altering the present relationship of fixed and variable expenses? Is this possible?
- Has the firm produced a break-even chart for annual operations?
- Has this chart been reduced to monthly periods?
- Could the break-even point in sales be lowered? How?
- Can any fixed expenses be made variable in order to reduce risks?
- How would profits change with a 10 per cent increase in sales?
- How would profits change with a 10 per cent reduction in fixed expenses?
- Is the firm approaching 100 per cent of capacity in its present quarters?
- Is the present percentage of capacity known? Can it be increased?
- Is each expense dollar providing a productive return to the firm?
- Can semi-variable expenses be controlled any better?

Dun & Bradstreet

Classification of Causes of Business Failures in Canada, Total Year 1981

Based on Sampling of Opinions of Informed Creditors and Information in Dun & Bradstreet's Credit Reports

LINE OF BUSINESS — ALL

METHOD OF OPERATIONS — ALL

Number	Per Cent	UNDERLYING CAUSES		APPARENT CAUSES	Number	Per Cent
				Bad Habits	8	0.1
				Poor Health	3	0.2
16	0.7	NEGLECT	Due to:	Marital Difficulties	4	0.1
				Death	2	0.3
				Other	1	—
				Misleading Name	—	—
4	0.4	FRAUD	On the part of the principals, reflected by:	False Financial Statement	1	0.1
				Premediated Overbuy	0	0.1
				Irregular Disposal of Assets	3	0.2
				Other	0	0.1
541	10.5	LACK OF EXPERIENCE IN THE LINE		Inadequate Sales	1,027	41.3
				Heavy Operating Expenses	1,414	46.9
399	9.0	LACK OF MANAGERIAL EXPERIENCE		Receivables Difficulties	20	0.9
				Inventory Difficulties	26	1.9
178	10.1	UNBALANCED EXPERIENCE*	Evidenced by inability to avoid conditions which result in:	Excessive Fixed Assets	31	1.2
				Poor Location	12	0.3
1,389	66.0	INCOMPETENCE		Competitive Weakness	142	5.6
				Other	26	1.6
				Fire	2	0.1
				Weather	2	—
15	0.3	DISASTER	Some of these occurrences could have been provided against through insurance.	Burglary	—	—
				Employees' Fraud	1	0.1
				Strike	—	—
				Other	10	0.1
56	3.5	REASON UNKNOWN	Because some failures are attributed to a combination of apparent causes, the totals of these columns exceed the totals of the corresponding columns on the left.			
2,598	100.0	TOTAL				

*Experience not well rounded in sales, finance, purchasing, and production on the part of an individual in case of a proprietorship, or of two or more partners or officer constituting a management unit

Although the last available figures are for 1981, the causes of business failures have not changed in the last decade. *Courtesy of Dun & Bradstreet Canada Limited.*

14 FOR EVALUATING CREDIT POLICIES

- Is the firm financially equipped to carry its own accounts receivable?
- What types of credit accounts are available to customers now?
- Should other types of accounts be made available?
- What is the cost of administering the present credit program?
- Would it be better for this firm at this time to discount all its receivables with a finance company or bank?
- Are credit card sales being collected efficiently? What is their cost?
- Should the firm issue its own credit cards?
- Does its credit policy reflect the fact that the company has both small and large credit sales?
- Has an aging of accounts receivable been made lately? What does it show?
- Has the writeoff of bad debts been realistic, too low, or too high?
- If the firm sells to business firms, has a sales discount been offered? Should it be?
- Has the firm taken advantage of purchase discounts offered to it?

15 FOR EVALUATING PROTECTION AGAINST RISKS

- Has the ownership truly analyzed all the major risks to which the firm is subjected?
- What protection has been provided against each of these risks?
- Is the incidence of risk properly considered in the protective action taken?
- Is self-insurance appropriate for this firm?
- How many risks are being absorbed? Should they be?
- Is co-insurance appropriate for this firm? How?
- Are there any recommendations for reducing risks or getting protection more economically?

16 FOR EVALUATING PERSONNEL POLICIES

- What has been the turnover of desirable employees?
- Are any outstanding reasons for resignations to be observed?
- Does the company provide training for new employees?

- Are company policies regarding personnel known to all new and old employees?
- Are there incentives in the personnel policy for employees to seek advancement?
- Does the policy reflect the generally agreed-upon objectives of all employees?
- Do opportunities exist for employees to work at different types of positions?
- Is the company image one that suggests this is a good firm to work with?
- Are pay scales and/or other advantages consistent with larger firms in the area?
- Is there any problem of employees being overtrained or undertrained?
- Are there any recommendations for changes in the present policies?

2

The Business Plan

3.1 The Business Plan—What Is it?

The business plan is a written summary of the overall activities of the business enterprise. It is a report on the company's sources and uses of funds, its management personnel and labour relations, its products and marketing strategy, its production techniques and research program. It describes the past, present and future of the enterprise. When it is properly prepared, the business plan becomes a blueprint for financing. It should be complete, organized and factual.

The business plan forces management to plan and to balance plans. If management promises a 100 per cent per annum growth in sales, then the business plan must prove that working capital is available to support this level of activity; that the plan can, or can be expanded to, handle that volume; and that adequate labour will be available at that production level. The business plan forces management to commit wild forecasts to a plan that balances all inputs—capital, materials, labour and productive capacity.

3.2 Why Bother With a Business Plan?

The business plan will be one of the most important elements in the presentation to the venture capitalist and a focal point for organizing the whole management effort. It is absolutely indispensable. A well-prepared plan:

1. induces realism in the founders. When founders are forced to sit down and really study and quantify the whole cost-volume-profit relationship—they are frequently made aware of their own over-optimism;

2. exposes management (especially non-financial professionals) to the whole planning, budgeting, forecasting and reporting process—its method and its merits;

3. helps to set the break-even point in profitability and cash flow;

4. helps to identify the users, the market, the pricing strategy and the competitive conditions under which the company must operate to succeed;

5. provides the budget that will be a

useful barometer for an early assessment by the venture capitalist of project feasibility and project attainment;

6. spurs prompt investigation of deviations or variations from plan before conditions become irreparable;
7. discloses the timing and amount of the sources and uses of funds, especially the timing of capital expenditures and the need for short-term bank borrowings;
8. provides a measurement of anticipated return on investment;
9. identifies the number of employees needed, the timing of their need and the balance of skills;
10. is testament to the ability of the management to plan;
11. reduces the time that it takes a prospective investor to assess and accept or reject the proposal;
12. helps establish optimal size and location of plant and facilities;
13. helps to identify the factors critical to the success of the concept.

Above all, the business plan is a tangible submission blueprinting management's dream. The venture capitalist will either take the dream apart or he will be convinced of its obvious merits when he reviews the blueprint.

3.3 The Business Plan—Its General Outline

The Mini-Proposal—

It is recommended that the plan be introduced by a one to three-page summary of the idea, the market need, the amount of capital required and the projected financial results expressed as a rate of return.

Table of Contents—

The contents should be comprehensive and well indexed for complete and easy reference.

Physical Condition—

The plan should be typed and set out in such a way that it invites examination (e.g. double-spaced and

well paragraphed). Frequently the most inviting reports are those which introduce each new idea with a question, the answer to which follows in the body of the text.

The business plan should be prepared in non-technical language wherever possible.

Playing the Devil's Advocate—

Every intelligent reader of the business plan will read it with scepticism. The contentious points should be anticipated with the business plan addressed to those points. The plan should discuss any special hazards or problems associated with the product. An experienced investor knows that every product and every company has some element of risk attached to it. There should be no attempt to gloss over the negative aspects of the product or the company.

3.4 The Business Plan Itself

3.4.1 Background—

A narrative description of the development of the business or the concept including the rationale for entering specific markets should introduce the plan.

3.4.2 Management—

The business plan must establish that management, capable of carrying out the business plan, is or will be available. The plan should include:

1. Personal resumes of the executives and senior supervisory personnel detailing
   age,
   academic background,
   positions held,
   shareholdings,
   functions,
   principal accomplishments,
   business references.
   a description of current remuneration.
   The plan should demonstrate that these people will be capable of growing with the company.
2. A discussion of back-up management and availability of replace-

ments. Does the plan depend on one man for its complete success or failure? Discuss in detail how each individual could be replaced in a crisis.

3. A comment on the extent to which product, goodwill or technical know-how may come to rest in a limited number of people who are not substantial shareholders.
4. A discussion of the need for employment contracts.
5. A description of why members of the management group left their former employers.
6. A schematic organization chart that describes the responsibilities associated with each major management position.
7. A comment on the demands on senior management in year five of the plan to ensure that management will be able to cope at expanded activity levels.
8. Identify the timing and the need for new management.

3.4.3   Labour—

The plan must identify:
i) the skills required;
ii) the timing of the need for labour;
iii) compensation levels both now and in the predictable future;
iv) the availability of labour;
v) the anticipated productivity of the labour.

The plan must bespeak its realism by building in training and a learning curve and by showing its flexibility and responsiveness to unanticipated disruptions and demands.

The plan should comment on:
1. The company's compensation including fringe benefits, comparing it to other companies in the same geographical area and/or in the same industry;
2. The current or anticipated status of union contracts, union demands and objectives;
3. Labour relations in the company and in the industry. It should

comment on the extent to which the company is exposed to further labour organization. It should name current and prospective unions;
4. The availabiltiy of skilled and unskilled manpower in the area to meet the most optimistic levels of demand;
5. Whether the company and the industry are becoming less labour intensive. Comment on labour turnover comparing the company's position to that of the industry.

3.4.4   Research and Development—

The business plan must demonstrate that the company has the technical capability to introduce and sustain products or processes. The plan must therefore:
1. indicate why the product or process is unique and worthy of financial support;
2. provide independent scientific support for the product or process (including laboratory reports and/or users' reports and endorsements);
3. indicate the anticipated costs of developing a working prototype (including timing);
4. set out anticipated research and development costs to advance prototype to production-line status (including timing);
5. comment on the state of the art among
   i) domestic competitors,
   ii) foreign competitors;
6. comment on ability to legally protect know-how and lead time over competitors (e.g. patents);
7. describe the scientific frontiers that are being advanced the most;
8. describe future pressures on research and development, commenting on probable product adaptations.

3.4.5   Marketing—

The marketing aspect of the business plan must convince the reader that the company has a product or process which is different and worthy of support. The marketing plan must identify:

  i) the customers,
 ii) size of the market,
iii) anticipated selling price,
 iv) methods of distribution,
  v) costs of reaching the market.

A well prepared plan should:

1. comment on the general condition of the economy and the industry. Comment on the degree to which the company's products or services are sensitive to short-term changes in the economy;

2. describe in detail the existing and proposed products or services including any patented or patentable features. Submit sales literature, photographs, drawings, etc;

3. describe the customer benefits and economic advantages over existing competitive products or services;

4. define the company's marketing philosophy;

5. outline with reasons, a detailed marketing plan including:
    i) analysis by product, by territory,
   ii) optimal distribution method, e.g. wholesaling, franchising, own sales force, agents, etc.,
  iii) price and credit structure, product line profit contribution,
   iv) break-even analysis by product and territory,
    v) market characteristics, market measurement,
   vi) identification and classification of principal customers,
  vii) product and packaging testing,
 viii) test marketing,
   ix) media selection for advertising,
    x) warranty policy;

6. indicate the present and potential size of the total market. What share do you hold or expect to hold?

7. provide an analysis of competitors, including an evaluation of their products, pricing, market share;

8. name potential customers who have been contacted. To what extent have they shown enthusiasm? Give actual names of people in company who may be contacted;

9. describe degree of exposure to changes in freight costs, strikes at carriers, customers and suppliers;

10. comment on the potential demand for the product or service in the export market. When and how should this demand be met?

11. estimate market start-up costs.

3.4.6   Manufacturing—

The manufacturing plan must identify:

  i) the need for physical plant;
 ii) optimal size and layout of plant;
iii) capacity of plant;
 iv) alternative uses;
  v) burden of fixed costs;
 vi) availability of a trade-off of fixed costs for variable costs (e.g. by sub-contracting component production);
vii) the cost of the fixed assets required.

1. The plan must include a complete bill of materials describing and costing each input and naming at least two suppliers. It must also indicate whether it is from domestic or foreign supply.

2. Comment on price trends of major raw materials, compared to trends in selling prices of the finished products.

3. Determine degree of reliance on one or few suppliers, carriers, etc.

4. Comment on utilities, degree of dependence, availability, usage

and rate trends.

5. Comment briefly on anticipated availability of all major items of raw materials consumed in operations.

6. Comment in detail on how you arrived at the following factors of manufacturing standards:
   i) size,
   ii) weight,
   iii) durability,
   iv) convenience,
   v) packaging,
   vi) quality,
   vii) colour,
   viii) customer service,
   ix) product standardization and compatibility.

7. Comment on how plant location has been or will be determined. Include references to:
   i) customer proximity,
   ii) supplier proximity,
   iii) manpower availability,
   iv) transportation services,
   v) investor preferences.

8. Describe and diagram the production process. The costs of all facilities and equipment should be substantiated by invoices or third party quotations from prospective landlords, contractors, equipment suppliers, etc.

9. Comment on qualifications to do a plan layout. Discuss scope for physical expansion at same geographic location.

10. Comment on production planning and scheduling procedures, including an estimate of plant startup costs.

11. Briefly describe existing plant and property. Comment on physical condition of plant and equipment including outstanding capital projects and probable costs of expansion. Give expansion time-table.

12. Provide a quarterly analysis of degree of unused capacity and where possible similar data for the industry and competitors.

13. Brief trend analysis of expenditures on maintenance and fixed asset additions (both owned and leased).

3.4.7   Other Information—

The other information that should be included in the business plan will be of a legal nature. It will include a description of authorized and issued shares, copies of relevant contracts and disclosure of all non-arm's length relationships. This information will be important to a prospective investor and his lawyer in determining that the company is legally capable of accomplishing its business purpose in the proposed way.

1. Give facts as to incorporation of company, date, province, the locations of executive officers.

2. Submit a photo-copy of the letters patent especially those sections dealing with the authorized capital structure (including rights, restrictions and preferences).

3. Include a complete listing of shareholders and number of shares owned.

4. Submit a chronological record of consideration received from prior sale of shares, number of buyers and identity of principal buyers.

5. Provide information on any predecessor companies, partnerships, trusts, if any, including financial statements, a copy of agreement of asset and know-how transfer, details of contingent liabilities.

6. Submit a copy of any:
   i) employment contracts;
   ii) pension plans including actuarial reports on extent of unfunded past service liabilities;
   iii) profit sharing plans;
   iv) options and warrants;
   v) patents, trademarks;
   vi) franchise and distributorship agreements.

7. Comment on whether there will be any non-arm's length relationships between the company and its landlord, customers, carriers, distributors, licensors, licensees and suppliers.

8. State whether the company's beneficial contracts are assignable.

Consider licences, royalty agreements, employment contracts, leases, suppliers' contracts, collective bargaining agreements.

9. Comment on any past, present or threatened litigation or proposed changes of laws which could adversely affect business, e.g.:
   pollution legislation;
   minimum wage law;
   new government production standards;
   tariffs;
   exchange controls;
   price controls;
   advertising and promotion.

10. Describe those aspects of the company's business now subject to government control and regulations. Is there a likelihood of additional regulation?

11. A trade secret may frequently be a very valuable asset. In many cases, industrial know-how will be the most important asset contributed by the entrepreneur and founder. There are two principal considerations surrounding know-how which the founder must be prepared to discuss thoroughly with the venture capitalist:

1. Does the industrial know-how legally belong to the founder?
2. Assuming that it is legally the property of the founder, to what extent is it patentable?

Services of a skilled lawyer will be required to clarify these points before the venture capitalist will make any commitment. Frequently, the venture capitalist will want his own legal counsel to consider these matters.

Founders forget that at some time in previous employment, they may have signed agreements at their former employer's request that:

i) they would not directly or indirectly own, operate, be employed in, or otherwise be connected in any manner with an enterprise competing with their former employer;

ii) that they would not communicate with or contact any customers of their former employer;

iii) that they agreed to assign and transfer to their former employer all inventions, discoveries or improvements made during their former employment.

There may be circumstances in which the industrial know-how which the founder represents as his own was once owned by predecessor corporations, partnerships or proprietorships. Although the former owner and partners may have, in discouragement, abandoned their active interest in the product, process or service, they may still have a legal claim to participate. These long lost claimants frequently do not appear until the concept is an assured success. While some of these claims may be unenforceable, legal counsel is highly recommended if the founder is to reduce his vulnerability to legal action from past employers, former partners and fresh investors.

3.4.8 Financial—

The financial component of the business plan will summarize in a visual form, expressed in dollars, all of the other elements of the business plan, marketing, production and personnel. It will demonstrate whether management's dreams, when expressed in dollars, are in integrated attainable projection. A well prepared financial plan must identify:

i) the sources of funds . . . in terms of timing, amount, cost and repayment;

ii) the uses of funds . . . in terms of timing, amount and return.

So many companies underestimate their needs. When their shortfall is finally identified, the expenditures have reached the point of no return. If the company is desperate, the cost of funds will be outrageous. Great care should be taken not to underestimate the necessary amount of funds. Always overestimate the need for money.

The financial plan should therefore include:

1. Actual audited financial statements for at least the most recent five years should be submitted. These statements, both balance sheets and income, should then be transferred to a five-year comparative summary for ease of study by investors.

2. Interim financial statements should be submitted for each of the last 12 months and for each of the last five quarters to facilitate month-to-month monitoring of operating results by means of comparison with forecasts submitted.

3. Detailed cash flow and income projections should be provided on a monthly basis for the next 24 months and quarterly for the following three years. These estimates must be realistic. It is advisable to prepare three separate forecasts: the most pessimistic, the most optimistic and the most probable. All assumptions should be described and cross-referenced to a document that supports these assumptions. The cash flow analysis will indicate the timing and amounts of sources and uses and funds. Determine the precise capital needs and comment on the anticipated sources of these funds— timing, amount and cost.

4. Pro forma balance sheets should be prepared for each of the next five years.

5. All costs should be broken down into fixed and variable components. The break-even point (both accounting and cash flow) should be determined.

6. Wherever existing loans are outstanding, identify:
   lender;
   terms;
   security;
   restrictive covenants;
   lending officer;
   details of options, conversions;
   audited financial statements for as many years as possible.

7. Complete description of accounting principles and policies including;
   i) Recognition of inventory obsolescence, disposal of inventory variances, treatment of fixed and variable overhead, inventory cost flow assumptions, e.g. LIFO, FIFO, average cost.
   ii) Treatment of prepaid expenses and deferred charges, e.g. supplies, uniforms, large advertising campaigns.
   iii) Treatment of research and development expenses.
   iv) Recognition and amortization of intangibles such as goodwill, patents, licences, franchises and know-how.
   v) Fixed asset accounting policies, including capitalization policy, maintenance policy and depreciation policy (straight-line vs. declining balance vs. sinking-fund).
   vi) Treatment of leased assets.
   vii) Treatment of government assistance and government grants (reduction of current expense, deferred revenue, reduction of cost of fixed assets, contributed surplus).
   viii) Basis of provision of liability for damaged goods, warranties, guarantees, servicing.
   ix) Recognition of revenue on installment sales, deferred servicing. Clear statement of methods followed in recognizing revenue in general.
   x) Treatment of other lump-sum non-recurring or abnormal outlays, e.g. lease termination, severance pay-

ments, special advertising, opening expenses, consulting studies.

xi) Impact of changes in accounting policies during period. Put all statements on a comparative basis. (Note: Also put statements of other companies being used in comparative study on same accounting basis, where practical.)

3.5   The Proof of the Pudding—
Is It in Your Business Plan?

Before the plan is submitted to a prospective investor, several independent parties should review it to determine those matters which may have been glossed over, misrepresented or left unanswered.

The independent parties should confirm that the plan demonstrates:
1. complete managerial ability;
2. realistic market identification and marketing strategy;
3. sufficient funds for long-term activity;
4. balanced productive capacity;
5. a technically feasible commercial product.

There are few smooth-talking promoters and entrepreneurs who can make up for an inadequate business plan. If the plan is not well prepared, the company does not deserve financing!

3.6   Helpful Tips for Attracting Venture Financing—a Summary

Someone once defined a "big shot" as a little shot who keep shooting. Keep shooting. Financing for most people is a time consuming, expensive, frustrating and demoralizing experience. The entrepreneur must:
1. Become the advocate of his product or service. He must sell, sell, sell. He should rehearse his presentation until it will withstand experienced cross-examination. He must be prepared and be persistent;
2. Place special emphasis on researching the market;
3. Get professional assistance, but only for those aspects of the presentation in which he may be expected to lack expertise;
4. Demonstrate his own financial commitment before expecting others to supply high-risk capital;
5. Try to scale down grandiose plans into identifiable stages. Frequently, a small-scale pilot project can be easily financed. If it is successful, other stages of financing become easier;
6. Consider acquiring a profitable going concern onto which the new product or process may be added;
7. Attract prestigious people to the product or process (e.g. backers, suppliers, customers, users);
8. Get advance cutomer commitment and document their acceptance of the product or service;
9. Include in the proposal the negative factors as well as the positive;
10. Keep partners to a minimum in early stages. Otherwise too many people must agree on every detail before any steps can be taken;
11. Be stingy with equity but be realistic. Avoid giving away too much of the concept in the early stages before the major financing has been raised;
12. Avoid delays. The entrepreneur must take a leave of absence from his current employment, if necessary, to really give the proposal the attention and dedication it deserves;
13. Check, double check and then check out again, finders and financial consultants. A reputable counsellor is worth his fee—but there are some finders who will waste time and prostitute the proposal.

Reprinted from *Sources of Venture Capital in Canada*, Revised Edition, Government of Canada, Industry, Trade and Commerce, 1978.

Appendix

▼▼▼▼▼▼▼▼▼▼

3

Business Plan for

Speedy-Lube

Speedy-Lube[1]

S.G. Hall

[1] This sample business plan was prepared by a student of Professor Szonyi. Names, dates, and prices have been altered to protect the author. Prices are consistent within the plan but do not represent 1991 prices.

1.0   Introduction

The objective of Speedy-Lube is to establish an operation that will provide a specific automotive service which is a regular and repeatable item of automotive maintenance. The service provided is termed "light automotive servicing," which includes oil changes, oil and air filter changes, full chassis lubrication, and fluid level checks (power steering, differential, and transmission).

Although the service to be provided is not new, it is intended to package the service in such a way that it will be attractive to the consumer. The main components of the service will be speed, efficiency, and cleanliness. Speedy-Lube will be known as an oil specialty shop and will specialize in performing an oil change and chassis lubrication in less than 10 minutes.

Several changes in consumer psychology and the automotive aftermarket have made this concept marketable. The consumer has become very time conscious and desires to reduce the amount of time and trouble spent performing the service items of life (grocery shopping, cleaners, drug store, etc.). It is believed that the consumer has the same approach to automotive servicing. Surprisingly enough, the automotive aftermarket has actually been moving away from the concept. Since the adjustment in world oil prices in 1973, the major oil companies have reduced the number of full-service station outlets and created the concept of the self-service gas bar. The consumer is now forced to go to large full-service outlets for his light auto servicing. This is quite often very frustrating because of the long waiting time and the continuous attempts of the service centre to sell additional tires, batteries, or accessories (TBA).

As a consequence, it is believed that the consumer will be highly receptive to an oil specialty shop that offers quick service and eliminates the apprehension of constantly being encouraged to purchase additional services.

The potential consumer is perceived to be a car owner who requests fast, efficient service at a predictable cost. Apartment dwellers, single women with cars, housewives with cars, and present do-it-yourself car owners are believed to be important characteristics of the potential consumer.

It is intended to commence the Speedy-Lube concept initially at one location with plans to establish additional outlets within two years of opening. In order to guarantee that the level of service can be achieved, it is felt that the service outlet must be designed from the ground up. The concept of converting an existing structure is not considered acceptable.

2.0 Organization and Management

Speedy-Lube is a new company that will be formed as a limited partnership between Ms. S. Hall and Mr. M.P. Adair. Resources of the managers is presented in Exhibit 1. Ms. Hall will be a working partner and will be responsible for the daily operations of the company. Mr. Adair will remain a silent partner; however, he will assume complete responsibility for the establishment of a comprehensive financial planning and control system along with policies for inventory control.

The partnership will be of equal equity contribution of $10,000.00 each. Ms. Hall will draw a salary of $15,000.00 per annum from the operation of the firm. Mr. Adair will remain at his present occupation and will draw no salary for services rendered. This arrangement will exist until the initial outlet has become profitable. At this time the arrangements for compensation will be reviewed.

3.0 Market Analysis

3.1 Demand Analysis

The geographic region that is being considered initially is the central Mississauga area because of:

1. high urban population

2. high population density due to apartments and condominiums

3. growth potential

4. company founders reside in area.

The area that is being considered is shown in Exhibit 2. The area is divided in accordance with the census tract delineation of the Canada Census. The census tracts that are considered are 505-513 and 520-526. These cover an area of approximately thirty square kilometre with a population density of 5000 per square kilometre.

United States market surveys for specialty auto services have indicated that the market area has a 5 km radius and requires 8000 households in the area. For the market area being considered in Mississauga there are 36 620 households within a 5 km radius of Dundas and Hurontario.

The Ontario statistics for the number of automobiles per household are as follows:

55% of all households have one car

21% of all households have two cars

3.4% of all households have 3 or more cars

From this data the total number of cars in the market area is estimated to be 39,256. An analysis of the following market information provided an estimate of the potential number of automotive oil changes that would be required if all auto owners were maintenance conscious:

Information from reference (4):

average annual miles driven by: men   - 18 300 km
                                women - 8 700 km

sex of principal drivers: male   - 53.8%
                          female - 46.2%

average distance between oil changes is 10 000 km.

product blow-by into the crankcase. Consequently, the 10 000 km interval may be too large and, as a result, the market size could be conservative.

3.2 Conditions of the Market

Several trends have occurred in the automotive servicing market that have created the conditions for the successful introduction of the specialty oil shop.

Prior to 1983 the full-service service station enjoyed 50% of the oil and oil filter market with the rest of the market split between car dealers, general repair shops, and the DIY auto owner. However, since 1973 there has been a major upset in the concept of automotive servicing due to the adjustment increases in world oil prices. The service station concept was affected due to the significant reduction in the margins on gasoline sales in the retail auto market. Margins were reduced by up to 50% in cases. This precipitated an action by the major oil companies to improve their efficiency by streamlining operations and increasing the sales volume at their outlets. As a result, numerous full-service outlets were either closed completely or completely converted to self-service gas bars with no service-bay facilities. The full-service service stations that still exist are much farther apart and are usually of a minimum of three service bays. The next five-year trend will see the average full-service service station with a 2,275,000 litres/annum gas sales with three or four service bays operating at 75% capacity.

The service station now only has 26% of the oil and oil filter market. This has resulted due to the decrease in service stations and an increase in the size of the DIY market segment. In the United States this segment accounts for 55-60% of the aftermarket oil sales. In Canada the size of this market has grown to 30-40% of the aftermarket sales. Early reports in 1990 indicate that the increasing trend in the DIY market has levelled off.

The changes in the automotive aftermarket have created a gap in light auto servicing. The auto owner has been forced to drive farther to larger full-service outlets for his light auto servicing. In many cases, due either to the inherent waiting time or the apprehension of being hounded to purchase additional TBA, the auto owner has omitted regular preventative maintenance procedures or converted to a DIY auto owner.

There is a definite decline in the serviceability of automobiles on the road today. The Manitoba Motor League has reported a significant increase in the number of vehicle failures due to the omission of regular vehicle inspection and maintenance.

The potential number of oil changes in the market area are:

for men-driven cars   - 42 652 oil changes/year

for women-driven cars - 14 983 oil changes/year

                          56 615 oil changes/year

Studies indicate that the do-it-yourself (DIY) segment of auto owners are males between the ages of 18 and 49; in Canada they are estimated as performing 30% of all oil changes. Adjusting for this factor, the total potential oil changes are estimated as being 44 825 per year, or 143 oil changes per day. This recognizes the potential fixed market size that exists due to the surrounding residential areas.

An additional market segment exists in the volume of captured passing trade that may reside outside of the 5 km radius area but frequently visits or passes through the zone for alternative reasons (fast food outlets, shopping malls, etc.). For studies conducted for car wash installations in the United States it was determined that a traffic count of 30 000 to 40 000 cars per day is required to ensure passing trade capture. This fact has been considered in selecting the location.

In summary, the market is perceived as being made up of three distinct segments:

1. fixed residential auto owners within a 5 km radius
2. potential passing trade
3. conversion of DIY auto owners in segments 1 and 2

The estimated sizes of the market segments were developed assuming all auto owners were maintenance conscious. It should be pointed out that it is not perceived that this is the present size of the market because many auto owners are not conscious of the benefits of regular preventative maintenance. However, it is felt that given proper promotional techniques more of the public can be educated and convinced of the need for the service of Speedy-Lube.

It should also be noted that the interval between oil changes has been estimated at 10 000 km. However, there is some seasonality to the frequency of oil changes. During the winter it is recommended that oil changes occur on the basis of time rather than miles because oil degrades faster due to the increased thermal cycling of the oil, greater tendency for crankcase condensation, extended operation with choke in operation, and increased combustion

3.3 Consumer

The potential consumer is perceived to be any private auto owner whose vehicle is off warranty. The most potential consumer is the non-DIY owner who requires someone else to perform the auto servicing. They would be people who did not have the DIY facilities or were not mechanically adept. They would be principally female auto drivers, apartment dwellers and non-DIY males.

The DIY auto owner is also a significant potential consumer because he represents 30% of the market, is obviously convinced of the need for vehicle maintenance, and statistically changes his oil every 8000 km, which is 2000 less than the national average. The DIY auto owner has evolved due to the increasing costs of automotive labour and dissatisfaction with the speed and quality of the work done. It is felt that a significant portion of this market can be captured provided that the components of speed, quality, and price are correct.

The lifestyle of urban living has placed an increasing demand upon the automobile. Ninety per cent of all vehicle transportation is performed by the private automobile. This dependence on the automobile has created a consumer who is extremely reluctant to part with the possession of their vehicle for any significant length of time. This, combined with the consumer's desire to maximize leisure time and minimize the time spent on performing the maintenance items of life, has created a consumer who requires speed and efficiency when obtaining these items. This explains the success of fast-food outlets, drive-in cleaners, automated banking machines, automatic car washes, etc. Extending this concept, it is perceived that the concept of a drive-through oil change will be well received.

It is recognized that not all consumers are aware of or convinced of the preventative aspects of regular oil and filter changes and chassis lubrications. The consumer must be educated in these aspects and constantly reminded of oil changes. In contrast to other automotive specialty services (mufflers, transmissions), it is not immediately apparent to the consumer when he has exceeded the recommended interval between oil changes. Continuous promotion will be necessary to remind the consumer.

3.4 Competition

The identified sources of competition are: other outlets of full service; other outlets that specialize in oil changes and lubes; and changes in the oil market.

The full-service outlets consist of car dealerships, oil-company sponsored service stations, or general repair outlets. The car dealership is not considered a competitive threat because they have very little of the market for cars more than two years old. The identified general repair centres in order of decreasing sales are: Canadian Tire Corporation, Dayton Tire (Family Auto), Firestone Stores, K-Mart Auto Centres, Woolco Auto Centres, and Sears Ltd. These outlets are heavily committed to the sale of TBA and do not offer the speed and efficiency that Speedy-Lube will be capable of.

At present, other outlets that specialize in the same service as Speedy-Lube are being backed by the major oil companies. All of these outlets also have a self-service gas bar on the site. Shell (Rapid-Lube) is presently heavily committed to the concept and has constructed nine outlets in the Toronto Area. Gulf (Heavy-Lube) is just beginning to become involved. Esso has not approached the concept at all. BP is waiting to see what happens.

Discussion with oil distributors has revealed that there is presently no private specialty oil and lube outlet in the Toronto market. There has been private development in other market areas in Canada. In Vancouver there is an operation called Minite-Lube, which has done well. In Ontario there is a private concern from Kitchener which has established outlets in Kitchener and Guelph. Trade information indicates that this concern does not intend to take on the Toronto market. The trade is presently not aware of any private operation opening up in Toronto. However, this does not eliminate the future possibility.

Another area where competition could become important is in the technological development of synthetic oils and long-life filters. These two products have been around for 5-10 years now, but still command a price premium that does not make them any more economic than standard equipment. Combined with this is the fact that the consumer has not been convinced of the credibility of the manufacturer's claims. Even the manufacturers do not feel that these extended life components are applicable to older engines. When the average age of registered automobiles is 6.2 years it is observed that a large part of the auto market is not affected by these product innovations. The potential competition from this source is not felt to be significant.

4.0   Service, Products & Location

4.1   The Service

The service that will be provided is as follows:

- oil change
- oil filter change
- all point chassis lubrication – front suspension
    – drive train
- inspection and sale of air filters and crankcase filters
- fluid level checks – power steering
    – differential
    – automatic transmission
    – windshield washer fluid
- visual inspection of most frequently replaced auto accessories and note to customer if requested
    – V-belt inspection
    – leaking oil seals or gaskets
    – leaking shock absorbers
    – broken muffler clamps

There is nothing new or innovative about the service to be performed. The main selling feature, however, will be the way in which the service is performed. The key components are speed, efficiency, quality, and cleanliness. The outlet will be designed in such a way as to ensure that these components can be satisfied.

4.2   Design of Outlet

A schematic of the layout of the outlet is presented in Exhibit 3. Efficiency of traffic flow is obtained by adopting a one directional flow-through pattern. In order to minimize time, a pit configuration for under-car servicing has been selected rather than utilizing time-consuming hydraulic or electric lifts.

The bay is of sufficient length to accommodate two cars end to end. During peak periods this allows the work to be divided into two zones: one man for the pit operations and one man for the surface operations.

The pit is designed for optimum efficiency. All the necessary supplies are in the pit in order to allow the pit man to operate on two cars continuously without, having to exit the pit for supplies. An operating stock of oil filters is located in the pit. The draining of crankcase oil is facilitated by a moveable oil drain tray, which drains to an underground tank. The chassis lube is stored in bulk and

transferred to the pit by hydraulic lines. Small quantities of gear oil are stored in the pit also.

The surface area is also designed for maximum efficiency. Two common types of oil will be stored in underground tanks and pumped by overhead lines through metered nozzles to the car. Air filters and uncommon oils will be stored on display in the bay area. The above ground man will also be responsible for the billing function.

The customer waiting area is readily accessible to the service bay. The customer is encouraged to be with his car during the servicing in case an air filter or crankcase filter is in need of replacement. The dividing wall between the waiting area and the service bay is glass for the purpose of maximizing visibility and contact.

The traffic flow will be facilitated by the installation of power operated entrance and exit doors. This will provide additional time for the crew to prepare for the next set of cars.

Cleanliness will be incorporated into the total building design. The pit arrangement keeps much of the potential dirt out of the customers' view. The waiting area and washrooms will be well appointed and maintained clean.

The total capacity of the outlet on an hourly basis is twelve cars per hour. While this capacity will be required during peak periods (Saturday mornings) the average daily through put has been forecasted for operation at 60% of capacity.

4.3   Products and Costs

The products will be name brand products for purposes of establishing credibility and justifying price.

Arrangements will be made with Quaker State for the supply of bulk oils along with a supply of uncommon grades of oil for special cases. As volume picks up negotiations with a major supplier such as Gulf Oil will be attempted. The quoted cost of bulk oil is $0.68 per litre.

Purolator will be the supplier of oil, air, and crankcase filters. The average filter costs have been quoted as follows: oil filters, $1.54; air filters, $1.70; crankcase filters, $0.50.

A distributor in Brampton has been contacted for the supply of chassis lube, gear oil, oil additives and transmission fluids. The cost of chassis lube has been calculated at $0.10 per car.

5.0 Growth Strategy

Speedy-Lube will initially be set up as one outlet and will enter one market area at a time. Additional outlets will be set up as soon as the initial outlet has established its market. Expansion locations will be concentrated in Mississauga and Brampton. It is felt that there are at least three potential locations in Mississauga and two in Brampton.

The first several locations will be set up and operated by Ms. Hall until they become viable. The management of the outlet will then be transferred over to either a part owner or a franchisee. Ultimately, it is intended to establish a chain of outlets which will operate under a franchising agreement. The company will negotiate volume contracts with suppliers on behalf of all franchisees. The extent of the chain will depend upon the perceived market potential in other centres.

4.4 Pricing Strategy

The price of an oil and filter will be a fixed value, regardless of the auto, provided that the standard oils are used. The oil and filter will be sold as a set. No oil changes will be performed with changing the filter.

The air filters and crankcase filters will be priced separately.

The chassis lubrication will be priced separately and will be constant for all passenger cars. Trucks and 4-wheel drives will command a premium price because of extra points for lubrication. A chassis lube will not be performed without an oil change.

It is felt that the consumer will be prepared to pay a premium for the provision of quick service and financial security. Speedy-Lube will not be in price competition with the full-service centres that use the oil change, filters and lube as a "loss leader." Such instances are Family Auto at $6.91, Firestone at $7.95, and Gulf at $8.95.

Speedy-Lube will price an oil change, filter and chassis lubrication at $10.99. Terms of payment will be cash or either of the two major credit cards, Visa or MasterCard. If future oil contracts are made with the major oil companies then use of their credit system will be negotiated.

4.5 Location

The three main parameters to be considered in selecting a location for Speedy-Lube were:

1. nearness to a dense urban population with a significant percentage of apartment dwellers

2. high visibility for the purpose of capturing the passing trade – location on a main traffic artery was preferred

3. location in an area where people are going, nearness to a plaza, fast food outlets or other auto specialty stores were considered ideal

The natural area is considered to be the Dundas, Dixie, Hurontario area as indicated in Exhibit 4. The expected traffic flows in the area are indicated along with an indication of the location of competition and perceived assets.

6.0 Marketing

Since the Speedy-Lube operation is selling a service which is fixed at a location, it is necessary to adopt marketing techniques that will stimulate the consumer to come to the outlet.

Area advertising will be carried out by zone advertising with flyers that carry a discount coupon for a limited time period. Newspaper ads will be taken out in the two city newspapers, Mississauga News and Mississauga Times. Exchange arrangements will be made with nearby fast-food operations or shopping malls.

On-site advertising will be of prime importance. The outlet sign will advertise that Speedy-Lube is a "specialist in auto lubrication." The concept of ten minute service will also be visibly displayed.

The price will not be visibly displayed outside but will be well displayed inside the bay in full view of the customer. This is his reassurance that there are no hidden costs or extras.

7.0 Operation

7.1 Location

The outlet will be located on 500 m^2 of leased land in the Dundas, Hurontario area. The terms of the lease are for 20 years at an annual fee of $12,000.00 per year.

7.2 Building

A 140 m^2 outlet will be constructed on the site. Quotes for construction were obtained and the structure cost, complete with lighting and heating, is estimated at $50,000.00. Utility costs have been estimated at $1,000.00 per year. Insurance costs were quoted at $600.00 per year.

7.3 Equipment

A quote was obtained from Lincoln Engineering for the provision of specialty oil service equipment. The equipment and costs are listed below:

```
- bulk storage tank system        $ 3,500.00
- waste oil tank (installed)        3,000.00
- crankcase draining system         1,000.00
- chassis lubrication system        2,000.00
- oil dispersing system             2,000.00
- compressor installation           3,000.00
- displays and shelving             5,500.00
                                   $20,000.00
```

7.4 Inventory Control

Material suppliers have indicated that inventory orders can be placed on a weekly or biweekly basis. The required lead time for orders is approximately two days.

7.5 Hours of Operation and Labour

The outlet will have the following hours of operation:

```
Mon. & Wed.      10-7
Thurs. & Fri.    10-9
Sat.              8-6
                   56    hours of operation
```

8.0 Finance

The cost of developing the outlet and installing the necessary equipment is $75,000. An additional $10,000 has been allowed for working capital at start-up. The total financial requirement is $85,000.

The principal partners have a combined equity contribution of $20,000. The remaining financing requirement of $65,000 must be obtained from other financial interests. It is estimated that these funds can be attained at an interest cost of 15% and can be partially secured by the building.

9.0 Financial Analysis

Pro forma financial statements and cash flow forecasts are presented in Exhibits 5, 6, and 7. The assumptions made in the development of the statements are presented below:

- sales forecast - sales were estimated to increase gradually over two years and stabilize at a monthly volume of 1200 vehicles for remaining years
- cash sales are estimated as 80% of total sales
- the term of accounts receivable was estimated at 30 days
- accounts payable were assumed paid in 30 days
- a starting working capital of $10,000 cash was available
- inventories were ordered on a monthly basis
- the required bank line of credit was available
- during the first year the month end and cash balance was maintained at a value equal to the forecasted cash disbursement for the next month; during the second year the cash balance was maintained at $7,000

Exhibit 7 indicates that a bank line of credit of $23,000 will be required by the end of the first year. The chart indicates that the operation will begin to cover costs in the 14th month of operation at a monthly volume of 600 cars. It is estimated that an after-tax return on equity of 20% can be established at a monthly sales volume of 650 cars. This represents the unit operating at a 35% capacity factor.

The initial bank line of credit will be repaid within 22 months of operation. Partial repayment of the long term debt could be arranged during the third year of operation if necessary.

During the first several months the unit will be operated by Ms. Hall only. Only one car will be serviced at a time. As volume increases part-time labour will be employed to assist during peak periods. It is expected that student labour will be used primarily. With increased volume (16 cars/day) an additional full-time attendent will be hired. The intention is to find someone who would eventually operate the outlet so that Ms. Hall could concentrate on future expansion.

Exhibits 5 and 6 indicate that the firm will achieve an increase in total net worth during the third year of operation. A return on net worth of 91% is estimated for the third and successive years of operation.

10.0 Risk Analysis

The financial analysis indicates a gross margin on sales of 50%, which is in excess of the industry average for repair centres of 24.7%. The material and labour costs are considered to be accurate. It is felt that the pricing strategy could be optimistic. The price premium for service may be excessive.

This margin does, however, allow significant downward flexibility in pricing in the event that competing outlets establish in the same market area.

The forecasted time to develop the sales volume is felt to be highly conservative. United States studies indicate that sales volumes of 20 cars/day can be achieved in less than 6 months' operation. The forecasted peak volume represents operation at 62% of the outlet capacity and is felt to be realistic.

In the event that sales do not achieve the maximum predicted value of 1200 vehicles per month, it is calculated that the outlet can exist on 650 vehicles per month with a pay-back period for the bank line of credit of 5 years. This level of operation represents a 30% capacity factor and a market penetration of 17% of the potential market within a 5 km radius.

Assuming that the forecasts are realistic, the firm will be in an economically stable position for expansion shortly after 2 years of operation. If consumer reaction to the business concept is more positive than predicted, the timing of the expansion plan should be advanced in order to minimize the possibility of loss of other potential market areas to competition. The concept of outlet franchising or the attainment of additional venture capital in the form of equity will be considered in order to ensure growth.

References

1. Motor Equipment Manufacturer's Association
2. National Petroleum News 1990 March
3. National Petroleum News 1990 April
4. Motor Vehicle Manufacturer's Association 'Motor Vehicle Facts & Figures – 1989'
5. Statistics Canada Reports

Exhibit 1

Morton P. Adair

Home Address

2595 Hillsdale Street #503
Mississauga, Ontario
L5A 2G5
Telephone: (416) 555-1012

Personal Data

Date of Birth: 24 November, 1959, Winnipeg, Manitoba

Married Status: single

Education

Bachelor of Economics, University of Manitoba, 1982

Work Experience

From 1982 – present:

Public Chartered Accountant with Abercrombie and White.
Specific experience in management consulting with clients
during last two years. Currently a group manager.

References available upon request

Exhibit 1

Susan G. Hall

Home Address

29 Derek Drive
Mississauga, Ontario
L5A 3M9
Telephone: (416)555-3210

Personal Data

Date of Birth: 15 June, 1961, Winnipeg, Manitoba

Marital Status: married, no children

Education

B.Sc. in Mechanical Engineering, University of Manitoba, 1983

Work Experience

From 1983 – present: Engineer with Torotek

Experience in plant operations and maintenance,
system design, and testing.

Before June 1985: student

References available on request

Exhibit 6

Speedy-Lube

Pro forma Balance Sheet
As At End of Year

	Year 1	Year 2	Year 3
Assets			
Current:			
- Cash	$ 7 365	$ 12 885	$ 64 371
- Accounts Receivable	1 248	3 120	3 120
- Inventory	3 785	6 000	6 000
Total Current Assets	$ 12 398	$ 22 005	$ 73 491
Fixed:			
- Building	50 000	50 000	50 000
- Less Accumulated Dep.	3 000	6 000	9 000
- Equipment	20 000	20 000	20 000
- Less Accumulated Dep.	2 000	4 000	6 000
- Furniture + Fixtures	5 000	5 000	5 000
- Less Accumulated Dep.	1 000	2 000	3 000
Total Fixed Assets	$ 69 000	$ 63 000	$ 57 000
Total Assets	$ 81 398	$ 85 005	$ 130 491
Liabilities			
Current:			
- Accounts Payable	$ 5 305	$ 11 110	8 800
- Income Tax Payable	0	5 244	13 260
- Bank Line of Credit	23 173	0	0
Total Current Liabilities	$ 28 478	$ 16 354	$ 22 060
Long Term Debt	65 000	65 000	65 000
Total Liabilities	93 478	81 354	87 060
Equity			
Shareholders' Equity	20 000	20 000	20 000
Retained Earnings	(32 080)	(16 349)	23 431
Total Equity	$ (12 080)	$ 3 661	$ 43 431
Total Liabilities and Equity	$ 81 398	$ 85 005	$ 130 491

Exhibit 5

Speedy-Lube

Pro forma Income Statements
for
Beginning 36 Months of Operation

	1-12 Mths	13-24 Mths	25-36 Mths
Sales	$ 42 120	$ 135 096	$ 187 200
Cost of Goods Sold	17 578	51 961	72 000
Direct Labour	17 022	22 560	22 560
Gross Profit	$ 7 520	$ 60 575	$ 92 640
Expenses			
- overhead:			
lease	$ 12 000	$ 12 000	$ 12 000
utilities	1 000	1 000	1 000
insurance	600	600	600
supplies	5 000	5 000	5 000
- advertising	3 000	3 000	3 000
- general and administrative	2 400	2 400	2 400
- depreciation	6 000	6 000	6 000
Total Expenses	$ 30 000	$ 30 000	$ 30 000
Earnings Before Interest and Taxes	$(22 480)	$ 30 575	$ 62 640
Interest Expense	9 600	9 600	9 600
Earnings Before Taxes	$(32 080)	$ 20 975	$ 53 040
Taxes	0	5 244	13 260
Earnings After Interest and Taxes	$(32 080)	$ 15 731	$ 39 780

Glossary

A

Absenteeism
An employee staying away from work without an acceptable reason.

Acceptance company
One which buys sales contracts from retailers, thus financing consumer credit.

Accounting
Classifying, analyzing, and interpreting financial data.

Accounting cycle
The length of time for which a company summarizes its financial transactions. Can be a month, a quarter, a year.

Accounts payable
Money owed by a firm for goods and services purchased. A current liability.

Accounts receivable
Money owed by customers to a firm for goods and services provided. A current asset.

Accrual accounting
The accounting method whereby revenues and expenses are recorded when the agreement to pay is made, rather than when money is received or disbursed. In standard use.

Acid test
The ratio of current assets minus inventory to current liabilities. Measures ability to meet debt. Also called liquid or quick ratio.

Actuary
A professional statistician who calculates insurance risks.

Ad valorem
Latin for "according to value." An *ad valorem* tax constitutes a percentage of the value of the item taxed.

Advertising
Techniques and activities involved in conveying information about a product or service, in order to persuade people to buy it.

Agent
Someone who legally represents someone else, and can act in that person's name.

Amortize
To pay off a debt over a stated time, setting aside fixed sums for interest and principal at regular intervals. A mortgage is an amortized debt.

Annual report
A financial statement made at the end of a fiscal year, presenting the financial transactions of the past year and their results.

Annuity
A payment of money every year for a stated number of years, from invested capital.

Appreciate
To increase in value.

Arbitration
The resolution of a dispute between two parties by a supposedly impartial third party. Used in disputes between labour and management when direct negotiations fail. The arbitrator's decision may or may not be final, depending on previous agreements

or, in the case of public sector strikes, government decisions.

Arm's length

In business, an arm's length transaction is one between two parties, each of which has no interest in the financial success of the other and therefore acts from self-interest alone.

Arrears

Debts that are in arrears are overdue.

Assessment

The valuation of land and buildings for tax purposes.

Assets

Anything whose value can be expressed in money, which can be owned, and therefore can be sold.

Audit

A check of an organization's financial statements by someone whose independence of the organization and professional qualifications create faith in his or her judgement. An audit testifies to the honesty and accuracy of the organization's records.

Authorized capital

The number of shares a corporation may sell, and their par value.

B

Bad debt

A debt the creditor no longer expects to collect.

Bad faith

An unspoken attitude on the part of one or more parties to a negotiation, that there is no need to negotiate seriously or to live up to any agreement made.

Bailee

Someone who is given possession of goods for a particular purpose.

Bailor

The legal owner of goods which are handed over to a bailee for a stated time and purpose.

Bait and switch

A selling device. A "special" is advertised, but "sold out" when the customer appears. The advertiser hopes the customer will buy something else. Illegal.

Balance sheet

A statement of assets, liabilities, and equity as of the end of an accounting cycle. A balance sheet is a statement of a firm's financial position according to the system of double-entry bookkeeping: assets always equal liabilities plus equity.

Bank draft

A cheque drawn on a bank's own funds, in the bank's name. As good as money as far as the creditor is concerned.

Bank of Canada

The agency of the federal government through which it implements and manages its money policies. It lends money only to the chartered banks and to a few recognized dealers in government securities.

Bank rate

The rate of interest charged by the Bank of Canada to chartered banks, thus generally passed on to all financial institutions.

Bankruptcy

The financial and legal position of a person or corporation unable to pay debts. A legal bankrupt must transfer control of any remaining assets to a Trustee in Bankruptcy.

Bargaining unit

Any group of employees recognized as an acceptable party to labour-management negotiation under federal or provincial labour law.

Barter

The exchange of goods and services for other goods and services rather than for money.

Base mill price

Price at the place a product is made; thus, the price of goods calculated on the cost of materials, labour, and overhead, without shipping costs.

Base rate

The lowest wage agreed to in a labour contract.

Basing point pricing

Setting the price of a product as the sum of a fixed price plus the cost of shipping from one particular place, not necessarily the place of manufacture, to the customer.

Bearer bond

A bond not issued in the name of any person, and thus the apparent property of anyone possessing it.

Beneficiary

Anyone named as a recipient of money or other property in a will or insurance policy.

Betterment

Any expenditure improving or adding to the life of a fixed asset.

Bill

Either a statement by a seller of money owned by a buyer, *or* a statement admitting the existence of a debt, that can be used like cash.

Blind trust

A means of managing a person's assets without that person having to know what is going on. Assets are turned over to an agent, or trustee, who reports to the owner on their current value, but not on actual transactions to the people and institutions involved.

Board of Directors

The senior officers of an organization, who supervise management and create policy. In a corporation, these officers are elected by the shareholders.

Bond

A statement or certificate of indebtedness, along with interest, terms, and date of maturity or repayment, issued by a government or corporation.

Bondable

A person whose trustworthiness is guaranteed by another person's willingness to make a financial commitment on the faith of it is said to be bondable.

Bonded area (warehouse, etc.)

An area on the soil of any nation within which goods may be kept without payment of duty, sales, or excise tax. These taxes are payable only when the goods are moved from the bonded area.

Bonded carrier

A commercial shipper, such as a truck or airline, that may bring goods into the country with import requirements being met at the final destination rather than at the border.

Book value

The value of a corporation or asset according to the balance sheet. Net book value is total assets minus total liabilities. It is not necessarily the same as real or market value.

Break-even point

The point at which the income derived from a product equals the cost of making it.

Bridge financing

Short-term financing arranged to carry a firm until long-term financing is granted.

Broker
Anyone who brings a potential buyer and a potential seller together, in return for a fee or commission charged to one, the other, or both.

Budget
A plan for spending. The expression in money of an organization's goals and resources.

Buffer stock
Goods bought when the supply is large and the price is low, in anticipation of a time when supply will be small and price high.

Business cycle
A term used by economists and business analysts, to refer to the fluctuations in economic activity between prosperity and hardship. Such people do not agree on the nature and causes of business changes.

Business expense
An expense of producing and/or selling a product, which can be deducted from gross income to arrive at net income for taxation purposes.

Business GNP
The segment of Gross National Product, the dollar volume of total goods and services a country produces, produced by business corporations, excluding the segments produced by government and chartered banks.

C

Caisse populaire
See *Credit union*.

Call loan
A loan which the debtor may repay or the creditor demand payment on, at any time.

Capital
Anything that can be used to produce goods and services and thus to earn money. Capital funds are funds invested to make the earning of money possible.

Capital asset
A possession such as a machine, which can be used to make money and has a reasonably long life, usually over a year.

Capital cost
The cost of using a capital asset. A capital-cost allowance in tax calculations is the same as depreciation.

Capital gain
Increase in the value of an asset that produces a profit if the asset is sold.

Capital-intensive
An industry that requires large quantities of funds and equipment and relatively less human labour.

Capital investment
Money spent on income-producing assets.

Capital loss
Decrease in the value of an asset that produces a loss if the asset is sold.

Capital market
The sources to which a borrower can turn for investment funds.

Capital stock
The money invested in a business, through founder's equity and shares bought by shareholders.

Capital tax
Tax levied on money or assets owned, not income.

Capitalize
To put an asset to use as investment capital.

Carrying charge
The cost, in overhead, insurance, interest, etc., of owning inventory.

Cash-based accounting
The opposite of accrual accounting. Income and expenditures are recorded at the time they are received or paid. Not in common use.

Cash budget
A plan of money to be received and paid out for a particular period of time.

Cash flow
The income and outflow of funds available for regular operating costs. The cash-flow statement presents all receipts and expenditures for a stated period.

Casualty insurance
Insurance other than accident and life insurance: fire, theft, general liability.

Certification
Legal recognition of a union as the agent of a particular bargaining unit.

Certified cheque
A cheque bearing a guarantee from the signer's bank that funds have been reserved to cover it.

Chain store
A store, generally retail, that is one of a group of similar stores owned and managed by one owner.

Channel of distribution
The physical means of conveying goods from producer to wholesaler to retailer to final consumer.

Charter
In business, a piece of paper declaring that a firm is a legal corporation, with its declared purpose and authorized capital.

Chartered bank
In Canada, a bank created by its own Act of Parliament. The federal government defines and regulates its activities. Other financial institutions may provide banking services, but only chartered banks may borrow from the Bank of Canada.

Chattel
Portable personal property.

Chattel mortgage
A loan made on the security of a chattel. Such a loan must be registered with the provincial government.

Check-off
The deduction of union dues from employees' paycheques. Most union contracts now include compulsory check-off, i.e., dues are deducted whether the employee joins the union or not.

Class action
A lawsuit brought on behalf of or jointly by a group of people with a common grievance against one offender.

Closed shop
A bargaining unit for which the employer may hire only members of the union. The union is often the hiring agent.

Codicil
A change or addition to a will.

Collateral
An asset pledged to a creditor. If a debt is not paid the collateral belongs to the creditor.

Collective agreement
A contract between employees through their union, and employer, that states the rights and obligations of both sides.

Collective bargaining
Negotiation over a labour contract between union representatives as agents of the employees, and management representatives as agents of the owners.

Combination

An agreement, explicit or implicit, among businesses in one industry, to manipulate production and prices so as to reduce competition to their own greater profit. A criminal offence.

Commodities

In business, raw or semi-processed materials.

Common carrier

A shipping or transport business whose service is by law available to all customers at the same price.

Common law

The precedents established by previous court decisions, which have all the force of written statutes unless Parliament passes a law to the contrary.

Common market

A group of independent countries that have abolished import and export taxes among themselves.

Common stock

A share of ownership in the assets of a company, which carries with it the right to receive dividends *if* the company decides to pay them, to vote at annual meetings *if* the company permits. See also *Limited company*.

Company union

An organization that represents the employees of one company only, and has no connection to any wider group.

Compound interest

Interest payment in which the interest already paid is added to the principal amount in calculating the next payment. Thus, the amount paid increases every year, since the principal increases.

Concession

The right to exploit a resource, build a road, or sell a product, granted by the owner, usually a government.

Conciliation

An attempt to *arbitrate* which neither side has to accept. In union bargaining conciliation occurs before a dispute degenerates into a strike or lockout.

Conditional sale

A sale made but not final until certain acts or events take place.

Condominium

An apartment or rowhouse building in which individual residences are not rented but purchased and owned.

Conflict of interest

A personal benefit that is available through a decision to be made by someone in a position of trust, whose decisions are supposed to be directed to the benefit of an organization or of other people.

Consignment

Ownership of goods by someone to whom they have been delivered for sale, who does not pay the supplier until the goods have been sold.

Consortium

A group of companies involved in a joint venture to the benefit of all. Controlled by law in domestic ventures, encouraged for export schemes.

Conspicuous consumption

Spending for the sake of impressing others, not for the sake of the goods or services bought.

Consumer credit

Credit given to the final buyer of a product, in installment terms, credit cards, or loans.

Contract

An agreement, usually but not necessarily in writing, between two or more people, to provide a good or a service in return for payment of some kind, that constitutes a legal obligation.

Contribution

The portion of the selling price of a good that covers the vendor's fixed costs and provides the vendor's profit.

Control

The system for and activity of measuring and reporting the actual transactions of a business in comparison with its plans. These measurements and reports are generally financial.

Convenience goods

Goods like milk and bread, bought regularly with little attention to brand or, within reason, price.

Convertible

Changeable into something else. Convertible money is money that can be exchanged for the currency of another country. Convertible bonds can be exchanged for common stock in the same corporation; convertible stock can be exchanged for another kind of stock.

Conveyance

The making over of ownership from one person to another, legally registered in the appropriate government office.

Co-operative

A business that is joined, not owned. Its members are its employees, managers, and/or customers, who share its profits and losses.

Copyright

The legal registration and ownership of the product of a writer, painter, singer, musician, choreographer, photographer, or other original creator. The owner of a copyright owns all rights to use the copyrighted material. Copyright laws are subject to international treaties.

Corporation

See *Limited company*.

Cost accounting

The description and control of the cost of making or selling one unit of the product dealt in.

Cost centre

Any division of a business whose activities are unique within that business, and whose costs can be measured separately.

Cost control

The measurement and reporting of all funds paid out.

Cost-plus agreement

An agreement or contract to provide a good or service at a price consisting of the total cost of providing it plus an agreed amount over. The full sales price is thus unknown to both parties when the agreement is made.

Countervailing duties

Duties imposed to cancel the effect of subsidies by foreign governments on the prices of imported goods.

Covenant

An agreement that can be understood as a legally binding contract. Certain kinds of words and actions in certain circumstances are accepted in common law as an unspoken agreement or implied covenant.

Credit

(1) A loan, in the form of deferred payment on goods, or in cash, in return for a promise to pay. *Or,* (2) an entry on the right side of a balance sheet, indicating income or liabilities acquired. See *Double-entry bookkeeping*.

Credit bureau

A business whose product is

information on the credit transactions and relevant personal lives of individual people, which it sells.

Credit rating

The opinion of a financial institution as to whether a given person or business should be lent money.

Credit union

A co-operative bank. Takes deposits and makes loans in the usual way, but is owned by and run for the benefit of its members.

Creditor

One to whom money is owed.

Critical path

The name of a method of finding the most efficient way of doing something. The critical path is the *longest* sequence of activities involved, thus indicating the total time it will take.

Crop yield

The average quantity of a crop grown per hectare of land devoted to cultivating it.

Crown corporation

A business corporation owned by the public through the provincial or federal governments, or both together. Extremely important in the Canadian economy.

Crown land

Land owned publicly through federal or provincial governments. Includes all land with no private owner.

Cumulative quantity discount

A discount given as a percentage of selling price, which goes up as the quantity bought goes up.

Current assets

An asset that is used as a means of production or exchanged for cash in a given accounting cycle. Accounts receivable, inventory, and short-term notes are current assets.

Current debt

A debt or liability payable within a given accounting cycle. Interest on loans and suppliers' bills are current debt.

Current ratio

Current debt as a proportion of current assets. Measures ability to meet recurring operating costs.

Cyclical industry

An industry such as base metals in which demand for the product depends on expansion or contraction in the economy as a whole.

D

Damages

Money that must be paid to someone who has been legally injured.

Debenture

A bond, corporate or government, with no security but the credit rating of the issuer.

Debit

An entry on the left side of a balance sheet, indicating an asset or expense paid for. See *Double-entry bookkeeping*.

Debt

Money that must be paid back to someone else, usually with interest.

Debt capital

Capital invested in a company which does not belong to the company's owners. Usually consists of long-term loans and preferred shares.

Debt-to-equity ratio
The ratio of all long-term debt to owner's equity. Measures overall profitability.

Debtor
One who owes money to someone else.

Deductible
(1) In an insurance contract, the amount of the cost of damage insured against that the insured person must pay. (2) In income tax, an amount that can be subtracted from total income in calculating taxable income.

Deed
A piece of paper that states legal ownership of physical property and its transfer from one person to another.

Default
Failure to meet the terms of a contract.

Deficit
The amount by which money spent exceeds money earned.

Demand
The desire of a particular group of consumers for a particular product, as demonstrated by their buying it.

Demand curve
The rise and fall in demand for a product. The curve may be based on price, season, fashion, or any combination of influences.

Demand loan
A loan that must be repaid whenever the lender chooses.

Demand pull promotion
Advertising a product to its final consumers, to create a demand that will encourage wholesalers and retailers to buy it.

Demand push promotion
Advertising a product to wholesalers and retailers, so that they will put it on the consumer market.

Demurrage
Charges levied by shipping and transportation companies to cover delays that create unforeseen costs in handling and storage.

Depletion
The writing-off of the cost of a *wasting asset* (see). The depletion allowance is a tax deduction permitted on income from ownership of such assets.

Deposit
(1) Money in a bank account or (2) a down payment.

Depreciation
The writing-off of the cost of using a *fixed asset*. Buildings, machinery, equipment, etc. may all be depreciated in calculating taxable income.

Derived demand
Demand for a good or service that is the result of demand for another good or service to which it is necessary. The demand for upholstery fabric is derived from the demand for furniture.

Desk jobber
See *Drop-shipper*.

Dilution
The shrinking of a company's profit in relation to the number of its shares, created by increasing the number of shares.

Direct cost
An expense that is necessary for the actual making or selling of a product, such as raw materials and labour. Same as *Variable cost*.

Direct investment
Buying or trying to buy a controlling share in a company. Same as *equity investment*.

Direct sales
Sales made directly to the consumer, without any intermediary such as a retail merchant. Door-to-door or mail sales are direct sales.

Direct tax
A tax paid to the government by the person on whom it is levied. Income tax, personal and corporate, is a direct tax.

Discharged bankrupt
One who has been declared legally bankrupt, and thus has no liability to debtors beyond what the *trustee in bankruptcy* declares.

Disclosure
The public statement of an individual's or a firm's financial standing, interests, and in the case of a firm, its directors, as required by law.

Discounting
Lowering a price in return for buying a large volume of goods, paying promptly, etc.

Discretionary income
The amount of money people have to spend after they have purchased the basic necessities of food, shelter, and clothing.

Disposable income
The amount of money people have to spend after they have paid their taxes and compulsory social insurance premiums.

Distressed inventory
Damaged inventory, to be discounted or written off.

Distribution system
The means and methods, physical and financial, of moving goods and services from producers to consumers.

Dividend
Money paid by a corporation to its shareholders. The shareholders' return on investment.

Double-entry bookkeeping
A method of keeping track of the financial state of an organization, which works through recording every transaction twice, as a debit (an asset given up) and as a balancing credit (an asset acquired). When the books are properly kept, they "balance": total credits equal total debits.

Drop-shipper
An agent wholesaler, who takes orders for a manufacturer. The manufacturer invoices the drop-shipper but delivers to the final customer.

Dumping
The selling of goods on the international market for less than their price on the domestic market.

Durable goods
Goods expected to last more than three years.

E

Earning power
The capacity of a *capital asset* to produce profit.

Earnings statement
A financial statement, usually part of an *annual report*, showing money taken in, its sources, and how it has been spent. The bottom line is the "net profit."

Easement
Rights in the use of land owned by someone else.

Economic life
Same as *Useful life.*

Employment standards
Labour laws that establish minimum wages, hours, overtime pay, childbirth leave, paid vacations, etc.

Energy efficiency
The fuel required to run a machine, in relation to others with the same purpose.

Entrepreneur
One who, insofar as this is possible in a human society, sets out to make a living independently of any existing economic institution. Sometimes used of those who seek to enlarge existing businesses.

Equity
Capital that constitutes the owner's share of a business.

Equity base
The amount of capital put into a firm that the firm owns, as opposed to capital put in through debt that must be repaid with interest.

Equity investment
The exchange of funds for a share of ownership.

Escrow
The deferment of an obligation to pay or right of ownership for a stated time or until stated conditions are met.

Estate
An individual's property after all debts are paid.

Estate freezing
The withholding of an estate from its apparent owners until outstanding debts are paid or legal ownership is decided.

Excise tax
A tax on specific goods or services, such as alcohol or tobacco.

Executor
A person appointed in a will to see that its terms are carried out.

F

FIFO
First In, First Out. A method of

inventory accounting that assumes that the first goods to enter inventory are the first to be sold.

F.O.B.
Free on Board. Goods delivered to the buyer without delivery charges.

Factoring
The sale of accounts receivable, at less than their full paper value, to a firm or bank which makes its profit by collecting at full value.

Failure
Going out of business because the business cannot be run at a profit. Not always equivalent to bankruptcy.

Fair value
The price a commodity can command on a "free" market, one in which there is no compulsion on buyer or seller to accept or reject a certain amount.

Feasibility study
The study of a project to see if it is technically possible and commercially profitable.

Featherbedding
Deliberately increasing the number of jobs in a project or organization, beyond what the work itself calls for.

Fiduciary
A note, contract, or other guarantee of value that is based on trust. Paper money like the Canadian dollar, issued by a government that will not exchange it for gold or any object of absolute value, is a fiduciary note. Also, one who manages property in trust for someone else, a trustee.

Financing mix
The particular combination of sources a firm chooses for the capital it needs—equity investment, debt, credit, mortgages, sale of stock, etc.

Fire-fighting
Dealing with the day-to-day problems and crises of running a business. Can get in the way of planning and control.

First mortgage
See *Mortgage*.

Fiscal year
An accounting cycle of twelve months. Usually Jan. 1 to Dec. 31; the Government uses April 1 to March 31.

Fixed assets
Permanent or long-lived possessions of a firm—land, building, machinery—used for production.

Fixed costs
The invariable costs of a business, costs such as rent, wages, and property tax, that are the same whatever the level of production or sales. Same as *Overhead*.

Fixed interest
Interest payments that remain constant despite changes in the profitability of the invested capital, or in the official prime interest rate.

Fixed pricing
Selling an article for a particular price regardless of changes in vendor's costs or in the market.

Fixed shift
In a business which has several shifts of workers, having the same people work the same shift permanently.

Floating rate
A floating rate, in currency exchange, interest, etc., is one set in response to changing external forces in the market. The vendor or creditor is not bound to any particular rate.

Footing
In accounting, adding a column of figures.

Foreclose
To sell or cause to be sold a property when the owner fails to meet mortgage, tax, or other debt payment on it. Must be approved by the courts.

Franchise
The right to use and/or sell a product, trademark, technique, or all three, sold by the owner to an approved buyer, usually in a stated area.

Fraudulent conveyance
A transfer of ownership from one person to another for the purpose of cheating creditors. A criminal offence.

Free market
A market in which the flow of goods and services is not impeded by anything other than natural, impersonal forces, and prices are set by supply and demand combined with the independent motives of equal individuals. A model for economic speculation; has never existed in the real world.

Freight forwarder
An export agent who moves goods through customs.

Frozen asset
An asset that cannot be used or sold, usually by court or government decision pending outcome of a dispute over ownership or indebtedness.

Functional organization
A management hierarchy in which each area, such as production, advertising, etc. is run by a specialist, so that subordinates may take orders from several superiors.

Funded debt
Debt incurred through the sale of securities, that must be repaid over the next year.

Futures

Commodities bought and sold before delivery is expected or even possible. A grain crop, for example, may be sold before the seed has sprouted. Futures trading is a form of speculation that makes funds available for production but may distort the market and/or divert profits from primary producers.

G

Garnishee

To deduct money from a debtor's wages to pay a creditor. The creditor obtains a court order directing the employer to make the deduction and pay the creditor.

Geographic pricing

Charging a selling price for the same product that varies according to where it is actually sold.

Go public

The action of a private corporation in offering its shares for general sale.

Good faith

An unspoken attitude, in parties to a deal or negotiation, of honesty and serious intention.

Goodwill

The earning power of a business that lies in its reputation and skill and thus on the value of its name or trademark. Accounting formulas exist to define it as a portion of a firm's total money value.

Grace

A short time, usually a few days, after the date on which a debt is actually due, in which payment can be made without penalty.

Gross profit

Total sales minus direct costs, but including indirect costs—taxes, overhead, etc.

Gross sales

Total sales. Income before deducting cost of production, overhead, or taxes.

Guarantor

A third party to a credit transaction. One who promises to pay a creditor if a debtor fails to pay back a loan.

H

Holding company

A company which exists to buy and own a majority of shares in other companies, and thus to control them.

Hypothec

A security advanced by a debtor on property, without transfer of title to the creditor, as in a mortgage.

I

Incentive

An offer or promise of something meant to persuade people to do something. The government uses the tax system to persuade business to invest within Canada, or in research and development.

Income averaging

A way of reducing income tax, used by people whose earnings tend to fluctuate from year to year. Rather than pay extraordinary tax in a prosperous year and little or none in the next bad year, it is possible to buy an annuity and pay tax only on the money paid out each year by the annuity.

Income statement

A statement of earnings, from all sources, and expenditures. The bottom line of an income statement is "net profit."

Incorporation

The setting up of a *limited company*.

Done through government charter. See also *Limited liability*.

Increment
An increase.

Indemnity
Money paid for *damages*.

Independent union
A union that has organized across company lines but is not a member of any organization or congress of unions.

Indirect cost
Overhead. Cost of doing business which cannot be identified with any one specific activity.

Industrial democracy
A very vague term, referring to employees' participation in the management of a business.

Industrial goods
Goods bought by manufacturers to produce other goods.

Industrial union
A union of all workers in an industry, regardless of the kind of job they have.

Inflation
A rise in the price of all products and services sustained over a significant length of time.

Insolvency
Lack of ready cash to pay bills as they come due. Not the same as *Bankruptcy*, since the firm may have reserve assets which it cannot or should not turn into cash.

Insurance
A contract entered into for protection against risk on one side, and profit on the other.

Intangible asset
Assets such as trade names or patent rights which are not physical objects or sums of money.

Intellectual property
Knowledge and information which can be legally owned, as defined by laws governing copyright, trademarks, patents, royalty obligations, etc.

Interest
The set percentage of a principal amount of a loan which must be paid along with the principal. Rent on the use of money.

Interim
In the meantime, not final. A report issued partway through an *accounting cycle*.

Inventory
The supply of goods, whether materials, parts, or finished products, owned by a firm at any one time, and its total value.

Inventory control
Planning, identifying, and reporting on the physical items held in inventory at any one time, and the amount of money involved.

Inventory financing
Obtaining funds on the future value of inventory, or by selling it in advance.

Inventory shrinkage
Loss in the value of inventory due to spoilage, damage, or theft.

Inventory turnover
See *Turnover*.

Invested capital
Total *equity* plus long-term debt, minus current *liabilities*.

J

Job description
The actual work done by a person holding this job, and the authority and responsibility involved.

Job evaluation
An examination of the work involved in a job to determine a fair wage for it.

Jobber
A small wholesaler, one who buys from producers and large wholesalers and sells to small retailers.

Joint account
A bank account containing funds that are the property of two or more owners, both or all of whom may make deposits and withdrawals, and are individually liable for overdrafts.

Joint venture
A partnership formed for the sake of one project only. Joint ventures may be undertaken by two or more companies, or by the government and private companies.

L

LIFO
Last In, First Out. A method of inventory accounting that assumes that the last or most recent goods to be put into inventory are the first or quickest to be sold.

Labour council
A local or regional association of union representatives.

Labour-intensive
An industry that requires large numbers of employees and relatively less *capital* funds and equipment.

Laid-down cost
Invoice cost of supplies, plus custom, excise, transport and delivery charge.

Laissez-faire
Let alone, let be. Refers to the notion that the ungoverned operation of selfishness produces the most prosperous economy.

Land assembly
The buying up and consolidating of neighbouring pieces of land, usually for some large commercial project.

Land registry
A government office where titles of ownership of all land and buildings in the province are recorded.

Last resort
The final appeal when all else fails. The lender of last resort is the lender a borrower tries after being turned down by all possible lenders elsewhere. In Canada, the lender and employer of last resort is the federal government.

Laundered money
The profits of criminal activity, made to appear legitimate.

Layoff
Depriving workers of their jobs, not through any fault of their own but because the employer cannot give them profitable work.

Lead time
The time between the making of a decision to act and the appearance of results of the action—thus, the time between deciding to manufacture a product and the appearance of the first profits from it.

Lease financing
A method of putting available funds to best use by leasing *capital assets* rather than buying them outright. A firm will thus preserve *working capital*, and frequently gain tax advantages.

Leaseback
The sale of a capital asset on condition that the vendor may then lease it from the buyer. Provides and preserves *working capital*.

Leasing
A contract in which the owner of a piece of property gives the exclusive

use of it to someone else, in exchange for a stated sum of money, for the duration of a stated time.

Ledger

A book of accounts. See *Double-entry bookkeeping; T-Account.*

Letter of credit

A bank document addressed to branches or foreign associates, stating that the person named may be paid a stated amount, for which the issuing bank will be responsible.

Letter of intent

A written proposal or statement indicating a serious interest in a business arrangement. It does not constitute a binding contract, but is a stage towards one.

Letters patent

Charter, documents issued by the government making a new corporation legitimate.

Leverage

The difference between the profit that can be made on borrowed money and the cost of using it—i.e., the interest payments. Relying on the leverage available in a particular market for a particular product is a deliberate calculated risk.

Liabilities

All debts, of any kind, including interest payments, taxes, etc. Total *assets* minus total liability equals owners' *equity.*

Lien

The claim of a creditor on some particular piece of property belonging to a debtor. If a debt is unpaid, the creditor may have the right to seize the property, though it may not be sold by either party without a court decision.

Limited company

A business firm incorporated as a person in law, with limited liability.

Limited liability

The limitation of the debt of shareholders in an incorporated company to the amount of their own investment. Since an incorporated company is a legal person in its own right, it is responsible for its own debt, and can be sued in court. But shareholders cannot be sued for the debt of the company, though they may lose their own investment if it fails.

Line and staff organization

Combines *line* and *functional organizations.* Used in organizations large enough to divide primary function (producing the product) from *planning and control.*

Line of credit

A bank's stated willingness to lend up to a certain amount of money to a particular person.

Line organization

A hierarchy of authority in which each officer is responsible for all those below and responsible to the officer immediately above. Each person reports to and takes orders from one person only.

Liquid assets

Cash on hand and anything that can easily and quickly be turned into cash.

Liquidation

Turning assets into cash. May refer to winding up a business by selling off all its assets.

Liquidity

The ability of a firm to muster sufficient *liquid assets* to handle *current debt.*

Listed stock

Stock traded on a stock exchange; therefore, stock that has met an exchange's standards of an honest risk.

Lockout
The reverse of a strike. An employer's refusal to let employees work and thus earn their pay.

Long-term assets
Same as *Fixed assets*.

Long-term financing
Loans or other credit on which the principal does not have to be repaid for at least ten years.

Loss leader
An item sold at a loss in order to attract buyers who will then buy other items as well. The capacity of certain large retail chains such as supermarkets to sell at a loss for the sake of eventual profit gives them an advantage over small independent retailers.

Lump sum
A single large amount, paid all at once.

M

Make-work
A job created for the sake of giving someone work, not for the sake of the work done.

Management by exception
An approach to management through budget control: as long as sales and spending are within the range forecast in the budget, do nothing.

Management by objectives
An approach to management through individual ambitions and involvement, on the theory that people prefer to be interested in what they are doing. The goals of each job are defined by employee and supervisor; the company's goals are met through the sum of all the goals within it.

Management information
The accounting, marketing, supply, labour, and all other facts that influence the fate of a business.

Manifest
The particular items carried in a shipping vehicle or stored in a warehouse.

Margin of dumping
The difference between the domestic market value and the export price. Taxed in Canada on imported goods which threaten Canadian industry.

Marginal cost
The cost per unit of increasing the rate of production.

Market economy
A situation in which government interferes as little as possible in economic life, and prices and incomes are dictated by impersonal laws of supply and demand. Has never existed. See *Mixed economy*.

Market research
The study and prediction of what sells, what will sell, where, and why.

Market value
The price a product or service brings at the moment.

Marketing board
In Canada, a group given power by the government to regulate production, distribution, and prices of any one product.

Marketing concept
The idea that since a business exists to make profit it should be consciously organized for the sake of achieving the most profitable (which is not necessarily the highest) level of sales.

Marketing mix
The particular combination of design, price, distribution, and advertising strategies chosen to profit from a given product.

Markup

The amount a vendor adds to the price of a product. The difference between what the buyer pays and its cost to the vendor. Not the same as net profit, since a small markup on a large quantity of goods sold may produce more profit than a large markup on a small quantity of goods sold.

Medium-term financing

Loans or other credit on which the principal does not have to be repaid for three to five years.

Merchant bank

A bank that exists to finance and invest in business ventures, and does not deal with the general public. Very uncommon in Canada, although foreign merchant bankers have large interests here.

Merger

The joining of two companies to make one. Involves combinations of assets, or absorptions of the assets of one company into the other.

Merit pay

Pay given for doing the job well, as opposed to pay given for doing the job satisfactorily or for seniority.

Mill rate

The percentage of each thousand dollars of assessed value by which property tax rates are set.

Minimum wage

The smallest hourly amount that the law permits an employer to pay an employee.

Misleading advertising

Advertising that lies, implicitly or explicitly, about the price, quality, or use of a product. Illegal.

Mixed economy

The economic situation of every advanced non-Communist country. Government and privately owned

business share economic power; government assumes the duty of defending the general good against private interests when the two are seen to clash.

Money market

The sources of short-term credit and securities. An organized, distinct industry, whose members are banks and other financial institutions, governments, and the *Bank of Canada*.

Money supply

The sum of money available for investment within an entire economy at any one time.

Monopoly

The domination of the entire market for a product by one supplier.

Mortgage

A loan granted on the security of land or buildings. The lender assumes ownership, though not possession, until the loan is paid off, and can, with legal permission, sell the land or other property if the borrower does not pay. The same property can be used more than once in this way, the holder of the first mortgage having a claim that takes precedence over the claim of the holder of the second mortgage.

Mortmain

Ownership that cannot be transferred or sold. Institutions such as churches may own land in this manner.

Mutual agency

A legal relationship in which two people may act for one another. A partnership is a mutual agency.

Mutual fund

A company that exists to invest in other companies. As distinct from a *holding company*, its primary purpose is not to take controlling interest in other companies, but to invest its equity to the benefit of its shareholders.

N

Nationalize

The transfer of ownership of a corporation from private persons to the government, because the government has decided such a transfer would be to the public good, not because the owners want to sell.

Near bank

A *credit union*, caisse populaire, or trust company. These institutions may not borrow from the *Bank of Canada*, though they perform the usual financial services of all banks.

Negotiable

Usable as money. A negotiable *security* that can be signed over by the owner to someone else, who can then turn it into cash.

Net profit

The amount remaining after all costs and taxes have been deducted.

Net worth

The *assets* remaining after deduction of total *liabilities*.

Normal value

Domestic price; the market price of goods in the country in which they were made.

Notary

An official legally authorized to administer oaths, certify that documents are valid, etc.

Note

A paper promising to supply funds. May or may not be negotiable.

O

Open market

A market in which sellers are free to set their own prices and buyers free to choose when they will spend. Does not exist.

Open shop

A bargaining unit, within a recognized union, in which newcomers may choose whether or not to join the union.

Operating budget

The financial plan that defines and allocates *working capital*, the revenues and expenditures of doing business from day to day.

Operating expense

Any part of the cost of producing a product or service.

Option

The right to buy a property, within a certain time. The potential buyer must pay for this right, but the owner of the property may not sell to anyone else until the agreed-upon time is past.

Outstanding shares

The number of shares in a company presently owned by the public.

Overdraft

A debt to the bank incurred by withdrawing more money from an account than it holds.

Overhead

The expenses – rent, heat, property tax, etc. – of keeping a business open. Same as *Fixed costs*.

Over-the-counter securities

Bonds and shares sold by private negotiations, rather than through stock exchanges.

Overtime
Hours worked over the weekly number agreed upon in a labour contract as set by law.

P

Paper loss
A loss that has not actually been paid for, because it is the result of a decline in market value of an asset that is still owned.

Paper profit
A profit that is not actually in the hand, because it is the result of an increase in the market value of an asset that has not yet been sold.

Partnership
A legal arrangement in which the ownership, profit, and liabilities of a business are shared between two or more people.

Par-value stock
Stock with its value printed on the certificate. This is not necessarily the market value of the stock.

Patent
The legal possession of an original invention and the right to use it.

Penetration pricing
Deliberately setting the selling price of a new item low, so that it will be able to enter a market dominated by better known brands.

Pension plan
An organized savings fund out of which an annual retirement income will be paid. A contributory plan is one to which the employer contributes on behalf of the employee, in addition to the employee's own contribution.

Personal selling
Face-to-face selling.

Piecework
Work for money paid by the quantity produced, not by the hours worked.

Planning
Setting goals, defining means of reaching them, and foreseeing obstacles.

Posting
In accounting, the transfer of an entry from one record to another.

Power of attorney
A document giving one person the power to act on behalf of or in the name of another.

Predatory pricing
Setting the price of an item so as to drive competitors out of the market. A criminal offence.

Preferred creditor
A creditor who must be paid first, in case of death, bankruptcy, or termination of a business.

Preferred stock
A stock or share bearing a constant rate of return.

Price cutting
Charging less to increase or maintain sales. If done to drive out competition, illegal.

Price-fixing
Collusion among businesses to refrain from competition in order to keep prices up. Illegal.

Price-skimming
Charging a high price for a new product for which there is no competition, to take advantage of a demand which cannot be met elsewhere.

Price spread

The difference between selling price and cost of production.

Price support

Assistance to an industry from the government to maintain the price of a product at a minimum level.

Price war

Reduction of prices by competing firms reacting to one another's actions in turn. Reductions are almost always temporary.

Prima facie

At first glance.

Primary industry

An industry that extracts or performs the first step in processing raw materials.

Prime rate

The interest charged by chartered banks on corporate loans. Ultimately determined through the *Bank of Canada*.

Private company

A limited company whose shares are not traded to the general public, and cannot be sold at all without permission of the board of directors. There are no more than fifty shareholders.

Private label

A label or brand name put on by the retailer, under agreement with the producer. Commonly used in food retailing.

Private sector

The economic institutions controlled by and for private individuals.

Pro forma **statement**

A financial statement that projects costs and profits from present assets and plans.

Producer goods

Goods used to make other goods.

Product differentiation

Details of design, promotion, and pricing planned to distinguish competing products in the minds of consumers.

Product life-cycle

The curve of profit in relation to costs and sales described by every product in the time between entering and leaving the market.

Product line

The particular combination of goods and services a business offers on the market.

Product mix

The combination of products that a business has to offer at any one time.

Production plan

The quantity of goods a business intends to produce in a given period of time, together with its sources of supplies, projected costs, and projected sales.

Productivity

The capacity of a machine, business, industry, nation, or human being to produce goods and services.

Profit

The sum of money shown on a financial statement after all costs of making revenue have been deducted from revenue.

Profit and Loss Statement

A financial statement showing sources and amounts of revenue, and sources and amounts of expenditure.

Profit centre

Any division of a business whose activities are unique within the business, and which brings in revenue that can be measured separately from revenue brought in by other divisions or by the business as a whole.

Profit margin
The figure that is the result of calculating *net profit* as a percentage of *gross sales*. Useful as a way of comparing one firm's performance against another's.

Profit-sharing
The paying, in cash or stock, of a proportion of business profits to employees as part of total wages.

Progressive tax
A tax in which those who have more pay more in proportion.

Project financing
Loans and credit organized for a particular business project.

Promissory note
An I.O.U. A promise to pay a specified sum at a specified time and rate of interest, signed by the debtor.

Promotion mix
The combination of types of advertising, advertising media, and means of selling chosen for a particular product.

Property tax
A tax levied on land and buildings at a percentage of their value as established by the taxing authority, usually a municipal government.

Prospectus
A set of financial and other statements concerning the nature, organization, legal and financial status, ownership, and management of a business.

Proxy
A declaration signed by a voter that permits another person to vote in his or her place.

Psychological pricing
Setting the price of an item so as to profit from the buyer's subjective attitudes to it. A car, for example, may fetch a higher than rational price if it appeals to the buyer's desire for prestige and luxury to pay such a price.

Public company
A company whose shares are for general sale on a stock exchange.

Public ownership
The ownership of an organization producing goods and services by a government in the name of its citizens.

Public relations
The various activities of an organization that are meant to make the organization known and approved of.

Public sector
All economic institutions that are ultimately run by and through government—utilities, transport and roads, hospitals, schools, housing, etc.

Public warehouse
A warehouse where anyone may have goods stored.

Publicity
Any news, activity, or advertising that makes a product or the company making or selling it generally known.

Pyramid sales
A sales device in which sales people are encouraged or required to make money by bringing in other sales people, as well as or in place of selling a product. Usually fraudulent.

Q

Quantity discount
A reduction of the selling price of an item made if more than a certain number are bought. Legal only if available equally to all customers.

Quick ratio
See *Acid test*.

R

Rack jobber
A wholesaler who sells discounted goods on consignment to a retailer.

Ratio analysis
The study of a business's or industry's financial position through various proportions of income to assets and to spending.

Real profit
The true purchasing power of the money made from a business, allowing for inflation as well as all costs.

Real wages
The true purchasing power of money earned, allowing for inflation and local living expenses.

Realization
In accounting, the recording of revenue only after it is earned.

Rebate
A refund, paid for buying a certain quantity, paying before a certain date, etc. Illegal if not offered equally to all customers.

Recapture
An amount previously deducted from taxable income as a *capital-cost* allowance taken back into income after the sale of an asset.

Receivership
The control of a business and its assets by someone other than the owner until debts are paid or the business is wound up.

Regressive tax
A tax in which those who have less, pay as much as or more, in proportion to their income, than those who have more.

Remainder
Stock sold off at a greatly reduced price, to get rid of a surplus.

Renewable resource
Live natural resources which replace themselves—fish, forests, fur-bearing animals.

Resale price maintenance
The dictation of retail prices by the supplier. Illegal.

Research and development
Projects meant to discover, improve, and establish the profit to be made through new products and techniques.

Responsibility accounting
Checking an organization's spending by comparing actual costs to budgeted costs down to the lowest unit in the organization that is responsible for spending or earning.

Retained earnings
The profits that are not spent or divided among the owners but reinvested in the business.

Return on investment
The percentage of an investment that it produces as profit.

Revolving credit
Credit given up to a regular stated amount as long as regular minimum payments are made.

Rigged bid
A bid on a project that is the result of conspiracy among the contractors bidding, to allocate the job to one of themselves and fix the price. Illegal.

Right-to-work
Laws which make the *union shop* illegal or impossible.

Rollover
Any financial transaction that has no tax consequences; one so conducted that it makes no difference to income.

Royalties
Payments made for the use of property owned by someone else.

S

Seasonal credit
Credit given to tide a business over a time of year in which it cannot take in enough revenue to keep going.

Seasonality
The dependency of a business or industry on conditions at a certain time of year.

Secondary industry
An industry that manufactures goods from materials supplied by primary industry.

Secured loan
A loan of which the repayment is guaranteed by *Collateral*.

Security
(1) An income-producing easily liquifiable asset, such as stocks and bonds, or (2) an *asset* used as *collateral*.

Seed money
Money provided to get a project started.

Seniority
The length of time an employee has worked for a firm.

Service life
The period in which a *fixed asset* produces profitable income.

Shop steward
The union representative for a certain division within a unionized organization, chosen by the workers.

Shopping goods
Goods bought relatively infrequently and hence with relatively more attention to price and quality. Meat, fruit, clothing.

Short-term credit
Debts to be repaid in a year or less.

Sinking fund
Money reserved from profits, usually invested in short-term *securities*, for paying off long-term debts or for foreseen large *capital costs*.

Social cost
The price of individual actions for which the public as a whole must pay—crime, pollution, etc.

Social overhead
The *capital assets* provided by public money by which business profits— roads, railroads, airlines, schools, water, etc.

Sole proprietorship
An unincorporated business, the assets of which are the property of one person, who is personally liable for all of its debts.

Solvency
The capacity to meet current debt; a surplus of *current* or *liquid assets* over current liabilities.

Span of control
The number of workers under a supervisor, and the work done; thus, the extent of the supervisor's authority.

Specialty goods
Goods bought infrequently, to satisfy an individual taste or desire, hence with less attention to price than to quality and image.

Speculation
Buying a commodity in the hope that it can be sold again fairly quickly at a profit.

Split shift
Working hours divided into two or more separate segments every day.

Stale-dated cheques
An uncashed cheque more than six months old. No Canadian bank will cash such a cheque.

Startup
The beginning of a business, including planning, forecasting, and initial investment.

Statement of change in financial position
A financial change that shows any increases or losses in capital funds owned by the firm from one year to the next.

Stock
A share of ownership in an incorporated business.

Strike vote
A vote, held a required time before a strike can be called, among union members giving their bargaining committee the right to call a strike.

Subsidiary
A company that is the property of another company.

Sweat shop
Any business that makes a policy of paying the lowest possible wage for the most possible work under the cheapest, from the employer's point of view, possible conditions.

Sweetheart contract
An agreement made between an employer and a corrupt union representative, that ignores the interests of the two parties to the deal, or any business agreement that puts the private interests of the negotiators above the interests of the people or organizations they are supposed to represent.

Syndicated loan
A loan made by a group of investors.

T

T-Account
The basic device of *double-entry bookkeeping* and modern accounting. All *debits* are listed on one side, all *credits* on the other. They equal one another if the books are properly kept.

Takeover
The buying of a controlling number of shares in a company.

Tangible assets
Land, machinery, buildings, materials—*capital assets* that are physical objects.

Tangible net worth
The value of all tangible assets after deducting *liabilities* and *depreciation*.

Tariffs
A tax levied on imports.

Tax base
The amount of money which is taxed under any particular law. Property tax, for example, is levied on the current assessed value of property owned, income tax on yearly income after deductions, sales tax on price.

Tax credit
An amount that can be deducted from income tax (not from taxable income).

Tax deduction
An amount that can be deducted from total income to arrive at taxable income.

Tax deferral
The postponement of paying a tax, permitted under certain conditions.

Term loan
A loan that need not be repaid in full until after a certain period of time.

Third-party liability
Insurance against damages claimed by another person for events due to negligence or other acts for which the insured person is legally responsible.

Title
Formal evidence of ownership.

Trade credit
Credit given by a manufacturer or

supplier to other businesses in the same industry.

Trade discount
A reduction of prices given by a manufacturer or supplier to other businesses in the same industry.

Trademark
A name, symbol, or other mark that identifies a product to customers, and is the legal product of its manufacturers or inventors.

Trading up (down)
Changing a product line to suit a price and quality range above or below the market now being exploited.

Trial balance
Adding all *credits* and all *debits* to see if the two sums are equal. A device used to check the accuracy of a company's books.

Truck jobber
A wholesaler who operates from a truck, going directly to customers with the goods for sale.

Trust
Money or property held by one person in the name of and for the benefit of another.

Trustee in bankruptcy
An official appointed by the courts to administer the assets of a declared bankrupt, and to see that creditors are paid.

Turn-key operation
A project, such as setting up a business, or an office, in which all work is done by a contractor and handed over in working order to the owner.

Turnover
The number of times a given item is replaced in *inventory* in a determined *accounting cycle*.

Tying arrangement
One in which a purchaser is not permitted to buy a product unless another is bought at the same time. Illegal.

U

Underwriter
One who takes responsibility for the financial risk of issuing new *securities*, by buying them for resale.

Unearned increment
An increase in the value of an asset that is not caused by anything the owner has done.

Uniform delivered pricing
The seller assumes all responsibility for delivery to any buyer; a single price includes all delivery charges. Also called postage stamp pricing.

Union shop
A *bargaining unit* in which all new employees must join the union after a certain time. Almost universal in union contracts in Canada.

Unit cost
The cost of producing one item or example of a product. Found by dividing total cost by number of units made.

Unit price
The price of an item per unit actually sold. Food retailing also prices items per unit of the weight by which they are sold.

Unsecured creditor
Someone who has lent money for no *collateral*. Last to be paid, if paid at all, in *bankruptcy*.

Useful life
The period of time in which a *capital asset* can be expected to produce profit.

Uttering
Using a forged document for one's own profit while knowing that it is forged.

V

Variable cost
A cost that rises and falls according to the level of production or sales. Costs of materials, supplies, and labour, for example, may vary.

Variable pricing
Letting the price of an item go up or down depending on production costs.

Venture capital
Investment capital made available to new businesses. More expensive, since the higher risk commands higher rates of return.

Vertical integration
The extension of a company's control over suppliers, distributors, and retailers. These independent businesses are absorbed by one central company to control costs and competition.

Volume discount
See *Quantity discount*.

W

Warranty
A promise to the buyer that the product sold is of good quality, and that if not, certain repairs and replacements will be made.

Wasting asset
An asset, such as a natural resource, which is lost by being exploited. A non-renewable asset.

Watered stock
See *Dilution*.

Wholesaler
One who buys products from producers for sale to retailers.

Wildcat strike
A strike held by the workers, without a formal strike vote and union approval and thus illegal.

Windfall profit
Profit that is completely unexpected and uncontrollable, not due to anything the owner has done or planned.

Winding up
The legal procedures of closing down a *limited company*.

Work-to-rule
A form of protest used by unionized workers, in which they do exactly what the contract says they must do, and no more, exactly as the contract says they must do it, and in no other way.

Working capital
What is left after subtracting total current liabilities from total *current assets*. The money available to run the business with.

Write down
Reducing the value of an asset, say old inventory, in the company's books, to reflect the real loss in value on the market.

Write off
Taking of a worthless asset out of a company's books.

Z

Zero-based budgeting
Drawing up a budget from scratch every time a budget is renewed or reviewed, rather than carrying funds and activities on automatically.

Zone pricing
Setting the price of an item according to where it is sold, to allow for extra shipping charges or other costs that vary from region to region.

Index

STUDENT REPLY CARD

In order to improve the quality of future editions, we are seeking your comments on *Small Business Management Fundamentals,* Fourth Canadian Edition, by Szonyi and Steinhoff. Thanks in advance for your feedback!

1. Name of school you attend: _____

2. If you are enrolled in a degree program, please indicate your field of study: _____

_____

3. Approximately how much of this text did you use for your course? _____

_____

4. What did you like best about this book? _____

_____

5. What did you like least? _____

_____

Other comments:

--- CUT HERE ---

--- FOLD HERE ---

BUSINESS
REPLY MAIL

No Postage Stamp
Necessary If Mailed
in Canada

Postage will be paid by

7115

Attn: Sponsoring Editor, Business and Economics
The College Division
McGraw-Hill Ryerson Limited
300 Water Street
Whitby, Ontario
L1N 9Z9

TAPE SHUT